THE ESSENTIAL GUIDE TO

MOTORCYCLE MAINTENANCE

TIPS & TECHNIQUES TO KEEP YOUR MOTORCYCLE IN TOP CONDITION

MARK ZIMMERMAN

Whitehorse Press
Center Conway, New Hampshire

ACKNOWLEDGMENTS

Books like this one take a lot of help. In no particular order I'd like to offer a heartfelt thanks to Alex Gifford at Branchville Motors; Frank, Greg, Pat and Art at Danbury Power Sports; Brad Banister at Yamaha Motor Corporation; American Honda Motor Corporation; Roy Oliemuller at BMW of North America; Kathe Killian at Yuasa Corporation; Racetech; Ray Mancini at Extreme Motorsports; and the entire crew at Danbury Harley-Davidson, for their technical help and in many cases for providing motorcycles and parts. If I've forgotten anyone, and I'm sure I have, it was not intentional.

I'd also like to offer a heartfelt thank-you to the folks at Whitehorse Press for giving me this opportunity, and especially to Lisa, Greg, and Matt for their help in whipping this book into shape.

Finally, a big thank-you to Jeff Hackett for his terrific photos. And, of course, to my wife, Brenda, for all of her help and support.

—Mark Zimmerman

Whitehorse Press books are also available at discounts in bulk quantity for sales and promotional use. For details about special sales or for a catalog of motorcycling books and videos, write to:

Whitehorse Press
107 East Conway Road
Center Conway, NH 03813
Phone: 603-356-6556 or 800-531-1133
Email: Orders@WhitehorsePress.com
Internet: www.WhitehorsePress.com

ISBN-13: 978-1-884313-41-7
ISBN-10: 1-884313-41-8

15 14 13 12 11 10 9 8 7 6

Printed in China

CAUTION: Your good judgment is essential for safe and successful service work. If you have doubts for any reason about your ability to perform safe maintenance or repair work on your motorcycle, have the work done at a qualified repair shop. The information in this book is true and complete to the best of our knowledge. All recommendations on parts and procedures are made without any guarantees on the part of the author or Whitehorse Press. Author and publisher disclaim all liability incurred in connection with the use of this information.

Front and back cover photos by Jeff Hackett.

Design and illustration by Jessica Armstrong.

Table of Contents

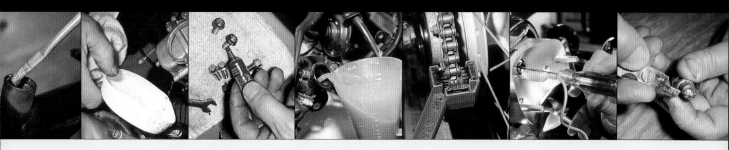

Table of Contents

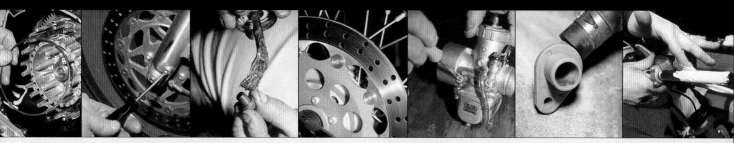

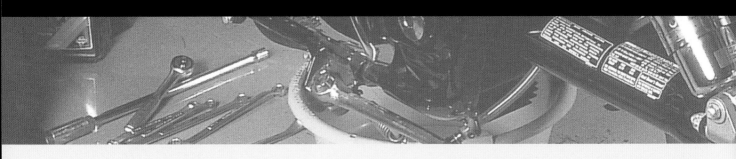

The purpose of this book is to show the novice motorcycle mechanic how to maintain and improve his motorcycle. I'm going to assume that you have little or no mechanical knowledge. I'll also assume that you have few tools and are going to be working under the old shade tree in your backyard, metaphorically speaking. And finally, since I assume you're interested in having fun, I'll try and make the learning process as entertaining as possible. Finally, since motorcycling is somewhat esoteric, a lot of strange jargon and odd technical terms may crop up to confuse you. I'll try my best to define them as we come to them.

Just as there is no such thing as a typical motorcycle rider, there is no such thing as a typical motorcycle mechanic. I've spent all of my working life (so far) as a mechanic; I've met children, women, and the prototypical "old geezers" that had developed an innate and profound understanding of things mechanical. I've also met many "mechanics" employed in the trade that would have been better suited to sweeping chicken coops. Fast approaching geezerdom myself, I've come to realize that anyone with the proper training and the right attitude can become a competent, if not excellent, mechanic. My goal in writing this book is to cut through the bull, so to speak. It shouldn't matter a whit if you're a 14-year-old with his or her first dirt bike, a grandmother about to embark on the adventure of a lifetime, or a genuine rocket scientist who's just

You're never too young, or too old to start learning. By the time young Wyatt is 14 he should be an ace wrench.

tired of paying someone else to service his bike. When you finish reading this book you'll understand how your bike works and you'll know what to do when it doesn't.

WHY YOU SHOULD LEARN TO MAINTAIN YOUR BIKE

Why perform your own maintenance, you might ask? A fair question, especially if you normally have the family sedan, your motorcycle, or your lawnmower serviced by a professional. The best answer is that to become a proficient motorcyclist requires a fair amount of human/mechanical interaction, and by performing your own basic maintenance you'll gain a much better understanding of how motorcycles function. You also develop a much better feel for the health of your bike. In time you'll be able to sense a small problem developing and deal with it before it becomes a big one, or worse, a serious safety issue.

Mechanics who service large fleets of vehicles and airplanes rely on a system of preventive maintenance to do just that. By learning and performing regular preventive maintenance you'll find that unexpected breakdowns will be few and far between. Your owner's manual will provide you with a list of items that should be inspected on a regular basis. This book will provide you with a better understanding of why those items should be inspected, and how to go about it.

In concert with preventive-maintenance inspections, I also recommend you always perform a pre-ride inspection, which consists of all of those little items that the owners' manual recommends you check before riding off into the sunset. I'd be lying to you if I said that I always perform this pre-ride ritual, but I do use a combination of preventive maintenance and a daily walk-around inspection of my bike to forestall unexpected problems. I'm going to teach you to do the same thing.

If that's not enough to convince you, maybe these three practical reasons for learning to maintain your bike will. First, a little practical knowledge can mean the difference between riding home and a long walk when you or your buddy's bike breaks down by the side of the road. Second, if you do take your bike back to the dealership for service, the staff there would

COMMON HAND TOOL LIST

This is just the minimum amount of tools you'll need to properly maintain your motorcycle. They should be sized to fit your bike, which means metric stuff for most you, and fractional sizes for the Harley guys (with a few odd metrics).

- Combination wrench set (6mm to 19mm metric or 1/4 to 3/4-inch fractional).
- Socket set, 3/8-inch drive (sized as above)
- Allen wrench set, either metric or fractional depending on your needs.
- 12-inch adjustable wrench
- Screwdriver set (#1, #2, #3 Phillips and common slotted blades from 1/8 to 3/8 inch).
- Spark plug socket sized to fit your bike.
- Common pliers
- Needle-nose pliers
- Diagonal-cutting pliers
- Locking pliers (Vise-Grip medium size #7)
- 16-oz. hammer
- Plastic-faced hammer (16 oz.)
- Impact driver (essential for removing stubborn case screws)
- Feeler gauges
- Spark plug gauge
- Tire gauge
- Battery hydrometer
- Antifreeze hydrometer (you can delete this if you own an air-cooled bike)
- Wire-crimping tool
- Test light
- Hacksaw and blades
- Gasket scraper
- 16-inch pry bar or small crowbar

Additionally, you should pick up any odd-sized wrenches pe-

Digital tire gauges are accurate, easy to read, and affordable.

This Sidewinder ratchet set should satisfy your fastener turning needs. Its unique design makes it extremely useful for working in tight spaces.

culiar to your bike. Trust me, it's much easier to loosen and tighten that 26mm rear axle nut with the right wrench or socket than it will be with an adjustable wrench.

The tools listed above in a nice sturdy toolbox should cover just about any maintenance or emergency-repair situation you're likely to come across. In fact, the box I carry to the racetrack every weekend contains just about what I've listed here, minus a few items.

■

much rather deal with a knowledgeable rider than an ignorant one. Third, it's comforting to have enough knowledge to understand what was

MOTORCYCLE-SPECIFIC TOOLS

While everyone's needs will differ depending on the make and model bike, here's what I'd recommend, at least for starters. This list will vary depending on how much of your own service work you intend to do.

- Plastic rim protectors
- Two tire irons
- Valve-adjusting tool (if required)
- Drain-plug tool
- Fork-level tool
- Spoke wrench
- Adjustable hook spanner (a perfect tool for adjusting steering-head bearings).
- Carb synchronizer

Kind of a small list isn't it? Don't worry, it'll grow. Just wait until you start rebuilding your friends' engines. ∎

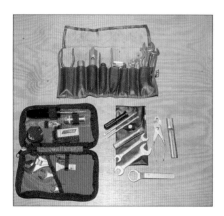

Factory supplied tool kits vary in quality and content. The BMW supplied kit (top) is one of the best. The CRUZ TOOLS kit, (bottom left) is a popular and high quality aftermarket item. The factory-supplied kit (right) found under the seat of my dirt bike works fine in emergencies.

done to your bike and why, as opposed to trusting in blind faith that it was needed and done correctly.

A PLACE TO WORK

Any realistic preventive maintenance program requires a few simple necessities. Foremost, is the desire to actually get your hands dirty. If you're still reading at this point, I'll take that as a given.

Next on the list is a basic understanding of how your motorcycle works; together we'll achieve that. Practical considerations boil down to a place to work and tools. Let's start with a place to work.

The expression shade-tree mechanic carries good and bad connotations. Among professional mechanics, it's come to mean someone whose work habits and skills are amateurish. To me it conjures up an image of someone content to work at a leisurely pace on his own equipment for his own pleasure. That's a good thing in my book (pun intended).

Unfortunately, working under the shade of a friendly maple is not the ideal situation. First, you're at the mercy of the elements. Second, if you're forced to stop in the middle of the job, you must package everything up and find a place to store it until you can come back to it.

While the shade of a friendly tree is fine if you're doing a real quickie job, like adjusting the chain or bolting on a new luggage rack, a far better solution is a permanent workshop. If circumstances force you into doing all your work outside, you can get by; but ask around, one of your friends may let you use a corner of his shop or garage.

Workshops are neat. They give you a place to store your tools and bike. They keep you warm and dry. And in the event you're forced to stop before the job is completed you can put your tools down, cover up any exposed parts, and lock the door. Your shop is also a great place to just get away from it all. Which is one reason why my shop door locks from the inside. One of my little pleasures is to go out to the shop at the end of the workday, pop myself a cold one, and just sit and look at my motorcycles.

Workshops can be as plain or as fancy as you want. Since I spend an obscene amount of time in mine, I've literally created a home away from home, complete with a refrigerator, comfy chair, and my favorite artwork: the ever-popular and suitably tacky poker-playing dogs.

At the very least a workshop suitable for working on your motorcycle needs to be clean, dry, bright, and adequately ventilated. A couple of inexpensive overhead fluorescent work lights can be installed to provide light. You can knock together a decent workbench or purchase one complete with tool drawers for $200. Throw up a pegboard and one or two steel shelves, hit the walls with a coat of semi-gloss white paint, and bingo! The old cave is now a workshop.

Creature comforts should include a radio and something to sit on. Standard shop fittings should include a decent workbench, a bench-mounted vise, at least one fire extinguisher, and a decent first-aid kit. One real important item, particularly if you work alone a lot, is a cell or extension phone. Not only can you relieve the tedium by calling a friend, but in the event of an accident or problem, help is readily available.

A few inexpensive steel shelves and plastic storage boxes will provide you some storage space, and can be purchased at any home-improvement center. If you want your shop to have a professional look, you can pick up cardboard "bin boxes" complete with the name of your local auto parts store emblazoned on them for about $0.50 apiece. A nice steel trashcan comes in handy, too. If you look, you can usually find an old 25-gallon drum somewhere that's free for the asking.

Good lighting is imperative. A few fluorescent fixtures hanging in the workplace will make it bright and cheery. A coat of semigloss white paint will make the place even brighter, and give you a nice backdrop for those poker-playing dog posters.

Try and pirate a few old cookie tins or baking pans from the kitchen. These are great for storing small parts while you're working on the bike. You'll also need an oil drain pan. Most auto parts stores carry drain tubs that also serve as storage containers. You can usually get several oil changes into one before it's full.

Some of you may be tempted to work on your bike in the basement. Off the cuff, I'd say the basement is not really the place to store or work on your bike. Outside of the entry and exit problems, which may prove daunting unless you're capable of carrying your bike up and down a flight of stairs, there are a host of real concerns.

Most basements contain the water heater or some sort of furnace, and these tend to come on at inopportune times, like right after you've spilled two gallons of gas on the floor. Furthermore, most basements are poorly vented. Any solvents you use will permeate the entire house. I'm not sure about your family, but mine's not real thrilled about the old man filling the house with eau-de-carb-clean.

There are other reasons why basements make lousy storage sites for bikes—we'll discuss those later on in Chapter 14.

WHY YOU NEED A MANUAL FOR YOUR MOTORCYCLE

The most basic tools when it comes to motorcycle maintenance are printed ones: books. With the right technical material and a little patience the average person (male or female) should be able to fix anything. The first book you'll need, outside of this one of course, is the owner's manual or handbook that came with your motorcycle. If you bought your bike used, it may be missing. If that's the case, go order one.

The owner's manual explains what you'll need to know about riding and using your bike. It tells you how to start it, how to turn on the lights,

BIG TICKET TOOLS

Last on the tool list are the big-ticket items. These should be purchased on an as-needed basis. Some of them you may never need, while others will prove useful for varied tasks around the house—at least that's what I tell my wife.

- 1/2 or 3/8-inch drill
- Drill index (drill bits from 1/16 to 1/2 inch)
- Bench grinder (and safety glasses to wear when using it!)
- Timing light
- Torque wrench (these can actually be purchased for under $50; start with a 3/8-inch drive model)
- Battery charger, suitable for motorcycle use.
- Digital multimeter (these range in price from $14.95 to $1,495; pick something you can afford)
- Air compressor (get one of at least 5 horsepower, capable of 120 psi)
- Small oxyacetylene cutting/brazing/welding outfit.
- Soldering gun
- Motorcycle lift (these range from shop-type lifts to small roll-around style lifts)
- Pressure washer
- Parts washer
- Tap-and-die set in the appropriate thread sizes

This category is limited only by your imagination, and your budget. I've seen a few home-hobby shops that were better equipped than some professional garages. ∎

Digital voltmeters are indispensable when it comes to troubleshooting electrical problems.

and what grade of gas to put in it. It tells you what the tire pressures should be, what spark plug should be used, and when to change the oil. The owner's manual also lists what maintenance is needed and when to perform it. It may even describe how to do some of the basic jobs like how to change the oil or remove the wheels. In fact, some owner's manuals are so detailed that they are in effect mini shop manuals. The ones that come with BMWs are particularly good, but they are the exception. In short, the owner's manual is a very basic and important tool that you should keep on or close to the bike at all times and read thoroughly at the first opportunity.

Unfortunately, what the owner's manual won't provide is a detailed procedure for repairing the motorcycle's components. For that you'll need a service manual. Service manuals are highly-detailed descriptions of every system and component on the motorcycle and the procedures for their repair. Good service manuals describe the repair procedures step by step. They also illustrate each step with clear photographs and blown-up drawings. Manuals contain all the information needed to overhaul your bike from top to bottom; if it's pertinent information, the factory shop manual will list it.

That said, factory shop manuals are written for the professional mechanic and assume you have reached a certain level of ability, own or have access to a fully equipped shop, and have all kinds of specialized tools. Shop manuals completely disregard the fact that some of us need our hands held occasionally. There's nothing more disconcerting to the novice mechanic than reading 'assemble in the reverse order of disassembly' after they've just dismantled their first gearbox.

You may also find the text of the factory shop manual a little daunting at first. In fact, I'd suggest asking your local dealer for a quick look at his before ordering yours, just to see if it's readable. Some poorly translated European manuals can be a little hard to follow, being translated into English "as she is spoken." If that's the case or if the price tag of the factory manual gives you a nosebleed, I'd suggest taking a look at one of the independently published manuals.

Chilton, *Haynes*, and *Clymer* all publish shop manuals that cover most of the popular models. Besides being a fair amount cheaper, the aftermarket manuals are usually written for the novice. Most aftermarket manuals also suggest alternative procedures and tools in cases where the factory-authorized tool may be unavailable.

Let me be blunt here, you don't have much choice. I've spent over 30 years employed as a professional mechanic, and I rarely work on a bike without having a service manual close at hand. Get a manual for your bike.

HAND TOOLS

I confess: I'm a fool for tools. I like tools, and I buy a fair number of them. However, I won't presume that you, perhaps never having had a profound need to use tools before, feel the same way. So here's the deal. Rather than giving the reader a long list of tools to buy, usually at a prohibitive price, I'm going to list the tools needed to perform a specific job when I describe that job. If you'd prefer to buy a complete tool kit, I've listed the basic required tools in the following pages. You'll find that as your interest and appreciation of mechanics increases so will the weight of your toolbox. If you're already a tool junkie then you probably own most of the basic hand tools required to work on your motorcycle, although you may want to fill in a few gaps here and there. If you're completely new to this then

This neatly arranged shop has plenty of storage and workbench space. Judging by the tools and posters, the owner is a vintage bike enthusiast. (This is the author's shop.)

you'll need to give serious thought to acquiring a comprehensive tool kit. You may be tempted to try to get by with the factory-supplied tool kit. If you've just bought a new BMW you may be able to do just that. With rare exceptions, most of the tools supplied with new motorcycles have all the structural integrity of Swiss cheese. Besides, the kits themselves are far from complete.

Tools can be good and moderately priced, good and very expensive, or cheap and probably not so good. Stay away from cheap bargain-basement tools. They don't fit the fasteners very well, which tends to round off the fasteners' edges, making them difficult to remove. Most of them feel awkward in your hand, and they seem to break at inopportune times, allowing your knuckles to crash into something solid. It's much easier to stay away from no-name tools than it will be to repair the damage to your bike and body caused when one slips or breaks.

If money is no object, then seek out the local Snap-On, MAC, or Matco tool truck and spend away. If you plan on buying everything you need in one fell swoop, you can probably get them to drive to your house for a private viewing. Sort of like your own little chrome-plated fashion show.

When I was a kid I was on a first-name basis with the local Snap-On dealer. I think I pretty much put his kid through medical school. Now I'm a little, not much, just a little, wiser. I buy most of my common tools through Sears Craftsman or the local home-improvement chains. Craftsman, Husky, SK, BlackHawk, and Proto are a few of the more reasonably priced tool lines available. All are excellent tools, carry lifetime, full-replacement guarantees, and are readily available seven days a week. For the price of one Snap-On ratchet, you can purchase a whole set of Craftsman sockets and ratchets, leaving that much more dough to spend on the bike (or more tools).

So, my recommendation is this: if tool status is your thing, buy Snap-On tools, which honestly are probably the best tools in the world from a standpoint of comfort, durability, and appearance. But, and I say this after 35 years of twisting wrenches, a Craftsman wrench is just as functional, just as durable, and often costs less than half as much.

EXPENDABLES

These are the things that get used up, worn out, and tossed away in daily use. Oil, spray solvents and lubricants, rags, razor blades, and about a million other things go on the expendable list. After awhile you'll see trends develop and decide just what to keep on hand. As you get more involved in maintaining your motorcycle you'll start to acquire lots of expendable items. Pretty soon they'll fill up your garage and you'll have to move.

HERE'S WHAT I STOCK:

- Single-edged razor blades. Handy for everything from scraping gaskets to slicing fuel line.
- Rags—you can never have enough, especially when you're changing the oil.
- Paper towels. Steal 'em from the kitchen or buy them by the roll. I get the cheapest, largest roll I can find.
- Waterless hand cleaner. Unless you like getting yelled at for leaving paw prints all over the house.

- Sandpaper
- Scotch-Brite pads. These have more uses than you can imagine, from removing gasket residue to polishing engine cases.
- Various weights of grease and oil. You'll accumulate everything from light, white lithium grease, (handy for assembly work) to heavy, copper-based anti-seize compounds used to assemble exhaust systems.
- Penetrating and moisture-displacing lubricants: WD-40, CRC-556, Bel-Ray 6-1; these will do everything from putting a shine on your tank to removing old stickers.
- Polish and wax
- Brake, carb, and contact cleaner
- Skin cream, unless you like wearing latex gloves while working around your motorcycle (I really don't), you'll find that sooner or later you'll end up with chapped hands. A little skin cream will go a long way toward making them more comfortable. ∎

Expendable items will accumulate faster than you can find space for them.

In addition to a set of common hand tools, the avid motorcyclist will require a few special tools. How many depends on how involved you plan to become with the mechanical end of motorcycling. By special tools I mean ones dedicated strictly to motorcycle maintenance tasks, such as chain breakers and clutch hub holders, as well as ones designed specifically for working on your particular motorcycle.

These are available through your local motorcycle shop or from sources listed in the appendix. I want to note that there are a lot of tools not listed: files for instance, and things like extendable magnets, flare-nut wrenches, and other semi-specialized tools. I figure if you need a file or whatever for a particular job, you'll be smart enough to go get what you need.

SAFETY CONCERNS

Before we delve into the nuts and bolts of theory and repair I do want to list a few simple safety dos and don'ts. One of my favorite quotes is from Ben Franklin. It sums up the safety issue in general and as it applies to motorcycles in particular: "Experience keeps a dear school, yet fools will learn in no other."

Working on motorcycles involves lots of flammable liquids and plenty of heat and sparks. Know where the fire extinguisher is at all times. If you don't have one, get one (with an ABC rating suitable for extinguishing fuel, electrical, and material fires) and mount it close at hand. An electrical spark, a careless cigarette ash, even a spark caused by a dropped tool can and has started devastating fires. Fires seem to occur when things are already out of control; if one does start, keep your head, and remember that your life is worth more than a burning motorcycle or shop.

No matter how careful you are, you're bound to skin a knuckle or two, so keep a first-aid kit handy. I like the fully equipped ones available through industrial supply shops, but you can probably find one just as good at the drugstore. It should be well marked and stored in plain sight.

Keep your work area neat and well organized. Clutter leads to slips, trips, and assorted mishaps. A few minutes spent policing the area during the course of a large job is always time well spent. Like granddad always said, "A place for everything, and everything in its place."

Whenever you grind or drill, use the appropriate eye protection. I've had a piece of wire that came off a wire wheel removed from my eye. It was painful, expensive, and I had to listen to a long lecture from the doctor on creeping socialism and the high cost of doing business while he was poking around in my eye with a tweezers. When the incident occurred, I had on safety glasses, but no face shield. The whole experience was about as grim as it gets. A $10 face shield would have prevented it from happening.

Batteries are nothing more than plastic boxes full of acid that give off explosive gases. Exercise extreme caution whenever you're working around or with them. Needless to say, never smoke when you're servicing one. Unless there is some compelling reason for not doing so, always disconnect the battery (from the ground side) when you're working on the fuel or electrical system. Be extremely careful whenever you're topping up the battery because battery acid is highly corrosive and will eat through your bike's metal frame, your clothes, and your flesh in short order.

Whenever you use a wrench (or any tool for that matter), take a moment to visualize what might happen to your tender knuckles if the tool slipped. Then reposition the tool accordingly. Whenever possible, you should pull on a wrench rather than push on it. By the same token, ill-fitting wrenches or any tool that's substandard should be tossed out. Tools that slip damage fasteners, paint jobs, and knuckles, not to mention your disposition.

Never leave a job half finished intending to return to it later. For example, you're in the process of replacing the front brake pads when you're called away on some urgent task, like taking the kids out for a Happy Meal. You've already installed the new pads; all you need to do is bolt the caliper back onto the fork. You hang the caliper on the fork, running the bolts in finger tight and head off to the local Mickey D's. Bad move!

Either leave the caliper off the bike or finish the job completely before stopping. It's easy to forget that the bolts are only hand tight, especially if they look tight. I can't tell you how many guys have installed a clutch hub or crankshaft rotor nut, spun the retaining nut on finger tight, and then gone to lunch. As you might imagine, upon their return they button up the engine, leaving the nut loose. Eventually, they discover their error, usually when the engine goes bang and self destructs.

Children are by nature curious beings. Young children especially love to poke, prod, and touch everything they can reach. That includes hot, sharp, and rotating parts. Mixing young fingers and motorcycles can lead to some very unpleasant situations. If you decide to work on your bike with youngsters present you'll need to be particularly aware of where everyone is at all times.

Safety is almost always a common sense issue. I shouldn't have to tell you not to stick your fingers into a rotating wheel. I definitely shouldn't have to tell you not to clean parts in gasoline. And I really shouldn't need to point out the dangers of running an engine in an enclosed area, so I won't.

WALK-AROUND INSPECTIONS

The Department of Transportation has something they want truck drivers to do on a daily basis known as a walk-around inspection. This is nothing more than a quick walk around their truck looking for any obvious problems. Normally, it takes less than a minute to perform.

As promised earlier, I'm going to teach you how to do the motorcycle equivalent of the trucker's inspection. You don't need to get down on your hands and knees and give the bike a complete inspection, but should be able to assess the general condition of your bike with a quick glance. After some practice, you'll do it unconsciously. In fact, you may already be doing so.

As you walk up to the bike a quick sweep of the eye should tell you that there are no large puddles under the bike indicating a leak, that the tire tread is good, and the chain has no excess slack. If your engine has an oil-level sight glass, now is the time to look at it. If it uses a dipstick, check it at least every other time you fill up the tank. A quick pull on the brakes tells you they're still connected. As the bike warms up, check the lights and clutch operation. As you roll out of the driveway the bike should feel familiar and solid. If it doesn't, stop and investigate.

Once a week give the bike a complete check-over, adjust the tire pressures, adjust the fluid levels, and lubricate and adjust the chain and cables. This applies whether you ride the bike on a

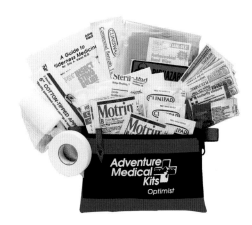

No shop should be without some sort of first aid or medical kit.

daily basis or just on Sundays. Of course, if you ride the bike infrequently, you can adjust the service schedule accordingly. I find the easiest way to perform my weekly check-over is to combine it with the bike's weekly wash.

As you become a more adept at mechanics, you'll find that you sense subtle changes in the way the bike behaves over time. As the tires wear, you'll notice that the handling is less precise, for instance. Or maybe you notice that vibration levels have increased, indicating that the carbs need synchronizing. The act of riding then becomes another phase of maintenance.

Finally, keep your motorcycle as clean as possible—one of my personal tenets of preventive maintenance. Regular cleaning helps you spot small problems before they become big ones. Oil leaks, for example, will make themselves known early on when the bike is kept clean. If your bike looks like something the cat dragged in, you may not even spot that blown gasket and leak until the oil light comes on and you're 50 miles from nowhere. Besides, clean motorcycles are more fun and easier to work on than dirty ones.

DO ME A FAVOR

I'm going to ask you all to do me one favor: after reading, or maybe struggling, through this book, I'd like you to share with me your comments, good and bad. To that end, you can contact me online at zimmemr@aol.com or through the publisher. In the meantime, have fun, work safe, enjoy yourself, and ride whenever you can.

The engine is the heart of your motorcycle. Depending on what year and type of bike you own, the engine will be of the four-stroke type or the two-stroke type. Since these two engine types differ so fundamentally, we'll split this chapter into two parts, one dealing with four-strokes and the other with two-strokes. For each, we'll discuss the basics of how they work and then we'll tell you how to maintain and improve each type. Since the four-stroke is by far the most common, we'll look at it first.

You can call it a motor, the mill, the lump, or the power plant. Whatever you call it, the engine changes energy into motion. In our case the energy is derived from the controlled burning of fuel inside of the engine. Hence, we call it the internal combustion engine. Over the years I've had more than one armchair engineer take me to task for calling an engine a motor. Sorry, but Webster's defines a motor as 'an engine; especially an internal combustion engine', so we'll use the term engine and motor interchangeably. Besides, who wants to ride something called an engine-cycle?

While some brave (or more likely foolhardy) pioneers experimented with steam-powered bikes, the norm has been to use internal combustion engines. Internal combustion engines come in a variety of designs: the two-stroke and four-stroke being the most common. The Wankel or rotary engine has also been tried, albeit with limited success. Over the years Yamaha, Suzuki, Norton, Hercules (a German marque) and Van-Veen (a Dutch company) have built rotaries. Of the four only Suzuki's sold in any real numbers, and even it discontinued the design after two

This Moto-Guzzi is of non-unit construction. Note the seam, just in front of the rubber plug, where the transmission is joined to the engine.

years. As motorcycling has passed the rotary by, so shall we.

All piston-powered internal combustion engines share a few fundamental characteristics. It doesn't matter if it's a tiny, single-cylinder, model-airplane engine with all the horsepower of a rabid bumblebee, or a huge 16-cylinder power plant designed to spin a locomotive dynamo, the basic principles remain the same. In essence, we need a way to get the fuel into the engine in a manner that allows it to be burned, some way of using that burning fuel to perform some useful work, and after the fuel is converted into energy, some means of exhausting the remains.

Before we can have a meaningful discussion on how an engine works, we'll need to define a few of the basic parts common to the internal combustion engine and briefly discuss how they work. Many of the parts we're going to discuss are common to both two- and four-stroke engines, and most of you probably have at least a passing acquaintance with them. Some of you may have only encountered the two-stroke in passing (generally by being awakened at 6 a.m. by some melonhead using a chainsaw running at 10,000 rpm) and may not realize that the two-stroke design uses neither camshaft nor valves (at least not valves of the conventional type).

TWO-STROKE BASICS

The two-stroke engine derives its name from the fact that only two strokes of the piston (one revolution of the crankshaft) are needed to complete the intake, compression, exhaust, and power cycles.

The two-stroke engine enjoys certain performance advantages over the four-stroke, which is why today it is used primarily in bikes requiring a very high power-to-weight ratio, such as dirt bikes. While the two-stroke is being gradually phased out of racing, in part because racing two-stokes are noisy and environmentally dirty, as of this writing it's safe to say that the "strokers" still dominate some forms of racing. Conversely, because the two-stroke employs fewer moving parts and is inexpensive to design and build for utilitarian purposes, it dominates the moped and commuter bike market, particularly in third-

PISTON-PORT TWO-STROKE ENGINES

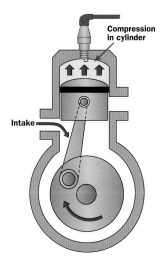

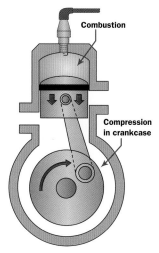

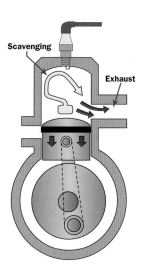

(TOP) As the piston moves up from bottom dead center, a partial vacuum is produced in the crankcase. As the piston continues moving upward, its skirt clears the intake port, allowing a fresh charge of fuel/oil/air mix to be drawn into the crankcase. The fuel mix fills the crankcase and starts to flow upward through the transfer ports (not shown). As the piston passes by the exhaust port, it seals it off. As it continues upward, the piston closes the transfer ports and starts to compress the mixture flowing from the transfer ports into the combustion chamber.

(CENTER) As the piston nears top dead center, a spark occurs across the plug gap, igniting the compressed-fuel mixture. The expanding gases drive the piston down. As the piston moves down it closes the intake port and compresses the air/fuel mix into the crankcase.

(BOTTOM) As the piston moves past the exhaust port, uncovering it, exhaust gases flow out. As the piston continues downward it uncovers the transfer ports. The compressed mixture in the crankcase begins to flow out of the transfer ports and into the cylinder, sweeping any remaining burnt gas out the exhaust port. After the piston reaches BDC, it starts upward again. As the piston passes the transfer and exhaust port, it seals them off, and the process repeats. ■

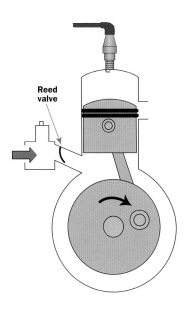

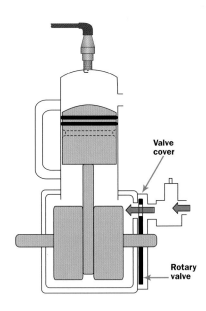

Reed valves are used in some two-cycle engine designs to prevent backflow of the fuel/air mixture when the piston begins its downward stroke. This refinement greatly increases power and rideability. The rotary valve is another improvement to two-stroke operation. In this design a disk, into which a slot has been cut, rotates with the crankshaft. The slot is arranged in such a location that it exposes the inlet port to the crankcase during the time when fuel/air should flow into the engine. At other crankshaft positions it seals the inlet port, preventing backflow of the fuel/air mixture.

world countries where cheap transportation is the motorcycle's primary function.

There are two principal differences between the two- and four-stoke designs. The first and most significant is that the basic two-stroke has no camshaft or valves; the fuel/air mix flows into the cylinder through holes or ports cut directly into the cylinder liner. The second major difference is the way the engine is lubricated. Unlike a four-stoke engine, the two-stroke uses its crankcase as a passageway for the fuel/air mix. Because the crankcase is sealed and used during one phase of the intake and compression cycles, it's impossible to use it to store oil as a four-stroke does (even dry sump systems store some oil in the crankcase).

Two-Stroke Lubrication

All two-stroke engines are lubricated by one of two methods, each of which has the same end result. Oil is either mixed directly with the fuel or injected by pump into the fuel as it leaves the carburetor. Some of the better systems also inject oil directly into the main bearings. Regardless of the system, most of the oil is consumed in the combustion process. Oil being heavier than the fuel, it drops out of the mix and coats the bearings and piston skirt. All of the bearings in a two-stroke engine are roller-, needle-, or ball-element bearings, rather than plain bearings because roller-

element bearings require much less lubrication. While it's true that many four-strokes are or were built with roller bearings, no two-stroke engines are built with plain bearings.

Because much of the oil is burned and what remains exits the exhaust pipe in its natural state, emissions are a big problem. Modern two-strokes are a vast improvement over their predecessors but they are still quite dirty. For that reason alone it's unlikely we'll ever see the large-bore two-stroke road bike again.

Piston-Port Two-Strokes

The most basic form of two-stroke design uses the so-called piston-port induction. In this type of engine the fuel/air mixture is drawn into the crankcase by the motion of the piston, passed to the combustion chamber through transfer ports, and then exhausted after combustion under the power of its own expansion. The flow of the fuel/air mixture and burnt gases is controlled entirely by a series of ports in the cylinder wall that are sequentially covered and exposed by the piston. See the sidebar for a step-by-step description of the full two-stroke cycle.

Reed Valves and Rotary Valves

More sophisticated two-strokes are fitted with reed or rotary valves. The basic problem with a piston-port engine is that as the piston moves down and begins to compress the mixture in the crankcase, the pressure in the crankcase soon exceeds that of the atmosphere. Once crankcase pressure is higher than atmospheric, the fuel mix will reverse direction and flow backwards out of the carburetor. This phenomenon can be overcome, or at least its effects can be diminished, by using very small ports and very moderate intake port timing, which reduces power.

A better way is to place a reed valve in the inlet tract to prevent backflow. Reed valves are just thin strips of metal or phenolic material, such as fiberglass or carbon fiber, that act as a one-way valve between the carburetor and the intake port. During the intake period the reeds are held open by the flowing fuel/air mix, when crankcase pressure overcomes atmospheric pressure, the reeds snap shut, preventing backflow. Because the reeds positively prevent the mixture from flowing backwards the port can open earlier and remain open longer, greatly increasing power and rideability.

In rotary-valve (also known as disk-valve) two-strokes, a partially cut-away disk rotates, opening and closing the intake port. The disk, or rotary valve, is typically attached to the crankshaft, and is timed to open on the upward stroke of the piston so that the opening in the disk permits the fuel/oil/air mixture from the carburetor to enter the crankcase chamber. The rotary valve then closes on the downward stroke of the piston. Carburetors are typically found on the side of the engine, allowing a more direct flow of the fuel/oil/air mixture through the hole in the disk into the crankcase.

Power Valves

The big leap forward in two-stroke performance came with the introduction of the power valve in the late 1970s. The power valve is nothing more complicated than a moveable restriction placed in the exhaust port. A small electric motor similar to a computer's disc drive may control the power valve, although there are many versions that are controlled by purely mechanical means. In essence, a large exhaust port is good for top-end power while a small port enhances midrange and low-speed running. The power valve is shaped like an eyelid. The control mechanism raises or lowers the eyelid depending on engine

rpm. Currently all performance-oriented two-stroke engines are equipped with some variation of the power valve.

FOUR-STROKE BASICS

The four-stroke engine is used in all current mass-produced automobiles, most motorcycles, and a few outboard motors. Technically speaking the four-stroke engine is called a four-stroke-cycle engine. Since we're all friends here we'll just call it a four-stroke. They're called four-strokes because it takes four separate strokes of the piston (two complete revolutions of the crankshaft) to complete the four cycles needed to make the engine run and accomplish one combustion cycle.

One piston stroke is the piston movement from the top of the cylinder to the bottom or from the bottom of the cylinder to the top. When the piston has reached the extent of its upward mo-

Power Valve Assembly
(1989-ON YZ250; 1989-1990 YZ250WR; 1991-ON WR250Z)

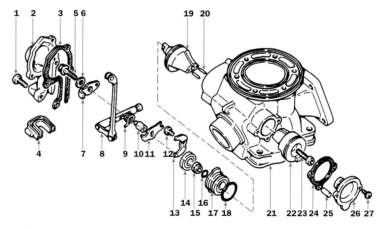

1.	Screw	15.	Collar
2.	Cover	16.	O-ring
3.	Gasket	17.	Holder
4.	Seal	18.	O-ring
5.	Bolt	19.	Right-hand Power Valve
6.	Washer	20.	Pins
7.	Lever	21.	Cylinder Block
8.	Pushrod	22.	Left-hand Power Valve
9.	Spring	23.	Bolt
10.	Boss	24.	Gasket
11.	Lever	25.	Pin
12.	Screw	26.	Holder
13.	Thrust Plate	27.	Screw
14.	Oil Seal		

The power valve is a device that increases or decreases the size of the exhaust port according to engine speed. A large exhaust is best for top-end power, while a smaller port is better for low and mid-range operation.
(Courtesy Yamaha Motor Corporation)

FOUR-STROKE ENGINES

In the four-stroke engine, the complete cycle of events—intake, compression, power and exhaust—requires four piston strokes, and the engine has an intake and an exhaust valve per cylinder head, plus a camshaft.

Theoretically, on the intake stroke, the piston moves down from TDC to BDC, and a partial vacuum is produced in the cylinder. Then the intake valve opens, allowing an air-fuel mixture to stream into the cylinder.

But in an actual engine, the intake valve opens just before the piston reaches TDC, and closes a little after the piston has started up from BDC in order to utilize the inertia effect of the incoming air-fuel mixture.

On the compression stroke, the piston moves up from BDC to TDC. Both intake and exhaust valves are closed and the air-fuel mixture in the cylinder is compressed.

As the piston reaches TDC on the compression stroke, an electric spark is produced at the spark plug. The spark ignites the air-fuel mixture, causing it to burn very rapidly.

Actually, the ignition is timed a little before the piston reaches TDC to allow the fire to spread to every corner of the combustion chamber, thus producing high pressure. This high pressure forces the piston to move down, and the movement is carried by the connecting rod to the crankshaft. The crankshaft is thus made to rotate.

On the exhaust stroke, the burned gases are forced out of the cylinder to permit a fresh charge of air-fuel mixture to enter the cylinder. For better exhaust efficiency, the exhaust valve is opened a little before the piston reaches BDC. ■

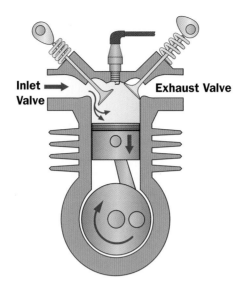

Inlet Valve   Exhaust Valve

1. INTAKE STROKE

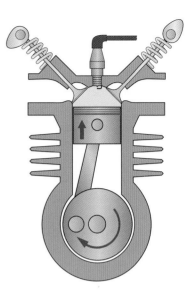

2. COMPRESSION STROKE

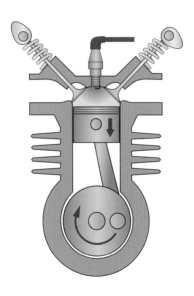

3. POWER STROKE

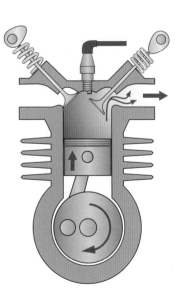

4. EXHAUST STROKE

tion, in other words when it's as close to the cylinder head as it's going to get, it's said to be at top dead center, or TDC for short. When the piston reaches the bottom of its stroke, (the point where it's as far from the head as possible) it's at bottom dead center (BDC).

The four-strokes are intake, compression, power, and exhaust. Here's how they work together on a running engine: on the intake stroke the piston heads toward BDC, the intake valve opens, and fuel-air mix flows into the cylinder. On the compression stroke, the piston rises toward TDC, compressing the fuel-air mix. On the power stroke, the spark plug fires the compressed mix, pushing the piston back down to BDC. On the exhaust stroke, while inertia carries the piston back toward TDC again, the exhaust valve opens and the burned gases are expelled. Let's start with a look at the four cycles needed to make an engine run.

The Intake Stroke

During the intake stroke the piston moves from top dead center to bottom dead center. When the piston moves down it leaves an open space above it. That open space, until recently occupied by the piston, is now empty, and because nothing has replaced the piston, that open space is an area of low pressure or vacuum. The intake valve then opens and a mixture of air and fuel from the carburetor flows into the cylinder.

Why does the fuel/air mix flow into the cylinder? As we all learned in high school physics (at least those of us not daydreaming about motorcycles) nature abhors a vacuum. Because the downward movement of the piston has created an area of low pressure between the closed intake valve and the piston, and the air on the other side of the valve (in the intake port) is at atmospheric pressure, which is 14.7 pounds per square inch. The instant the intake valve opens the higher pressure air in the inlet port will flow toward the low pressure area in the cylinder.

Now in reality, the process is slightly more complicated. The intake valve actually opens before the piston reaches top dead center and it closes some time after the piston reaches bottom dead center in order to take advantage of the inertial effects of the flowing air. But for the time

being we'll assume that the valve has opened slightly after top dead center and closed slightly before bottom dead center.

The Compression Stroke

The piston comes to a brief stop when it reaches the bottom of the intake stroke. It then begins to travel upwards. Both the intake and exhaust valves are closed during the compression stroke. The fuel-air mixture in the cylinder is compressed into an ever-decreasing volume as the piston moves toward top dead center.

The Power Stroke

This is when all the good stuff happens. As the piston reaches top dead center the ignition system creates a spark at the spark plug tip. If every-

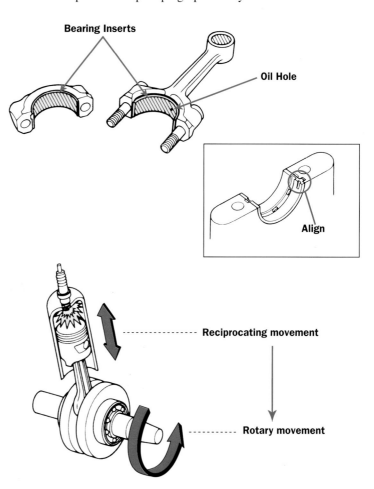

The crankshaft converts the reciprocating motion of the piston/ connecting rod into a rotary motion. Built- or assembly-type cranks generally use roller-type bearings. One-piece, or unit-type, forged cranks employ split-plain bearings. Unit cranks require two-piece connecting rods that are bolted together. (Courtesy American Honda Motor Corporation)

thing goes according to plan the spark ignites the fuel-air mixture inside the cylinder.

As the mixture burns it expands. The expansion of the burning gas creates very high pressures inside the cylinder, pushing the piston back down. How high? Anywhere from four to six tons depending on the engine's design parameters.

Make no mistake about it, when I say the gases burn at a controlled rate they do just that. The last thing you want and the very last thing an engine will tolerate is an explosion in the cylinder. Engineers equipped with some very expensive and powerful computers spend enormous amounts of time ensuring that what you get is in fact a controlled burn.

The Exhaust Stroke

The piston has once again reached bottom dead center. It now starts to move upward, and as it does the exhaust valve opens and the piston forces the spent gases from the cylinder. When it reaches top dead center the whole process begins again.

It may occur to you that we need something to help keep the engine turning over smoothly between strokes. If we relied solely on the inertia provided by the piston and crankshaft assembly, the rotary motion of the crankshaft would proceed in fits and starts. It would be very difficult to keep the engine running, particularly at low speed. A perfect example of this is a common

Four-stroke cylinders are nothing more than a precision-machined tube surrounded by air cooling fins or a water jacket.

lawnmower. Remove the blade sometime and try to start the mower, chances are you won't even get the thing to turn over. Energy is stored in a large mass bolted to, or manufactured as, part of the crankshaft. This mass is called a flywheel.

The purpose of the flywheel is to store energy between power strokes. Essentially it uses the stored energy to keep the engine turning over smoothly and prevent it from stalling. The lighter the flywheel the less energy it stores. Bikes with light flywheels tend to stall more often than engines with heavy flywheels, but an engine with a light flywheel will also respond to changes in engine rpm a lot quicker.

As a rule of thumb, high rpm engines, like those found in sportbikes and race bikes, will have light flywheels, while touring bikes and cruisers will have heavier flywheels. By the same token, single-cylinder engines require a heavy flywheel to keep their one big piston moving up and down smoothly. Multiple-cylinder engines with proportionally smaller pistons and a fair amount of crankshaft mass, needed to accommodate the extra hardware required for their multiple cylinders, can make do with lighter flywheels.

The preceding description is vastly oversimplified and sure to give anyone intimately familiar with the internal workings of a four-stroke engine heart palpitations, but at least it's better than thinking there must be seven little dwarves in there making the piston go up and down.

The astute among you probably have a whole bunch of questions by now. For instance, how does the movement of the piston turn the wheels? How is the engine lubricated and cooled? Patience, Grasshopper, all will be revealed.

Now that you have a fundamental understanding of how a four-stroke works, let's look at the parts that make it all happen. These parts can be thought of as two major systems: the bottom end and the top end, as well as a bunch of auxiliary systems. First, let's look at the top and bottom ends.

THE BOTTOM END

An engine bottom end consists of the crankcase, crankshaft, main bearings, rod bearings, and connecting rods. These parts convert the up-and-down motion of the pistons into the round-and-round motions needed to power the transmission. All those parts are housed in the crankcase, along with anything else the designer decides to stuff in there. On some engines, the oil is stored in the crankcase (these are called wet-sump engines). On others it is stored in a separate tank (these are called dry-sump engines).

Also, many modern motorcycles also house the transmission and clutch assembly inside of the crankcase (these are called unit-construction engines). On others, the clutch and tranny are in a separate case (these are called non-unit engines). Most modern bikes use the unit-construction design; the exceptions that come quickly to mind are BMW, Moto Guzzi, Harley-Davidson big twins, and the Honda Gold Wing.

All engines begin with a crankcase. Most motorcycle crankcases are built in two pieces, incorporating a vertical or horizontal seam to facilitate assembly, and are commonly referred to as "cases."

The backbone of the crankcase is the crankshaft. The crankshaft converts the up-and-down motion of the piston into a rotary motion that's used to drive the motorcycle. Motorcycle crankshafts may be made of several separate pieces that are pressed or bolted together. These are known as pressed, built-up, or less frequently assembly crankshafts. Or, the crankshaft may be forged from a single chunk of steel alloy, these are usually called a forged or unit crankshaft.

The crankshaft is supported in the crankcase by main bearings. There may be as few as two in a single-cylinder or twin-cylinder engine and up to six on a four-cylinder engine. The main bearing may be either automotive-type shell bearings, generally known as plain bearings, or ball- or roller bearings. Some designs even use both. Due to their peculiar lubrication requirements ball- or roller-bearings must be used to support two-stroke crankshafts.

If the crankshaft is the backbone then the connecting rod must be the leg bone. The connecting rod connects the piston to the crankshaft. The rod needs to be both light and strong and it must be able to transmit the heavy loads imposed on it by the piston without deflecting. The end of the connecting rod that fastens to the crankshaft is

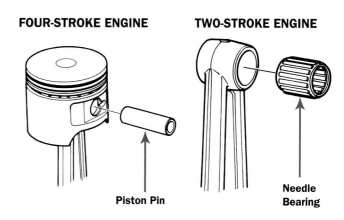

FOUR-STROKE ENGINE   **TWO-STROKE ENGINE**

Piston Pin   **Needle Bearing**

Due to their unique lubrication requirements two-stroke engines require a needle bearing between the rod and wrist pin. four-strokes can use a plain bearing, although in the past some four-strokes did use needle bearings at the wrist pin. (Courtesy American Honda Motor Corporation)

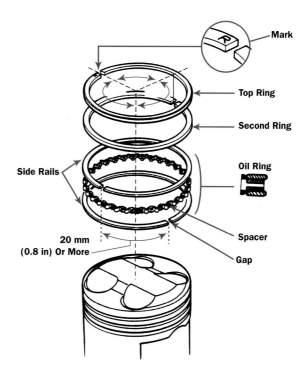

Mark

Top Ring

Second Ring

Side Rails

Oil Ring

20 mm (0.8 in) Or More

Spacer

Gap

Most four-stroke pistons use three rings; two compression rings and one oil control ring. The oil ring may be cast in one piece, or the design may use two thin rails separated by a spacer. As the inset shows, many rings are directional and need to be installed with the indicator facing up. (Courtesy American Honda Motor Corporation)

sometimes called the big end because it has a larger diameter than the end of the rod that is connected to the piston, which is called, as you

The Desmodromic method of opening and closing valves, wherein the valves are opened and closed by the rocker arms, is peculiar to Ducati.
(Courtesy Ducati)

might have guessed, the small end. Rods intended for use in plain-bearing engines are constructed in two pieces; the bottom cap is removable so the bearing can be installed into the rod and the rod onto the crankshaft. One-piece rods normally use a roller bearing. Depending on the designer's whims a built-up crankshaft intended for four-stroke use may have connecting rods that use either plain or roller bearings. However a one-piece, forged crankshaft, due to its construction, must use rods with plain-bearing big ends. The crankcase assembly, along with the crankshaft, rods and in some cases the camshaft is collectively referred to as the bottom end.

THE TOP END

The top end is everything that fits above the crankcase assembly, including the cylinders, cylinder head, pistons, valves, and cams (if an overhead-cam design is being used). These are the parts that control the flow of gases in and out of the engine and turn combustion energy into the up-and-down motion of the piston.

Set atop the crankcase is the cylinder, or in the case of multiple-cylinder engines, the cylinder block. Each piston moves up and down in the cylinder bore, which is a precisely machined hole in the cylinder. Most motorcycle engines use a cylinder or cylinder block with a pressed-in-place liner made of steel alloy. If the liner becomes damaged it can be re-bored to accept an oversize piston. Some engines use plated bores instead of liners. The aluminum cylinder is bored almost to size, and then the bore is plated with chrome or nickel-silicon to give a hard-wearing surface.

Such cylinders are lighter than the traditional two-piece style and tend to cool slightly better. In general, they resist wear better than a steel liner as well. On the downside they are more expensive to make than a standard cylinder and cannot be re-bored if damaged, although there are some specialists that will re-plate them or install a conventional liner. Chrome bores were once used exclusively on race bikes but today are found on quite a few street bikes.

There are a few motorcycles that use a cylinder block cast directly into the upper portion of the crankcase. The outer portion of the cylinder block is made of aluminum alloy (some older bikes used cast iron), and contains the coolant passages depending upon whether the engine is liquid cooled or if the engine is air-cooled.

Technically a piston is any disc or small cylinder fitted into a hollow cylinder that is acted upon by fluid pressure and used to transmit motion. Throughout this book we'll run into a variety of pistons that serve other purposes, but this one is the main man, the Big Kahuna. This is the guy that does the work.

The piston pin connects the piston to the connecting rod. The piston rings are used to maintain a gas-tight seal between the piston and the cylinder. Piston rings are also used to control the oil that lubricates the piston skirt and assists in cooling the piston. About one-third of the heat absorbed by the piston during the combustion process passes from the piston through the rings and into the cylinder walls. While many different materials have been used to manufacture piston rings, cast iron has proven as good as any. Other materials used include chrome and cast iron with a molybdenum alloy used as a face material.

There are two types of rings found in a four-stroke engine. The upper rings are the compression rings; their job is to prevent combustion gases from leaking past the piston during the compression and power stroke. Normally two compression rings are used. Below the compression rings lies the oil ring. In the past some en-

COMMON VALVE CONFIGURATIONS

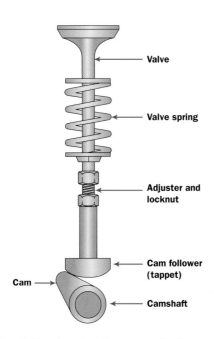

Valve

Valve spring

Adjuster and locknut

Cam follower (tappet)

Cam

Camshaft

In a flathead engine, the cam and valves are located in the block, below the cylinder head.

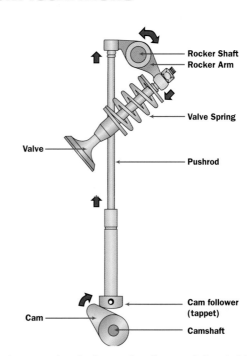

Rocker Shaft

Rocker Arm

Valve Spring

Valve

Pushrod

Cam follower (tappet)

Cam

Camshaft

In an overhead-valve engine, the cam is located in the block, the valves are positioned in the head.

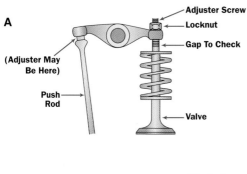

A

Adjuster Screw

Locknut

Gap To Check

(Adjuster May Be Here)

Push Rod

Valve

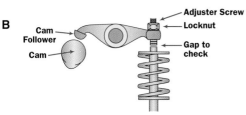

B

Adjuster Screw

Locknut

Cam Follower

Gap to check

Cam

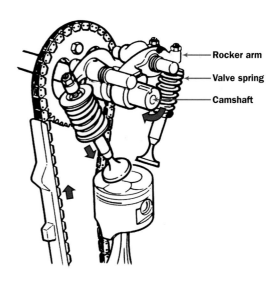

Rocker arm

Valve spring

Camshaft

(A) Pushrod engines may have their valve adjusting mechanisms located at either end of the rocker arm or built into the pushrod.
(B) Where a single or double overhead cam design is used the cam is located in the head, adjacent to the valves.

Cams may be driven with gears, chains or toothed rubber belts.

(Courtesy American Honda Motor Corporation)

TWO-STROKE ENGINE TOP END

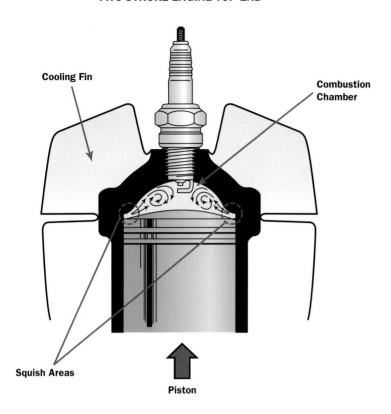

Cylinder head construction is pretty straightforward where a two-stroke is concerned. **(Courtesy American Honda Motor Corporation)**

gines used two oil rings, one below the compression rings and one at the very bottom of the skirt. Current practice is to employ one oil ring below the compression rings.

All rings are split so they can be easily installed on the piston. Because the splits don't form a perfect seal the ring ends are staggered during assembly so that no joints are directly above each other. In a four-stroke engine the rings are free to rotate. Allowing the rings to rotate prevents carbon from building up between the ring and its seat, which would degrade the ring's ability to seal. Because a two-stroke engine has ports cut into the cylinder wall, the rings cannot be allowed to rotate; if they did, the ends would likely spring out into the port, destroying the ring, piston and cylinder.

The piston pin connects the piston to the rod. Pins are made of steel alloy that's been case hardened (a process that creates a tough outer layer of material surrounding a relatively soft inner core). Usually the pin is also given a layer of chrome plate to increase its wearing qualities. The tubular, hollow construction allows the pin to be both strong and light. Four-stroke engines generally employ a replaceable bushing in the small end of the connecting rod, while the two-stroke engine uses a needle bearing. Again this is because two-strokes have much different lubrication systems than four-strokes.

The portion of the piston that the pin passes through is a reinforced area called the piston-pin boss. All modern motorcycles use a full-floating piston pin. In the full-floating design the pin is free to move in both the rod and piston. It is prevented from working its way into contact with the cylinder bore by clips or buttons pressed into the piston bosses. While there are other methods of locating the pin they are not currently used in motorcycles.

VALVES AND CAMS

Engines need some way of allowing the fuel and air mixture into the cylinder, sealing it and then expelling it once its job is done. In a four-stroke that's the job of the camshaft and valves.

Every cylinder of a four-stroke engine has at least one intake valve and one exhaust valve. They can have more if the designer feels it's warranted but they must have at least one of each. High-performance engines generally have two of each for each cylinder, and some even have three intake valves.

Today all valves are located in the cylinder head. This design is known as OHV (short for overhead valve), meaning that the valves are located above the piston. This wasn't always the case. Prior to World War II many motorcycles had the valves located in the cylinder block. The cylinder head held only the spark plug. These designs were called flatheads or sidevalves. Today, the only place you're likely to find a flathead, outside of an antique show, is on a lawnmower and even these are being phased out.

The cylinder head of a four-stroke engine contains the valves, the intake and exhaust ports, and in the case of an overhead-cam engine, the camshaft. It also contains the combustion chamber, a carefully shaped depression where the fuel-air mix is actually burned. A two-stroke head contains only the combustion chamber and the spark plug. Heads are either bolted directly to the cylinder, or they may be fastened to the crankcase with long studs that sandwich the cylinder between the head and crankcase. Often, a combination of the two are used.

The valves used in motorcycle engines are called either poppet valves, because they pop open, or mushroom valves, due to their appearance. Valves are made in either one- or two-piece configuration. Two-piece valves are created by spinning the valve head in one direction, and the valve stem in the opposite direction. A negative current is passed through one piece, a positive charge through the other. The pieces are spun at very high speeds and then brought together. Friction and the opposing charges weld the valve head to the stem.

To enhance flow through the cylinder the intake valve is always larger than the exhaust valve. Ordinarily intake valves are made of chromium-nickel alloys. Because they run so much hotter, the exhaust valves are constructed of silichrome alloy or some derivative material such as stainless steel.

The valve seat is the circular opening in the port where the face of the valve rests between strokes. The seat is precision machined to ensure a positive seal. Valve seats are replaceable, although it takes a fair amount of use and abuse to wear one out. Normally when a valve seat needs renewing it is simply recut with a special tool.

Prior to 1980, lead was routinely added to gasoline to increase its octane rating. The lead was also thought to act as a cushion between the valve and the valve seat preventing wear. When unleaded fuel was phased out, manufacturers scrambled to install hardened seats, designed to work with unleaded fuel. As an aside it's worth pointing out that initial concerns over rapid valve seat failure when leaded fuel was withdrawn from the market turned out to be much ado about nothing. In the end it was found that with rare exception unleaded fuel had little or no effect on valve seat wear.

It doesn't make good engineering sense to just drill a hole through the head and install the valve. Valve guides provide a hard-wearing and accurately-machined surface to guide the valve. Guides may be made as an integral part of the

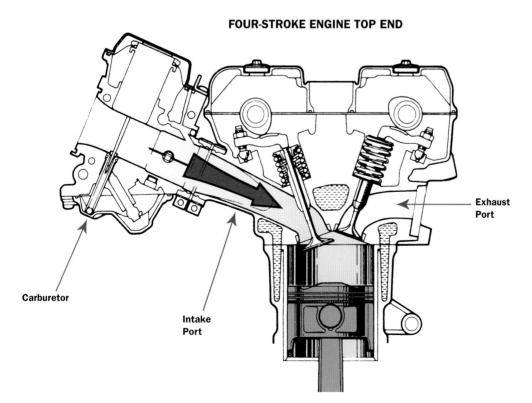

FOUR-STROKE ENGINE TOP END

Carburetor

Intake Port

Exhaust Port

In a four-stroke engine the fuel/air mix enters through the intake valve via the intake port; spent gases exit through the exhaust valve and port. This one is an overhead-cam design. (Courtesy American Honda Corporation)

head or they may be replaceable. All motorcycle engines use replaceable valve guides. Valve guides are normally made of cast iron or bronze phosphor alloys.

The valves are opened by the camshaft; springs return them to their seats. Common practice is to use two concentric springs to close the valve. You'd think one stiff one would be up to the task and you'd be right, if closing the valve were the spring's only job. By using two valve springs harmonic vibrations that might cause the spring to fail are reduced. Furthermore, two springs help to prevent valve float. Valve float results when engine rpm gets so high that the valve can no longer be controlled by the camshaft. In essence, the valve floats in the combustion chamber, where it can become tangled with the piston, or even other valves, resulting in extensive damage.

The other parts of the valve system or train include the valve collar, which retains the valve springs, and the keepers, which are little half-moon shaped cotters or locks used to hold the spring and collar assembly in place on the valve.

As I said, the valves are opened by the camshaft (or cam for short), which usually has individual cam lobes for each valve. Let's digress for a moment: a cam is nothing more than a wheel

Pushrods may be located within the cylinder or in external tubes, as on this engine.

with a lump on one side to give it an irregular motion. Cams are used to bump or lift all types of things from switches to valves. When you place one or more cams on a shaft you have a camshaft. I've already mentioned that the valve springs close the valve; let me expand on that a bit. The springs provide closing pressure. The cam profile controls the closing rate; if the cam didn't prevent the valve from slamming violently into its seat, valve life would be incredibly short. The camshaft may be located in the head directly over or adjacent to the valves, or it may be located in the engine block.

When the camshaft is located in the head it's called an overhead-cam (or OHC) engine. An overhead-cam engine may use one cam to open the intake and exhaust valves, in which case it's called a single-overhead-cam (SOHC) engine. Or the designer may opt for separate cams for the intake and exhaust, particularly if the engine is so wide that using a single cam would present problems. An engine using two overhead-cams is called a double-overhead-cam (DOHC) engine. When the cam is located immediately above the valve it works directly upon the valve stem, usually through an inverted bucket placed over the valve stem, or a pivoted finger. When the cam is adjacent to the valves it works the valve through a rocker arm.

Engines with the cam located in the crankcase are called pushrod engines. They take their name from the long rods that transfer the motion of the camshaft to the valves. All pushrod engines use rocker arms to transfer the motion of the pushrod to the valves. Pushrod engines may use one, two or four cams depending on the type of engine.

Cams are spun by the crankshaft at half the engine speed, so if the engine rpm is 4,000 the cam is only turning 2,000. Why? Because during the four cycles of a four-stroke engine the valves are only opened and closed during two of the cycles. The cam(s) are turned either by gears, chains, or rubber belts, depending on the designer's preference and the engine's intended use.

Camshaft design is quite complex. The cams control when the valves open, how long they stay open, and how high they open. By and large the cams control how well the engine breathes,

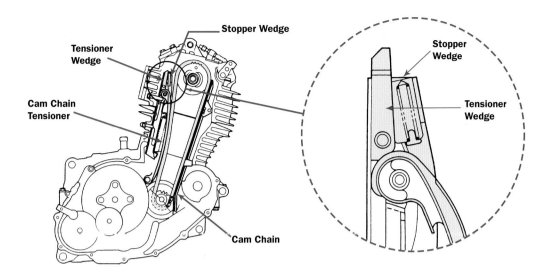

Cam chain slack is controlled by either a manually adjusted (shown here) or automatically adjusted tensioning device. (Courtesy American Honda Motor Corporation)

which is tantamount to how much horsepower the engine is capable of producing.

There are several variations on the two basic cam designs I want to touch on. One is the cam-in-head design, which is essentially an overhead-cam design using very short, rigid pushrods to open the valves. This system was used by Moto Guzzi on its four-valve engines and is still used by BMW on its oilhead engines. The other is the Desmodromic method of valve actuation employed by Ducati, which uses rockers both to push the valves open and pull them closed.

The cam-in-head design as used by Moto Guzzi on their four-valve engines places the cam slightly below and inboard of the valves. The cam is driven by a belt and operates the valves through a short pushrod and rocker-arm arrangement. The basic idea was to keep the engine height down, and to avoid using long and flex-prone pushrods in what was a high performance engine.

The Desmodromic system is a somewhat complicated system peculiar to Ducati. Ducati uses a conventional camshaft above the valve to open it through a rocker arm. Another rocker arm is located below the first. The second rocker arm has a forked end on it, which rides just below the valve stem tip. Removable keys positively locate the forked end in place. The second rocker is used to close the valve without using

springs, although on street versions light springs are used to seat the valves at starting speeds. At one time the Desmo system had some real advantages on the racetrack. Today it's a Ducati tradition, and a bit of signature engineering. Now that you're conversant with the basic parts of a four-stroke engine let's look at how they actually work.

ENGINE LAYOUT

By engine layout I really mean cylinder arrangement. Let's start at the bottom and work our way up.

The single-cylinder engine is used when weight, simplicity, and a strong, wide power band outweigh the need of almost anything else. Single-cylinder engines are built in every displacement from 50cc to the appropriately named Suzuki Dr Big which displaces 800cc. Single-cylinder bikes are easy to maintain, make good power, and are light and narrow. The disadvantages are moderate-to-high levels of vibration (overcome with balance shafts) and, for the most part, a power band and basic design that makes them unsuitable for high-speed touring.

The parallel twin, in which both cylinders are located side by side, was a popular design used by everyone from Ariel to Yamaha. The parallel twin design originated in the 1930s. Triumph is generally given credit for building the first, commercially successful parallel twin. The idea behind the parallel twin was to reduce vibration. The somewhat flawed reasoning was that two small bangs would be less objectionable than one big one. In the parallel design the pistons either rise and fall together, in which case the engine is said to use a 360-degree crankshaft, or they may have a one-up-one-down pattern, the 180-degree crank. Triumph, BSA, Norton, and Yamaha were the main proponents of the 360-degree parallel twin engine, a design characterized by a fair amount of vibration. Current examples of parallel twins may be found in such diverse bikes as the 250cc Honda Rebel and the 800cc Triumph Bonneville. Parallel twins are a nice compact design capable of churning out some real horsepower. Mounting the exhaust and carburetors is easy because the cylinders are next to each other. Manufacturing costs are kept low, in part because you're building two single-cylinder engines on a common crankcase. The big problem with the parallel twin is vibration; many of them rattle hard enough to shake your fillings loose.

The opposed-twin design locates the cylinders 180 degrees apart. The best example of an opposed-twin design is the BMW twin-cylinder engine. Because the cylinders are located parallel to the ground or wheel axles, the design is known as a flat twin or pancake. Since the flat-twin crankshaft lies parallel to the frame rails and at 90 degrees to the rear axle, the opposed-twin design facilitates the use of a shaft drive. As the pistons move in and out together (reaching both BDC and TDC together) vibration levels are extremely low. The big problem with an opposed engine is that the cylinders intrude on space needed for foot pegs, and building the intake manifold may require some creativity. However, they are smooth and easy to design for use with a shaft final drive, which makes them an attractive engine for touring bikes. A variant of the opposed twin is the opposed multi, the Honda Gold Wing being the primary example.

Harley-Davidson, Moto-Guzzi, and Ducati illustrate the diverse nature of the V-twin design. The Harley uses a 45-degree V-twin with a unique knife-and-fork connecting rod arrangement utilizing a single crank pin. Vibration levels and torque are high, power output moderate. The Guzzi uses a 90-degree V-twin mounted longitudinally, that is, with its crankshaft inline with the frame, so a drive shaft can be used.

Ninety-degree twins have perfect primary balance so vibration levels are low. Ducati also uses a 90-degree V-twin, but it is mounted with the cylinders fore and aft. Both the Guzzi and the Ducati use offset cylinders, the connecting rods running side by side. The 45-degree cylinder angle used by Harley Davidson makes it easy to mount the carburetor, both cylinders being close

(TOP) Cams may be driven with gears, chains or toothed rubber belts. This GL Gold Wing engine shows how Honda used a flat-opposed six-cylinder design to achieve a compact but powerful package. Its camshafts are driven by toothed rubber belts. (BOTTOM) This gear-driven camshaft design is used on Honda's V-four engines. (Courtesy American Honda Motor Corporation)

together. The 90-degree version used by Ducati and Moto Guzzi results in smoother engine operation. The V-twin design provides good torque, is narrow, and has a good look, making it a popular choice for cruisers. The "V"-design, especially the 90-degree, can make the chassis problematic, because the front cylinder may intrude on space required for the front wheel.

The V-4 exemplified by the Honda VFR is a refinement of the V-twin idea, one that works exceptionally well. The V-4 is practically vibration-free. It's compact, no longer than a V-twin, and barely any wider. Its only real disadvantage is that shoehorning the engine and its peripheral bits into the frame can sometimes compromise maintenance.

Inline transversely-mounted, (crankshaft sitting at right angles to the frame) multiple-cylinder engines, multiple in this sense meaning three or more, came to the forefront as the 1960s were ending. Inline three-cylinder four-strokes were available from Triumph, BSA, or Laverda, while inline three-cylinder two-strokes were available from Kawasaki or Suzuki. Honda, of course, set the motorcycling world on its ear by introducing the legendary four-cylinder CB750. The transversely-mounted multiple-cylinder engine has a lot going for it. More and smaller cylinders mean less vibration and higher rpm, which translates into high horsepower.

Offsetting the advantages are increased manufacturing and maintenance costs. Early multis often had annoying high-frequency vibrations especially at high speeds; however, modern designs have more or less eliminated the problem.

The other disadvantage to the inline transversely-mounted design is excess width. Again, refinement has taken care of much of the problem, but they can still be a little wide. While several manufacturers have tried to market inline transverse sixes I personally see four cylinders as the practical limit. Since no one is currently marketing an inline transversely-mounted six, I think I'm probably right.

Triumph's venerable parallel-twin was developed in the 1930s. The same basic layout was used by most manufacturers at one time or another.

The V-twin layout has become synonymous with the laid-back cruiser style. This Honda Shadow is a modern rendition of a time-tested engine configuration. (Courtesy American Honda Motor Corporation)

This photo of a BMW opposed-twin engine shows the lovely—and functional—symmetery that inspired this design. Putting the twin cylinders out in the wind was also a great aid to engine cooling. (Courtesy BMW North America)

Motorcycle engines are cooled by one of three mediums, or more accurately by a combination of the three. Air, oil, and water are used to keep our engines at the correct operating temperature over a wide range of conditions.

Bear in mind that internal combustion engines work most efficiently when the engine is kept hot. Hot, of course, being a relative term. An engine that runs too cool wastes fuel and won't work efficiently. An engine that runs too hot will soon melt itself into scrap. If all the heat generated by an engine could be conserved and put to work, it would develop a lot more power and use a lot less fuel than anything currently available.

So why do we struggle to keep our engines cool? Good question. The short answer is that the materials currently used to build engines just won't take the kind of temperatures needed to build our super-efficient theoretical engine. Not if we want those engines to be affordable, and as a side note this is one reason why many engine designers have been experimenting with ceramics. A ceramic piston, for example, can withstand temperatures that would vaporize even the best alloy ones.

The amount of heat created by our engines is considerable. And what's worse is that only about 30 percent of the caloric value of the fuel is actually turned into useful work. Which actually isn't bad considering that only about 10 percent of my caloric intake is turned into work of any type, but I digress. The other 70 percent must be shed in some fashion. About 35 percent of the

The water pump is generally mounted externally and in a protected position; on this Honda MXer it's located between the clutch cover and the frame, with coolant hoses attached.

excess combustion heat flows out the exhaust pipe. The other 35 percent needs to be absorbed in some fashion by the cooling system.

AIR AND OIL COOLING

Some engines are designed to be cooled primarily by air. These engines have fins on the cylinders and sometimes on the valve covers and crankcases to increase surface area for better cooling. Oil circulating through the engine also picks up heat and sheds it through the finning on the oil sump. This generally is all you need for low- and medium-performance engines under normal conditions, so almost all motorcycle engines were air-cooled until the manufacturers began increasing the number of water-cooled models in the 1980s.

More power means more heat. As motorcycle engines got larger and more powerful, some manufacturers began augmenting their air-cooling systems with jets to spray the underside of piston crowns and other hot spots to cool them with oil. To help cool the oil, these systems include an oil cooler. A thermostat in the oil cooler shuts it off until the oil temperature reaches about 180 degrees.

Air and oil cooling work fairly well, and a lot of new motorcycles continue to use it. Maintenance is practically nil, there is nothing to break or leak in the event of a spill, and aesthetically it looks right. That said, before we take a look at the mechanics of the cooling system, keep in mind that the cooling system of an air- or oil-cooled motorcycle engine includes every single exposed surface of your the engine. From the crankcase to the valve cover your engine radiates wasted heat. Let me overstate the obvious here: if you chrome your engine covers, if they are highly polished, or if they are dirty and covered with spooge (spooge being the technical term for grease, dirt and oil mixed into a form of mung), they will not conduct or radiate heat very efficiently. The best finish for your engine is a thin coat, no more than 0.015-inch thick, of matte black paint. Of course matte finishes rarely win shows, and I've been known to polish a case cover or two myself, but the bottom line is a clean engine works better than a dirty one and a matte finish better than a polished one.

SYNTHETIC VS. MINERAL OILS

The synthetic versus mineral oil debate has been raging for some years now, and it's certainly not going to end here, but maybe I can shed some light on the subject. Synthetic oils have some proven advantages over mineral oils. Particularly when engines are subjected to high stresses, high heat, and/or extended oil change intervals. But they are expensive and in many instances laboratory testing has proven that a top shelf mineral oil may work just as well, particularly when it is changed frequently.

Here's my take on it. First, if the OEM recommends that you use a synthetic oil, follow that recommendation. If the manufacture is ambivalent on the subject, my advice is to use a synthetic if you run the bike hard, under extreme conditions, or if you sometimes inadvertently over-extend your oil change intervals. On the other hand, a mineral-based oil works just fine if you adhere to the manufacturers recommended grade and viscosity, assuming the bike is ridden normally and the oil and filter changed on a regular basis. Finally, unless the manufacturer specifically recommends breaking in a new motorcycle on a synthetic oil, I'd wait until you've put at least a thousand miles on the engine before switching from a mineral oil to a synthetic, to ensure that the rings seat properly. ∎

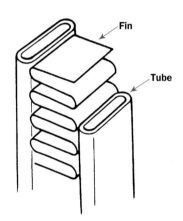

Heat is dissipated by flowing the warm coolant through the tubes; The heat is transferred into the fins, where it passes into the atmosphere. The larger the fins' surface area, the more efficiently the radiator will cool. (Courtesy American Honda Motor Corporation)

The material used to construct the engine also plays a critical role. When engines used cast-iron cylinders and heads, overheating was common. Eventually, engine designers realized that aluminum alloy was lighter and dissipated heat better and thus alloy heads, cylinders, and pistons became the norm.

Despite its seeming complexity liquid cooling is simple and works exceptionally well. (Courtesy American Honda Motor Corporation)

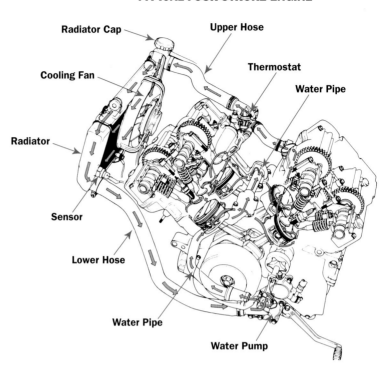

Radiator Cap — Upper Hose — Cooling Fan — Thermostat — Water Pipe — Radiator — Sensor — Lower Hose — Water Pipe — Water Pump

Air Cooling

Air is a pretty neat cooling device; it's free, it's everywhere, and it's easy to replace when it's hot. On the downside, to remove an equal volume of heat requires four times the weight and four thousand times as much volume of air as of water. The other problem associated with air-cooled engines is that they need to be built a little heavier and wider than a comparable liquid-cooled model. This is because the wide, thick fins of the air-cooled engine need more room between them than the narrow passages of a water jacket. The cylinders of an air-cooled engine also need a considerable space between them to allow a good cooling draft to flow around them. Not a problem in a single or twin, but a very real concern in a four-cylinder model, particularly when you consider that with the extra width you need a longer crankshaft, wider cases and so on. Air cooling also creates problems with a V-design simply because airflow to the rear cylinder is impeded. An air-cooled V-twin may work fine; however, a V-four would be out of the question.

Heat flows out of the combustion chamber through a variety of avenues. Some is absorbed directly by the cylinder head; a portion flows from the piston into the rings into the cylinder wall. A big chunk goes from the exhaust valve into the valve seat and thence into the head. In short, the heat flows out into the surrounding metal and into the fins. The fins then radiate the heat into the flowing air stream, which carries it off.

Air-cooled engines are generally set up to run slightly richer than liquid-cooled engines as well. By running a little richer, the combustion chamber temperature is reduced, less heat is created, so less needs to be removed. Fin spacing is also a consideration: as a rule of thumb, small closely spaced fins cool better than large coarsely-spaced ones. The design of the forks and front fender may also come into play. If the front fender creates a lot of turbulence, disrupts, or even blocks airflow, the engine will be starved for cooling air. When it's all said and done, air-cooled engines work well.

LIQUID COOLING

Water cooling has a couple of advantages over air cooling. Because the water can take care of localized hotspots and the overall engine temperatures are kept more consistent the carburetion can be run leaner, keeping the EPA happy and at the same time producing better power and a crisp throttle response. The water jacket surrounding the cylinders also keeps noise down. Since engine noise is figured into the total when noise limits are established, a quiet engine means the designer has a little more leeway when designing the intake and exhaust systems. Liquid-cooled engines don't overheat when they get stuck in traffic or when they're covered with a sportbike or touring fairing.

All those benefits come at the price of complexity. Water-cooling systems require a pump to move the fluid, hoses and water passages to carry it, a radiator to cool the fluid, and often a cooling fan to help cool the bike when it is at a standstill. Also required are an expansion tank for overflow, a thermostat to regulate temperature, and the fluid itself, which is a 50:50 mix of water and antifreeze. This adds weight and complicates placement of components and styling. Nevertheless, water cooling is almost the rule today.

In a liquid-cooled system, coolant is circulated through the engine by a water pump. A water jacket surrounds the cylinder and the cylinder head is cast with passages that permit the water to flow through it. As the water flows around and through the engine, the water absorbs the heat generated by the combustion process. When the water flows through the radiator it gives up much of its heat to the atmosphere.

When we talk about liquid cooling systems what we're really talking about is a water-cooling system. But—and this is a big but—unless there are special circumstances involved, we rarely run pure water in our bikes. As stated earlier, most of the time we use a 50:50 mixture of water and antifreeze. So technically we're talking about something other than water most of the time. To make it easy on ourselves, or at least on me, we'll use liquid and water interchangeably in this section.

Liquid-cooled motorcycles are nothing new. The Scott, an imaginative British two-stroke built from 1908 until the late 1950s, utilized water cooling from the beginning. The first modern water-cooled street bike was the Suzuki GT 750 LeMans, introduced in 1972. Suzuki was deter-

mined to prove that a big two-stroke was a viable alternative to the large displacement four-stroke engine. They used liquid cooling to ensure reliability. So much for history.

While air works well as a cooling medium it does have a few inherent problems. We've already discussed engine width. Another problem is the inability of cooling air to reach deep down into the dark recesses of an engine. This is where liquid cooling really shines. Competent design-

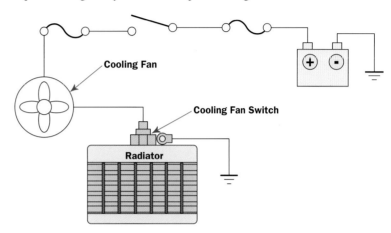

When temperatures exceed a predetermined limit the cooling fan switch will close and the fan will come on, increasing airflow through the radiator. When the temperature drops the fan will turn off. Most cooling fans turn on and off independently of the ignition switch. If you are working in or around the fan it's a good idea to disconnect it or remove the fuse, particularly if the bike is still warm. (Courtesy American Honda Motor Corporation)

DETERGENT VS. NON-DETERGENT OILS

Some old geezers, particularly some old motorcycling geezers, like to rattle on about what a great thing non-detergent oils were and how terrible modern detergent oils are. Well, since I'm more or less in the geezer class myself, I'm going to set the record straight.

Detergent oils are oils that have an additive package designed to hold small particles of dirt in suspension until the oil filter can remove them. Non-detergent oils have no such additives. The dirt and small chunks that normally end up in the filter end up deposited throughout your engine, eventually blocking oil passages, impairing heat transfer, and creating all sorts of mischief. Non-detergent oils have no place in a modern motorcycle engine. In fact, I can't remember the last time I saw a non-detergent oil on the shelf, outside of a lawnmower shop. ∎

ers route the coolant where it'll do the most good. A well-designed cooling system routes water to the exhaust valve area, around the spark plug bosses or to any other area deemed critical by the engineer.

In the beginning motorcycle designers relied on a thermosiphon system to circulate the coolant. The most basic of systems, the thermosiphon doesn't use a pump to circulate the coolant. Instead the radiator was mounted as high as was practical. As the engine temperature rose so did the coolant temperature. The hot coolant would rise to the top of the radiator while the low temperature coolant would drop down. While the thermosiphon system does work, the addition of an engine-driven pump to circulate the coolant greatly improves the efficiency of the cooling system as a whole.

Let's look at and define the parts that make up a liquid cooling system.

The Radiator

The radiator is a contrivance designed to dissipate the heat that the coolant has absorbed from the engine. Common practice is to build a box shape out of lots of small tubes. The tubes are connected at the top with a receiving tank and at the bottom with a dispensing tank. Sheet metal fins are installed over the tubes. Heat flows from the water into the fins where it is dissipated by the air stream. The larger the radiator or the

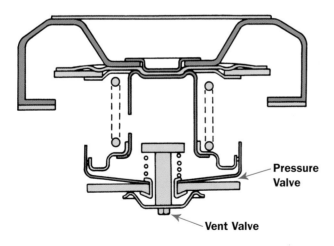

Pressure-type radiator caps increase the boiling temperature of the coolant and retain pressure within the cooling system. (Courtesy American Honda Motor Corporation)

greater the surface area of the fins, the greater the cooling capacity. In operation, water flows from the engine to the top of the radiator. A baffle plate is usually positioned directly under the inlet hose to help the hot water find its way into the tubes. As the hot water trickles down the tubes, convection causes the heat to flow from the water into the tubes and from the tubes into the fins. Remember heat always flows toward cold. As the water cools it contracts and becomes heavier; it drops to the bottom of the radiator and then flows to the pump where it is picked up and recirculated

In principle, the radiator in your motorcycle is exactly like the baseboard hot water heat in your bathroom. Of course, the one in my bathroom doesn't seem to give off nearly as much heat. Radiators may be constructed with copper or aluminum tubing with the tanks made either of aluminum, brass, or plastic.

Cooling Fan and Switch

The cooling fan works in conjunction with the radiator. As a rule of thumb a cooling fan is only found on a street bike. As I said, heat always flows toward cold. If the air surrounding the radiator becomes stagnant the difference between the atmospheric temperature and the coolant diminishes.

For example, if you become stuck in traffic on a summer day the ambient air immediately around the radiator may well approach 130 degrees or better. The engine then runs hot and overheating becomes a real possibility. To prevent overheating a small, electrically operated fan is positioned to move air through the radiator. The fan is switched on by a temperature sensor or fan switch. When the sensor reaches a preset temperature the switch closes a circuit and energizes the fan.

Caution: lots of bikes have self-energized cooling fans that may come on anywhere from a few seconds to a minute or more after the bike has been shut down. The cooling fan is rigged like this to prevent the bike from overheating when it's shut down with a hot engine. The fan will normally run for a few minutes until the engine has cooled off, then it shuts down. If you get your finger(s) caught in the fan it's going to hurt

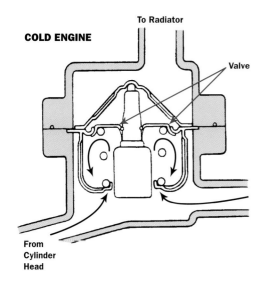

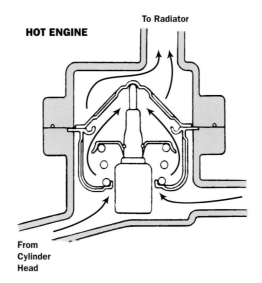

The thermostat is installed between the cylinder head and the radiator. It's really nothing more than a temperature-sensitive valve. At low temperature it stays closed, preventing coolant flow. As the coolant warms up, wax inside of the thermostat expands, forcing the valve open. The coolant now flows through the radiator, regulating the engine temperature. (Courtesy American Honda Motor Corporation)

like hell. Always unplug the fan before working anywhere near it.

Radiator Caps and Expansion Tanks

Because the boiling point of water increases under pressure a radiator cap is used that's designed to increase the pressure in the cooling system. As the coolant heats up it also expands, which increases the pressure even more. When the pressure exceeds a preset limit a valve inside the cap opens and excess coolant (remember the coolant volume has increased due to the heat) is allowed to flow through a hose connection into a small reservoir called an expansion tank.

After the engine cools off another valve in the cap, called a vent valve, is opened by atmospheric pressure. Since the coolant volume is now reduced, a slight vacuum is created in the radiator and coolant flows from the expansion tank back to the radiator.

Another function of the expansion tank is to remove the air bubbles from the coolant. Aerated coolant doesn't work nearly as well as the non-aerated variety, because the air bubbles tend to act as little insulators.

Thermostats

To keep the coolant temperature consistent a thermostat is installed between the water-jacket outlet and the radiator. The thermostat stays closed until the engine reaches operating tem-

perature. Once the engine is up to temperature a wax pellet inside the thermostat expands opening the thermostat valve and coolant flows from the engine to the radiator and back again.

If the coolant temperature drops off the thermostat will close until it again reaches the correct temperature. If the thermostat sticks open the engine will fail to reach the correct temperature and will probably run too cool. If the thermostat fails in the closed position the coolant won't be able to circulate and overheating will be the end result.

Water Pumps

To make the cooling system more efficient an engine-driven water pump is installed. The pump ensures that water is delivered at a uniform rate to the cylinder and head. The pump also forces the coolant to circulate throughout the entire system. Normally the pump is driven from the crankshaft. The centrifugal motion created by the pump impeller (which is nothing more than a multi-bladed propeller designed to drive the fluid forward) pulls the coolant in from the bottom of the radiator and then discharges it into the water jacket. Water pumps are sometimes built with a small discharge hole. If the pump fails internally the coolant will leak out of the hole rather than be pumped back into the engine, contaminating the oil. Any fluid leak from the hole is a cause for concern. Chances are the pump's

DIV *Changing Coolant*

You'll need:

- *Shop Manual*
- *Fresh Coolant*
- *Catch basin*
- *Screwdrivers to fit the radiator hose clamps*
- *Pliers for squeeze-type clamps*
- *Antifreeze hydrometer*
- *Funnel*
- *Rags*

Coolant degrades over time and should be replaced, as should the hoses. Your owner's manual or shop manual will give you the replacement intervals, usually two years for coolant and four years for the hoses. There will also be occasions when the coolant must be drained and replaced as part of another job or to effect a repair, a bad thermostat for example.

The antifreeze protection level should also be checked periodically.

Do yourself a favor and pick up a hydrometer that actually measures the specific gravity of the antifreeze. Those little $2.00 antifreeze testers that use floating balls are little better than nothing. Most hydrometers will give the freezing temperature as well as the specific gravity. I'd recommend those over the type that just list specific gravity just because they're easier to use. ■

Once the bike is warmed up, drain the coolant from the lowest point in the system. In this case the coolant is drained by removing the hose to the pump. Careful, it's hot.

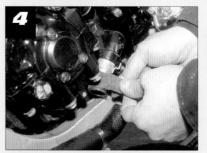

Let the coolant drain until it stops flowing.

Your shop manual will also point out any other areas that should be drained. This Yamaha engine has two drain points located in the cylinder block.

Clean any corrosion from the hose fittings before reinstalling the hose. If your bike uses a drain cock or some other type of drain plug you won't need to remove any hoses.

A little anti-seize will prevent the hose from sticking to the pipe connection, and help prevent leaks.

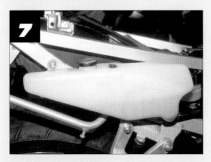

Using the specified mixture of antifreeze and water, (or a premixed coolant) refill the radiator to the top, run the bike long enough to bring it up to operating temperature, then check and top off the radiator.

Top off the overflow tank as well.

Last, check the antifreeze solution and make certain that the freezing point is as specified in your manual.

internal seals have failed and total pump failure is about to occur.

Coolant

Plain old water works fine as a coolant. It's cheap, easy to find, and has a high enough boiling point to keep our engines cool under most circumstances. Unfortunately, pure water has a couple of disadvantages. First, it has a distressing habit of turning into a solid at temperatures below 32 degrees. As you can imagine this can create quite a problem. Second, water has a tendency to corrode the various parts of the cooling system. What's needed is something that won't corrode and won't freeze. That something is, of course, antifreeze.

Antifreeze is a generic term. It is basically an additive that lowers the freezing point of water. In effect, it acts as a catalyst. Antifreeze is created from a variety of glycol bases, chiefly ethylene glycol, or propylene glycol. Other additives are mixed in with the base stock to prevent internal engine corrosion. Inhibitors are added to prevent rust and scale from forming in the water passages and the radiator. Ethylene glycol is the preferred base, because it has an extremely high boiling point of 330 degrees Fahrenheit, doesn't evaporate in use, is non-corrosive, has no odor, and furnishes complete protection when used in the correct proportions.

The correct proportion is the important part. Depending on the type, straight antifreeze may have a freezing point that's only somewhat below that of pure water. When mixed in a 60:40 ratio, (60 percent antifreeze to 40 percent water) the freezing point drops to minus 65 degrees. Personally, when it's that cold, I'm staying by the fire.

The worst problem associated with traditional ethylene-based antifreeze is that it's highly toxic and even worse has a sweet taste, making it attractive to children and pets. Any spill, no matter how small, should be mopped up immediately. If that's not practical, flood the area with water until no trace of the antifreeze remains.

Water

Ninety percent of the time, plain old tap water is added to antifreeze. Bad move, as tap water contains a host of impurities that will promote cooling system corrosion. A better bet is to mix your antifreeze with distilled or demineralized water available at any grocery store.

If you're not up to measuring and mixing your own coolant it can be purchased pre-mixed at most motorcycle shops or auto parts outlets. Make sure the container is specifically labeled "for use in aluminum block engines." There are plenty of good ones out there, including Spectro Year Round Coolant and Silkolene Pro-Cool, as well as a brand sold by Honda. I mention these three only because I've used them.

Safety Precautions

Because you're dealing with toxic liquid that's contained under pressure at boiling temperature, extreme caution should be used when working on the cooling system, particularly if it's hot or if the engine is overheated. People have been scalded to death because they didn't follow a few simple precautions.

Never remove a radiator cap when the engine is hot. If the engine is overheated, that coolant is well above the boiling point. As soon as the pressurized radiator cap is removed, that scalding fluid is going to make Old Faithful look like a koi pond and if you're in its way you're going to get burnt. If the bike is overheated or even just hot, let it cool down; go get a soda or take a nap, and when it's cooled off a little you can investigate the problem.

As I said, antifreeze, particularly when it has an ethylene glycol base, is highly toxic. Always store antifreeze in a clearly marked, tightly shut

Antifreeze comes pre-mixed and straight. Motorcycle manufacturers may specify a particular type or brand.

container. Used antifreeze should be treated the same way you'd treat any other deadly poison. Drain it, contain it, and dispose of it responsibly.

Oil Cooling

Part of the engine oil's purpose is to remove a portion of the heat generated by internal friction and the combustion process. Oil cooling functions in exactly the same way that liquid cooling does: convection. The oil picks up heat wherever it's generated. As it flows through the engine it gives up the heat to the cooler surrounding surfaces, the oil sump being the main one, and this is why oil sumps have fins. Under some conditions the oil may not be able to transfer heat out of the engine quickly enough. If that seems likely, an oil cooler will be installed. Oil coolers are nothing more than a small radiator and are normally equipped with a thermostat.

The thermostat gives the oil time to warm up (normal oil temperature is about 180 degrees) before circulating it through the cooler. If the oil temperature drops, or the ambient temperature is particularly low, the thermostat shuts down, bypassing the cooler. Oil-cooling systems incorporating a separate radiator are used on both air- and liquid-cooled engines. Some oil-cooling systems also use small jets to spray a cooling stream of oil on a particular hot spot, such as the underside of the piston.

ENGINE OIL AND LUBRICATION

The basic function of engine oil is to prevent the engine's internal rotating, sliding, and reciprocating parts from grinding themselves into paste or welding themselves into one large lump. If it weren't for the lubricant continually circulated by the oiling system, they would do just that.

Most current four-strokes use a wet-sump lubrication system, the major exceptions being Harley-Davidson air-cooled twins, and some off-road bikes. As we've already said, wet-sump engines carry all of their oil in the crankcase. Oil is pumped from the sump through a screen or filter and then pressure-fed to the engine components.

Gravity returns the oil to the sump. The wet-sump design is nice and compact and does away with the need for external oil lines. It also lends

DRY AND WET SUMP TYPE SYSTEMS

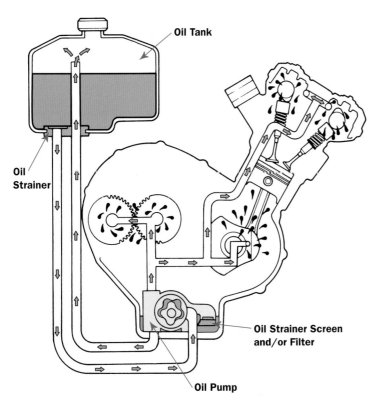

Oil Tank

Oil Strainer

Oil Strainer Screen and/or Filter

Oil Pump

Dry-sump systems use an external oil tank and dual-function oil pumps. In this system, the pump draws in oil for delivery to the various components and pumps oil out of the sump and back to the oil tank.

Since this design eliminates the need for space to contain the oil within the lower portion of the crankcases, the engine can be positioned lower than would otherwise be possible. This design often incorporates routing and oil storage configurations that aid in lowering oil temperature.

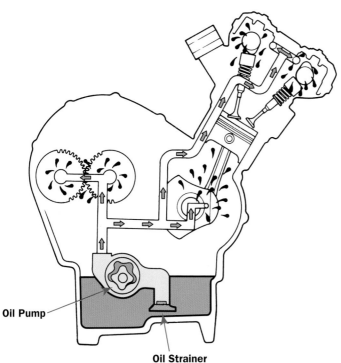

Oil Pump

Oil Strainer

Wet sump systems use the engine to contain the oil. This eliminates the need for an external oil tank and the attendant, leak prone lines that go with it. On the downside it creates a taller engine and may lead to higher oil temperatures. Which in turn, may create the need for an oil cooler with external lines that may leak! *(Courtesy American Honda Motor Corporation)*

■

DIY Oil Change

You'll need:

- *Owner's manual*
- *The correct weight and quantity of oil*
- *A new oil filter*
- *Any required gaskets*
- *The appropriately sized wrench or socket to remove your engine's oil drain plug*
- *An oil filter wrench or substitute if the filter is a spin on type filter or the correct*
- *wrenches needed to remove the cover if it's a cartridge style filter.*
- *A drain pan large enough to hold the used oil.*
- *Anti-seize compound.*
- *Brake or contact cleaner.*
- *Rags or paper towels.*
- *Latex mechanics gloves (optional)*

Oil changes are where most of us start our mechanical careers. It's a basic but very important job. It can be a little dirty if you aren't careful but that's part of the fun.

Start by reading the appropriate section in your owners or shop manual. While the basic procedure is generally the same for all motorcycles, some bikes, particularly those with dry sumps, or those that use the frame to store a portion of the oil may require slightly different techniques.

Because warm oil drains more readily than cold, start by warming the bike up to its normal operating temperature. Dirt particles that may have dropped out of the oil while it was cold will also be picked up and held in suspension when the oil is warmed up and re-circulated. By draining the oil when it's warm these dirt particles are removed along with the oil. ∎

Locate and remove the drain plug

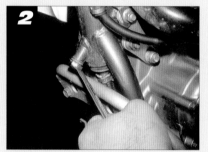

This particular bike has two, one in the sump and one in the frame.

Remove the oil filter cover (or oil filter if the engine has a spin-on type filter). This off-road model also had an oil filter cover guard installed.

Allow the oil to drain.

Allow the filter cavity to drain.

DIY *Oil Change*

6

Thoroughly clean the drain bolts. Replace the drain plug gasket with a new one if need be.

7

Clean filter cavity or gasket surface.

8

A little lubricant doesn't hurt. I prefer a copper based anti-seize compound.

9
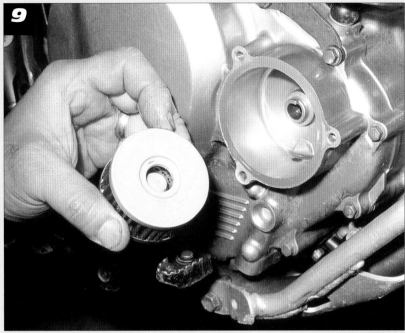

Install the new filter. If it's a cartridge type make sure you install the correct end on the filter mount.

10

Install the new O-ring.

11

Reinstall the oil filter cover and torque it down evenly.

12

Fill the sump, run the engine for a few minutes, check for any leaks and then recheck the oil level.

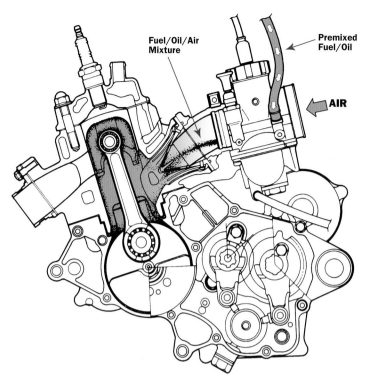

Fuel/Oil/Air Mixture

Premixed Fuel/Oil

AIR

Premix lubrication is most widely used on competition two-stroke engines and lawn equipment, go figure. Oil injection removed most of the headaches from two-stroke street bike ownership; pity they're all gone now. One of the better oil injection systems, Suzuki's Posi Force system, injected the oil directly into the bearings and cylinders. (Courtesy American Honda Motor Corporation)

itself well to use with designs that lubricate the engine and transmission from a common oil supply.

Bikes that use a dry-sump system have external oil tanks. On some models the tanks may be incorporated into the frame itself. Since the dry-sump design eliminates the engine-oil sump, the engine can be mounted lower in the frame than it might be otherwise. Dry-sump systems normally have their tanks and plumbing designed to help cool the oil as well.

In a dry-sump system, the pump is forced to do two jobs. First, it must draw oil in from the tank and distribute it throughout the engine. Second, it has to return the oil that falls into the sump back to the tank. Dry-sump oil pumps are usually described as having a pressure side and a scavenge side. The pressure side pressurizes the engine, and the scavenge side picks up the oil from the sump and returns it to the oil tank.

Choosing the Right Motor Oil

Motor oil has a tough job. It not only has to lube parts, but it must also carry off a fair amount of the heat generated by those same parts, remove some of the heat generated by combustion, and hold in suspension a whole slew of nasty by-products created by the combustion process. It must be thin enough at low temperatures to flow readily through the engine on cold start, and thick enough at high temperatures to prevent metal-to-metal contact.

Furthermore, it has to perform under tremendous heat and pressure and cost less than $5 a quart. In order to perform all these functions in all the various engines, oil manufacturers have formulated a bewildering number of motor oils. So which should you choose?

We need to look at two things when buying oil. First, is the oil the correct weight for our application, and second, is it the correct quality? Your owner's manual will spell out in great detail exactly what is required; some will go so far as to specify a particular brand. In fact, at one time some manufacturers actually embossed the oil-filler cap with a selection of name brands and grades. So, off you go to the local shop, owner's manual in hand, but when you arrive things get a little more interesting. For starters, there are at least ten different brands at varying prices, none of which are listed in the manual.

The first thing to look for is the grade designation. Usually, it's right on the front in big bold numbers that say 10W40 or 20W50, and so on. Your owner's manual will tell you in no uncertain terms: "This motorcycle is designed to use 10W40," or whatever weight oil. It will also tell what oil rating it should be (we'll discuss that in a few paragraphs). My advice is to stick to the manufacturer's recommended weights at all times. Going to heavier or lighter weight oil won't accomplish anything and may cause engine damage or accelerated wear.

If you're buying your oil from a motorcycle dealership, chances are you're either buying a motorcycle oil specifically formulated for motorcycle use, or one that the dealership knows has a proven track record and recommends. If you purchase dedicated motorcycle oil such as Spectro, Maxima, Bel-Ray or Silkolene to mention four, you can be certain that the oil you're getting is good quality. But what if you're out on the road when it's time to change the oil, a million miles from the nearest motorcycle shop?

All reputable oil will carry either an American Petroleum Institute (API) or its European equivalent the ACEA (Association des Constructeurs Européens d'Automobiles) rating. Somewhere on the package is a sentence that says "meets or exceeds API specifications XX." If it doesn't, think long and hard about pouring that oil into your bike.

The package may also display the API seal, which looks like a little donut. The top half of the donut describes the oil's performance level, its quality, so to speak. In the center of the donut will be the oil's viscosity. The bottom of the donut will tell you if the oil is considered "energy conserving."

As we mentioned earlier, your owner's manual lists your bike's required oil performance rating. Every manufacturer has their own preferences, but most currently call for oil with an SF or better rating (such as SG, SH, SI, or SJ, which is the current standard). To sum it all up, you should choose an oil of the correct viscosity and specified or higher service rating, from a reputable manufacturer.

Quick Oil Facts

Multi-viscosity oils are created when polymers are added to a light base of 5W, 10W or 20W oil. At low temperature the polymers are coiled up like little snakes. The oil flows at the low number rating. As the oil warms up the polymers unwind into long chains. The chains prevent the oil from thinning out as far as it normally would.

Most of today's oil is very good, if you know what to look for you can find the best. Here's a quick list.

The viscosity index, or VI, is a number that indicates an oil's viscosity change within a given temperature range. The higher the VI number the less change, and the lower the VI the greater the change. Viscosity is crucial to bearing life. Therefore a high VI number, all things being equal between oils, is a real strong point. But be advised that VI is only a valid comparison within a given viscosity range; it won't tell how well the oil resists thermal breakdown outside of that range.

The flash point is the temperature at which the oil can be ignited with a flame. Oils with low flash points vaporize easily and burn off. Flash point is an indication of the quality of the base oil used. The higher the flash point, the better the oil.

The percentage of sulfated ash is how much solid material is left when the oil burns. High ash contents form sludge and leave deposits in the engines. The lower the ash content, the better your engine will like it.

The percentage of zinc. Zinc is an extreme-pressure additive. It protects your engine during brief periods of metal-to-metal contact. Motorcycle engines, particularly those used in sportbikes, like big shots of zinc.

Oil Additives

Three words: don't use them. Every so often a miracle additive comes along guaranteed to add horsepower, enhance engine life, and whiten your teeth. Engine oils are thoroughly researched and painstakingly compounded; nothing you can add will improve them. In fact, the

The API donut will tell you all you really need to know about a particular oil.

additives may actually have an adverse affect on the oil's performance. Of course, if you really want to whiten your teeth. . .

ENGINE LUBRICATION: FOUR-STROKE ENGINES

How Lubrication Works (why our engines don't grind themselves to bits)

Engine lubrication exists in three forms: hydrodynamic, boundary, and mixed. The three conditions overlap depending on the function of the part being lubricated and what the engine is doing at the time.

Hydrodynamic is just a ten dollar word meaning "fluid in action." When applied to machinery, it refers to the wedge of oil that develops between certain moving parts. The wedge of oil prevents the parts from ever making metal-to-metal contact, which as you can well imagine would greatly shorten the engine's life. Hydrodynamic lubrication only exists when the engine is running and only between moving parts. The best examples of hydrodynamic lubrication in action are the crankshaft bearings and connecting-rod bearings.

The why and wherefore of hydrodynamic lubrication can get pretty complex. The short version is that as the crankshaft rotates oil is fed through it under pressure. Oil flows out of a hole in the crank directly under each bearing. As the crank rotates, the oil, due to its adhesive nature, sticks to it and is quickly pulled into a wedge shape. The oil wedge rotates along with the crankshaft, interposed between the crankshaft bearing surface (the journal) and the connecting rod bearing. The rod bearing actually floats above the crankshaft journal supported by the wedge of oil. Oil pressure at the most heavily loaded portion of the bearing may reach several thousand pounds per square inch. Technical guru Kevin Cameron refers to hydrodynamic lubrication as "metal surfing."

Boundary lubrication occurs when you start your engine. Most of the oil has run off and there are no moving parts to create hydrodynamic action. The only thing left to carry the load are a few measly molecules of oil stuck to the parts, and oil additives (primarily zinc) that were designed to form a protective coating between wear surfaces. Boundary lubrication protects your engine during cold starts and when the bike sits for any length of time. Considering that most engine wear takes place during cold starting, an oil that offers good boundary protection is worth using.

Mixed lubrication is a combination of hydrodynamic and boundary. It occurs when parts are moving too slowly to take full advantage of hydrodynamic action—the best example being the cam and tappets or rocker arms when the engine is idling. The cam just isn't spinning quickly enough to develop the kind of hydrodynamic wedge it needs to support the tappets. So it depends upon some boundary lubrication to prevent galling.

Another, perhaps more dynamic, example would be the piston. As the piston approaches both TDC and BDC it must slow down and actually come to a stop. As it does, the hydrodynamic wedge protecting the skirt-rings and cylinder wall disappears leaving only boundary protection.

Bear in mind that during periods of mixed lubrication some protection is provided by hydrodynamic action and some from boundary; this is why oil additives are important. Taking this a step further, we can see that an oil with the right additive package (extra zinc, for example) may prove beneficial.

OIL PUMPS

There are three broad types of oil pumps: piston pumps, which aren't used much any more, gear pumps, and georotor pumps, which are a rotor-type pump.

Piston pumps, as the name indicates, use one or more piston(s) to pump oil. They were often seen on old British bikes and some old Hondas. They didn't put out much pressure or volume, but worked well enough on the modestly powered bikes they were fitted to.

Gear pumps use two meshing gears inside a tight fitting case. Oil is drawn in one side and discharged through another. Gear-type pumps are simple and inexpensive to build. One rung up on the evolutionary scale from the piston pump, they are somewhat inefficient.

THE TROCHOID OIL PUMP

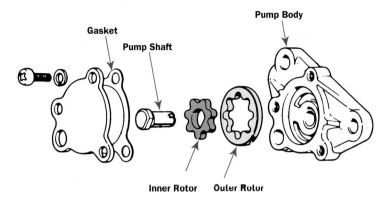

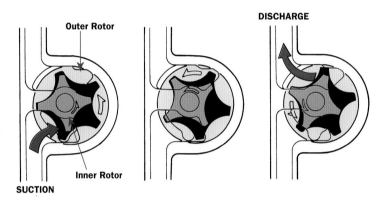

The trochoid-type oil pump is the most common oil pump design used in 4-stroke engines. It is designed to turn two rotors within a casing, with and inner rotor fixed on the pump shaft (drive shaft) and an outer rotor on its circumference. When the inner rotor is turned by means of the oil pump shaft, the outer rotor also turns, with the clearance between the two rotors varying. Lubricant is drawn through by suction when the clearance is enlarged. Oil is delivered to the opposite side through this clearance and is then routed into the discharge passage when the clearance lessens. The more teeth the inner and outer rotors have, the less the amount of pulsation. The oil flow volume increases in direct proportion with the increase in thickness of the rotor dimension.

Some models have a double rotor trochoid-type oil pump with collects oil directly from both the oil cooler and the sump. ∎

The trochoid type oil pump is compact, efficient and pumps a boatload of oil. All good reasons for its popularity.
(Courtesy American Honda Motor Corporation)

The predominant georotor pump in use today is the trochoid, or Eaton-style, pump. It is also the most common oil pump found in modern motorcycles. A shaft-driven lobed inner rotor rotates inside an outer rotor. The outer rotor has female recesses machined to match the inner rotor's lobes. The female recesses are larger than the lobes, and there is always one more recess than lobe. As the inner rotor turns it drives the outer rotor. The clearance between the lobes and the recesses constantly changes. When the clearance is large, oil is drawn into the pump through the appropriate port. It is swept around to the opposite side of the pump, and as the rotor clearance diminishes, it is discharged. While trochoid pumps are somewhat complex to machine, they do produce high volume and pressure, making them the best pump for most situations.

3 *Ignition*

The sole purpose of the ignition system is to create a spark capable of igniting the fuel/air mixture inside of the cylinder, at precisely the right time, which varies with engine rpm, and it must do it hundreds of times a second. It ignites the mixture by creating an electric arc at the tip of the spark plug (which we'll discuss later). And if you take nothing else away from this chapter I want you to learn this one simple fact: the fuel/air mixture inside of the cylinder does not "explode" when the spark plug ignites it; it burns, at a steady and controlled rate. If it didn't, the engine would destroy itself in a matter of moments.

There are several means used by various motorcycle engines to light the fire. Most common are battery-and-coil systems (including points, transistorized, and others), CDIs, and magnetos.

so let's look at each in turn. In this chapter we'll look at all the various components of your motorcycle's ignition system and tell you how you can maintain and improve them.

BASIC BATTERY AND COIL IGNITIONS

Since the majority of you probably own motorcycles (or at least cars) that use direct-current (DC) battery-and-coil ignition systems that's where we'll start. And we'll make it even simpler by starting with a single-cylinder engine.

The basic battery and coil ignition system as used on a motorcycle consists of two separate circuits: the primary and the secondary. They are independent but work together to make a spark. First, we'll describe these two circuits and then tell how they pull together to light your bike's fire.

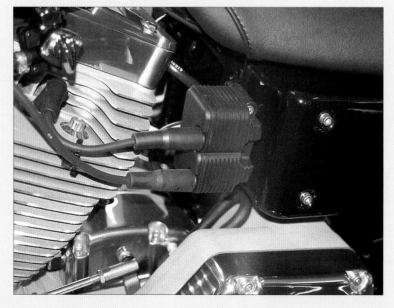

The twin-tower coil is used on wasted spark ignition systems. Both spark plugs fire at the same time, but since one cylinder is on the exhaust stroke while its companion is on the compression stroke the excess spark has nothing to ignite.

The Primary Circuit

The primary circuit is the low-voltage circuit, meaning its components all operate at the nominal 12 volts of the battery. This circuit includes the battery, the ignition switch, the primary windings in the ignition coil (the coil also has secondary windings, which are part of the secondary ignition circuit), and a mechanism for triggering the spark, which could be a system of points, condenser, and breaker cam on an older machine or the electronic ignition of newer machines.

The battery is nothing more than a storage unit for the electricity needed to fire the ignition. The ignition switch is the gateway that connects or disconnects the battery from the rest of the primary circuit. When the switch is in the open position the circuit is off; when the switch is closed the circuit is on.

The primary windings of the ignition coil consist of several hundred turns of wire approximately the same diameter as a common steel pin (0.4–1 mm). One end of the primary winding connects to the positive terminal of the coil, the other end to the negative terminal.

The trigger mechanism is just a form of switch that interrupts the primary circuit at specific intervals. That switch can be either mechanical (ignition points) or electronic (a transistor), but it still serves the same function. On a four-stroke motorcycle the trigger signal is timed to occur every other rotation of the crankshaft, on the compression stroke. On a two-stroke engine the trigger signal is timed to occur on every rotation of the crank, on the compression stroke.

The Secondary Circuit

The secondary circuit is the high-voltage circuit, meaning its components operate at the higher voltage supplied by the ignition coil, which is anywhere from 20,000 to 30,000 volts. This circuit consists of the secondary windings in the ignition coil, the spark plug wires, and the spark plugs. On some older bikes, the secondary circuit also included an automotive-type distributor. For the most part motorcycle distributors were phased out in the early '70s. Nevertheless, we'll discuss distributors after we've finished with the basics.

DIY Adjusting Ignition Timing

Adjusting the ignition timing used to be a routine part of servicing your motorcycle. No longer, in fact on many newer bikes the timing isn't even adjustable. However that doesn't mean it shouldn't be checked every once in awhile. A radical shift in ignition timing could mean you're on the verge of an ignition component failure, and give you a chance to correct the problem before disaster strikes.

Most timing lights have an arrow on the pickup lead that indicates which direction the pickup should be installed on the spark plug. Install the lead, with the pick-up facing the

(continued next page)

You'll need:

- *Your shop manual*
- *Tools to remove the timing inspection cover*
- *A timing light; these can be purchased at an auto parts store, Sears department store or through any good tool outlet.*
- *Optional, a fully charged 12 volt battery*

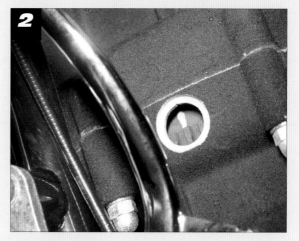

The manual will provide all the information you'll need. Timing lights can be purchased for $50 or less.

A dab of paint on the timing mark will make it much easier to see.

DIY Adjusting Ignition Timing

right direction on the #1 plug (#2 on some machines; see your manual). Next, connect the timing light leads either to the bike's battery or your spare. Remove the appropriate cover to gain access to the timing marks. Start the engine and aim the light at the marks; when the trigger is pulled the marks should be clearly illuminated. Check the marks position against the shop manual specifications, both in the retarded position (idle), and at full advance (about 3,000 rpm). If the marks are off consult your manual for the correct adjustment procedure.

Tip #1: sometimes the marks are hard to see, but a dab of paint will make spotting them a lot easier.

Tip #2: some bikes tend to sling oil out through the timing plug (Harleys are particularly prone to doing so). There are special clear timing plugs available, but not for every bike. If your bike's timing marks run "wet" be prepared for a spray of oil. ∎

Try to focus the light directly on the timing mark and the datum point. If the light is tilted the mark may appear higher or lower than it really is.

The secondary winding of the ignition coil is made of several thousand turns of very thin, hair like wire (0.05–0.1 mm). The secondary coil wires are wrapped around a laminated iron core. The core may take the form of an iron bar, in which case the primary windings surround the secondary windings. Or the secondary windings may be wrapped around a horseshoe shaped frame, in which case the primary winding fits inside of the secondary. One side of the secondary winding connects to the positive terminal; the opposite end of the secondary is connected to the high-tension terminal, right where the spark plug lead plugs in.

The spark plug lead is a heavily insulated piece of wire that carries the high voltage generated by the secondary circuit to the spark plug. Its inner core may be made of solid copper wire or it may use strands of fiberglass impregnated with graphite.

The spark plug is simple device that uses a gap between its two electrodes (one connected to the plug wire and the other grounded through the engine) to turn the high voltage from the coil into a spark to ignite the fuel/air mixture in the cylinder.

Lighting the Fire

Here's how the primary and secondary ignition circuits work together: first, you turn on the ignition switch, which routes battery voltage to the to the coil's positive terminal, through the primary windings to the negative terminal and out to the trigger mechanism (points or electronic ignition).

If the trigger mechanism is closed, current flows from the battery and through the primary windings to ground. As the current flows through the primary windings it induces a magnetic field in the secondary coil windings.

When the points or electronic ignition circuit opens, current flow through the primary circuit stops, causing the magnetic field created in the secondary windings to break down. As the magnetic field collapses it generates a rising voltage in the secondary windings. Because there are so many more coils of wire in the secondary windings than in the primary windings the voltage is increased proportionally, somewhere on the order of 200:1. When the voltage rises high enough, the electrical current from the secondary jumps the gap between the spark plug's two electrodes, and the current flows to ground

When the breaker cam then allows the points to close, current again starts to flow through the primary windings, and the whole process is repeated up to 300 times a second or more!

Now that you know the fundamentals of how all battery-and-coil systems operate, it's time to go into greater detail on all the systems that are necessary to make fire on all the many different types of motorcycle engines. These include timing, distributing, and advancing systems.

Timing and Advancing the Spark

Here's the problem. It takes some amount of time for all of this making and breaking of circuits to occur. It also takes some time for the spark to ignite the mixture and it takes some time for the mixture itself to burn. That means we have to time the spark to occur as the piston reaches some distance before top dead center (TDC). At an idle speed of 800 rpm, for instance, we may be able to compress and burn all of the fuel in our cylinder if we ignite it at, say, 10 degrees before TDC. This is called base timing or the retarded position.

As engine speed increases, however, we have less time in which to burn the fuel. The answer is to light our mixture earlier. Therefore, as engine speed increases we must advance the timing of the spark so that it arrives at the plug tip a little earlier, for example to 38 degrees before TDC at 3,000 rpm.

As engine speed increases, so does the burn rate of the fuel, which is called the flame speed. This is the reason we don't have to continually advance the timing as engine rpm increases. At some point, usually around 3,500 rpm or so, we can stop advancing the timing. When the timing has reached its point of maximum advance it's said to be at full advance.

To get both base and full-advance timing, engines are designed with advance units, which provide a means to advance and retard ignition timing based on rpm. On the earliest motorcycles, the timing unit was manually actuated by a lever or twistgrip control.

The first automatic-advance units were just a mechanical governor that used springs and bob weights. Centrifugal force flung the weights outward against spring tension as engine rpm increased. The weight forced the points cam to rotate forward, advancing the point at which the cam nudged the points open.

On more modern machines, the advance is controlled electronically, giving the engine designer much wider latitude in designing the advance curve or rate at which the advance occurs. By measuring throttle position, engine speed vs. road speed, coolant temperature, and almost any other thing he wants, the ignition engineer can map a computer-controlled advance

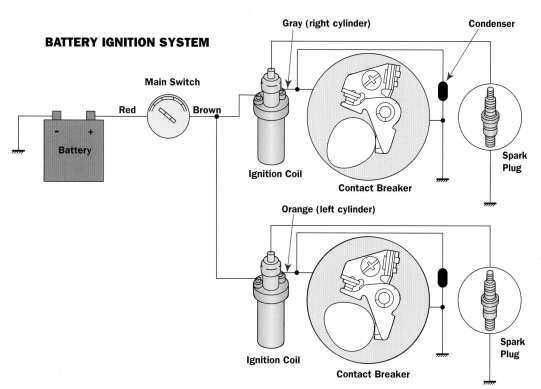

BATTERY IGNITION SYSTEM

The basic DC battery and coil ignition system. The system shown is typical of the design used on many twin-cylinder motorcycles. Note that the points are wired in series with the coil's primary circuit. (Courtesy Yamaha Motor Corporation)

progression that adjusts the timing for optimum performance at virtually any engine rpm.

A FINAL WORD ABOUT ADVANCE

Lots of bench racers will tell you that advance is good, the more advance you dial into your ignition the faster the bike goes. Wrong; the better your engine design, in terms of its ability to burn fuel, the less ignition advance you'll need. Think about it. If the charge burns quickly and efficiently you can light the fire a lot later. If the charge burns slowly you have to light the fire early. NASCAR engine builders routinely set their full advance at less than 30 degrees.

Igniting Multiple Cylinders

Igniting and timing the ignition get even more complicated on multi-cylinder engines.

One early solution was to use a distributor. The distributor, as its name implies, was nothing more than a rotary switch that distribute to each cylinder in turn the electrical energy produced in the coil.

A more common solution was to add another set of points and another coil that could fire each cylinder in turn without the added complexity of a distributor.

An even simpler and more common solution was to fire two cylinders from one coil. Designers accomplished this by arranging the cylinders so that when cylinder number one was on the power stroke, cylinder number two was on the exhaust stroke. They connected two spark plug leads to a common terminal (a twin-tower coil) and connected the coil to one ignition trigger.

When cylinder number one was on the power stroke and the spark plug ignited the mixture, the spark plug in cylinder number two fired as well. But since the exhaust valve was open and there was no mixture in cylinder number two to burn, nothing happened. These were known as wasted-spark ignition systems and are still used by some models today.

DETONATION AND PRE-IGNITION, THE TWIN TERRORS

Let me make one thing clear from the start: while detonation and pre-ignition are closely related and one may be caused by the other, they are really two separate phenomena. Unfortunately, if allowed to continue for any length of time the end results are the same: severe engine damage.

Most of us have experienced detonation at one time or another. It's become quite common since lead was removed from gas. In the U.S. we call it knock or ping; in England they call it pinking. Personally I think it sounds more like the tinkling of broken glass (or broken engine parts).

Usually the scenario goes something like this. You're driving or riding up a hill, or putting the engine under some other severe load, as you accelerate you hear a noise coming from the engine that sounds a lot like someone beating it with a hammer. As you back off on the throttle the noise goes away. That, my friends, is detonation. It's caused by excessive heat and pressure causing the fuel/air mixture to auto-ignite, and detonation always occurs after the spark has ignited the mixture.

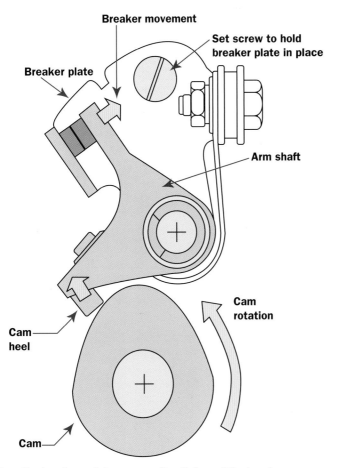

Picture the breaker points as a small switch, and the breaker cam as a finger pushing them apart. (Courtesy Yamaha Motor Corporation)

Labels in figure: Breaker movement · Set screw to hold breaker plate in place · Breaker plate · Arm shaft · Cam heel · Cam · Cam rotation

The big problem from the engine's point of view is that when auto-ignition occurs the mixture truly does explode instead of burning smoothly. The explosion generates a shock wave that hammers the piston, cylinder head, connecting rods, and bearings.

Anything that causes the engine to run hot, that heats up the fuel/air charge, or that raises compression can cause detonation. Overly advanced ignition timing, too lean a mixture or fuel with too low an octane are also prime suspects. Lugging the engine, which is loading it heavily at very low rpm, can also cause it to detonate.

Anything that keeps the engine running cooler or promotes rapid burning of the fuel-air mixture makes detonation less likely. These include richer mixtures, retarded ignition timing, low compression, more efficient engine cooling (read that as water cooling), and cylinder and intake systems that develop lots of gas turbulence, which helps promote a rapid burn.

Engines that have had severe detonation problems have pistons and cylinder heads that look like they've been sandblasted. If the engine detonates long enough and hard enough it will be destroyed in short order.

Pre-ignition occurs when some unusually hot object inside the combustion chamber ignites the fresh mixture before the spark plug has fired. Normally pre-ignition is caused by either a glowing piece of carbon in the combustion chamber or by using a spark plug that's too hot for the conditions. Using an overly hot plug can literally turn the spark plug electrode into a glowing chunk of red hot metal.

Pre-ignition overheats the gas just as overly advanced ignition timing does. In very short order pre-ignition causes detonation which leads directly to a torched motor. A hole burnt through the center of the piston is a pretty good indication the motor suffered from pre-ignition.

Points and Condensers

Most motorcycles built from the 1930s through the 1960s have breaker points to trigger the ignition. After that, electronic ignition became more common and finally became universal in the 1990s.

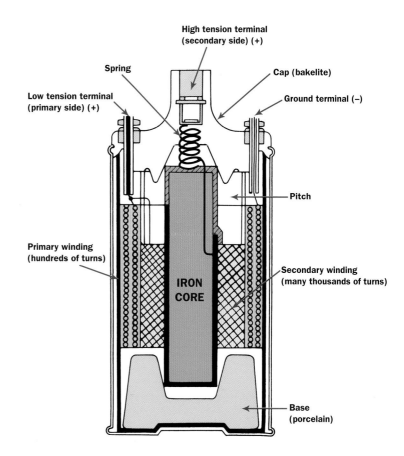

The open magnetic circuit case coils aren't as popular as they used to be. (Courtesy Yamaha Motor Corporation)

Picture the breaker points as a small switch and the breaker cam as a finger pushing them apart. Spring tension holds the points together, and the breaker cam pushes them apart. On most four-stroke motorcycles the breaker cam is driven by the camshaft and turns at one-half engine rpm. On a two-stroke engine the breaker cam is turned by the crankshaft and spins at engine rpm.

When the points are together, current flows through the primary circuit. As the points begin to separate, the current flowing through the primary circuit tries to jump across the points, in the same way the spark jumps the gap in the spark plug. While we want a spark at the spark plug, we don't at the points because the spark will burn and erode the surface of the points, wearing them out prematurely. To prevent such sparking, almost all motorcycle points systems also include

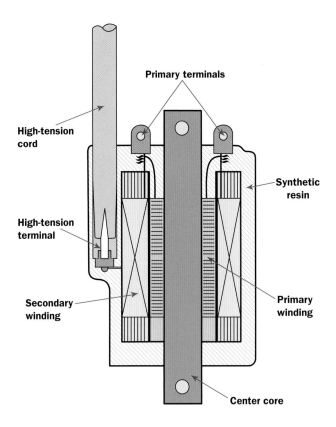

Due to its compact construction and superior reliability, the open magnetic circuit molded coil has become the standard type for motorcycle use. (Courtesy Yamaha Motor Corporation)

a capacitor (or condenser) wired in parallel with the points. Here's how it works:

The condenser has the ability to absorb and store a small amount of current. Since it's easier for the current to flow into the condenser than to jump across the quickly widening point gap, that's what it does.

There is another reason that point fired ignitions include a condenser: the quicker the primary circuit collapses, the stronger the induced voltage in the secondary circuit becomes, which in turn creates a healthier spark at the plug tip. Because the condenser starts to absorb current the instant the points begin to separate it prevents self-induction from continuing current flow in the primary circuit. Since the condenser cuts off flow in the primary almost instantaneously, the voltage induced in the secondary circuit is considerably stronger than it would be if no condenser were installed. In general, condensers last

much longer than points do. That said, they do fail.

Problems with Points

Points had a few inherent problems. Being a mechanical device they were subject to wear, which meant they required fairly frequent attention. Most twin- and four-cylinder bikes had two sets of points and triples three sets of points. Some twins were equipped with a single set of points as were all singles (duh). A normal tune up at the time meant that all of the points were adjusted or replaced. If they were replaced, condensers were usually replaced along with them.

Also, because the intensity of the spark depended on the amount of time it took to open and close the points and how much current could pass through them, the quality of the spark was to a large degree limited by the points.

To function properly the points had to start with an initial setting. This is called point gap and is usually between 0.012 and 0.016 inch. Once the correct gap was set. The position of the points was adjusted relative to piston position. During normal running, the points wore, especially the rubbing block, which is a block of fiber that rubs against the contact-breaker cam and opens the points. Other wear spots included the point pivot itself as well as the advance unit. As the points wore the gap tended to close up, retarding the timing.

Electronic Ignitions

Electronic systems with no moving parts eliminated problems with wear and the need for frequent adjustment. Also, because they employ solid state technology very high voltages can be used. The higher the voltage the better the spark, the better the spark the better the bike runs. Furthermore, an ignition advance curve that suits the engine's requirements at any and all engine speeds can be precisely mapped. At the same time a rev limiter can be installed to prevent over-revving the engine.

The first electronic ignitions weren't all that great. In some cases they were actually worse than the magneto systems they were designed to replace. In most instances they just needed a little fine tuning; today the electronic ignition is practically universal, in fact even my lawnmower is fitted with a simple electronic ignition. Currently (no pun intended) electronic ignition systems can be divided into two groups: transistorized (which use a battery) and CDI type (most of which do not require a battery). There is also a practical limit to what you need to know so we'll just hit the basics here.

Transistorized Ignition Systems

In a transistorized ignition system, current flows from the battery to the primary side of the coil and to a transistor in the ignition control module. A signal from the pulse generator turns the transistor on and off. When the primary circuit is turned off, induced current flows through the secondary circuit creating a spark.

With any ignition system, as engine speed increases the on-off cycle through the primary side of the coil occurs more frequently. As the duration of the current in the primary side drops off, a correspondingly lower current is created in the secondary side. As a result the spark created at the plug tip may not last long enough to ignite the mixture or it may not be strong enough to even jump the gap at the plug tip. The result is usually a high-speed misfire.

The transistorized ignition compensates for the voltage drop by using the ignition timing control circuit to increase the length of time the primary side stays energized as rpm increases. Because the primary side is energized for a longer period of time it increases the voltage induced in the secondary coil, creating a hotter spark.

Digitally Controlled Transistorized Ignition Systems

Now we're getting to the good stuff. Digitally controlled or mapped ignitions are the hot tip, no doubt about it. CDI ignitions were among the very first of the pointless ignitions and are still used on everything from trail bikes to tourers. An adaptation of the transistorized ignition system, the digitally controlled system uses a microcomputer to calculate the perfect ignition timing at every engine speed and condition. Some systems are more sophisticated than others, especially those used on the latest fuel-injected bikes, but all of them are pretty good. Most of these systems also incorporate some kind of fail-safe

mechanism that kills the engine when timing, engine speed, or fuel delivery goes off the scale.

Digitally controlled ignitions use an ignition pulse generator rotor, one or two pulse generators, the black box (and in this case it truly is a mysterious component), ignition coils, and spark plugs.

The ignition generator rotor has small projections on it that look like teeth; these are called reluctors. The generator rotor is mounted to the crankshaft. As the reluctors sweep past the ignition pulse generator a signal is sent to the black box telling it exactly what the crankshaft position and rpm are. A signal receiver inside the control module converts the pulse to a digital signal. The signal is sent to the microcomputer, which compares it to the ideal timing point for that situation, which is stored in the computer memory. If everything looks good to the computer it turns off the transistor controlling the primary side of the coil and fires the plug. If things are a little off the computer advances or retards the timing to suit the engine requirements.

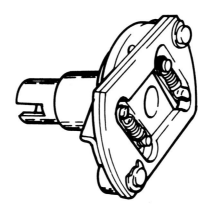

Like the points that they opened, mechanical advance units have all but disappeared. (Courtesy American Honda Motor Corporation)

"Why pay extra for premium? My bike runs fine on regular." This piston was destroyed by a combination of overly advanced ignition timing, and low octane fuel.

The latest systems include throttle position sensors, coolant sensors and anything else the engineers can come up with to help the computer determine the optimum ignition point.

CDI

CDI stands for capacitive discharge ignition. These were the first real electronic systems, initially appearing on off-road two-strokes. The CDI produces a quick and stable high secondary voltage that is extremely resistant to spark plug fouling. A big advantage is that voltage increases as engine rpm increases. The original CDI systems and the ones still used on off-road and dual-sportbikes are based in part on the flywheel magneto used on many older bikes.

The CDI system incorporates a crankshaft-mounted rotor, which is nothing more than a heavy external flywheel fitted with magnets. Mounted either around the rotor or inside the rotor is a stationary coil called the exciter coil. As the rotor spins, an alternating current (AC) is induced in the exciter coil. In some modern CDI systems the induced current is converted to DC by a rectifier. The current flows into a capacitor located in the ignition control module, which most people refer to as the black box.

Power is stored in the capacitor until the rotor magnet passes another coil called the ignition pulse generator. The pulse generator is nothing more than a triggering device. It is connected to the ignition trigger. When the trigger is turned on the capacitor receives an electronic pulse telling it to discharge current into the primary side of the coil. The current flowing through the primary induces a high voltage surge in the secondary side of the coil followed by a nice fat spark at the spark plug.

Because the CDI system is light, reliable and doesn't require a battery to function, it is often used on off-road bikes and race bikes.

Let's digress for a moment. I mentioned that the pulse generator is nothing more than a trigger. You should also be aware that pulse generators take many shapes. In some CDI ignitions they are mounted integrally with the rotor and coil assembly. In others they look like a little toothed wheel with a black box located next to it. Some systems even use light emitting diodes or photocells to trigger the ignition. Keep your eyes peeled, you never know what you'll find under those covers!

Older systems were serviceable and often had adjustable timing. Modern systems are limited to component replacement and many now have fixed timing with no adjustment. However this is a grey area, so consult your service manual as to any possible adjustments.

DC-CDI

A variation on the CDI is the DC-CDI. The DC-CDI is identical in most respects to the plain old CDI except that the bike's battery is used as the primary current source. Inside the black box is a DC to DC transformer, which converts battery voltage to about 220 volts. Power is then stored in the capacitor. From there the system functions just like a standard CDI. Since the initial voltage is provided by the battery independent of engine speed, the DC-CDI provides a better low-rpm spark than a standard CDI. Since a DC-CDI system requires a battery it is found on mainly on street bikes. It is also used on dual-sportbikes that have electric start.

Magneto Ignitions

Being an old sentimentalist, I just had to include this. Early motorcycles had big problems with battery ignitions. The batteries themselves weren't very good and the recharging systems worse.

The solution was the high-tension magneto. Since magnetos disappeared from the scene around 1970 and in fact had been on the way out since the early '60s, it's unlikely you'll be running into any in the near future unless the restoration bug bites you.

Magnetos were completely self-contained ignition units, requiring neither a battery nor a separate ignition coil. They were driven by a chain or gear connected to the engine crankshaft or camshaft. Essentially a magneto uses a set of electrical windings called the armature, which includes both the primary and secondary windings. The armature rotates between high-strength horseshoe magnets, although in some designs the magnets rotate past the windings. This induces a current as the windings cut the magnetic field. A set of points makes and breaks

DIY Installing Spark Plugs

I think it's safe to say that lots of plugs are improperly installed right from the get-go. Here's the right way to install one. First, unless it's a dire emergency let the engine cool down until you can work on it barehanded without burning yourself. Remove the plug cap; most pull straight off but you may need to give it a twist as you

Remove the spark plug lead. Since I have access to a compressor, I blow the dirt out of the plug recess the easy way before removing the spark plug.

pull. Pull only on the cap itself, never on the wire. Before removing the old plug thoroughly clean the surrounding area to prevent dirt from entering either the combustion chamber or lodging in the threads. Use a soda straw and lung pressure to blow the dirt away.

When the area around the plug is clean remove it by turning the wrench counterclockwise. If the plug resists or stops after a few turns spray the threads with WD-40, let it sit for a while, then try again. If the plug won't turn, stop right there and seek the advice of a professional mechanic before proceeding. Once the plug has been removed lay a clean rag or paper towel over the hole to keep any dirt out until your ready to install the new plug.

The spark plug box will probably say that the plug is pre-gapped. Maybe it is, but you should still check it anyway. In my experience the gaps are correct only about half the time.

(continued next page)

You'll need:

- *The correct sparkplug socket or wrench, which hopefully came in your bike's tool kit.*
- *A spark plug gapping tool—available at every auto-parts and tool supply shop in the world.*
- *Anti-seize, available at hardware stores, auto supply stores and tool outlets*
- *The correct plugs for your bike*
- *An ordinary drinking straw—Steal that at the burger joint on your way back*
- *from picking up the plugs.*
- *A 3/8-inch drive torque wrench. The torque wrench is optional, if you have access to one and it'll fit your plug socket by all means use it. However your bike may require a special socket that won't fit with the torque wrench or there may not be enough room to use it without dismantling half the bike.*
- *Brake or contact cleaner or WD-40*

Remove the old plug, and cover the hole with a clean rag or paper towel.

Measure the gap of the new plug.

If the gap isn't correct, use the tool to open it slightly by bending only the side electrode. If the gap is too large, lightly tap the ground electrode against something solid.

DIY   *Installing Spark Plugs*

5

Coat the threads of the new plug with anti-seize.

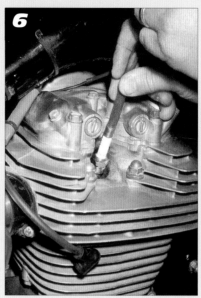

6

If you're afraid of cross-threading the plug, slip a piece of fuel line over the top and use the line to hold the plug while you thread it in. If the threads catch, the line will slip on the plug body before any damage is done.

7

Run the plug in until it bottoms out. Once the plug seats, check the plug manufacturer's instructions for tightening—these are often printed on the box. Normally a new plug should be given an additional half- to two-thirds of a turn after the gasket seats.

Check the plug-gap setting in your manual. Find the appropriate gauge, and insert it between the center electrode and the ground electrode. Use only a wire spark plug gauge to set the gap, flat feeler gauges will give you a misleading feel, making it hard to set the gap.

If the gap is too large gently tap the center electrode against a hard object like a vise or even the concrete floor. The operative word here is gently. You're probably only going to close the gap by 0.002 or 0.003 inch, so there's no need to hammer it.

If the gap is too small, position the gapping part of the tool against the ground electrode and open it up slightly. Never use the porcelain insulator as a fulcrum point to adjust the gap. Not unless you want another bad plug.

The next is a controversial point. I use anti-seize compound on my plugs. Some will tell you it insulates the plug from the head, preventing heat transfer. I don't buy it; in fact I'd argue that it enhances heat transfer. But anti-seize definitely prevents stripped threads and makes the plug much easier to remove the next time. The choice is yours, but in the 30 years I've been using it I've never stripped a spark plug. If you do use it, apply it sparingly.

Once you're satisfied with the gap, thread the new plug into the hole by hand until it seats on its gasket. Then tighten it to the manufacturer's recommended torque specifications. Proper torque for a spark plug in-serted into an aluminum head is 18–21.5 lb.-ft. for a 14mm plug and 10.8–14.5 lb.-ft. for a 12mm plug.

If you have no torque wrench or don't have the room to use it or the plug socket is not adaptable to the torque wrench don't sweat it, run the plug in until the gasket seats and then give the plug an additional one-half to two-thirds turn with your wrench.

Lastly, the spark plug is our window into the engine. Used plugs can tell us a great deal about the internal workings of our engines. ∎

the primary circuit. Secondary current flows through a set of carbon brushes that contact the armature. The spark plug wire is connected to the brushes via a pick-up connection. As engine speed increased the mag made more power, at least until engine speeds got so high that the magneto started to fling windings off the armature, a problem cured by the adaptation of the rotating-magnet models.

The magneto's big drawback was its poor sparking ability at low rpm. This unfortunate feature could make starting a problem, especially when the temperature was cold, the engine oil thick, and the rider not up to the task of kicking over a big single or twin. Magnetos also fell out of favor due to their large size, which took up a chunk of engine space, and their maintenance requirements, which while not outrageous, are still more trouble than the battery-and-coil systems that replaced them.

A variation on the theme is the flywheel magneto. Mainly used on small two-stroke engines, flywheel magnetos incorporate the magnet into the engine flywheel. The coils are located under the flywheel along with the points and condenser. Generally the secondary coil is located outside the flywheel. We'll go into a little more depth on these in chapter 11.

Spark Plugs

Spark plugs are one of the simplest yet most misunderstood components of an engine. They are the subject of more speculation and rumor than any other component I can think of (except maybe oil). They are often replaced needlessly and probably just as often left in an engine long after their useful life as expired.

Spark plugs play two roles, and both are equally important: they ignite the fuel/air mix and conduct heat from the combustion chamber.

To be efficient at lighting the mix, the plugs need to be clean, properly gapped, and still within their service life.

Heat Range

When a plug conducts the right amount of heat, it is said to be in the correct "heat range." Heat range is one of the more confusing things associated with spark plugs, but it's really very simple: a spark plug's heat range refers only to its ability

to transfer heat out of the combustion chamber. A cold plug transfers a lot of heat out of the combustion chamber quickly. A hot plug transfers less heat and takes a longer time to do it.

Hot plugs are used in mildly tuned, low-speed engines. Because their tip temperatures stay high, they burn off carbon deposits that are associated with slow running. Cold plugs are used in high-speed and severe-use circumstances such as racing or high-speed, long-distance touring, circumstances in which the plug must transfer as much heat as possible out of the chamber and into the surrounding metal of the cylinder head.

Selecting the correct heat range is crucial; the working end of the plug operates between 450 and 850 degrees Centigrade. At 950 degrees the piston melts. Below 450 degrees the plug fouls and stops working. The rule is, a hot plug for a cold engine and a cold plug for a hot engine.

Numbering Systems

Stamped on the body of every spark plug is a string of letters and numbers. Some may be

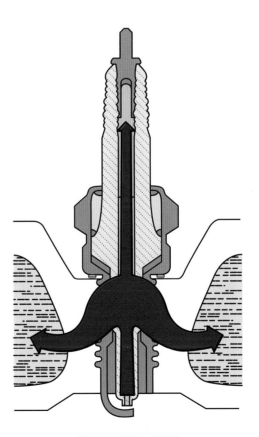

The heat flow path is through the insulator, into the metal body and from there into the cylinder head and atmosphere. (Courtesy American Honda Motor Corporation)

HEAT DISSIPATION

short. For instance a common NGK plug is stamped B8ES. Others aren't so short, for example DPR7EA-9. The alphanumeric code tells you exactly what the physical characteristics and the heat range of a given plug are, but bear in mind that each manufacturer has its own code. Even the numbering system that describes the heat range, which according to common sense should be standardized, varies. For example, NGK motorcycle plugs are generally numbered from 2 to 10. The lower the number the hotter the plug, with 4 actually being the hottest practical plug. On the flip side, both Champion and Bosch go the other way: the high numbers are hot, the low cold.

There are cross-reference charts available that show equivalent plugs. You need to be a little careful here. Because materials and methods of construction do vary you may find a listed equivalent plug to be slightly hotter or colder than the specified plug. While crossover charts are generally accurate, my advice is to always consult the plug manufacturer's catalog before substituting another makers spark plug for the recommended original equipment brand.

Resistor Plugs

Some bikes use resistor spark plugs to avoid interrupting reception of nearby TVs and radios.

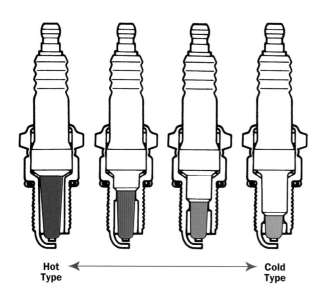

Hot Type ⟵――――――――――⟶ Cold Type

The length of the porcelain determines the heat range of the spark plug. **(Courtesy American Honda Motor Corporation)**

Resistor plugs generally cost a few cents more than non-resistor plugs, so you may be tempted to replace them with their less-expensive equivalents. That may not be such a good idea, because switching to a non-resistor plug can confuse your bike's ignition black box and other electrics.

Your owner's or service manual should list the specific spark plugs recommend for your engine. My advice is to only use those plugs or their equivalents. Beware of advertisers that claim huge horsepower gains and whiter teeth from their trick plugs. Chances are that a brand new set of stock plugs will produce the same results.

Ignition Coils

Some new models have the coils that attach directly to the spark plug without wires. These integrated coils can fire the plug at a much higher voltage than a traditional coil and high-tension wire can. They also cut down on radio wave emissions. I suspect we'll be seeing a lot more of these in the future.

MAINTAINING YOUR IGNITION SYSTEM

Bad grounds, loose connections, and corroded terminals cause many ignition problems. If your bike suddenly develops a pain in its electrical innards check the connections first, especially if you like to wash the bike with a high pressure hose.

Maintaining Spark Plugs

As I mentioned above, plugs nowadays seldom need attention beyond their scheduled replacement intervals. But what if you don't know when your plugs were last replaced? The first thing to look for is lots of dirt and carbon buildup on the spark plug insulator. If the thing looks really crusty, bin it and install a new plug. I feel that cleaning a plug is a waste of time. But how can you tell if the plug is simply worn out? Take a look at both the center electrode and the ground electrode. If they are nice and square on the edges the plug is fine. However, if the edges are well rounded and particularly if the center electrode looks as if it's shrinking into the porcelain insulator, consider the plug to be on it's last legs. Finally, one genuinely good indication that it's time for plugs is a slight high-speed misfire or hiccup.

Misfire and Fouling

A plug misfires when it fails to ignite all of the fuel/air mix in the cylinder. A slight misfire causes a loss of performance; a severe one causes large problems and can eventually lead to engine damage. Misfiring may be caused by a variety of ignition system problems. Bad coils, bad ignition system components, overly retarded timing or fouled plugs are all things you should check for.

The most common spark plug problem, fouling, occurs when the spark plug tip temperature is too low to burn off the by-products left over from the combustion process. Oil and carbon create an electrical path to ground. Instead of the spark jumping the gap, it leaches through the plug. The spark is either too weak to fire the mixture or there is no spark at all. A plug may be wet-fouled, which means it has raw gas or oil dripping from it, or dry-fouled, meaning it has fluffy carbon or soot all over it. A wet-fouled plug needs to be manually cleaned or replaced. A dry-fouled plug may clean itself once the engine is up to operating temperature.

Before replacing a fouled plug always determine why it fouled. Common causes include using a heat range plug that is too cold, extended or improper use of the choke, lots of low-speed driving, and overly rich fuel mixtures (caused by dirty air filters, or a poorly adjusted carb, for instance).

Improving the Ignition System

We've touched on this a bit already. The state-of-the-art in ignition systems is, for the most part, very good indeed, so realistically making any concrete improvements may prove difficult. sportbike owners have it the easiest in that regard: there are replacement chips available for many bikes that will allow you to bypass the OEM fuel and igniton maps for more power. Other tricks include clipping certain wires used to control restrictor circuits or replacing your ignition module with one that contains either a dif-

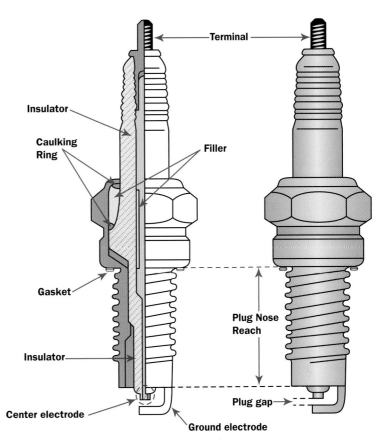

Most sparkplugs are constructed in a comparable fashion, using similar techniques and components.

ferent ignition curve or perhaps a modified (raised) rev limiter. If, heaven forbid, you're still running a points-fired ignition, consider an upgrade to an electronic system. Aftermarket coils are also available, particularly for popular older bikes. Installing a second spark plug used to be a popular modification, especially on older two-valve motors. If it's ultimate power you're after you may want to consider that option.

Aftermarket Advancers

Aftermarket ignition advancers that provide a little more timing advance are the hot item. Do they work? The answer is yes and no. They do advance the timing slightly, usually about 5 degrees, and yes, the factory does retard the timing slightly from the optimum. They do it to prolong plug life in fact; the more advance an ignition uses, the shorter the plug life.

On early bikes intake, fuel, and exhaust systems were as simple as could be. Gasoline from the tank flowed by gravity to a simple carburetor that often fed as many as four cylinders, and the exhaust flowed out the exhaust port or a simple pipe. Through the years, however, these systems have become increasingly sophisticated and complex. Some of the latest motorcycles have electric fuel pumps and gas tanks in such odd places as under the seat; separate fuel injection for each cylinder; charcoal canisters to reduce evaporative emissions; complex tuned air boxes to reduce intake roar, and variable-valved exhausts that give great power and a quiet exhaust note. Whether ancient and simple, or modern and complex, these systems work together toward one purpose: to move gases through the combustion chamber. In this chapter we'll look at all the various components of these systems,

starting with carburetors, and tell you how you can maintain and improve them.

CARBURETOR TYPES

Carburetors fall into two broad categories: variable venturi and fixed venturi. Variable-venturi carburetors come in lots of shapes and styles and are by far the most popular carburetor for motorcycle use. At one time fixed-venturi were the carburetors of choice for most American-made motorcycles, but today fixed-venturi carbs are only found on lawn equipment, some older bikes, and personal watercraft. Since this book isn't about lawnmowers, personal watercraft, or old Harley-Davidsons, we'll leave you to mull over fixed-venturi carburetors on your own.

Variable-venturi carbs are the most popular, and for a good reason. They are easy to build, simple to maintain and adjust, and adaptable to a

The dyno never lies; am I making more horsepower or just more noise?

wide variety of conditions. In many respects, the best of them work as well as some fuel-injection systems.

Variable-venturi carbs have sliding throttles, or what we now call a slide. The throttle slide moves across the venturi at a right angle, altering the size or cross section of the venturi. The side of the slide facing the incoming air is slightly beveled. This portion is the cutaway, and the cutaway is always placed toward the incoming air. The slide can be either round, square, or flat. As the slide lifts, more fuel and air are admitted to the engine, and the engine speed picks up.

While all variable-venturi carbs function in the same basic manner, there are several variations on the theme. The most profound difference being between the basic slide carburetor and the constant-velocity (CV) version.

Slide Carburetors

Slide carburetors are so-called because they feature a slide that connects directly to the throttle cable. Twisting the throttle pulls up the slide, which increases venturi size and allows more fuel-air mix into the engine. These were the most common type of carburetor from the 1950s through the early 1980s. They are still the most common carb type for dirt bikes and racing machines because slide carbs can be tuned to produce more horsepower than a CV carburetor.

Slide carburetors have one inherent shortcoming. All slide-type carburetors, unless they are of very sophisticated design, will have a tendency to stumble whenever the throttle is suddenly yanked open. Slide carburetors also have a somewhat abrupt response at times. This can be problematic, especially under conditions where traction is less than optimum and horsepower high. We'll deal with this phenomenon more thoroughly in the section to follow on accelerator pumps.

CV Carburetors

Today's carbureted bikes are almost universally fitted with CV carbs because they automatically adjust the venturi size to meet engine demand. Visually the CV looks a little different than a garden-variety carburetor. Situated on top of the carb body is either a large flat area (Stromberg type) or a dome (S.U. type). Since both instru-

DIY Installing an Inline Fuel Filter

I like inline fuel filters, especially since I fuel a lot of my bikes from five-gallon Jerry cans. Inline fuel filters are cheap insurance.

Under normal conditions, an inline fuel filter should prevent any debris from reaching the float bowl. But no matter what, some junk always finds its way in. Obviously any foreign matter in the float bowl is detrimental to your carburetor's good health. The most common thing found in the float bowl (besides fuel) is water. Water enters in any number of ways. Two of the more common means are through the vent hoses or air filter when the bike is washed. Because the water is heavier than gasoline, it settles to the bottom of the float bowl, where most carburetor manufacturers have thoughtfully provided a drain.

Use your shop manual to locate and identify the drain screw or plug. Not all carburetor float bowls have drain plugs in them. Some older carbs make you remove the float bowl to clean it. Since most of those were made prior to 1972 we won't get into them here. All modern carburetors should have a small hose attached to the float-bowl drain. Locate that as well and place a small container under it. Turn the petcock off.

Loosen the screw until fuel runs out. When fuel stops flowing snug the screw back down. Examine the fuel that you caught in the container. See those globules of water and dirt? That's what we're after. If none are present, so much the better. Repeat the process for each carburetor. Please dispose of the drained gas in a responsible manner, such as safely burning it. Pouring it down the nearest storm drain is not acceptable. ∎

Draining the float bowl every so often keeps carburetor related problems at a minimum. Most drain screws are easy to access, like this one. They are located at the lowest point of the float bowls.

FLOAT SYSTEM

The float chamber holds a constant level of fuel so the engine is provided with a stable supply of the required air-fuel mixture.

As fuel is consumed and the level in the chamber falls, the float and float valve are lowered and the chamber is immediately refilled to a specified level. A rise in fuel level causes the float and its valve to rise, the valve contacts the valve seat and the fuel supply is cut off. This operation repeats while the engine runs.

The float valve contains a spring which lightly depresses the valve so that it does not become dislodged from the seat by vibration when the vehicle is running. To keep the inside of the float chamber at atmospheric pressure, there is a connection to the outside of the carburetor known as the air vent passage.

An overflow tube is provided to drain off any excess fuel to the outside of the carburetor, should the valve and seat become separated due to the intrusion of dirt or other foreign matter. ■

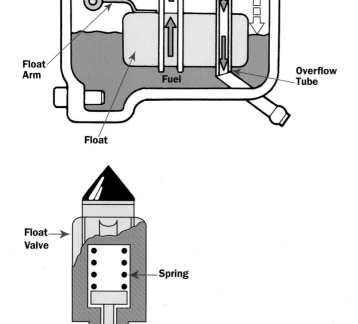

(Courtesy American Honda)

ments function in the same basic manner a discussion of one is as good as the other. Because the Stromberg design is the more compact, making it more popular for motorcycle use, that's what we'll look at.

The CV works just like the slide carburetor with one important difference. The slide is not connected to the throttle cable. Instead, the cable is fastened to a butterfly valve located in the venturi. The slide is connected to a rubber diaphragm located in the chamber above the carb body. The diaphragm chamber is connected to the venturi by a small passage. When the throttle cable moves the butterfly valve, air flows through the venturi, creating a vacuum above the diaphragm and pressure below it and the slide raises.

The neat thing is that the slide will only rise in proportion to the engine's demands. If you grab a big handful of throttle at idle, the slide will only move upwards as engine vacuum dictates. In other words engine speed and the carburetor's slide position are in always in balance, which in turn provides the optimum fuel mixture for every situation, at least in theory.

The CV solves a bunch of little problems. Because slide position adjusts according to the engine's demands, rather than the rider's whims, fuel economy and overall performance are improved. CV carbs are also altitude compensating; because air pressure drops off at high altitude, the slide won't lift as high for a given throttle position. And finally if you're one of those guys that just loves to whack open the throttle, with a CV carb you can do it in complete confidence, knowing that the engine won't spit and sputter, nor will it suddenly light up the rear wheel.

CARBURETOR CIRCUITS

Like the motorcycle itself the carburetor can be broken down into subsystems or circuits. There are five on most carburetors: the float circuit, low-speed circuit, high-speed circuit, accelerator-pump circuit (which isn't always present), and the cold-start circuit (or choke). To best understand how a garden-variety carb works, let's first take a very brief look at the basic principle behind its function. We'll then take a look at the circuits and how they operate. Finally we'll give you some tuning and maintenance tips.

Briefly, air flowing through the venturi creates a vacuum. Fuel outlets are placed at strategic points in the venturi, those points being where vacuum is greatest. Atmospheric pressure forces the fuel to flow from those outlets. The fuel mixes with the air and is drawn into the engine where it is ignited.

Float Circuit

The float circuit's job is to ensure that all of the other circuits have the fuel they need. Fuel is contained in a chamber called the float bowl. A small buoyant plastic or brass float fits inside the bowl. The float bowl is always vented to the atmosphere, either directly (on older bikes), or through a charcoal canister.

Fuel flows from the fuel tank through a small inlet valve in the bowl. As the fuel level rises, the float pushes against a small lever that closes the inlet valve once the fuel reaches the correct level. When the level drops, the float drops with it, opening the valve and allowing fuel to flow in from the tank. Fuel exits the float bowl through openings provided for the high- and low-speed circuits; those openings are located in the main body of the carburetor (the venturi) at points of high vacuum.

The level of the fuel in the float bowl is critical. If the level is too high, too much fuel will be positioned in the high-speed discharge passage; more fuel than is necessary will be drawn into the engine, making it run rich. If the fuel level is too low, not enough fuel can be pulled in, resulting in an engine that runs lean.

Jets and Jet Needle

Since we'll be talking a lot about jets I thought I'd better define them. Jets are small replaceable orifices screwed or pressed into the various passageways drilled in the carburetor body. Normally, the jets are used to control fuel flow, but there are some used to control air flow. Jets are made of brass and have numbers stamped on them indicating their size. They also come in different shapes and sizes, yet they all function the same way.

The pilot jet is a very small jet used to control fuel flow at idle and very low throttle openings.

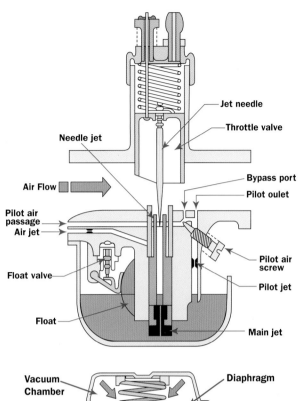

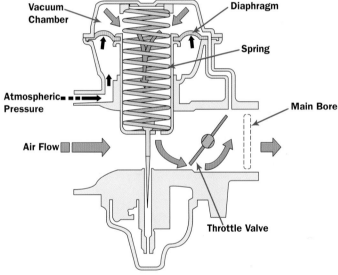

The basic slide carburetor (TOP) is simplicity itself. When you twist the throttle the slide goes up and the laws of physics take over, supplying the fuel/air mixture to the engine. Their principle weakness is a tendency for the engine to stumble when the throttle is opened abruptly. To overcome this problem, engineers developed the constant-velocity (CV) carburetor (BOTTOM). Instead of activating the slide directly, the throttle cable on a CV carb is connected to a butterfly valve which controls vacuum in the caburetor throat. This vacuum acts on a diaphragm whose movement controls the position of the throttle slide. This indirect control of the throttle slide keeps it in the correct position according to engine speed and the rider's throttle input. The result is more consistently accurate fuel mixtures under various engine conditions. (Courtesy American Honda Motor Corporation)

FUEL FLOW BY THE NUMBERS

At very low engine speeds, from zero throttle opening to 1/8 throttle, fuel flow is regulated by the pilot or slow speed circuit. At any speed above that the carburetor's main fuel circuit is utilized. Here's how it works:

When the throttle is opened past idle a greater amount of fuel and air is obviously required. From 1/8 to 1/2 throttle airflow through the carburetor venturi creates low pressure above the discharge tube (needle jet holder). This allows atmospheric pressure to act on the fuel in the float bowl and force it past the gap between the needle jet and the jet needle.

As the throttle opens past 1/4, the taper of the needle begins to play a greater part. As you can see from the illustration the needle is tapered, consequently the higher it rides in the jet, the more fuel it allows to pass through the jet. On some carburetors the needle adjustment may be fine tuned by raising or lowering the small clip that positions the needle. Lowering the clip causes the needle to ride slightly higher creating a richer mixture and vice versa.

Above 3/4 throttle the needle is nearly withdrawn from the needle jet. At that point fuel delivery is regulated by the main jet. Although it may not be obvious there is some overlap between the various jet circuits as they make the transition from idle to wide open throttle.

(Courtesy American Honda)   ■

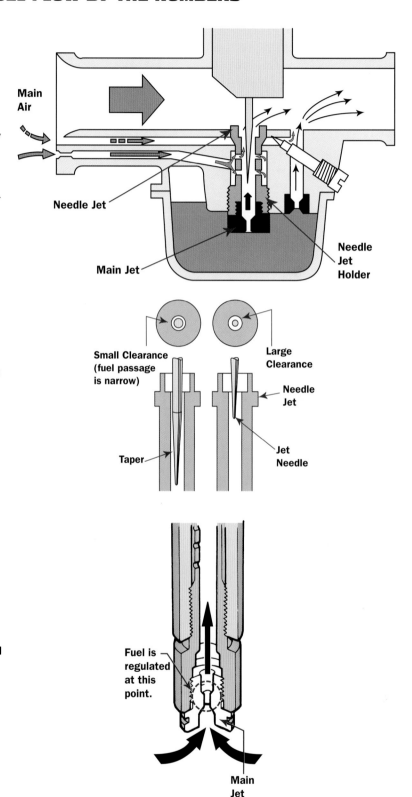

It is connected directly to the pilot-adjustment screw. The screw controls the strength of the mixture flowing from the pilot orifice. Depending on the carburetor, the screw may control fuel, air or both. The needle jet is screwed into the carb body and may be considered the main fuel-discharge tube. At anything above one-eighth throttle the majority of the fuel passes through the needle jet.

The jet needle is a thin, tapered needle that hangs from the slide. As it moves up and down with the throttle, the taper controls the amount of fuel flowing out of the needle jet. The main jet screws into the bottom of the needle jet. It determines how much fuel flows when the throttle is wide open.

Slide Cutaway

Let me digress for a moment. If you look at the back of a variable-venturi carburetor's throttle slide, the portion that faces the air cleaner, you'll notice the bottom of it has a slight scallop or cutaway to it. The slide cutaway affects the transition between the pilot circuit and the high-speed circuit. The size of the cutaway determines how much initial vacuum is available: a small cutaway creates a lot of restriction; hence, a lot of vacuum; a large cutaway creates less restriction and vacuum. The more vacuum the richer the mixture.

Low-Speed or Pilot Circuit

When the throttle is closed, not much air flows through the venturi. Indeed, unless the carb is of a very special design, not enough air flows to pull fuel out of the needle jet. A separate circuit that bypasses the throttle is used instead. The pilot circuit feeds fuel to the engine when it's idling and during very low-speed riding. Because even identical engines have different fuel requirements, especially at idle, the pilot circuit is controlled by an externally adjustable screw.

Depending on the designer's whims, the screw may control fuel, air, or the fuel-air mix. Current EPA regulations require manufacturers to seal the screw on street-legal bikes after the mixture has been adjusted. But trust me, the screw is hiding under that little aluminum plug just waiting for you to give it a tweak.

High-Speed Circuit

The high-speed circuit controls fuel delivery and mixture at cruising speed and above. The main jet, the needle jet, and the jet needle comprise the bulk of the high-speed circuit. At the outset fuel flow is controlled by the needle jet. As the throttle is opened further the tapered needle moves further out of the jet, allowing more fuel to flow. Finally, as the throttle is opened past three-quarter throttle, all fuel flow is controlled by the main jet.

Accelerator-Pump Circuit

It used to be quite common on bikes equipped with non-CV carbs for the engine to stumble or

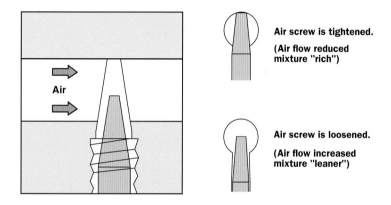

The pilot screw regulates either air or fuel depending on the carburetor. On the VM Mikuni the screw regulates airflow.
(Courtesy American Honda Motor Corporation)

ADJUSTING IDLE SPEED

Occasionally you may find that your bike idles too fast or too slowly after it's been warmed up. A word of caution here: sudden changes in idle speed are usually indicative of some other problem, which may or may not be carburetor-related. If your bike is idling fine on Monday morning but stalls at every stop on Monday evening, the problem is probably not idle-speed adjustment. On the other hand, if your service manual calls for an idle speed of 1200 rpm and you notice that after the bike is good and warm the idle speed is 1400 rpm, adjusting the idle speed is certainly permissible. Idle speeds tend to creep up a little as motors loosen up with mileage. Also, manufacturers usually allow some variance in the idle speed. A particular manual may call for an idle speed of between 1000 rpm and 1200 rpm. If you'd rather set your idle to the low side, by all means do so and vice versa. Most bikes use a single adjuster screw to regulate idle speed. Find the idle-speed screw. This is usually a large knurled knob that can be turned by hand or a screw. With the engine fully warmed-up, adjust the screw until the desired rpm is indicated on the tachometer. ■

DIY *Synchronizing Carburetors*

You'll need:

- A long thin, flat blade screw driver
- Small wrenches (usually 8mm or 10mm)
- Vacuum gauges or manometer
- An auxiliary fuel tank, this can be purchased or fabricated.
- A floor fan (optional, but recommended)

Carburetor synchronization requires patience, a few special tools, and some experience. You may want to leave this job to the pros, at least the first time. The best way to synchronize multiple carbs is with a vacuum gauge set.

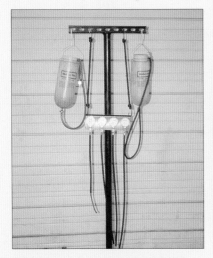

This rig mounts the vacuum gauges where they can be easily seen and holds two fuel bottles.

Occasionally you may find it necessary to synchronize the carbs either before adjusting the idle or as part of the idle-speed adjusting procedure.

Synchronizing just means making certain that the throttle slides all lift at the same time. Most modern bikes use a linkage to ensure that all the throttles work in concert. As wear and vibration take their toll, play develops in the linkage and the slides start to go up at different times. Even though the differences are usually slight, out-of-sync carbs cause all sorts of problems, including poor idle, decreased performance and fuel mileage, and increased vibration.

Older British and European twins, or any other motorcycle that uses a separate throttle cable for each carburetor, must have both throttle cables and idle speeds synchronized. This can be a lengthy and tedious project if done without vacuum gauges. While it's true that old timers, myself included (I'll modestly add), can sync old twin-cylinder engines by ear, it's not something you want to try as a novice mechanic.

The carburetor adjusting screws can be tricky to reach. Follow the screwdriver blade (to the left of the brass tube).

HERE'S THE RIGHT WAY TO ADJUST AND SYNC OLDER (AND SOME NEWER) TWINS.

Start the engine and using the throttle-stop screws, adjust the idle speed to the recommended settings. (It may seem silly to adjust the idle speed first, but don't forget that the idle screw determines slide height. If one slide ends up slightly higher than the other, it will throw your cable adjustment off.) Because the process make take some time and air-cooled engines don't like sitting and idling for extended periods of time, set up the floor fan to blow cool directly at your engine before beginning, to prevent any overheating problems. There are two methods; one uses a set of vacuum gauges or carb sticks, the second is the by-guess-and-by-golly method.

VACUUM GAUGE METHOD:

Warm the engine up to operating temperature. Disconnect the balance tube and install the vacuum gauges. Back the cable adjusters all the way off. Set the pilot screws at the recommended settings, and adjust as needed. Start the engine and let the engine idle, noting the readings on the vacuum gauge. Adjust the throttle stop screws until the vacuum gauge readings are identical. Stop the engine and adjust the free-play in the throttle cables to the recommended specs. Restart the engine and note the vacuum gauge readings as you open the throttle. If they differ greatly the carbs are out of sync. Hold the engine at one-quarter throttle. Adjust the cable free-play until the vacuum-gauge settings are identical. Let the engine idle and gently accelerate the engine while watching the gauge. If the carburetors are in sync, the readings will remain the same from idle to full throttle; although there is really no practical need to raise the speed past half throttle.

Synchronizing Carburetors

IF YOU HAVE NO VACUUM GAUGE:

Turn the idle screws in until they bottom out. Now turn them both out by exactly the same amount. I'd suggest five turns. Set the pilot screws to the recommended spec. Back the throttle cables all the way off. Start the bike. It may over-rev or idle at a very high speed, so stay alert. If the idle speed is really roaring kill the engine and turn the idle screws out another turn or two. Turn each screw in or out by the same amount until the idle speed is where you want it.

Adjust the throttle free-play. Open the throttle slowly while listening carefully. If it sounds as if one cylinder is lagging, turn the cable adjuster one-quarter of a turn and recheck the pick up. Continue until both cylinders pick up at the same time. This method is not as accurate as the vacuum gauge method but it will get you in the ballpark. ■

Motion Pro can supply their economy carb sticks for under 50 bucks. The carb sticks use a column of mercury to indicate manifold vacuum. You have to be a little careful with this type of gauge, if you snap the throttle shut at high rpm some of the mercury can be sucked into the engine. But in many cases, the carb sticks prove easier to use than the manifold gauges. Remember, mercury is a heavy metal and extremely toxic, so don't play with it, touch it or let get on your skin. These photos show the gauge before the carbs were synced (LEFT) and after (RIGHT). Not a perfect job, but one that is darn close.

hesitate for an instant if the throttle was snapped from idle (or very low speed) to wide open. Because the air is lighter than the fuel it starts to flow through the venturi before any fuel can flow out of the discharge port. The engine runs lean for an instant before fuel flow can catch up to air flow. We feel it as a slight hesitation in the seat of our pants. The most common way to avoid this is to include an accelerator pump in the carburetor.

Accelerator pumps are small mechanically- or vacuum-operated devices that provide a brief shot of fuel to the engine whenever the throttle is opened suddenly. Since most accelerator pumps fitted to motorcycle engines are mechanical and will operate when the engine isn't running, twisting the throttle, even with the engine off, pumps a small shot of fuel into the intake tract. This is not a good practice, as the raw fuel tends to foul the plug and dilute the oil. Accelerator pumps, while not uncommon, are not fitted to all motorcycles.

Cold-Start Circuit

When engines are cold, fuel tends to condense (rather than vaporize), in the inlet tract. Since little fuel actually makes its way into the engine, an exceptionally rich mixture is required until the engine warms up. As the engine approaches operating temperature, the mixture can be returned to normal.

Early carburetors employed ticklers to create the rich mixture needed for cold starts. A tickler is nothing more than an external plunger used to hold the float down until fuel overflows into the inlet tract, creating the rich mixture needed to start the bike.

As you can imagine, having raw fuel spew all over your engine and evaporate into the atmosphere is not really in our best interests from either a safety or environmental standpoint. Nevertheless, ticklers were used on street bikes right up until 1980 and even later on some off-road machines.

ACCELERATOR PUMP

When the throttle valve is opened suddenly, the air-fuel mixture drawn into the cylinder momentarily becomes lean. Because the vacuum at the venturi drops, air flow at the venturi slows down and the drawn-up fuel becomes too little compared with the air. To avoid thinning of the mixture under these conditions, an accelerator pump is used for temporary enrichment.

The principle of operation of the pump is as follows: As the throttle valve is opened, the pump's diaphragm is depressed by the pump rod. At this time the inlet check valve is shut, so the pump chamber undergoes a rise in pressure. The outlet check valve is then opened and fuel is supplied to the main bore via the pump hole.

As the throttle valve closes, the accelerator pump's diaphragm is returned by spring action. At this time the inlet check valve is opened and fuel from the float chamber enters the pump chamber. The outlet check valve is closed at this point to prevent air being drawn in through the pump hole. ∎

THROTTLE VALVE OPENS

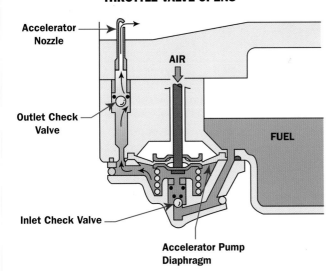

Accelerator Nozzle

AIR

Outlet Check Valve

FUEL

Inlet Check Valve

Accelerator Pump Diaphragm

THROTTLE VALVE CLOSES

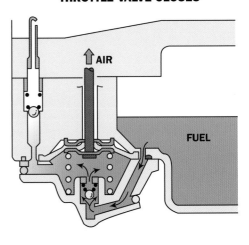

AIR

FUEL

(Courtesy American Honda Motor Corporation)

Some carburetors employ a mechanical choke to restrict airflow during startup. Chokes are moveable steel or aluminum plates that are placed in the venturi. When the choke is turned on, it enriches the mixture by restricting airflow and raising vacuum at the venturi. Chokes are commonly controlled by either a carburetor-mounted lever that acts directly on the choke or a handlebar-mounted lever that uses a cable to control the choke. Lately, mechanical chokes have fallen out of favor, having been replaced for the most part by an enrichener-starting device.

The enrichener starter is sometimes called a starter-jet system. An independent jet is connected by a passage to the venturi and by another passage to the float bowl. During normal running, a rubber-tipped plunger is held against the jet, preventing any fuel from flowing. During cold starts the plunger is lifted, and fuel flows from the jet, richening the mixture. Because the enrichener jet needs a fair amount of vacuum to work properly, the operator should keep the throttle closed when it is being used.

HOW CARB CIRCUITS WORK TOGETHER

Now that you know how each of the carb circuits work, let's look at how they work together. The simplest way to do so is to look at what's happening within the carb at various stages of throttle opening.

One-Eighth Throttle and Less

At idle or very low speed the pilot jet supplies most of the fuel-air mixture, aided by the slide cutaway. Theoretically, the engine runs at a richer than correct mixture when the pilot circuit is feeding it because there is not enough airflow to fully atomize the fuel.

When the engine is at idle the throttle slide rests against a moveable stop. This stop screw provides a method of regulating the slide height and controlling idle speed. Since every engine, indeed every cylinder of every engine, may require a slightly different mixture an adjusting screw is also provided to adjust the strength of the pilot mixture.

One-Eighth to One-Half Throttle

As the throttle is opened a little further, the slide cutaway takes over from the pilot jet and smoothes the transition between the pilot circuit and the high-speed circuit. The slide cutaway reduces the need for an accelerator pump (although supplementary pumps are sometimes fitted).

As more air starts to flow through the venturi the mixture leans out slightly. To prevent the engine from stumbling, some carburetors also include a pilot bypass to give the engine a little dollop of extra fuel as the throttle is opened.

One-Half to Three-Quarters Throttle

Between one-half throttle and three-quarters throttle, fuel flow is controlled by the combination of the needle and needle jet. At small throttle openings the straight section of the needle is positioned in the needle jet. Hence, fuel flow is determined by the size of the jet.

As the throttle position approaches three-quarters throttle, the tapered portion of the needle raises into the jet, so the taper takes over as the main influence on fuel flow. As the needle raises and its taper is reduced more fuel flows through the needle jet.

Needles are normally height-adjustable, at least they used to be before the EPA mandates became the law of the land. Raising the needle in the slide richens the needle. However, to richen the needle you need to put the retaining clip in a lower position.

Another problem with needles is this: because a needle is tapered its fuel delivery characteristics are an average. In other words, a "richer" needle may actually be leaner in some places then a lean needle, however, overall it delivers more fuel.

Full Throttle

At wide-open throttle the needle is so high in the needle jet that it no longer restricts fuel flow. The main jet now controls fuel delivery.

It may seem like the carburetion steps are clean breaks. In reality, there is quite a bit of overlap between stages. For example, while the influence of the pilot jet gradually tapers off as the throttle opens it never ceases to have some effect on fuel delivery. The point is that a bike with

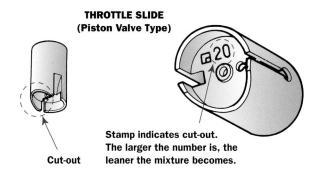

THROTTLE SLIDE
(Piston Valve Type)

Cut-out

Stamp indicates cut-out.
The larger the number is, the
leaner the mixture becomes.

The throttle slide. **(Courtesy American Honda Motor Corporation)**

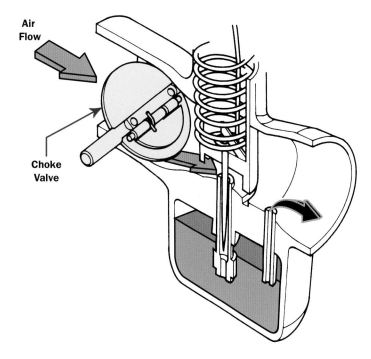

Air Flow

Choke Valve

The simplest form of cold start mechanism is the mechanical choke,
nothing more than a flat plate that restricts air flow, increasing vacuum
and creating a rich mixture. **(Courtesy American Honda Motor Corporation)**

STARTER CARBURETOR

Because the tickler and choke have an intimate relationship with the main circuit, the use of either requires some experience if flooding and fouled plugs are to be avoided. To eliminate this inconvenience, the starter carburetor was developed. It ensures a proper mixture for starting the engine without requiring any operating skill.

The starter carburetor is incorporated in the main carburetor body, but it is independent of the main circuit.

OPERATION

As the starter lever is pulled, the starter plunger moves up. This opens the air passage closed by the starter plunger, and the air streams into the starter air inlet. The air stream produces a partial vacuum around the starter jet nozzle, thus causing the fuel to stream out of the starter jet.

The plunger is cylindrical and has a rubber pad on its bottom.

Both mixture and air passages are on the same level, and when the plunger moves up, both passages are opened at the same time. ■

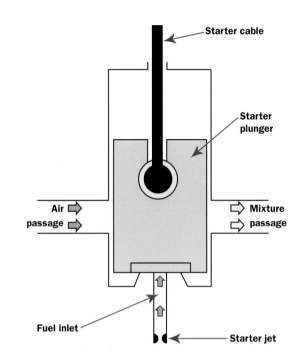

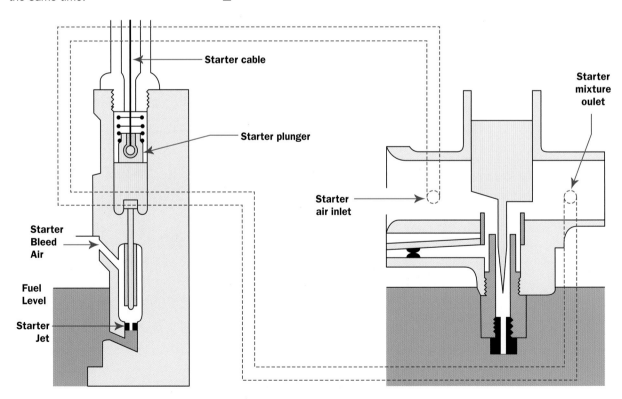

DIY — *Adjusting Idle Mixture*

Before the EPA became involved, adjusting the pilot mixture was pretty simple: you found the idle-mixture screw, gave it a turn, and the idle speed either picked up (meaning the mixture was slightly off) or it decreased (meaning it had been correct and you just screwed it up).

The usual procedure was to lean the screw setting out until the idle speed picked up and then either leave the screw set at that position, or perhaps richen it up a quarter turn for a little better off-idle pickup.

Thanks to the EPA, mixture screws are adjusted at the factory and then sealed with an aluminum cap. It is a violation of federal law to change this setting on a street bike. For off-road use only, the procedure is as follows:

Generally speaking, most bikes come with the mixture screw set on the lean side. A slight enriching will work wonders during warmups and eliminate the popping from the mufflers during deceleration.

To adjust the mixture, locate and remove the screw cover (if it hasn't already been done). Your service manual should tell you if the screw controls air flow, fuel flow, or both. Then, warm up the engine. Procedures vary between single- and multi-carburetor motorcycles. We'll go through the single-carburetor procedure first:

With the engine off, lightly seat the pilot screw, counting the turns as you go. When the screw stops, stop applying pressure; lightly seat means just that: *lightly*.

Note the number of turns (it's probably between one and two), and see how it compares with the recommended setting in your manual. Set the screw to the recommended position, and restart the engine. Open the screw one-quarter turn at a time until the engine idles smoothly. Don't be afraid to experiment. Try both directions. Snap the throttle one time or two and make sure the engine

doesn't cough or hesitate. If it does you adjusted it too lean, and you'll need to richen the mix slightly. If the bike has dual carbs, adjust each side in turn.

After the highest idle is reached reduce the idle speed using the stop screw(s). If the bike has multiple carbs, proceed as follows: With the engine off, adjust all the screws to the same setting. If the idle is ragged lean the screws out a quarter turn at a time until the idle smoothes out. If there is popping on deceleration, or coughing and spitting when the throttle is opened, you'll need to richen the mixture a quarter turn at a time. Reset the idle speed using the master screw. ■

You'll need:

- *Shop manual*
- *3/8 or 1/4-inch drill and bits*
- *Common hand tools*
- *Special adjusting tools (make access to the pilot screw easier)*

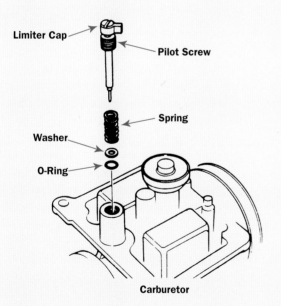

Carburetor

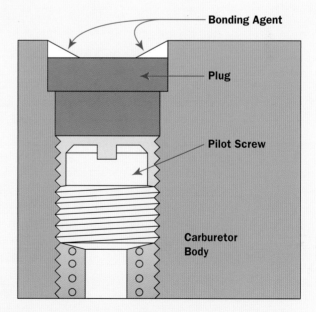

(LEFT) Limiter caps are generally made of plastic and can be easily removed with a gentle tug. (Courtesy American Honda Motor Corporation) (RIGHT) In some cases, the pilot screw will be sealed with a Welch plug and you'll have to drill through the plug to remove it.

one phase of its carburetor screwed up will never run right, no matter how well the other circuits function.

FUEL-INJECTION SYSTEM

Carburetors, no matter how sophisticated, all leave a little bit to chance. Fuel injection doesn't. Fuel-injection systems aren't new. BMW used a mechanical fuel-injection system on their Rennsport race bike in the early 1950s, but it's only in the last ten years or so that motorcycle fuel-injection systems have really started to take hold.

Motorcycle fuel-injection systems generally consist of an injector, a fuel pump to supply the system, a computer to make everything happen, and several sensors to provide the computer with the input it needs to make its decisions. The throttle plate, generally a butterfly, is connected in traditional fashion to the twistgrip via cable. The computer contains a "map" of the engine's fuel requirements.

The computer constantly measures a host of variables, including engine rpm, throttle position, atmospheric temperature and pressure, and engine temperature. The computer deciphers all of the inputs and decides when the engine needs fuel and just how much it needs. It then turns the injector on. When the injector is on, a high-pressure electric pump forces fuel through it. There are no jets, and the nozzle is non-adjustable. If the computer decides a richer mixture is in order, it tells the nozzle to stay open longer. The longer the nozzle is open, or on, the more fuel it delivers. Most injection systems are not owner adjustable, which may complicate things if you decide to change or modify your engine. If you need to modify the map, you'll either have to burn or purchase a new chip.

Injection systems have many real-world advantages, and only a few disadvantages compared to carburetors. On the plus side, when they are properly mapped, they provide excellent throttle response, good fuel economy, and reduced emissions. Fuel-injection systems also require less maintenance than carburetors. Altitude and weather have no effect on them. And, they can also have a cold-start mode programmed in, doing away with the need for a choke. On the downside, they can be difficult to troubleshoot when things go wrong, and as I pointed out, they can be difficult to adjust when they are used on modified engines. Still, my prediction is that within the next ten years most, if not all, motorcycle engines will feature fuel injection.

MAINTAINING FUEL INJECTION

Fuel-injection-system maintenance is pretty straightforward. The cables and throttle bodies need periodic adjustment and synchronization, just as old-fashioned carburetors do. Both procedures are more or less identical to those used to set carburetors, so refer to the carburetor section for the basic procedure. Your shop manual will fill in the specifics. Many fuel injection glitches can be traced to dirt, either in the fuel system itself or between the electronic connections. Periodic replacement of the fuel filter should forestall most fuel-related problems. If the bike is often used in wet conditions, or is stored in a humid environment, an occasional cleaning of the electrical connectors and the application of some dielectric grease should prevent any electrical gremlins from fouling up the system.

IMPROVING FUEL INJECTION

Everybody loves to tinker. When fuel-injection systems first made their appearance, there was some fear that everyone's tinkering days were about to end. Fortunately the aftermarket responded quickly. In some cases, software is available to simply reprogram the existing computer. In other instances, a new chip can be installed. The most common method of modifying an electronic fuel system is the insertable "black box." These are nothing more than a plug-in module that is inserted inline with the OEM computer. Some are fixed and non-adjustable, while others have trimming screws that allow you to fine tune the unit to your needs. Others have downloadable programs premapped for a given application. In some instances, the units can be adjust via a laptop and dyno to customize the mapping to your bike. Popular units include the Cobra FI 2000, which is a non-adjustable plug-in unit popular with cruiser owners; the Power Commander, which is available in several

DIY   *Adjusting Throttle Cables*

Cables require a certain amount of free-play or slack to operate correctly. If there is too much play, the reaction time between twisting the grip and the moving of the throttle slide is delayed. If there is not enough free-play, the slide will be yanked open whenever the bars are turned, causing the idle to soar. Too little free-play will also make the bike hard to ride, every twitch of the throttle making the bike leap forward. Most current street bikes use a push-pull throttle system. The pull cable opens the throttle; the push cable closes it. Some new motorcycles, older bikes, and off-road machines use a single pull cable. A heavy return spring does the closing.

To adjust the cable free-play on the pull cable, proceed as follows: note the amount of free-play by twisting the grip until it picks up the load. You can use the grip itself as a visual aid by noting the free-play at the grip's outer flange. Locate the adjuster and its lock nut. Adjust the cable free-play to the manufacturer's specifications. With the bike idling, turn the bars from side to side and make sure that the idle doesn't change. If it does, check the cable routing and recheck the free-play adjustment. The push cable should be adjusted to ensure positive closing of the throttle. As long as there is a slight amount of slack in the push cable, say 2–4mm, it'll be fine. If the push cable is too tight, it will make the throttle action heavy and may prevent you from fully opening the throttle. The push-cable adjuster is usually located at the carburetor end of the cable and should be checked whenever you adjust the pull-cable free-play. ∎

> **You'll need:**
> - *Wrenches to fit the cable adjusters*

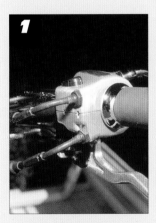   

Locate and identify the freeplay adjuster according to your manual.

Loosen the locknut.

Adjust the freeplay.

Tighten the locknuts.

different formats designed to accommodate everything from cruisers to Superbikes and beyond; and the Rev-Tech DFO, a popular Harley unit that features screwdriver adjustment.

AIR BOXES AND FILTERS

It wasn't too long ago when a motorcycle air filter was little more than a hunk of steel wool or pleated paper designed to keep chunks of gravel, low-flying birds, and small children out of your engine. Today, all current motorcycles are sold equipped with an air filter, and most also include an air box to enclose the filter. Three types of air filters are commonly used on motorcycles: paper, oiled foam, and oiled gauze.

Most new motorcycles are fitted with paper filters from the factory because they are the least expensive type and generally considered the best at keeping dirt out of the engine. However, they can restrict air flow when dirty, and they can't really be cleaned to function as new because they must be kept dry.

Some high-performance bikes are fitted with oiled-foam or oiled-gauze filters, which generally are less restrictive of airflow for engine horsepower. Modern air filters are extremely

A composite filter courtesy K & N.

good at protecting your engine, and they do it efficiently with a minimum restriction to airflow. There is no practical reason to run a motorcycle without one.

Paper Air Filters

Paper air filters consist of a band of porous paper, which is pleated to increase the surface area. This allows a relatively large surface area to fit into a small case. The paper is often treated with resin to strengthen it and to increase its water resistance.

Paper elements can be cleaned by tapping them on a hard surface to dislodge any big chunks and then blowing or brushing off any leftover dust and dirt. As the filter ages the pores in the paper will eventually become blocked with debris. Eventually it'll be time for a new one; figure about six cleanings to one replacement.

Foam Air Filters

A more efficient filter is the oil-impregnated foam filter. An internal wire frame supports a band or panel of open-celled foam. The holes in the foam are too large to trap the fine particles of dust, so the foam is impregnated with oil. In essence, the foam is only there to hold the oil. The oil is sticky and does the actual filtering by trapping the smallest dust particles.

At recommended intervals the filter should be removed, washed in solvent, and re-oiled. You can use almost any type of oil, but I'd recommend using a dedicated air-filter oil. These particularly sticky oils can be purchased in any motorcycle shop and come in either a squeeze bottle or an aerosol spray can. Foam filters can

be reused indefinitely, as long as they aren't torn or damaged.

K&N Filters

There is actually a third type of filter available. K&N markets an aftermarket filter that consists of cotton fabric sandwiched between aluminum screens. The filter is pleated and resembles a paper element. Like the foam filter, the cotton is doused with oil. K&N offers direct replacement filters as well as custom clamp-on models. While it's not my place to shill for any particular product, I swear by K&N filters. They combine all of the best features of both paper and foam elements; they are infinitely reusable, filter like nobody's business, and are much less restrictive than stock elements.

IMPROVING AIR BOX AND FILTER

One of the most popular modifications among motorcyclists is to switch to a less restrictive foam or gauze air filter, either the type that fits into the stock air box, or the type that clamps onto the carburetor. Why would anyone switch to a filter that lets in more dirt? Three reasons:

First, because the foam air filters are much less restrictive, so they may unlock a few extra horsepower in your engine. This is most important if you are making other modifications to increase horsepower.

Second, foam filters can be cleaned and re-oiled to function just as well as new, and they can be run longer between servicing. That can be a real advantage if you ride a lot and plan on keeping the bike forever, or if the air box is difficult to get to.

Third, few street bikes see enough dirty air to worry about the difference in filtering capability. If yours does, you may want to reconsider whether a switch is wise, or commit yourself to more frequent oil changes.

The K&N is the most popular gauze-type filter, and the UNI filter is the most popular foam type. These manufacturers offer direct replacement filters as well as custom clamp-on models. Which is better, gauze or foam? Both filter and flow about the same, but there's one other factor that gives the gauze type an advantage: oiled gauze is less flammable than oiled foam. If your bike sometimes backfires through the carb, be safe and go with gauze.

No matter what type of air filter you use, there are a few essential rules. Unless the air filter is clean and properly mounted, it will have a profound affect on the mixture. As the filter packs full of dirt, the mixture will become richer. If the filter is damaged, or if the connections between it and the carburetor are leaking, dirt and dust will be sucked into the engine. It will also cause the engine to run lean, resulting in overheating, or worse.

If you decide to replace the stock filter with an aftermarket one, consider the consequences. Most aftermarket filters are less restrictive then their OEM counterparts and may require re-jetting. In my experience re-jetting isn't usually required if you're only replacing the air filter but it never hurts to ask. And before you remove the air box to fit clamp-on filters, ask yourself whether you really want to live with a giant sucking sound roaring in your ears. If you only ride for short periods, it probably won't be bothersome, but over a 600-mile day, it will compound your fatigue.

In decades past, the first thing most riders did was to replace the air box with clamp-on filters. Generally, that strategy netted more horsepower, but on today's machines the benefits of doing so are not so certain and it's not so easy to do, because the air box is probably an integral part of the engine's breather system. It's also illegal if you plan to ride on the street. Nevertheless, it's still a popular option.

PETCOCKS

The petcock is nothing more than a three-position valve. There's an ON, OFF, and RESERVE position to get you to the nearest gas station when the tank runs low. While the manual petcock used to be the industry standard, today's street bikes commonly use vacuum-operated petcocks. Dirt bikes, for the most part, still rely on the manual version.

Vacuum-operated petcocks have a vacuum line tapped into the intake manifold. When the engine is running, intake vacuum is used to open a diaphragm in the valve, which allows fuel to flow. To help start the bike if you run out of fuel,

the valve has a prime setting. Moving the lever to prime bypasses the diaphragm, allowing fuel to flow without starting the engine. Vacuum petcocks are left in the ON position when the engine is not running. Very few bikes use an electric petcock. A small electric solenoid turns the petcock on whenever the ignition switch is energized. Finally, if your bike does use a manual petcock, make it a habit to turn it off whenever the engine is stopped for more than a few minutes.

MAINTAINING THE FUEL SYSTEM

Warning: Many of these procedures involve a highly flammable liquid and hot engine parts. Presumably you're all big boys and girls, but be careful, pay attention, and always keep a fire extinguisher close at hand. Unless they leak, petcocks require little maintenance. Some older ones are fitted with an inline filter or strainer that requires periodic cleaning. Other than that, no attention should be required. If the petcock does start to leak you may be able to obtain a rebuild kit from your local dealership. These generally contain all the perishable parts, such as gaskets, O-rings, and seals. If a rebuild kit isn't available you have two options: you can take the thing apart and try to find or make a gasket or seal that will fit, or you can buy a new petcock.

EXHAUST SYSTEM

An exhaust system, like everything else in the world, behaves according to rules formulated a long time ago by Mother Nature. Basically, any well-designed exhaust system works like an air pump. It helps empty and refill the cylinder. When the exhaust valve, opens a blast of high-

The foam filter is efficient and has an added advantage in that it can be cleaned and reused. (Courtesy Uni Filter)

pressure, high-temperature gas bursts out of the cylinder. The gas pressure will be anywhere from three to seven times that of atmospheric. The exhaust temperature will be in the neighborhood of 1,700 degrees. In essence, you've just converted a fair amount of potential energy into heat and kinetic energy. Since only about one third of the fuel's potential energy does any real work, the rest being converted into heat and noise, you can imagine how much more efficiently our engines would run if we could harness the exhaust's power. That's exactly what a well-designed exhaust system tries to do.

In this section, we'll discuss the functions of the various exhaust components. Then, we'll tell you how you can maintain and improve the whole system.

SCAVENGING POWER

Ideally, an exhaust system can harness the energy left in the hot exhaust gases to help increase engine power using a phenomenon known as scavenging. As the exhaust valve starts to open, the spent gases race down the pipe at around 1,800 feet per second, depending on their temperature. As our gases rush down the pipe they eventually reach a portion of the pipe that's larger than the exhaust port. When this pulse of exhaust gases hits the expansion area of the pipe the gases slow down and expand, which then cre-

Moto Guzzi uses an electrically operated petcock. When the ignition is on, so is the petcock.

ates a negative wave that flows back toward and into the exhaust port.

If the engineers did their homework correctly, the negative wave hits the exhaust valve during the valve overlap period and flows in through the open exhaust valve. Its low pressure helps evacuate any residual exhaust gases hovering around the combustion chamber. It also helps pull fresh mixture in through the opening intake valve. This jump starting of the fresh mixture that occurs before the piston has begun to descend on the intake stroke can provide a substantial torque boost.

Now here's the rub; while engine speed constantly varies, exhaust-gas speed remains constant. Therefore our scavenging effect will only work over a fairly limited rpm range, say a few hundred at best in narrow-spectrum competition engines. It's also important to remember that these pulses, both negative and positive, resonate back and forth from the port to the exhaust's open end until they more or less run out of energy on their own.

PIPE DESIGN

Normally, the muffler of a street bike damps down exhaust pulses. It also increases the range over which the negative pulses do their thing. On a race bike, particularly one that uses individual pipes for each cylinder, a tapered megaphone performs the same function.

A megaphone allows the exhaust wave to gently transition from the round pipe to the atmosphere. Because the effect of the megaphone moderates the exhaust pulses the bike becomes much easier to ride. By placing a reverse cone at the megaphone outlet we can reflect a positive wave back when we need it. A properly designed reverse-cone megaphone uses the negative wave to pull the fresh charge through the cylinder during overlap. Intact, it pulls so much charge (along with some help from inertia) that a portion of it spills into the pipe.

A nice side effect is that the fresh charge cools the exhaust valve. Before the exhaust valve closes the reverse cone reflects a positive wave back up the pipe, where it stuffs the spilled mixture back into the cylinder; the valve closes and bingo, free horsepower!

DIV *Cleaning Petcock Strainers*

This one is a breeze and should be done at every tune-up. The petcock strainer is out of sight and for the most part out of mind. Hidden in the dark recesses of the fuel tank it's often overlooked at tune-up time. Problem is if the strainer does plug up, you're not going anywhere. Worse yet, if it plugs up on your way to anywhere, you may be stuck somewhere, while your buddies are looking for you everywhere.

Note that not all bikes will have strainers. Also note that some petcocks have a strainer above the valve. On these, you must drain the tank and remove the petcock to clean the strainer. Your shop will fill in the details as to the location and the proper removal sequence. ■

You'll need:
- Small catch tank
- Appropriate wrench
- Contact or brake cleaner

The petcock strainer is one of those little things that is very easy to overlook. If it becomes clogged your bike will stop running, so service it at every tune-up. This petcock filter screws into the top of the petcock and is located inside the fuel tank. The clear tube next to it is the reserve fuel pipe. Most older bikes will have a strainer located in the petcock itself.

Remove the bowl.

Expose the screen and O-ring.

Remove and clean the screen with solvent, then reassemble using a new O-ring if possible.

As you can imagine, this calls for some serious cooperation between the pipe and the cam. Get it wrong and you're riding a slug, get it right (most tuners do, eventually) and you're on a rocket.

Crossover Tubes and Collectors

Street systems are the same but different. One way to enhance a street bike's exhaust system and quiet it down at the same time, is to join the head pipes together with an intermediate pipe. This works wonders in quieting the bike down, primarily because you're using the volume of the

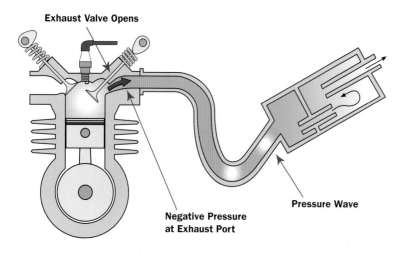

During the exhaust stroke a negative pressure (vacuum) is created at the exhaust port.

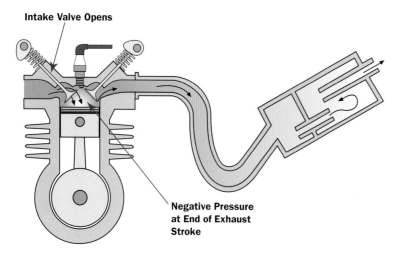

During the valve overlap period, when the exhaust valve hasn't fully closed and the intake has started to open the vacuum pulse in the exhaust system helps pull the fresh charge into the combustion chamber.
(Courtesy American Honda Motor Corporation)

entire exhaust system, which may include multiple mufflers, to quiet each exhaust pulse.

At first it was thought that by simply joining the pipes together at some point the flow of gas from one cylinder would create suction in the adjoining pipe. It was some time before designers realized that the balance pipe needed to be as close as possible to the exhaust ports, and that the head pipes needed to be restricted slightly just downstream of the balance pipe. If the restrictions were left out, then noise was reduced but the power was unchanged. When the restrictions were added, power and torque increased.

Currently the situation seems to be a bit more fluid. Some systems, particularly those found on twin-cylinder bikes, often seem to have their pipes joined wherever there is room, usually somewhere under the engine. Multiple-cylinder engines, particularly those used in sportbikes, generally have their pipes joined at a single point, commonly called a collector. The collector is located just forward of the muffler or exhaust power-valve.

Mufflers

There are two basic types of mufflers: the absorption type and the baffled muffler. Some mufflers combine both methods into one. In the good (bad?) old days of motorcycling the "fishtail" muffler was the hot tip if your neighbor wanted to sleep late on Sunday morning. Fishtails work by forcing the exhaust to flow through a small vertical opening. By forcing the exhaust pulse through the thin, vertical tail, the energy was removed from the exhaust pulse along with the noise.

Not a bad system, in fact. It works fairly well on an engine designed for moderate performance. Latter-style mufflers may employ mechanical baffles, fiberglass packing, concentric cylinders, or a combination of all three to reduce bark.

Absorption mufflers allow the gases to pass through a long perforated tube surrounded by fiberglass packing. The fiberglass absorbs much of the high-frequency elements of the exhaust; what issues forth then becomes more of a drone.

Baffled mufflers force the exhaust to exit through a series of welded-in baffles. The baffles

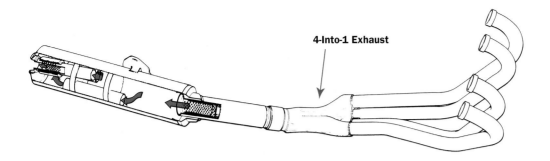

Typical four-stroke baffle-type muffler. As the exhaust forces its way through the baffles sound energy dissipates. (Courtesy American Honda Motor Corporation)

tend to block the low-frequency spectrum, leaving the harsh crack. Obviously, a better solution is to combine the two designs into one, and that's how most modern mufflers are built.

As a side note, the more cylinders the bike has, the easier it is to muffle, particularly when all the pipes feed into a common muffler. This may seem counter-intuitive. After all, a four-cylinder bike running at 2,000 rpm pumps out the same amount of exhaust as a single running at 8,000 rpm. The reasoning is simple; the exhaust pulses on the four are much closer together, resulting in a hum rather than a bang. If they are all fed into a big canister-style muffler, the gases are cooled, reducing their velocity. This lets the gas emerge from the muffler as a smooth continual stream, rather than a large pulse.

As a final note, let me leave you with a little food for thought. The old idea that a high-performance exhaust has to be loud to make big power was discredited a long time ago. Overly-loud pipes say more about the rider than they do about his motorcycle.

Performance Pipes

When I was a kid, I couldn't wait to fit my 1966 Bonneville with a set of megaphone exhausts, and as soon as I scraped up the $20 that they cost, I did. What a difference, I thought! In reality, all they were was loud. When I found out how exhaust systems really worked, I bought a set of Dunstall pipes and jetted the bike to work properly. Net result? A quieter bike with more horsepower that still sounded really neat.

Today's stock exhaust systems are amazingly efficient. They are quiet and make big horsepower. Some aftermarket pipes, when combined with properly jetted carbs, can increase power. Or they can decrease power and increase noise. Or they can provide more power over a very small rpm band to the detriment of usable power everywhere else.

If you're simply looking for a racy appearance and a little noise, almost any pipe will do. If you're looking for real performance or performance gains in a specific area, you have a few options. The first is to enlist the aid of a good shop, preferably one with a dynamometer. Find out what they have had experience with and what they would recommend. The second path is to perform your own experiments until you come up with a package you like. I've done it both ways and can tell you that the first option works best nine times out of ten.

An aftermarket pipe can save you a lot of weight, which in itself is a good thing. It will also enhance your and everyone else's aural experience. That may not be such a good thing. As far as power increases go, the answer is a qualified maybe.

Modern motorcycles use clutches of varied design. Some use a single- or multiple-plate automotive-style clutch, others a wet or oil-bath multi-plate clutch, and still others a dry multi-plate clutch. Small bikes such as scooters, mopeds, and minibikes often use a centrifugal clutch. There are also several variations on each theme. Each style has its advantages and disadvantages.

Whatever style of clutch your bike has, you can maintain, fix, and possibly even improve it yourself. This chapter will show you how. First,

though, we'll describe each type. Feel free to skip right to the section on the type used in your bike.

AUTOMOTIVE-STYLE CLUTCH

These clutches are mainly found in cars and BMW motorcycles. The engine flywheel is bolted to the end of the crankshaft. The driven plate, often called the clutch disc in this style clutch, has its center splined to fit over the transmission-input shaft. A large steel plate known as the pressure plate replaces the drive plates. The

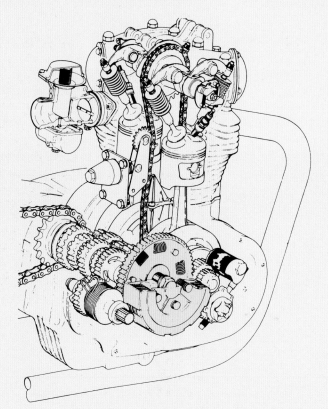

The clutch allows us to disconnect the engine from the transmission. It also allows us to gently engage the power, preventing damage to the driveline. In this drawing the clutch has been partially cut away to reveal the damping springs. (Courtesy Yamaha Motor Corporation)

spring is a diaphragm-type contained in the clutch cover. The cover bolts solidly to the fly-wheel. The spring forces the pressure plate to bear down on the disc. When the engine turns, the flywheel naturally turns, spinning the clutch cover. When the clutch is engaged, spring pressure forces the pressure plate and the disc together causing them to rotate as one unit. The splines on the disc rotate the transmission input shaft and down the road we go.

Your Multi-Plate Clutch

Multi-plate clutches are used most commonly on bikes with their crankshafts running crosswise in the frame, such as Japanese inline fours and the V-twins from Ducati, Harley-Davidson, and others. The overwhelming majority of bikes built have these, so it's likely your bike has one as well. The major parts include a clutch basket, several drive and driven plates, a clutch hub, a release mechanism, clutch springs, and a pressure plate.

Here's how they work together when the clutch is engaged: gears or a chain transfer engine power to the clutch basket. The basket transfers the power to the drive plates through the mating slots in the basket and tabs on the plates. The clutch springs and pressure plate clamp the drive plates to the driven plates, transferring engine power through them. Mating splines on the driven plates transfer that power to the clutch hub, and the hub transfers the power to the transmission.

Here's how they work together when the clutch is disengaged: the release mechanism releases spring pressure, so the drive and driven plates are no longer clamped together. This breaks the drive-transfer link between them, so the engine and clutch basket can spin independently of the clutch hub.

Some multi-plate clutches are designed to work while bathed in oil. These are known as wet clutches. Others are designed to operate dry and are appropriately known as dry clutches. Wet clutches are far more common than dry ones, and each type has its advantages and disadvantages. Wet clutches are more prone to slippage on engagement because the plates must displace any oil between them before they're

Adjusting Clutch Cable Free-Play

Most of you probably know or can guess what free-play is. No, it's not like recess. Free-play might be defined as the amount of clearance a mechanism requires to avoid self-destruction. From the text and your own experience I hope you've realized that any tension placed on the clutch springs will cause the clutch to begin to disengage. Continued partials lip will accelerate wear. It follows then that a clutch that is adjusted properly will have a better chance at long life than one that isn't.

The first line of adjustment is the cable itself. You might think that a clutch cable that has no free-play in it, yet doesn't exert pressure on the clutch-release mechanism, would be properly adjusted. If the engine parts always remained at a constant temperature you might have a case. In real life, as the clutch and engine parts heat up, their dimensions expand. If we don't have some clearance in our clutch cable, it won't be long before there is

Locate the adjusting screw and adjust.

Adjust the cable free-play.

DIY *Adjusting Clutch Cable Free-Play*

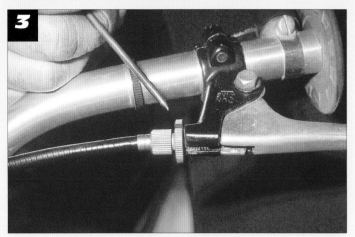

3

Make the final adjustment at the handlebar.

pressure on the clutch with the resultant slip, and eventually a prematurely worn-out clutch.

The converse is also true. If there is too much free-play in the clutch cable, the clutch will be difficult to disengage. Gears will protest with a clash and the bike may creep forward when the clutch is held in.

Most cable-operated clutches call for around 3mm or 1/8-inch free-play in the cable (your owner's or shop manual will provide an exact figure).

During normal use the clutch cable will stretch somewhat and the internal components of the clutch will wear. This usually takes place so gradually that most of us don't even notice it. After a while there is noticeably more free-play or slack than is necessary. At this point you may notice that shifting has becomes difficult or in an extreme case that the clutch refuses to disengage completely.

Adjust the cable for the recommended free-play using the adjusters on the clutch lever, inline with the cable, and at the clutch housing.

The obvious solution is to remove some of the slack from the cable. If the cable is only slightly out of adjustment you can bring it back into spec by twiddling the adjuster mounted at the clutch lever itself. Loosen the lock nut and turn the adjuster out until the free-play is properly adjusted. If the adjuster only takes a few turns, fine. However, if more than half the adjuster is now dangling from the bracket a little more work is required. Many bikes have an additional adjuster either built into the cable or located where the cable enters the clutch housing. If your bike does, try taking up some of the additional free play with the second adjuster.

Keep in mind that the clutch-cable adjusters should only be used to make minor adjustments. If the cable adjuster(s) are threaded out past their halfway points, the clutch itself needs adjusting. ∎

fully engaged. There is also less friction between plates. The designer overcomes this inherent flaw either by adding plates or stiffer springs.

Dry clutches can be built with fewer plates and lighter springs because there is no oil to evacuate from between the plates. These clutches are popular on some pure sportbikes. Ducati, for instance, installs them on some of its high-end track and street models. A dry multi-plate clutch gives off a very distinctive rattle at idle, and some owners find this attractive, feeling that it lends the bike a sporting cachet.

Centrifugal Clutch

Centrifugal clutches are commonly used on small scooters, mopeds, and minibikes, although some off road and touring bikes have used them in the past and still do. They may be considered automatic clutches; in most cases they cannot be overidden by any manual control.

Clutch Springs

Two types of springs are used in clutches. By far the most common is the coil spring. Coil springs look like any and every other coil spring in the world. There are usually three (older motorcycles) to six or even eight springs arranged around the circumference of the pressure plate.

Less popular on motorcycles, although quite common in cars, are diaphragm springs. A diaphragm spring is technically a truncated hollow spring cone sandwiched between two fulcrum rings. It looks like an inverted pie plate with slots cut in it made of spring steel. Diaphragm springs can exert enormous pressure for their size, yet are also light and easily balanced. This becomes an important consideration when they are used in single-plate automotive-style clutches, which rotate at engine speed. Furthermore, they have a very low release effort for a given clamping force, meaning that they require less lever pressure than a conventional spring. Currently, diaphragm springs, though not as common as coil springs, are used in a variety of single- and multi-plate designs, most notably on Harley-Davidsons.

Release Mechanisms

Release mechanisms work by pushing or pulling the pressure plate away from the clutch plates,

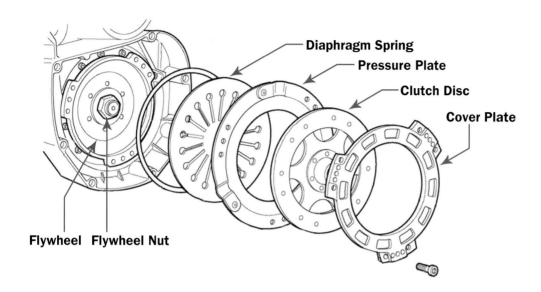

Diaphragm Spring
Pressure Plate
Clutch Disc
Cover Plate

Flywheel Flywheel Nut

The engine speed, single-plate clutch as used by BMW works well, but can make for clunky gear changes. The clutch disc is splined to the transmission input shaft; The diaphragm spring applies pressure to the pressure plate and the cover plate. The cover plate and pressure plate are bolted to the engine flywheel and revolve with it. The flywheel is secured to the engine with a large nut. When the clutch is disengaged the cover plate, pressure plate and spring rotate with the engine, while the clutch disc remains either stationary (bike in neutral or at a stop) or rotates with the transmission (bike moving and in gear). **(Courtesy BMW North America)**

compressing the springs. Some use a pushrod inserted through the hollow transmission main (input) shaft to push the plate. Others use an eccentric lever activated by a cable that forces the rod against the pressure plate. Still others use a mechanism installed in the crankcase cover; these can either push or pull on the clutch-pressure plate, depending on the design.

Hydraulic Clutch Actuation

Currently, many motorcycles come equipped with a hydraulic clutch release. Basically, this is nothing more than a handlebar-activated master cylinder controlling a small slave cylinder that activates the clutch-release mechanism.

Hydraulic clutches are popular because they seldom need adjustment and have relatively low maintenance requirements compared to a cable-released clutch. They are unaffected by temperature and cable routing, which has a major impact on a cable-operated clutch's feel.

On the other hand, many riders, particularly sportbike riders, complain that hydraulic clutches have a vague feeling, making release

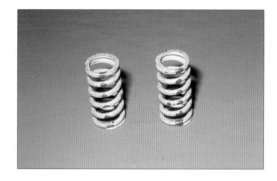

Spring tension may be applied by several, small coil springs (TOP) or one large diaphragm spring (BOTTOM).

SPRAG CLUTCH

The clutch system functions to disconnect and connect the power of the crankshaft. Most clutches are placed between the primary reduction and transmission. With some models, however, they are attached directly to the crankshaft.

The actuation of the clutch can be roughly divided into two types: the manual clutch controlled by the rider and the centrifugal clutch which connects and disconnects power according to engine rotation.

The clutch controls the transmission of power by frictional force. When the clutch is completely disengaged, power cannot be transmitted to the rear wheel. When the vehicle is started, the clutch gradually increases its frictional force and smoothly transmits power to the rear wheel. When the clutch is completely engaged, the power of the crankshaft will be directly transmitted to the rear wheel.

If the clutch is partially released with the engine at high rpm, the reduction in friction force caused by heat or wear in the clutch causes the clutch to slip even when completely engaged. As a result, power transmission is lost.

WET MULTIPLATE MANUAL CLUTCH

This is the most conventional clutch type used on motorcycles. The primary drive gear of the crankshaft drive the primary driven gear integrated in the clutch outer. The clutch discs and the clutch outer rotate with the crankshaft, because the claws of the clutch disc are engaged with the grooves of the clutch outer.

The mainshaft of the transmission and the clutch center are fixed with a lock nut. Furthermore, the clutch center and the clutch plates are engaged with splines. Thus, the clutch plates rotate with the rear wheel through the transmission.

When the clutch lever is pulled in, the clutch lifter mechanism presses the pressure plate through the lifter plate, resulting in a gap between the

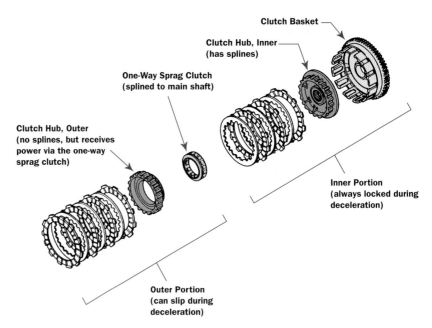

Clutch Basket
Clutch Hub, Inner (has splines)
One-Way Sprag Clutch (splined to main shaft)
Clutch Hub, Outer (no splines, but receives power via the one-way sprag clutch)
Inner Portion (always locked during deceleration)
Outer Portion (can slip during deceleration)

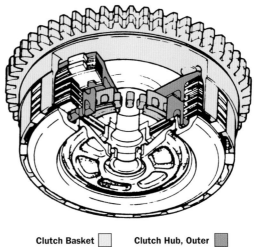

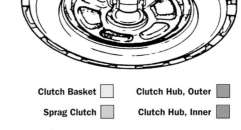

Clutch Basket ☐ **Clutch Hub, Outer** ☐
Sprag Clutch ☐ **Clutch Hub, Inner** ☐

During hard deceleration the sprag clutch releases, allowing the clutch to slip. This prevents the rear wheel from locking, yet still allows some engine braking.
(Courtesy American Honda Motor Corporation)

discs and the plates. The power of the crankshaft is now not transferred to the rear wheel.

When operating the transmission gear and gradually releasing the clutch lever, the pressure plate begins to press the disc and plate by the tension of the spring, and the discs and the plates begin to transmit

power by sliding contact. At this time, the vehicle will start to move.

When the clutch lever is completely released, the discs and plates are completely caught between the pressure plate and the clutch center, and no longer mutually slip. The power of the crankshaft is thus completely transmitted to the rear wheel. ∎

difficult. There are now kits on the market to convert your hydraulic clutch to cable operation and your cable-operated clutch to hydraulic operation. Some people are never happy, are they?

Wet Versus Dry

Originally, all clutches ran dry, cork being the preferred friction medium. Cork didn't tolerate much abuse though, so asbestos-based fabrics gained popularity. During the 1930s, oil-bath primary-chain cases became popular. Asbestos didn't handle the oil well, so cork was tried again. The combination of oil and cork was almost perfect. The oil gave the cork clutch a sweet action and kept it cool.

The downside? Oil-soaked plates also had a tendency to stick when they were cold. If you've ever wondered why many vintage motorcycle riders kick over a bike with the clutch pulled in, wonder no more, they're freeing up the clutch. And if you don't? Crunch goes the gearbox. In fact, I'd recommend warming up the bike with the clutch pulled in for at least ten seconds before shifting into gear, even on current models.

Sprag Clutches

Occasionally, you'll run into something called a sprag clutch. These devices are often referred to as back clutches or overrunning clutches. Normally, a sprag clutch is used in a starter motor or other device that needs to engage and disengage automatically, based on torque or speed.

Because a quick downshift may allow the engine's compression braking to lock the rear wheel, some motorcycles utilize a sprag clutch to prevent wheel lock under hard braking or downshifting. Sprag clutches are technically called back-torque-limiting clutches. The major difference between a standard clutch and back clutch is the two piece inner hub. When the engine is driving the bike the clutch acts normally. It also works normally during routine cruising and decelerating. But if a high torque load occurs during deceleration, which could potentially lock the rear wheel, the sprag portion of the clutch disengages. It will only disengage in an amount proportional to the amount of traction. You'll still have plenty of engine braking to help you slow down. So rather than being a simple on-off device, which would put the rider at a serious

DIY   *Adjusting the Clutch*

Due to normal wear and tear the clutch itself may need some periodic adjustment. The usual sign is excessive play that can't be removed with the cable adjuster(s). This is a good indication that the clutch-release mechanism or the clutch plates themselves are starting to show some wear. In most cases, it does not mean that clutch destruction is imminent, or that wholesale clutch replacement is going to be required.

These days few bikes have a provision for actually adjusting the clutch spring tension. What you're actually going to be adjusting is the clutch release mechanism. In some few cases you may find that your particular bike has no clutch adjustment other than the cable, an unfortunate situation that seems to be occurring more frequently. If that turns out to be the case and cable adjustment doesn't solve your problem try replacing the cable before moving onto the clutch.

Since every bike uses a slightly different procedure, you're going to have to refer to your shop manual, but a typical adjustment goes something like this:

Back off all the cable adjusters. Remove any covers needed to gain access to the adjusting mechanism, which is usually a threaded screw that contacts the end of the clutch pushrod. You'll probably find a lock nut securing what looks like a small screw. The normal procedure is to loosen the lock nut and turn the screw inwards until it contacts the clutch pushrod and then back it out anywhere from one quarter to one half-turn. Your service manual will give you the exact setting.

After the adjustment has been made, retighten the lock nut. Readjust the cable free-play to specifications. Road-test the bike. If the clutch slips or grabs, recheck your adjustment. If you adjusted the clutch to remedy a slipping problem and the results were less than satisfactory, proceed to the next section. ∎

You'll need:

- *Shop manual*
- *Deep sockets*
- *Screwdriver*

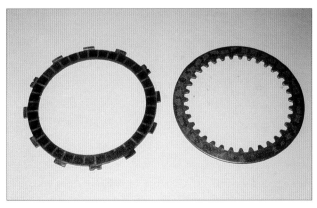

The drive plates (left) are generally made out of some type of fiber material, the driven plates (right) are usually steel.

DIY · *Replacing the Clutch*

You'll need:

- Impact driver and bits
- Hammer for use with the impact driver
- Soft-faced mallet, plastic or rawhide
- Clutch-cover gasket
- Oil and new filter (no sense putting clean oil in with a dirty filter)
- Clutch plates and springs
- Shop manual
- Pair of calipers (for measuring springs and steel plates)
- Oil pan
- Rags
- Brake or contact cleaner
- Razor blade
- Gasket sealer, if recommended in the shop manual

On most bikes, replacing the clutch is a simple job well within the capabilities of the novice mechanic. A word of advice, if you own a late model Moto Guzzi or BMW: replacing the clutch involves a lot of work and a few special tools. Basically, on both bikes you've got to remove the transmission from the engine (which on some requires removing the engine and transmission from the frame) before you can replace the clutch. A novice can do it, but it's a lot of work. My suggestion is to read through the manual beforehand; if the job seems within your capabilities, by all means proceed.

Ninety-five percent of the bikes in the world use the wet multi-plate clutch, and I suspect most of you own one of these, so that's what we'll tackle.

As a rule of thumb, you're only going to be replacing the fiber drive plates. Normally those are the ones that wear out first, so it's always a good idea to have new ones on hand before you dismantle the clutch. Replace the steel driven plates only if they are scored or warped. These are more expensive and may need to be special-ordered through your dealership.

Since they usually don't need to be replaced, my suggestion is to wait until the clutch is apart; if they're shot you'll need them, but chances are they'll be good enough to reuse.

Springs can be reused if they measure up, but they are cheap and it's worth it to replace them as a matter

After draining the oil, remove the clutch cover.

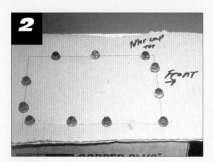

Since the bolts are all a different length some method of identifying them is helpful, such as a cardboard template.

A plastic mallet can be used to remove stubborn cases.

Allow the cavity to drain for a few minutes.

DIY Replacing the Clutch

5

Loosen the springs in a diagonal pattern, a little bit at a time.

8

Be on the lookout for any spacers or anti-shudder springs.

6

Remove the pressure plate and springs. Try not to lose any of the pieces.

7

Inspect the inner clutch hub nut and its retaining washer. Remove the clutch plates. Inspect the clutch hub splines and basket fingers for damage.

9

Clean the driven plates in mineral spirits or other solvent. Note the dark areas; that's where the plates have been rubbing.

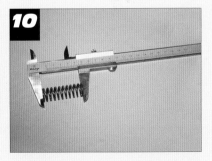

10

Measure the springs and compare them to the specifications listed in the manual. Measure the driven plates as well.

of course. Assuming your bike uses a wet clutch, most manufacturers recommend soaking the new clutch plates in fresh oil for anywhere from half an hour to twenty-four hours before use. This allows the fiber plates to absorb some oil and swell up to their full working thickness. Presoaking prevents the new plates from overheating, which could cause their early demise. It will also ensure a more accurate initial adjustment.

Most manuals (or the package the plates come in) will remind you to soak the plates. If for some reason it's not spelled out, take my advice and do it anyway. Do it now before you start taking out the old clutch.

DIV   *Replacing the Clutch*

Now, drain the oil from the clutch housing. In most cases that means draining the engine oil. Replace the drain plug, torque it, and set the drain pan under the clutch cover to catch any leftover oil. Next, release the

If you're running a wet clutch, soak the new plates in the same weight and brand of oil you'll be using to lubricate the clutch.

clutch cable by backing off all of the adjustments.

Remove any obstructions in the way of the clutch cover. Depending on the bike that could range from a footpeg, to a muffler, or to nothing at all if you're lucky.

Remove all of the bolts or screws from the clutch cover. These are probably going to be several different lengths. My suggestion is to draw a rough outline of the cover on a piece of cardboard. Punch holes in the approximate locations and push the cor-

Identify the sharp edge of the plates.

responding screw through the cardboard. This will make it a lot easier to get the right screw back into the right hole during reassembly.

Once all the bolts are out, the case should wiggle free. If it doesn't, don't don't try to pry it off with a screwdriver. Prying off aluminum cases puts deep gouges in them. The case will never seal against the gasket and the end result will be a perpetual oil leak. Instead, give it a smart rap with your soft-faced mallet. Whacking it with a steel hammer will probably remove it as well—in several large chunks. Don't do it! Once the cover is off, you should be staring at the clutch pressure plate and its retaining bolts.

Loosen the bolts in a transverse pattern, a few turns at a time, to prevent the pressure plate from warping. When all the bolts are loose, remove them with their springs. Remove the pressure plate. Remove the clutch push-rod or push-piece and any hardware that goes with it.

Remove the clutch plates one at a time, inspecting them as you go, and noting the order so you can put them back properly. Chances are good that the reason you've taken your clutch apart is because the fiber drive plates are worn out. If that's the case, your inclination may be to simply toss them out. Before you do, take a moment or two to look at them and compare them to the new ones. That way you'll know what a worn one looks like. Clean the steel driven plates in solvent, and wipe them dry. Use your caliper to measure the plates. If they have worn under spec, they're due for replacement as well. If the plates are discolored or blued they've been overheated a time or two. Overheating warps clutch plates. Check for warpage by laying the plates on a good thick, straight piece of glass. While holding the plate down, see if you can slip a feeler

Install the plates in the correct order, with the sharp edges facing outward.

DIV — *Replacing the Clutch*

gauge under it. If a gauge of more than a few thousandths can be inserted under the plate (your shop manual will tell you exactly how many), the plates are too warped and should be replaced.

Give the clutch hub and the clutch drum a good visual once-over. Look for grooves or notches worn into the working surfaces. Any nicks will make the clutch difficult to disengage and also prevent it from releasing cleanly. Small notches can be dressed smooth with a file. If the parts are deeply notched, replace them. If everything looks and feels good, remove all traces of gasket material from the clutch cover and the engine.

Before you reinstall the clutch plates run your finger along the tabs of the drive plates and the inner edges of the driven plates. Because the plates are stamped one edge will be sharp, the other rounded.

When the plates are reinstalled all of the sharp edges should face outwards. This will prevent them from binding against the hub, the basket, and eachother whenever the clutch is disengaged or released. Soak the new fiber drive plates in fresh oil for 30 minutes or so. This lets them swell to their working dimension. In fact if you have a little foresight you can pop them in a pan full of oil as soon as you get them.

Install the clutch plates in their proper order. Making sure all of the sharp edges face outward (away from the center of the clutch). Install the release hardware and pressure plate. Install the springs and retaining bolts. Torque the bolts in stages using a criss-cross pattern to prevent warpage. Install a new gasket and replace the clutch cover. Replace the oil (and filter, if required). Adjust the clutch as your manual says. Test-ride the bike. Be on the alert for slippage or any other abnormal behavior. ∎

Install the release/push piece followed by the pressure plate. Identify any balance marks and position the plate accordingly.

Install the springs. The bolts should be torqued down a turn at a time, again in a diagonal pattern. Check the clutch operation, install a new gasket, replace the cover, and refill the engine (or primary case) with the correct weight of oil.

Once you've disassembled the clutch for inspection or replacement, be sure to examine the splines on the clutch basket for excessive wear, as well as the inner clutch hub-nut (CENTER) and retaining washer. In this case, everything appears to be in good shape.

disadvantage during braking, the sprag clutch determines the correct amount of slip for the available traction and adjusts itself accordingly. Sprag, or as they are called in racing circles, "slipper" clutches are generally found on large twin-cylinder sportbikes.

MAINTAINING THE CLUTCH

There are really only two problems that can affect your clutch. When the clutch fails to transmit torque from engine to the transmission, the clutch is said to be "slipping." Most of us have experienced a slipping clutch at one time or another.

The first inkling of impending clutch failure, slippage is generally an increase in engine speed while the motorcycle's road speed stays constant or starts to drop off. This usually occurs when you call on your bike to accelerate in high gear while heavily loaded, at least initially. Keep it up, though, and pretty soon you'll have trouble just pulling away from a stop.

Worn out clutch plates or springs, or improper clutch adjustment, may cause the clutch to slip. Try adjusting your clutch (if it's adjustable) and adjusting the cable for free-play before deciding the clutch needs to be replaced. One thing to bear

in mind though, the clutch, just like a spark plug, oil filter, or tire, should be considered an expendable item to be replaced on more or less regular intervals. Regular abuse of the clutch will certainly speed the wear process. If you like to do burnouts or slip the clutch a lot on take-off be prepared to replace your clutch more frequently.

Clutch drag, on the other hand, may be characterized as not enough slip. Clutches that refuse to release cleanly or completely are said to "drag." The first symptom of a dragging clutch is usually a loud cry of anguish from the transmission when you try to engage low gear. If you persist by forcing the bike into gear, it may show its displeasure by either stalling, or if you're on a loose surface and the revs are high enough, taking off on its own. Note, though, that as I explained earlier, it's absolutely normal for a wet clutch to drag when it's cold. So don't panic if your bike experiences an occasional fit of "dragitis."

Other causes of drag are improper adjustment, worn release mechanisms, and the wrong weight oil in the primary, bent or warped plates, oil contaminating dry clutches, and worn splines in the clutch basket or hub (or both). If your bike's clutch starts to drag, try lubing and adjusting the cable first. If it's a dry clutch, try cleaning the plates. On some bikes this can be done with no more effort than pouring some mineral spirits into the clutch housing. Start the bike up, work the clutch, and drain. Only then should you think about disassembling the clutch and replacing parts.

The cables that operate the clutch also require maintenance. You need to periodically lube them and inspect them for proper free-play. During normal use the clutch cable will stretch somewhat, and the internal components of the clutch will wear. This usually takes place so gradually that most of us don't even notice it. After awhile there is noticeably more (or less) free-play or slack than is necessary.

If there is too much free-play in the clutch cable, the clutch will be difficult to disengage. Gears will protest with a clash, and the bike may creep forward when the clutch is held in. If the cable doesn't have sufficient free-play, it will put tension on clutch springs causing the clutch to begin to disengage. Continued partial disengagement of the clutch will cause the clutch to slip and accelerate wear. For tips on adjusting your clutch, see the sidebar.

Clutch Cables

It's safe to say that the clutch is only as good as its cable. If your clutch cable is improperly routed or dry as a bone it's not going to work very well. It's going to take a lot of effort to pull the clutch in. And it's not going to release very cleanly. The solution is to periodically inspect and lubricate the cable (if it's designed to be lubed, that is, not all cables are). Remember, a little preventive maintenance at the cable end will help keep your clutch healthy. Cable lubrication will be covered in the Appendix.

Hydraulic Clutch

There's not much maintenance involved with hydraulic clutch releases. A change of the hydraulic oil every couple of years is a good idea. The procedure is exactly the same as changing the brake fluid, so I would direct your attention to the brake section.

IMPROVING YOUR CLUTCH

When it's time to replace your clutch should you go OEM or aftermarket? If you do go aftermarket is it better to go with stock or heavy duty?

Good question; the aftermarket is full of heavy-duty clutch plates, reinforced clutch drums and hubs, super zooty pressure plates and heavy duty springs. In general if you're going to abuse the clutch in any way, whether through hard riding, or more horsepower, you should consider upgrading to at least heavy-duty springs and plates. These are available through your local dealership so start your hunt there.

Be advised that heavy-duty clutches will require more oomph to disengage. To that end some riders may feel it advantageous to install an aftermarket hydraulic release.

On the other hand some hard core sporting riders feel that hydraulic clutch releases lack feel and they may want to convert the hydraulic system to an old-fashioned cable system. In either case kits are available through the aftermarket to suit your needs. Find them at your local dealer or through the Internet.

Once upon a time motorcycles had no transmissions. Early motorcycles, which in reality were nothing more than bicycles with some sort of primitive engine lashed into the frame, relied on a simple flat leather belt or perhaps a V-belt to transmit power from the engine to the rear wheel.

The obvious question at this point: why do we need a transmission in the first place? A fair enough question. Internal combustion engines, be they gasoline or diesel powered, are fundamentally unsuited for use in any type of vehicle that requires varying speeds, i.e. a motorcycle, automobile, truck, or what-have-you.

The problem is that internal combustion engines only develop enough torque to propel a vehicle over a fairly narrow engine speed range. Initially it was thought that a motorcycle could

use a simple reduction gear system. These were used in machine shops of the day to power lathes, drill presses, and milling machines. It was a simple matter to adapt the basic principles to motorcycle use and initially at least it worked fine. Bear in mind that those seminal motorcycles also used a common bicycle type chain and pedal set up for starting and providing what was euphemistically known as LPA or light pedal assistance. In essence, you pedaled the thing up to the point were the engine could make enough power to propel you along on its own. Hills obviously needed a little LPA as did low speed turns or any other situation that called for a little extra torque. Just riding a motorcycle at the time required a fairly robust constitution.

It was soon obvious that a better system would be required. One footnote in the develop-

As horsepower increased so did the width of the primary chain. This older Bultaco two-stroke race engine used a double row primary chain. Apparently the owner went through a lot of lower fork legs as well.

CONSTANT MESH TRANSMISSION

Constant mesh transmissions consist of the following components: the mainshaft, with its fixed and sliding gears; the countershaft, with its fixed and sliding gears; the shift forks; the shift drum.

Power is transmitted through the clutch to the mainshaft. From the mainshaft, power may be transmitted through several gear sets to the countershaft. M1 through M5 are the gears on the mainshaft and C1 through C5 are the countershaft gears.

The gear sets are comprised of opposing gears, one gear on each shaft. The illustration on the right shows the gear sets, pairing the mainshaft number with the countershaft number (M1/C1, M2/C2, etc.). Selection of the proper gear set is done by moving a sliding gear into contact with the gear set desired. Connection of the sliding gear and the gear set is done using dogs and dog holes on the sides of the gears. In the illustration, gears M3, C4 and C5 are the sliding gears. The sliding gears are moved by shift forks which ride on the shift drum. Cam grooves cut in the shift drum move the shift forks as the drum rotates. Rotation of the shift drum is accomplished by moving the gearshift pedal. ■

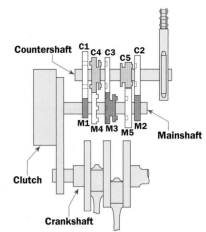

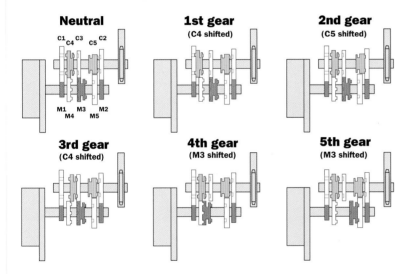

Neutral

1st gear
(C4 shifted)

2nd gear
(C5 shifted)

3rd gear
(C4 shifted)

4th gear
(M3 shifted)

5th gear
(M3 shifted)

The constant mesh transmission consists of the mainshaft, with its fixed and sliding gears; the countershaft, with its fixed and sliding gears; the shift forks, and the shift drum.
Power is transmitted through the clutch to the mainshaft. From the mainshaft, power may be transmitted through several gear sets to the countershaft. M1 through M5 are the gears on the mainshaft and C1 through C5 are the countershaft gears. The gear sets are composed of opposing gears, one gear on each shaft. The illustration shows the gear sets, pairing the mainshaft number with the countershaft number (M1/C1, M2/C2, etc.). (Courtesy American Honda Motor Corporation)

ment of the transmission was the Megola; built in Germany between 1921 and 1925 the Megola used a 5-cylinder 640cc engine laced into the front wheel. It had no clutch or gearbox but the sidevalve engine developed an enormous amount of low-end torque.

When you came to a stop the engine simply stalled, you then pushed it along to get it going again. Not a very elegant solution perhaps but far better than several early designers who tried coupling their engines to the rear wheel through a system of rods and joints like a steam locomotive. Before a transmission could be installed a means of disconnecting the engine from the drive wheel (rear in most cases) had to be found.

In the beginning the clutch was usually some form of idler pulley that could be controlled by a foot pedal or lever. Fine when your power transmission is composed of flat belt, legs, and lungs, not so good for torque-multiplying systems.

At first, simple two-speed gearboxes were tried, designs that were based on the back gearing of a lathe. Later, planetary gear trains based on bicycle practice were tried. Fitted to the rear hub these "hub shifters" had about as much mechanical integrity as a cheese omelet.

The designers of early motorcycles were by no means dim bulbs; quite the contrary. However, they were charting unexplored territory, so a number of false starts had to be expected.

SHIFTING GEARS

The gearshift mechanism consists of three gearshift forks, a gearshift drum, a gearshift arm, a shift drum stopper and a gearshift positive stopper. When the gearshift pedal is depressed the gearshift spindle rotates, causing the gearshift arm to rotate the shift drum. When the shift drum rotates, the shift forks move sideways due to the cam action of the groove cut into the shift drum body. ■

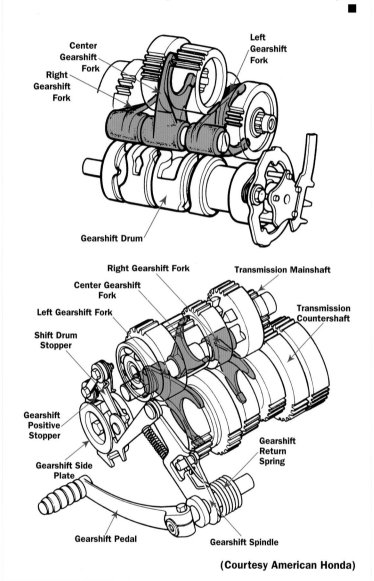

(Courtesy American Honda)

BASIC TRANSMISSION THEORY

Most transmissions use two shafts; the input, which may be called the mainshaft, and the output, which can also be called the layshaft, the driveshaft, or the countershaft. There are some transmissions, particularly those used in shaft-driven bikes, that utilize three shafts. Typically those transmissions separate the input shaft from the mainshaft. All of those names and terms can get a little confusing, so for our purposes we'll stick with the most popular terms: mainshaft and countershaft.

All modern motorcycles equipped with manual transmissions use a constant-mesh design. This means that all of the gears on the mainshaft (the shaft receiving power from the engine via the clutch) are in mesh all of the time with their counterparts on the countershaft (the shaft transmitting power to the rear wheel).

The gears on the shafts are either fixed or free to turn. Some of the gears are able to slide laterally while remaining in mesh. Pegs projecting from one side of the gear fit into sockets machined into the face of the gear it sits next to. When the gear slides over, the pegs engage the sockets, locking the gears together. Gear shifting is accomplished by locking various combinations of gears together, causing the shafts to turn at different rates.

Depending on the overall reduction, the transmission multiplies the engine's torque dependent upon our needs. In the low gears we need a lot of torque to overcome inertia and get the bike moving. Accordingly, a first-gear ratio may be something around 12:1, meaning the engine revolves 12 times for every turn of the countershaft. In the high gears we need less torque but more speed. A fifth-gear reduction may be 4.7:1 or less. Bear in mind that these are transmission ratios. We must also take into account the reduction in gearing between the engine crankshaft and the clutch, and the overall final-drive ratio, including the tire diameter, to arrive at our overall gear ratio.

How Gears are Shifted

As I said, some gears are able to slide on their shafts while other gears are fixed in place. The sliding gears have small collars machined into one side. One end of a fork, appropriately called a shift fork, rides in the collar. The other end of a shift fork has a peg on it. The peg engages a groove cut into the shift drum. The shift drum, as its name implies, is a hefty steel drum that's rotated whenever the shift lever is activated. The grooves (technically, they are called cams) are cut in an s-shaped pattern.

When the drum rotates the cam forces the peg to follow the groove, moving the shift fork to either the left or right. When the shift fork moves, it slides the gear into engagement with an adjacent gear, changing the ratio.

A variation of the shift drum uses a large plate with grooves machined into it. As the plate rotates, the grooves position the forks exactly like a drum does.

Shift Detents

To hold the shift drum in position after the gears are shifted, and to provide a better feel to the mechanism, a spring-loaded plunger, called a shift detent, is often used. A ball- or bullet-shaped plunger is forced against the shift drum by a sturdy spring. Milled into the shift drum are a series of shallow craters. The craters are positioned to correspond with the gears. When the gears are engaged, the detent plunger is forced into the appropriate crater, locking the shift drum into position. The little notch that you feel when you shift your bike into gear is the detent falling into place. Alternative designs may feature a small roller or bearing that drops into a notch machined into the gear shift mechanism.

Some bikes have a separate detent for neutral as well. Lots of times these take the form of a small spring-loaded ball or pin.

THE FINE POINTS

The slower a gearbox turns, the easier it will be to shift. By the same token, small, light gears are easier to shift than big, heavy ones.

This is because the gears themselves are subject to the laws of inertia. As the inertia builds up it gets harder to speed up or slow down the gear that's to be shifted, the speed between the gear and its engaging dog must match, to ensure proper meshing. The ideal situation would be one where the gears were light and spun slowly. However if we reduce gearbox components in size we have to turn them faster (to reduce torque loads) and if we spin them too fast we're right back where we started, slow shifting. Remember, a gearbox multiplies torque so the closer a gearbox gets to engine speed the less torque it

A simple chain-driven primary is efficient and compact.

has to deal with. At some point though, that torque must be multiplied. If not in the transmission, then in the final drive, which creates its own problems.

A well thought-out gearbox will have gears that are light enough to shift quickly and smoothly, without being so small that ultra-high input-shaft speeds are required to cut down substantially on torque multiplication.

There is a strong case to be made for designing a chain-driven motorcycle (primary and secondary) so that both the primary chain and the drive chain ride on the same shaft and on the same side, thus balancing the load caused by chain pull. Unfortunately, such an arrangement makes replacing the counter-shaft sprocket a real pain in the butt as the entire clutch assembly must be removed before you can access the sprocket.

Normal practice is to spread the reduction from engine to rear wheel as evenly as possible throughout the entire power train.

Gearing

When an engineer selects the gearbox ratios several factors must be considered, among them engine power, or lack thereof, the bike's intended usage, and the production budget. A designer will try to gear a pure sportbike so that its maximum speed will coincide with the engine rpm where the most power is produced. A sportbike will also use a gearbox with closely spaced ratios to help the pilot keep the engine "on the boil." A touring bike will have wider spaced ratios, in part because a mildly tuned touring engine develops lots of torque over a fairly large range of rpm. A touring bike will also be somewhat over-geared in top gear, providing a relaxed pace and good gas mileage; of course, passing a truck may require a down shift or two to bring the revs up, but that's an acceptable trade-off for most of us.

You may have heard the expression close-ratio gearbox or wide-ratio gearbox being bandied about and wondered what it meant. In a close-ratio box the numerical spread between the gear ratios is kept small. This keeps the rpm drop between gears at the bare minimum. Using closely spaced ratios ensures that the engine is always kept at or near its torque peak. sportbikes normally have very close or "tight" ratios. First may be 2:1, second may be 2.2:1, third 2.5:1, and so on (these are hypothetical numbers). A close-ratio box makes it easy to keep the bike in the fat part of the power band.

A touring bike or cruiser will have a gearbox that has fairly wide ratios. If first is 2:1, then second may be 2.75:1 and third 3.25:1. Normally, these type bikes have very broad power bands and their owners tend to ride them in a relaxed manner. Because they make lots of torque over a wide rpm range, the rpm drop between gears is of little consequence.

When I first started to ride, a four-speed box was the norm. Nowadays, five speeds are normal and six are common. The more gears in a box, the closer you get to having an ideal ratio for every situation. On the other hand, an engineer may under-gear a bike, particularly a cruiser or standard, perhaps sacrificing a bit of top end in order to endow it with a little more lively performance in high gear. As a general rule of thumb, the more tractable an engine, the fewer ratios it needs in its transmission. For example, an old 74 cubic inch Harley with a power band as wide as the Missouri River gets by very nicely on 4 ratios. Conversely the 50cc Suzuki that won the 1962 FIM road-racing world championship had a power band that was less than 800 rpm wide; it utilized a 16-ratio gearbox, and needed every gear it had just to get rolling.

Primary Drives

There are only two types of primary drive: direct and indirect. A direct primary drive couples the engine to the transmission directly through the clutch. Your family grocery-getter is the perfect example. The flywheel and clutch assembly bolts to the crankshaft. The transmission-input shaft fits into the friction disc of the clutch. The crankshaft to input-shaft ratio is 1:1. All gear reduction takes place in either the gearbox or the rear end.

A direct drive primary offers the designer several advantages. As we discussed in chapter 4, because the clutch turns at engine speed it can be made lighter and smaller. Since no intermediate gears are required, manufacturing costs are reduced. Finally the direct primary is highly efficient and power losses are cut considerably.

For a motorcycle direct primary drive to work efficiently the crankshaft and transmission shafts must run longitudinally; that is, in line with the direction of travel or, in fact, with the frame itself. Direct primary drives are popular with designers who intend to use a drive shaft as a final drive. BMWs and Moto Guzzis are the best examples of motorcycles that utilize a direct primary drive and a shaft-driven as opposed to a chain or belt final drive.

Indirect Primary Drive

Problems crop up when the engine crankshaft lies transversely, or across the frame rails. Transverse engines require the primary drive to rotate 90 degrees before the power can be fed into the transmission. This rotation requires an indirect primary drive. All transversely-mounted engines use an indirect primary of one form or another. An indirect primary simply takes the torque arriving at the crankshaft end and passes it on to the transmission input shaft. The indirect primary may take the form of a belt, chain, or

OIL ADDITIVES

As a rule I don't recommend using oil additives of any sort. Either in the engine, the transmission or the primary drive. Motorcycle engineers spend a lot of time researching the oils that they recommend for their bikes. In every case that I've ever seen, routine oil changes, using the manufactures recommend viscosity and grade of oil, will do far more to prolong the life of your motorcycle than some mysterious elixir of dubious parentage. ∎

gear(s). Examples of indirect primary drives are everywhere. In fact most motorcycles in the world use some form of indirect primary drive.

Standard practice usually mounts the primary sprocket or gear on the end of the crankshaft, and the secondary sprocket or gear on the clutch. As an alternative, some designers mount the primary-drive sprocket or gear somewhere toward the center of the crankshaft. Mounting the drive gear toward the center of the crank reduces the likelihood that stresses imposed by the combined action of the primary and secondary drives will twist the crankshaft out of true. As you may realize, this can become a serious problem on high-performance, transverse, multi-cylinder engines.

The clutch is secured to the transmission input shaft. Torque flows from the crankshaft into the belt, chain, or gear and then into the clutch. It's then passed through the gearbox and into the final drive, which is usually a belt or chain; although some manufacturers, notably the Japanese, have used an indirect primary with a shaft final drive. Since the engine turns faster than the clutch, the torque is multiplied by the difference between their respective sprocket sizes. Therefore, an indirect primary requires a heavier, stronger clutch than a direct primary.

Belts, Chains, and Gears

Once a clutch was first installed between the crankshaft and the gearbox some means of driving it was required. The roller chain was perfect for the primary drive—able to transfer lots of torque and more or less trouble free, though it was a bit messy and could be a bit dangerous. A shot of oil every so often and some periodic adjustment, and you were home free as far as maintenance was concerned.

Once unit construction became popular, it was a simple matter to install either an automatic or manual method of tensioning the primary chain. Simple in its construction and application, the primary chain needs nothing more than a little oil and some occasional adjustment to keep it happy.

Gear-Driven Primaries

While you might think that a gear-driven primary drive would be the most efficient way to

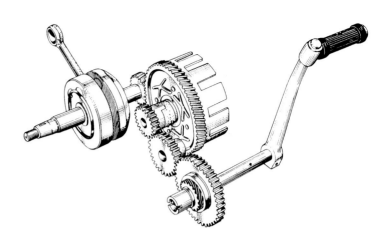

Most modern bikes use gears to transfer power from the crankshaft to the clutch. **(Courtesy American Honda Motor Corporation).**

transmit power you'd be wrong, at least in theory. Theoretically the roller chain is the most efficient way to transmit torque although there is strong argument to be made in favor of the toothed rubber belt currently used on some motorcycles (though more often as a secondary drive).

Gears are less efficient then chains or belts. Why? The answer is a little complex, but it boils down to the fact that when gears are used, only one tooth at a time transmits torque, as opposed to a chain or belt drive where the load is shared by at least half the teeth.

But as a practical matter, the gear-driven primary drive has a lot going for it and that's why they are currently the most common type of primary-drive system. They are incredibly robust and very quiet. The gears are in mesh, as opposed to being some distance apart, as they would be if a chain and sprockets were used, and the engine can be built to be a bit more compact. We may only be discussing millimeters here, but every millimeter is important when you're building a world-class motorcycle.

While toothed secondary-drive belts are popular, belts do have one major flaw when used as a primary drive. Clutches work best when covered in oil. When drive belts are run in oil they deteriorate in short order. Belts also generate a fair amount of heat. If the belt is run where it can constantly get a blast of fresh air, no problem. Enclose it in an aluminum cover next to the en-

Ouch! I hate to admit it, but this one came out of one of my transmissions.

gine and you've got a predicament. The other problem is width. Belts wide enough to transmit the engine torque are generally too wide to fit conveniently under the primary cover. As it now stands, I don't expect to see toothed belts used as part of a primary-drive system on anything but custom-built motorcycles and some race bikes.

In general, transmissions don't require much maintenance. In reality, there's not much you can do to them without performing some major surgery. Keep the box full of oil, keep the clutch adjusted, try to avoid hammering on the shift pedal, and your tranny should last darn near forever.

MAINTAINING TRANSMISSION AND PRIMARY DRIVE

Most motorcycles today are built with unit-construction engines with a common oil source for both the engine and transmission. On these machines, you'll never have to change tranny fluid because you change it every time you change the engine oil.

That doesn't mean you'll never need any maintenance, however. Depending on the year and model you own, you may still have to adjust the primary chain and change its lubricant.

Primary Oil Changes

Outside of Harley-Davidson and India (Royal) Enfields, not too many current motorcycles have a primary chain case. If yours does, it will need the occasional oil change. A primary oil change should be done anytime you change the transmission oil. Since the procedure is identical I think we can skip the fine details (see sidebar.)

Adjusting the Primary Chain

If you own a bike that has an adjustable primary chain, e.g., a vintage bike or Harley-Davidson, some routine inspection and adjustment is required. Your shop manual will detail the amount of slack or free-play the primary chain should have.

Let the engine cool completely before checking the primary chain and make sure the key to the bike is in your pocket. You can imagine the consequences of accidentally bumping the starter while your fingers are in the chain case. Check the chain at several points. Procedures on adjustment vary. In some cases, mainly bikes built before 1963 (I'm certain a lot of you own those models!) you'll have to move the transmission to adjust the chain. Some later bikes have an externally adjustable tensioner that can be accessed through an adjustment port. In other cases, you may have to remove the primary cover to access the chain tensioner shoe and adjust it.

TROUBLESHOOTING YOUR TRANSMISSION: HOW TO TELL IF THERE IS A PROBLEM

Transmission woes can manifest themselves in several ways. Signs of impending doom can be found in hard shifting, jumping out of gear, or big chunks of metal floating around in the oil. In the first case make certain that the clutch is properly adjusted. A dragging clutch or one that's worn out completely can make changing gears an uncertain proposition at best. If you suddenly have trouble finding neutral or the bike develops a balky shifter, check the clutch adjustment before proceeding any further. If the bike refuses to stay in a particular gear, it usually means a shift fork has been bent or the gear dogs have worn or are broken. Usually, the bike will either pop out of gear as soon as it's engaged and you let go of the shift pedal, or it'll jump out when you try to accelerate the bike. Occasionally the problem may be found in the external shift mechanism, but it's more likely that the problem will be found inside the gearbox. With rare exception, any and all chunks of metal found in the oil are cause for concern. Metal chips are generally an indication that something is in the process of wearing out. It may be a bearing or it may be the

DIY *Transmission Oil Change*

For those bikes with separate transmission lubricant, changing the transmission oil is as easy as changing the engine oil—easier, in fact, since there is no filter to deal with. Start by identifying the correct drain plug. I once saw a guy drain the engine oil out of a BMW when he intended to drain the transmission. Fortunately, he caught the mistake when he undid the transmission fill plug and realized that it was still full.

The first step is to take the bike out for a ride to warm the bike up to operating temperature the tranny lube. Remove the drain plug and drain out the old stuff. Gear lubricants tend to be pretty heavy so let the oil drain for at least 15 minutes or so.

If your transmission plug has a magnetic tip on it, use a rag or paper towel to clean off the accumulated metal chips. Unless you see some really big chunks (like a gear tooth or dog), don't be concerned. Metal chips and filings are a normal by-product of transmission use. If your bike doesn't have a magnetic plug, don't panic. The chips will collect in the lowest part of the transmission and won't cause any harm. Install a new drain-plug gasket. Give the drain-plug threads a taste of anti-seize or white grease, and reinstall it. Torque the bolt to the manufacturer's specifications.

Drain bolts can be a little tricky; first, you're threading a heavy steel

You'll need:

- Drain pan
- Funnel
- Shop manual
- Socket or wrench to fit the drain bolt
- Fresh oil
- New drain-plug gaskets
- Torque wrench, preferably 3/8-inch drive, 5-25 ft-lbs. (optional)

bolt into soft aluminum; second, they are often in awkward spots; and third, you're usually trying to compress a new copper or steel drain-plug washer. If you strip the case threads, you're in for a rare treat, especially since we haven't reached the section on thread repairs yet.

Compounding the problem is everyone's fear that if the drain plug does come out, it'll lube the rear tire with gear lube at some inopportune moment. All of these may seem like valid reasons to really bear down on that drain plug. Don't! Just snug it down, and then torque it to spec. If you don't have a torque wrench, just snug it down until you feel the washer compress.

Refill your transmission with the correct weight and amount of oil, and you're done. Easy, wasn't it? Do it at least once a year to keep in practice, and your gearbox should live happily ever after. ∎

Locate the fill plug.

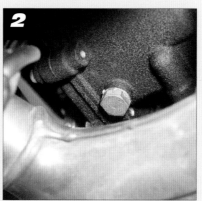

The drain plug, located directly above the hot exhaust, is far less convenient.

gear facing, but you'll need to investigate further.

Here's the catch: on some motorcycles, the gearbox oil will routinely accumulate microscopic bits of material. Don't just assume you've got a problem. Before you tear down the bike, take an oil sample to your dealer or someone that has experience with that model. On the other hand, if you find a good-sized chunk of machined material, chances are you'll be tearing down the gearbox in the near future. Every so often, some youngster brings his dirt bike to my

house complaining that the bike suddenly stopped shifting. Usually his bike had broken after a good fall. A quick look usually reveals that when the little urchin bailed, his bike landed right on the shifter. It may have just bent the shaft, making for stiff shifting, or it may have broken an internal part of the linkage. Minor open-case surgery will usually put things right. My point is this: if you've dumped your bike and the gearbox suddenly starts acting up, don't forget to check over the linkage, both inside and outside the case.

7 Final Drive

Your motorcycle will have one of three types of final drive: chain and sprockets, belt and pulleys, or driveshaft and rear drive. All three have advantages and disadvantages and have been in use for decades. In this chapter, we'll tell a little about each type of drive, and how to maintain, troubleshoot, and improve your final-drive box.

CHAIN DRIVE

Chain drive is used on more motorcycles than belt or shaft, because the system of a chain and two sprockets is lightweight, efficient, and allows easy changes of gearing.

Chains

Drive chains are constructed of links, pins, and rollers. The rollers mesh with the sprocket teeth to drive the motorcycle.

The chain's ends are joined with a master link. The master link may be staked, which is the strongest and safest method, creating an "endless" chain, or it may use a spring clip. Staked master links require special tools to install and remove, while a spring clip can be installed and removed with nothing more than a pair of pliers.

Unfortunately, a spring clip can also be unintentionally removed by anything that gets in its way, which is why master-link spring clips should always be installed with their closed end facing the direction of travel. Which type is better? My recommendation is to use a staked master link on any bike originally equipped with one.

The one innovation in chain design that really matters is the O-ring chain. This was created when some bright spark realized that by packing the spaces inside the chain with high-pressure grease, and then sealing the inner and outer links with rubber O-rings, chain life was greatly enhanced. The O-ring not only keeps the grease in, it keeps water and dirt out. The latest innovation is the X-ring chain, which is a variation of the standard O-ring chain. The X-ring purportedly has less drag than an O-ring, while offering the same level of reliability.

Poor sprocket/chain alignment will ruin even a new high-quality chain and sprocket set. Always check to make sure that the rollers are centered on the sprocket teeth, not misaligned, as shown here.

Sprockets

A sprocket is nothing more than a gear cut with sharp teeth. Rather than being in mesh with each other, sprockets transmit power via a chain. Your motorcycle will have two sprockets: the countershaft sprocket at the front, and the wheel sprocket at the rear.

Sprockets are commonly made of hardened carbon steel, chrome-plated mild steel, and aluminum alloys. As with the chain, stick to the manufacturer's recommended units.

Gearing

Together the countershaft sprocket and rear wheel sprocket make up the final drive. They also control the final-drive ratio, which controls acceleration and top speed. Given that both sprockets are easily changed, you can modify the final-drive ratio on a chain-driven motorcycle with a modest investment in time and money.

If you increase the number of teeth on the rear sprocket or reduce the number of teeth on the countershaft sprocket, raising the overall ratio between the two sprockets, the gearing is "lowered." The engine will now turn faster for a given road speed. The acceleration will improve, but in most cases the top speed will drop.

If we go the other way, that is, add teeth to the countershaft sprocket or remove teeth from the rear sprocket, lowering the ratio between the two gears, then we raise the gearing and the bike will go faster (in theory), but accelerate slower. Here's the catch: sometimes a bike is geared too highly and consequently may not be able to pull full rpm in high gear, meaning that the top speed drops. If that's the case, a change to lower gearing may let the engine turn more rpm, increasing the top speed.

Just remember, when dealing with gearing ratios, the higher the ratio number the lower the gearing. For example, a vehicle with a 5:1 final-drive ratio is geared lower than a vehicle with a 3:1 ratio.

MAINTAINING CHAIN AND SPROCKETS

Chains run in one of the harshest environments imaginable. They're constantly pulled, twisted, and covered in grit that makes grinding compound pale in comparison. Most of us can hardly

Chain Cleaning & Lubrication

Chains should be lubed more often than they're adjusted. In fact, the more you lube them the less likely they are to need adjustment. That being said, we'll start out by cleaning and lubing (they go hand in hand) the bejeezus out of one.

First, park the bike on its center or work stand, with the engine off and the transmission in neutral. Clean the chain and sprockets. Resist the temptation to spray it with water, especially from a pressure washer. High-pressure cleaners, steam cleaners, pressure washers, and the like do more harm than good. They can damage the O-rings in a chain and contaminate the lubricant. If the chain is really crusty use a natural bristle brush and douse the chain with a moisture-displacement lubricant such as WD-40. Then use a rag to wipe it clean.

An alternative would be one of those chain-cleaning kits that come with a brush and solvent. I wouldn't recommend using a wire brush to clean an O-ring chain for the obvious reason, although I have no problem cleaning a standard chain with one.

Then, check the alignment. If it appears to have changed drastically since the last time it was checked, take a good look at your swingarm bearings and your wheel bearings.

Common sense should tell you that the place to spray the lube is along the inside run of the chain, so that centrifugal force will help work the lube into the bushings and rollers. Lathering chain spray all over the outside of the chain does nothing but coat your chain, your bike, and your rear tire with sticky, dirt-attracting goo. In the case of chain lube, less is generally more. Jab the extender straw right down there between the inner and outer links on one side of the chain. Spin the wheel at least six times to ensure thorough application. Then switch sides and repeat.

Here's a few tips. I like to lube my chain after the ride. That way, the chain is warm, making it a little easier for the oil to get into all the little nooks and crannies. I also place a leftover pizza box under my chain when I lube it, to catch the overspray. ■

You'll need:
- *Shop manual*
- *Your favorite chain lube*
- *An old pizza box (optional)*

I generally remove the chain from the bike to clean it. But then all my bikes have chains held in place with spring clip master links. This photo shows a chain-cleaning brush in action.

CHAINSPEAK: WHAT DO ALL THOSE NUMBERS MEAN?

Chains are described by a series of numbers: 420, 428, 520, 525, 530 and 630, followed by a series of letters that the various manufacturers use to designate type, style and strength. As far as motorcycle drive chains go, the first number (at least currently) will always be a 4, a 5, or a 6. These numbers are more than just an arbitrary means of describing a chain. They correspond to the chains' physical dimensions.

Chains are measured in pitch. The pitch is the center-to-center distance between any two adjacent pins. The first number is the pitch measured in eighths. For example, a 4-series chain measures 4/8 inch between pins, or 1/2 inch. A 5-series chain measures 5/8 inch between pins and a 6-series 6/8 inch, or 3/4 inch.

The next digits represent the nominal width of the chain between the inner plates or the nominal width of the bushings, again measured in eighths. For example, a 2 would represent 1/4 inch, a 25 would represent 5/16 inch, and a 30 would represent 3/8 inch. To boil it all down, a common 530 chain would measure 5/8 inch from pin to pin and be 3/8-inch wide between the inner plates. These are nominal measurements. The dimensions do vary slightly from manufacturer to manufacturer. They also vary between chains of the same dimen-

sion, but of a different grade or style made by the same manufacturer.

The letters after the number are the chain manufacturers way of describing any special characteristics that particular chain may have. For instance, Tsubaki lists several different 530 chains in their catalog; the first is 530QR, which is their standard issue 530 chain, the tensile strength being somewhere in the neighborhood of about 7,500lbs. For high performance work they offer the 530HQR, which is a high performance chain rated at 10,600lbs. By the way, this is the same chain that BUB'S Denis Manning uses to spin the wheel on his land-speed-record

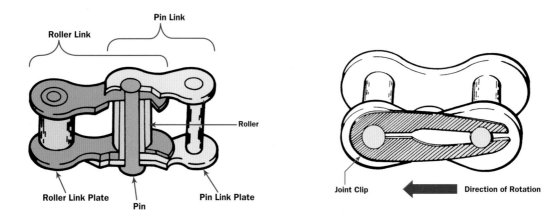

Pin Link

Roller Link

Roller

Roller Link Plate

Pin

Pin Link Plate

Joint Clip

Direction of Rotation

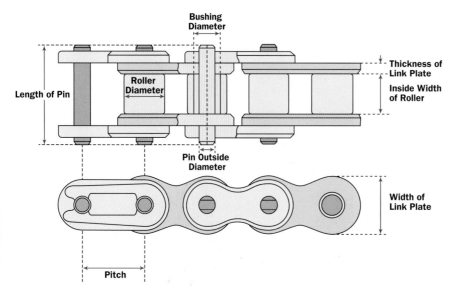

Bushing Diameter

Thickness of Link Plate

Inside Width of Roller

Length of Pin

Roller Diameter

Pin Outside Diameter

Width of Link Plate

Pitch

Chain size is indicated by its pitch, and the inside width of the roller link. Since the other measurements do vary between manufacturers it's inadvisable and dangerous to mix and match chain parts from different manufacturers. The most common mistake is trying to use a manufacturer's master link in someone else's chain. Due to variances in pin length and side plate width, it's difficult to obtain the proper fit, a situation that can lead to the master link disengaging from the chain at its earliest opportunity.

streamliner at Bonneville, reaching speeds over 300 mph, so it should work just fine on your hot-rod street bike. They also offer an O-ring chain, the 530 Sigma, (Don't jump to any false conclusions, they list a lot more 530 chains, I've just picked these three to illustrate my point.) All three chains will fit the same set of sprockets, although I have run into the occasional clearance problem when fitting O-ring chains to vintage bikes.

Here's the confusing part. Pitch is pitch: if you order a 530 chain from any manufacturer the pitch will always be the same, as will the roller diameter. Unfortunately, everything else may be and probably is different. Chain width between the roller-link plates may vary slightly as will the overall width. The plates themselves may be thicker or thinner, the pin length will probably be different and so on.

As you can see one maker's master link probably won't fit another's chain. By using matched chain and links you can be sure the fit is correct, as well as the tensile strength. Remember the old saying about a chain only being as strong as it's weakest link? Nothing will drive that point home like a master link rated for 5,000lbs. used in a 10,000lb. application.

The bottom line is never mix and match chain pieces. If you're using a Tsubaki 530 Sigma sealed O-ring chain, then you need a 530 Sigma master link; not an HQR, not an HSL, and certainly not some other manufacturer's master link.

Since manufacturers generally offer several grades of chain in each size, how do you select the one right for your application? Rule one: stick with either the motorcycle or chainmaker's recommendations when replacing the drive chain. Rule two: if you want to upgrade, fine; you can generally replace that standard roller with an O-ring or heavy-duty chain without any problems. Going the other way, is a major no-no. Believe me, that $25 bargain chain won't seem like such a great deal when it snaps in half and saws through your cases while you're touring the Rockies. ∎

be bothered to lube the chain, let alone adjust it. The result is a "stretched" chain and worn-out sprockets. However, a little common sense and some periodic routine maintenance will alleviate most problems and greatly enhance the life of your drive chain components, not to mention save you some hard-earned cash in the long run.

Do Chains Really Stretch?

Chains don't really "stretch." What happens is that as the chain does its job, the lubricant between the pins and bushings is burned off by heat and friction. Lose enough of it and rapid chain wear takes place as the various pieces grind away at each other. Once enough play develops between the pins and bushings, the chain elongates.

The two big problems that shorten a chain's life are improper alignment between the chain and sprocket and lack of, or improper, lubrication.

The signs of a poorly aligned chain are easy to spot. A shiny spot on the inside of the link plate is a dead giveaway; that's where the sprocket teeth have been rubbing it (check both sides!). Even easier, sight down the rear drive sprocket; the chain rollers should be centered on the sprocket teeth. If they run to one side, the rear wheel is misaligned.

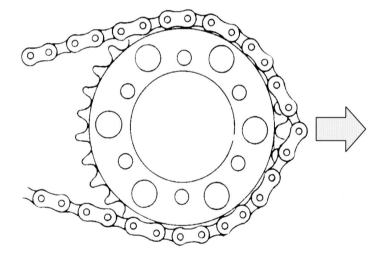

One way to check for chain wear. Too much freeplay between the rear sprocket and the chain means it's time for replacement. (Courtesy American Honda Motor Corporation)

You should lubricate the chain, even if it's an O-ring type. Since an O-ring chain's internal components have high-intensity grease injected at the factory, the lubricant plays a slightly different role. It's primary job is to keep the O-rings pliable. It must also act to displace moisture and prevent rust. In my experience, any good moisture-displacing lubricant works just fine on an O-ring chain, and yes, that includes stuff like

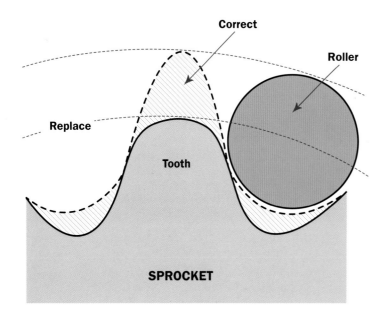

They don't get much worse than this. Badly worn, with a missing tooth.

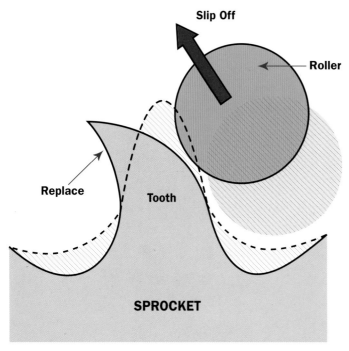

Installing a new chain over worn sprockets is a waste of time and money. If your sprockets are worn as shown, you'll want to replace both the front and the rear.

WD-40 and CRC-556. For standard chains, I'd recommend a dedicated chain lube available at any motorcycle shop.

While misalignment and neglect cause the majority of problems there are other reasons behind rapid chain wear, battery acid being one of them. Always make certain your vent tube is routed as far from the chain and as close to the ground as practical.

Are Your Chain or Sprockets Worn Out?

How do you know when the chain's worn out? If you can lift the chain more than one half of the way up a tooth on the rear sprocket it's had it. And, quite possibly, so has the sprocket.

Normally, you'll wear out two chains for every set of sprockets. Nevertheless, many manufacturers recommend replacing the sprockets whenever you replace the chain; in part, to ensure maximum driveline life, and to avoid personal-injury lawsuits.

Occasionally, the new chain wears out quicker than its predecessor did. Assuming that the new one was equal in quality to the old one, the most likely causes are worn sprockets and/or bad wheel, countershaft, or swingarm bearings.

Sprocket Maintenance

Sprockets also wear out and need occasional replacement. In the meantime, as long as the chain is properly aligned and lubricated there really isn't a whole lot you can or need to do for the sprockets. A periodic check of the mounting hardware is about all the maintenance most sprockets require.

As the sprockets wear, the teeth become hooked in profile and will wear down. At that point the sprockets should be replaced. The cardinal rule is to always replace both sprockets as a pair. As I stated previously, a good rule of thumb is that you'll replace a set of sprockets with every second chain.

DIY *Chain Adjustment*

Normally, the first step in adjusting the chain should be to clean and lubricate it. If you've been keeping up with your maintenance program this step may be omitted. If your chain is rusty, crusty, and dry as the proverbial bone reread the preceding paragraphs.

Chains develop tight and loose spots. This is because the individual links wear at different rates and the sprockets are never perfectly round. The first rule of chain adjustment is to always check the adjustment at the chain's tightest point. Find the tight point by rotating the rear wheel and watching the bottom run of the chain. If you need to, mark the chain with a crayon or piece of tape so you know exactly where the tight spot is.

If you have any doubts as to how much slack the chain has, use your tape measure. It's time for adjustment if the slack is double what's recommended by the manufacturer. Again this is something you'll develop

a feel for in time. This would be a short how-to if the adjustment is correct, so let's assume it isn't.

Remove the rear-wheel cotter pin, and loosen the rear axle nut. Not all bikes have a cotter pin securing the nut. If yours doesn't, then just loosen the nut up a turn or three. Some bikes use a pinch bolt to secure the axle. If your bike has one, loosen the axle nut before loosening the pinch bolt. Some axles have the end opposite the nut drilled to accommodate a drift, a punch, or an old hunk of rod to keep the axle from turning.

Generally, there are three types of chain adjusters in current use. The first is a bolt and locknut. To adjust the chain, you loosen the locknut and turn the bolt in to reduce slack, and out to add a little. A variation of that design uses a stud welded to the adjuster. The second type of adjuster is the snail cam. As its name implies, this is a half-moon shaped device that can be rotated to move the rear

axle. The third type of adjuster is the eccentric-axle adjuster. This design utilizes an eccentric-bearing carrier, or axle carrier, held in place by a clamp. When the clamp is loosened the eccentric rotates, moving the axle and wheel assembly in or out.

The first rule for chain adjustment is simple; a little slack is preferable to even marginally tight. Set the slack to the recommended figure by turning the adjuster or rotating the snail. Once the adjustment feels correct, check the datum points to make sure both sides are equal. Remember you need to adjust both sides of the axle equally.

I'm a big believer in using a torque wrench on axle nuts. I recommend

> **You'll need:**
> - *Shop manual*
> - *A tape measure*
> - *Basic hand tools*
> - *A torque wrench*
> - *Socket that fits the torque wrench and the rear axle nut*
> - *A new cotter pin to fit the rear axle nut*
> - *An old pizza box (optional)*

Different methods are used to hold the axle while loosening the axle nut. This axle has a hole bored through it for a tommy bar. But since Tommy went home early I just used a drift.

The cam style adjusters make it much easier to adjust the chain, all you need do is make certain both sides are set to the same position.

DIY *Chain Adjustment*

that you get into the same habit. When you torque down the axle nut, the wrench may have a tendency to pull the adjuster away from the stops, changing the chain adjustment slightly. You can avoid this by either pulling up on the lower run of the chain, or pushing the wrench so that the motion forces the wheel toward the swingarm rather than away from it.

After the nut is tightened, double-check the chain tension and the alignment.

Now, check that the chain is running true. You can do the job quickly by simply spinning your wheel and watching the chain move over the sprocket. The chain should be centered on the sprocket teeth. If it isn't, recheck your alignment marks and make sure they are equal. If they are, and the chain is still off-center, make sure the wheel is correctly positioned in the swingarm. If the wheel was removed for any reason you may have inadvertently mixed up a spacer or two. If the wheel wasn't removed or if everything is correctly assembled, it's permissible to twiddle the adjusters slightly to center the wheel.

Once the chain tension is correct and the chain runs centered, recheck your datum points. If they are off by any appreciable degree you'll need to check the wheel alignment before you ride the bike. In all honesty, it would be unusual for a modern bike to have alignment problems, unless something has been bent or broken due to hard use or an accident.

Once you're happy with the adjustment, you can install the cotter pin and bend its ends over. If your bike has a lever- or cable-operated-drum rear brake, you'll need to check and adjust the free-play before riding the bike. Likewise, before riding the bike make certain that the chain-adjuster bolts are tight and that they are seated in their respective slots in the swingarm. ■

Toothed belts have become increasingly popular because they are strong, clean, quiet, and as a bonus, require little maintenance.

BELT DRIVE

Today, toothed rubber belts are the drive of choice for moderate-horsepower street bikes, for a variety of reasons: low maintenance, long life, quiet running, and low initial cost of construction. They also have a tendency to absorb engine-power pulses better than a chain; one reason they're often seen on such diverse machinery as Harley-Davidson's V-twins and the Suzuki Savage 650cc single.

Belts do have a few drawbacks, though: they are one-piece construction, (which can make the belt difficult to change), they are wide (which makes it difficult to use with the fat tires currently so chic with the custom crowd), and there is a lack of readily available sprockets (which complicates gearing changes). For a stock application, though, especially one that's staying stock, a belt is tough to beat.

One criticism leveled at the toothed rubber used to be the "what if." As in, "What if the belt breaks while I'm on the road?" Since no one has ever pointed out to me how you'd be better off if a drive chain broke, I tend to ignore such questions. Besides, I'd rather have a rubber belt break than have a chain snap and crash through my crankcase cover. The reality is that rubber drive belts seldom break.

MAINTAINING THE BELT DRIVE

Belt maintenance is pretty straightforward. Adjust it once in a while, check it for rips, cuts, and stone penetration or any other damage. Replace it when it wears out or is damaged. Otherwise, change it at the manufacturer's specified mileage, or just run it until it breaks (just kidding, folks!).

Frankly, I've never seen a set of worn-out belt cogs, not under normal circumstances. That said, inspecting a cog is similar to inspecting sprockets. Make sure there is no damage to the serrations, particularly nicks or sharp spots that might cut the belt. Likewise, check for rust or corrosion that might cause the belt to fail.

Alignment should also be checked during routine service; a belt that's running off-center will wear prematurely and is more likely to break and leave you stranded. A severely out-of-line cog may also mean that wheel-bearing or

DIV *Sprocket Replacement*

Two rules here: always replace both sprockets at the same time and always replace the chain with the sprockets.

The first step is to remove the countershaft cover. This may involve removing a footpeg, shift lever, or whatever applies.

Then, remove the countershaft sprocket. Countershaft sprockets are secured to the countershaft by any of several means. Some use a circlip (snap ring) or E-clip to hold them in place. A few use two bolts to secure a retaining plate, and the rest use a large nut that threads onto the end of the countershaft.

The first two are easy to remove. You can use a screwdriver to pop the E-clip off, and snap-ring pliers will to remove a circlip with ease. If your

bike uses two bolts and a retainer, the appropriate size socket will do the trick. Trouble rears its head when you're suddenly faced with a huge nut securing the sprocket. How do you loosen the nut? In a fully equipped motorcycle shop they'd just zip that bugger off with a big air gun and socket. Or maybe use a special factory tool to lock everything in place. Since you're new to this game, I'll show you a little trick.

Remove the countershaft cover.

(continued next page)

You'll need:

- A socket for the countershaft nut
- New lock tabs for the sprocket retaining bolts
- A new countershaft sprocket lock washer (if your bike uses them)
- A chain-riveting tool if you plan to use original equipment riveted chain.
- Brake cleaner
- Rags
- Latex mechanic's gloves, available at any auto-parts store (optional)

My friend Joe Bolger invented the Grab-it tool many years ago. I've had mine since he came up with the idea.

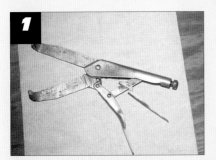

Honda likes to use two 6mm bolts and a keyed retainer to hold on some of their countershaft sprockets.

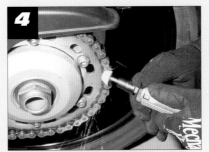

Grind through or remove the master link. Since the Hawk uses an endless chain, we ground through it. (Don't forget to wear eye protection.)

If you elect to grind, take the pins right down to the side plate.

DIY Sprocket Replacement

The first step is to flatten out any lock tabs that may have been installed. Use a sharp chisel to pry up the portion of the tab that's been folded over. The lock tab may be reuseable, or it may not. Your manual will specify which is the case. Just pry the sucker up and away from the nut; there is no need to hammer the washer flat. Make sure that the socket fits firmly on the nut. A word

Use a punch to remove the link. Remove the old chain. (If you're only replacing the drive chain, fasten the new one to the old and pull it through.)

of advice here: if your bike uses something like a nut that's 36mm across the flats, trot on down to the local tool store and pick up a nice long 1/2-inch drive breaker bar and socket. Even a 3/4-inch drive will do. There is no point in using a 3/8-inch drive ratchet and an adapter. That nut is going to be mighty snug.

Of course, we need to keep the sprocket from turning before we remove the nut, right? That's why we left the chain on and fully assembled. Place the bike in high gear, and either step on the rear brake or have a friend do it for you. With the rear brake engaged, the engine is locked and you should be able to spin the nut right off.

If for some reason you can't lock the sprocket with the chain and rear

Unbolt and remove both sprockets (rear only shown). Two machined surfaces mate.

wheel, there is a tool available through motorcycle shops called a Grab-it. The Grab-it is essentially a locking pliers with two tangs meant to engage slots or teeth. The Grab-it will secure all sorts of odd shapes; including sprockets, flywheels, and clutch hubs. They don't cost much, and no serious motorcycle mechanic should be without one. (Besides, a very good friend of mine invented it.)

Once the countershaft sprocket is out of the way, inspect the seal and replace it if it's leaking. Oops, sorry I haven't told you how to remove and install seals yet. Well then, skip ahead to the Appendix and read the section on seal replacement.

Next, remove the chain and pop off the rear wheel by following the instructions in your shop manual. Most rear sprockets are held on with nuts, studs, and lock tabs. This is dirty work, but not too tricky. Your shop manual will spell out the details, but basically you're going to unbolt one sprocket and bolt on another. If your hub has dampers or a cushion drive under the sprocket, inspect the rubber spacers for any overt signs of damage. If there is any doubt, install new ones. Replace them all, even if only one is bad.

When installing the sprocket, check that any offset is facing the correct way. If the manual recommends new lock tabs or the use of a

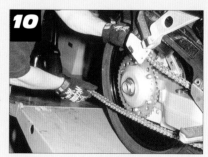

Loctite the securing bolts or nuts only if the manufacturer recommends doing so.

The bolts should be securely torqued into place.

The new chain is threaded into place.

DIY Sprocket Replacement

Because the Hawk uses a single-sided swingarm and eccentric adjuster, a spanner is required to adjust the chain.

Adjust the rear wheel until it's as far forward as it will go. Since we used a non-stock chain it will have to be cut to length. If in doubt, leave it a little long. It can always be cut shorter. Coat the new master link with grease or chain lube.

Adjust the slack in the chain according to the instructions in your manual. The factory-supplied tool makes adjusting the chain on this Honda Hawk a snap.

thread-locking compound, believe it. There are few worse experiences in motorcycling than having a rear sprocket come off at high speed.

After the rear wheel has been installed, install the countershaft sprocket and its retaining hardware, followed by the chain. Adjust the chain, and torque down all of the appropriate hardware. If you need to

lock the rear wheel to tighten the countershaft nut, do it now and then bend the lock tab over the nut. Double-check your work, then reinstall any covers and so on.

After a spin around the block, give everything the once over. After the first 100 miles or close to it, recheck the chain and adjust as required. ■

Once the adjustments are made, tighten the pinch bolt.

swingarm bushing failure has occurred. Belt adjustment is a little more complex than chain adjustment. All of the toothed belts I'm familiar with require use of a special tool to measure the belt's tension.

There are two styles of tool. One fits between the belt and the swingarm. The tool resembles a small telescope, with a stiff spring holding the inner and outer sections apart. The tool is inserted, and the belt adjusted until the mark on the inner piece lines up with the edge of the outer barrel.

Another type, the one supplied by Harley-Davidson, resembles a small fishing scale, what

LUBING DRIVE SPLINES

Anytime the rear wheel has been removed from a shaft driven motorcycle, or at least once a year, the rear drive splines should be inspected and lubricated. If the edges have a sharp look or edge to them it's possible that they've passed the point of no return; if that's your suspicion have a qualified technician inspect them. If they look okay give the splines a good coating of either high pressure grease or a molybdenum type anti-seize compound. The lubricant will act as a shock absorber to prevent loading shocks from wearing away the teeth as well as preventing corrosion. ■

DIV *Rear-Drive Oil Change*

You'll need:

- A drain pan
- Fresh oil
- A funnel or two
- The appropriate wrenches
- Drain plug gaskets
- Rags

About the only other maintenance chore peculiar to a shaft-driven bike would be the occasional lubing of the wheel or pinion-gear drive splines. Do it whenever the rear wheel is off the bike and you'll never have any problem. At least once a year the drive-shaft/rear-end oil should be changed.

Locate the rear-end filler plug and remove it.

Warm up the oil by taking the bike for a ride; the best way to change any oil is when it's warm. That's double the case when it comes to driveshafts and rear ends, mainly because the oil is so thick.

In practice, the procedure is exactly the same as changing the transmission or engine oil. Like a transmission, many rear drives use a magnetic drain plug which needs cleaning.

Don't be alarmed at the metallic swarf built up on the plug. That's normal; a swipe with a rag should remove it. Of course if you find big chunks of ring gear or pinion gear stuck to your drain plug a little investigation may be called for, but that's a rarity. If that unfortunate situation does a occur, a visit to your local dealership is in order. Rebuilding final drives is not a task that should be taken lightly.

The oil-change procedure is simple. Drain it into the pan, clean the plug and replace the gasket, lube the plug with a little anti-seize or white grease, and reinstall it. Refill with the correct grade and amount of oil and you're all done; after you reinstall the fill plug, that is.

■

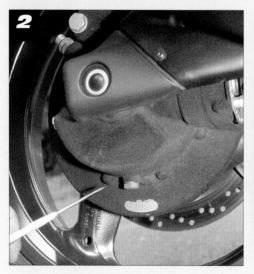

Locate and remove the drain plug.

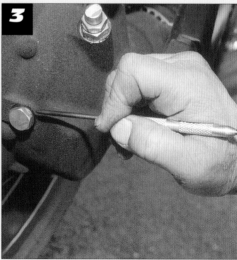

Some rear drives also incorporate an oil level plug.

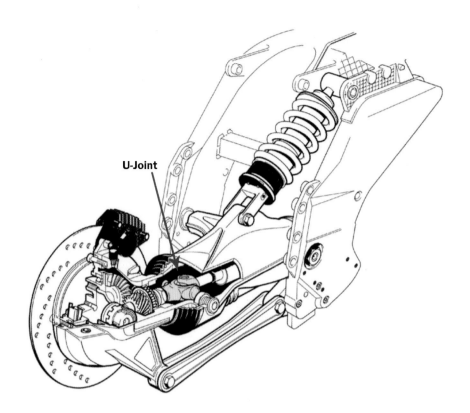

U-Joint

we used to call a "de-liar." This scale is used to apply ten pounds of pressure to the belt. The deflection is then measured and compared with the specifications listed in the service manual. The belt is then adjusted accordingly.

SHAFT DRIVE

Once somewhat of an anomaly, shaft drive has caught on in a big way in recent years, especially on touring bikes. In theory, it works exactly like you'd expect. An automotive-style U- or constant-velocity joint takes the drive from the rear of the transmission. A steel shaft transmits the drive to another joint at the rear-drive wheel housing (sometimes through another U-joint in front of the rear drive), where it's splined or bolted to the pinion gear. The pinion gear turns the ring gear, and down the road you go.

Driveshafts have become popular because they are easier to maintain, require less mainte-

nance, and are cleaner than chains. They also facilitate easy tire changes, a major plus on a large touring bike.

They do have a few slight drawbacks, however. Shafts are more expensive to manufacture, and they make it difficult to change overall gear ratios. They gobble up more horsepower than belts or chains and, in some cases, they can affect the bike's handling. As the pinion gear tries to climb up or down the ring gear during acceleration and coasting, the rear of the bike will tend to rise and fall, which causes changes in the bike's ride height and overall geometry.

This may take some getting used to, but it's more of a curiosity than a real concern. Besides, current suspension systems and clever driveshaft designs have eliminated or greatly reduced the phenomena on late-model, shaft-driven bikes.

If your motorcycle was built in the 1950s or later, it will most likely have some form of damped-fork suspension at the front and a swingarm-and-shock(s) suspension at the rear. In this chapter, we'll describe how the components of your front and rear suspension systems work together to cushion the ride and then tell how you can maintain those components and improve that action.

Before we discuss the suspension we need to discuss the concepts of springing and damping because that's really all your front and rear suspension does.

HOW SPRINGS WORK

The main functions of your suspension springs are to support the motorcycle above its wheels and to isolate the chassis and rider from the up-and-down motion of the wheels as they roll over bumps.

A spring's ability to absorb impacts is expressed as its spring rate and is normally given in pounds per inch (at least in the United States). A common spring rate is 100 pounds per inch. This simply means that it takes 100 pounds of force to compress the spring an inch, 200 pounds to move it two inches, and so on, until the spring is completely compressed, at which point it is said to be coil-bound.

Ideally, the spring rate on your suspension is stiff enough to keep the bike from bottoming out (fully compressing the suspension) on all but the very worst bumps, yet soft enough to provide a comfortable ride.

| STRAIGHT-WOUND | PROGRESSIVE-WOUND | COMBINATION TYPE | AIR-ASSISTED TYPE |

The four most common types of rear springing. The air-assisted type can be pressurized via an air pump or compressor to adjust the preload (some forks also use air assist). These are more popular on touring bikes. (Courtesy American Honda)

Unloaded   **Loaded**

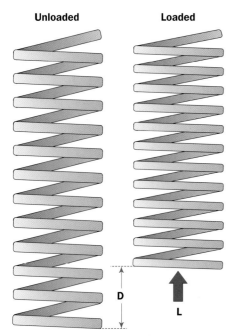

Spring rate is calculated by determining how much of a load it takes to compress the spring a given amount. In the drawing, D is the distance (usually one inch), L represents the load, (normally expressed in pounds).

Springs come in two basic varieties: straight-rate and progressive-rate. Straight-rate springs compress at one rate until coil-bound. Progressive-rate springs are built to have a spring rate that increases as the spring compresses (for example, from 100 pounds per inch at the beginning, to 300 pounds per inch when near coil-bound). The result is a spring (and suspension) that reacts well to light hits but becomes increasingly stiff when a big jolt occurs.

Many bikes come standard with straight-rate springs, and just as many with progressive-rate springs. There are also lots of aftermarket springs available to custom tailor your suspension to your requirements. We'll look at those upgrades later in the chapter.

What's Preload?

A related concept you also need to know is spring preload. Preload means simply that your suspension unit (shock absorber or fork) has a means to apply a force to compress the spring a bit independently of suspension movement. In other words, it has an adjuster, or collar, that loads the spring to alter the point at which the

DIY *Conventional Fork Oil Change*

You should change the fork oil at least once a year, or whenever your manual specifies. At the same time, you should examine the seals and springs and replace them if necessary.

The first step is to give your manual a read through and determine exactly how your fork is constructed. Most forks will have a drain bolt or screw somewhere near the bottom of the fork. Those that don't, primarily cartridge or male-slider forks, will have to be removed from the bike for servicing. If your fork has drain screws, start by loosening one fork cap; back it out until it's finger tight. Position the bike so that the front wheel is clear of the ground. Most bikes with centerstands will be fine as they are. The rest of you will need to jack the bike up until the front forks are completely unloaded. Remove the drain screw of the leg with the loosened cap. Once the drain screw is out, remove the cap the rest of the way. Be careful here; the cap may still be under a fair amount of spring tension. Let the oil drain into your

(continued next page)

You'll need:

- Shop manual
- Wrench to fit the top fork nut
- A basin or good-sized oil drain pan (preferably two, one for each fork leg)
- Fork oil
- New sealing washers for the drain bolts
- Clean rags
- A fork oil-level tool or garden variety turkey baster
- Small graduated cylinder
- Small funnel
- Tape measure
- Small flashlight
- Common hand tools
- A means of propping the front wheel clear of the ground
- New seals
- Snap ring pliers (if you're replacing the seals)

The shop manual has all the specifications. Loosening the upper pinch bolts will make removing the fork caps a lot easier.

Use a the appropriate wrench to remove the fork caps.

DIY Conventional Fork Oil Change

Remove the drain screw.

The oil will gush out, so have the drain pan ready. A little air will chase out any residual oil, or you can pump the fork a few times.

If you elect to pump the fork, only remove one fork cap at a time or replace the springs and caps before pumping the forks.

Use a new washer on the drain screw. Measure the correct amount of fork oil, pour it in slowly, and let it set for a few minutes to purge any air bubbles.

Install the cap, but leave it a little loose.

Pump the fork to remove any residual air. With the fork held down, tighten the cap. This can be tricky; a third hand may prove useful.

pan. You may find that on some bikes you can only remove the cap if the handlebars are unbolted. If that's the case make sure your fuel tank is protected with a towel or rags, to prevent it from being scraped. If you have compressed air available, it's okay; shoot some into the fork to flush out any residual oil. Repeat the process for the other side.

Some mechanics will reinstall the fork caps and springs at this point and place the bike back on its wheels. Holding the front brake on, they pump the forks a few times which should expel any remaining drops of oil. This won't hurt anything, so go ahead and try it if you want.

With the bike back on its stand remove the caps, fork springs, and any attendant spacers, noting the order in which they were installed. Replace the drain bolts, using new sealing

Torque the fork cap to specifications, and tighten the pinch bolt.

THREAD-TYPE ADJUSTER

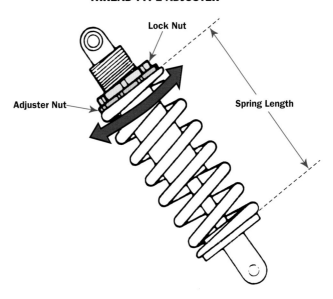

On a typical threaded adjuster, loosen the lock nut then use the adjuster nut to change the preload. These are more commonly found on single shock systems. (Courtesy American Honda)

A typical cam type preload adjuster, easily adjustable using a special wrench included in the bike's tool kit.

washers. It's always a good idea at this point to inspect the fork springs; even if they look perfect, measure them, and compare them to the free length listed in the service manual.

It used to be that all fork leg refills were given in ounces. That is no longer the case. Your manual may specify refilling the fork legs in ounces or cubic centimeters, or it may give the measure as specific height. If your manual lists a refill volume, use your graduated cylinder and refill each leg with exactly that volume. If you are installing an aftermarket spring kit, follow the manufacturer's instructions. The new springs may be directional, especially if they are progressively wound. Many spring kits include additional spacers to shim the fork. Again, follow the instructions. If the stock parts are going back in, install them in the correct order. Reinstall the fork caps, but don't tighten them.

Roll the bike back onto its wheels, and again holding the brake on, pump the forks several times. Listen for a hiss of air escaping. While holding the fork down, tighten the nut; this may require the help of a pal. This procedure will bleed trapped air from the fork giving it a more progressive action and working any air out of the damping valves. ■

spring begins to compress. For example, if you preload a 100-pounds-per-inch shock spring one inch, then it will take 200 pounds of force to make the shock compress its first inch from full extension (rather than 100 pounds without preload). I must emphasize this point about preload: it does not alter the spring rate, just the amount of force needed to begin compression of the fork or shock when fully extended. Altering the preload does not change the spring rate.

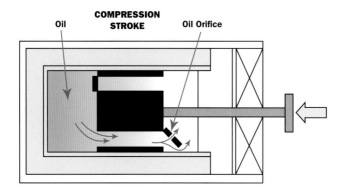

COMPRESSION STROKE

Oil Oil Orifice

As the shock compresses, the damper piston must force oil through a narrow oil orifice, slowing travel.

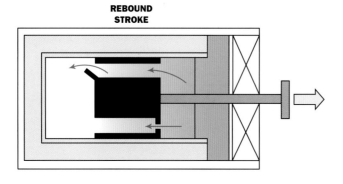

REBOUND STROKE

On rebound, oil escapes easily through a spring-loaded flap.

Why is preload useful? Because you can choose a spring that is the right weight for a comfortable ride and then preload it so that the weight of rider and bike doesn't compress the suspension (called suspension sag) more than is desirable. (How much sag do you want? About one third of total suspension travel or less.) If preload is adjustable, you can use it to set sag or ride height for riders of different weights. We'll show you how to make use of this later in the chapter.

How Damping Works

Your suspension absorbs or damps (not dampens, which means "to make wet") much of the energy transferred to it by the wheel when it rolls over a bump by pumping oil through small orifices as the suspension goes through its motions. For the same sized orifice a thin oil gives less damping action, and a thick oil more. Similarly, for the same viscosity oil, a large orifice gives less damping and a small orifice more. Today's

dampers use valving instead of orifices, which allows them to be compliant over small bumps and yet provide enough damping for large ones.

Modern suspensions also damp in both directions: when the wheel strikes an object and is driven upward (compression), and when the wheel is forced downward by the springs and gravity to its normal position (rebound). Naturally enough, these are termed compression damping and rebound damping.

Ideally, you want rebound damping to be about four times as powerful as compression damping. Why should compression damping be so soft? Overly stiff compression rates prevent the wheel from following the pavement, so it's better to let the spring rate control the majority of upward wheel movement, rather than oil flow.

Your suspension uses springs and damping together, in the form of forks up front and shock absorbers in the rear, to soak up the bumps and keep the wheels on the ground. Damping and spring rates must always be in balance.

If the bike has too much damping, it will overwhelm the spring and the suspension will be unresponsive, forcing the wheels to hop and bounce over every little obstruction. If there is too little damping, the bike is said to be oversprung, and the bike wallows and pitches through the turns and after the least little bump. In either case, both ride and handling suffer. Let's look at how you can optimize your front and rear suspension to get that balance.

FRONT SUSPENSION

Almost all motorcycles built in the last 40 years are fitted with some form of telescopic front forks. The most common of these consists of a pair of male tubes fixed to the triple clamp and a pair of female sliders affixed to the wheel by the axle. The slider telescopes up and down over the tubes as the wheel moves over bumps. Springs, damper rods, and damping oil inside the tubes absorb the shock and damp the movement. Seals in the slider keep dirt out and the damping oil in. More modern forks often include adjustable dampers, adjustments for spring preload, and other refinements.

Two recent variations on the telescopic fork design are worth noting. The first is the male-

DIY   *Cartridge-Type Fork Oil Change*

All inverted, male-slider forks that I've encountered have used the cartridge design; however, not all cartridge forks are inverted. Changing the oil in both types is easy. The only difference is that the forks will have to be removed from the bike to drain the fork oil, as the cartridge design precludes the use of external drain plugs.

I'd recommend loosening the fork caps before removing the tubes from the clamps. It's also a good idea to note the spring preload, the fork height in relation to the clamp, and the damping settings. Here's another tip: sometimes the pinching action of the top clamp can make removing the fork cap tough, if not impossible. Sliding the fork tubes up in the clamps a few inches will make the caps a lot easier to remove.

Follow the procedure listed in your shop manual concerning fork-leg removal. In general, you'll need to remove the wheel, front fender, and speedometer drive, along with the brake calipers. Remove each fork leg. Next remove the cap and spring. Note that a damping rod is attached to into the fork cap. Hold the damping-rod lock nut with a wrench while unscrewing the cap from the rod. Invert the fork, and drain the oil. If you plan to completely strip the fork, your shop manual will walk you through the procedure. In the main, you'll need a special tool to remove and install the cartridge unless you can devise an alternative.

Forks can be flushed using a little WD-40 or other mineral-based solvent. Resist the temptation to rinse anything in gasoline.

Refill the fork with the recommended weight and quantity of fork oil. Slowly pump the fork tube a up to ten times to purge the air. Next, pump the damping rod pump slowly, at least ten times until the resistance in both directions feels consistent.

Let the fork sit for at least five minutes to let the oil settle and to give any air bubbles time to come to the surface.

Recheck your fork oil level using a tape measure or an oil-level syringe. Oil-level syringes are available at any motorcycle shop. They are nothing more than a large syringe and a level stop. Set the stop at the distance listed in your manual. Overfill the fork slightly, then set the syringe in place. Then draw fork oil into the syringe until it starts sucking air. It's a simple and neat way of setting the level, and it will work on conventional forks as well.

Once the oil level has been established, the forks can be reassembled and replaced in the clamps as the case may be. ∎

You'll need:

- *Shop manual*
- *Wrench to fit the top fork nut*
- *A basin or good-sized oil drain pan (preferably two, one for each fork leg)*
- *Fork oil*
- *New sealing washers for the drain bolts*
- *Clean rags*
- *A fork oil-level tool or garden variety turkey baster*
- *Small graduated cylinder*

- *Small funnel*
- *Tape measure*
- *Small flashlight*
- *Common hand tools*
- *A means of propping the front wheel clear of the ground*
- *Snap ring pliers (if you're replacing the seals)*
- *New seals*
- *Seal driver (optional)*

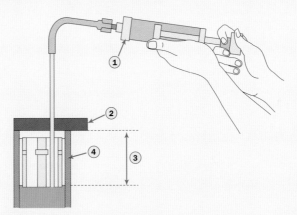

Fork oil syringes are the most accurate way to adjust the fork oil height. (1) syringe, (2) gauge stop, (3) oil level, (4) fork tube.

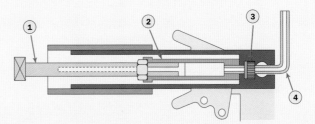

Cartridge forks require special tools. The damper holding tool (1) slips over the cartridge damper rod or adjuster to hold the cartridge. (2) Damper cartridge. (3) Retaining bolt. (4) Allen key. The tool holds the cartridge and prevents it from turning while the Allen bolt is unscrewed.

DAMPING-ROD & CARTRIDGE TYPE FORKS

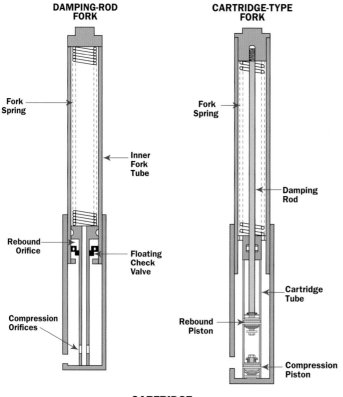

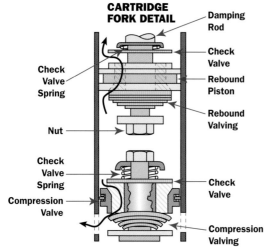

Located inside the cartridge-type fork are a separate cartridge tube and additional damping components. Note that with the conventional fork design, compression damping is for the most part controlled by the damping rod orifice, which is fixed and non-adjustable. In the cartridge design compression damping is controlled by a dedicated piston and shim stack located at the bottom of the fork. Cartridge forks are highly tuneable, and almost infinitely adjustable.

slider or inverted forks. Standard forks locate the small-diameter tubes in the triple clamp, right where the bending load is the greatest. This makes them prone to flex under strenuous riding conditions, such as heavy brake loads or when crossing rough terrain at high speed. Inverted forks place the large-diameter outer tube in the triple clamp. This gives the front end a lot more support and they resist flex extremely well.

The second innovation is cartridge forks, so-called because they feature small self-contained damper units called cartridge dampers in each fork leg. Inverted forks are sometimes referred to as cartridge forks because they all use cartridge dampers, but many conventional telescopic forksalso now feature cartridge-style dampers.

Many of today's forks feature adjustable damping. If your forks are adjustable, your manual will show you how. Even if they're not adjustable, you can adjust the damping by means of heavier or lighter oil, by changing the size of damper orifices, or by using aftermarket damping units or cartridges. We'll cover these techniques in the later section on improving your suspension.

While telescopic forks have proven the most viable in the long run, they aren't without their problems. The complaints are centered on two major issues. The first is that telescopic forks are flex prone and lack sufficient rigidity. This was true until the advent of large-diameter fork tubes and male-slider forks.

The other problem is that telescopic forks compress during braking and whenever a bump is encountered. This reduces both rake and trail at a time when both would be useful to have. As a result, some forks on bikes built in the 1970s and 1980s have anti-dive valving. To address these issues (and for other reasons), some manufacturers use alternative forks.

Alternative Forks

Late-model BMW motorcycles use a unique fork design called the Telelever. It features a cast aluminum A-arm between the engine case and fork sliders, and a single external damping unit. The design resists fore-and-aft flexing better than conventional forks. It also provides 7.5

(TOP LEFT)
The BMW Earles-type fork, which featured adjustable trail for sidecar use.

(TOP RIGHT)
The Harley-Davidson Springer fork actually works very well despite its dated design. In fact, it outperforms the telescopic design in several respects.

(BOTTOM LEFT)
The inverted, cartridge type fork is very popular for sportbike use due to it's rigidity and wide range of adjustment.

(BOTTOM RIGHT)
The offset axle helps reduce the seat height of this off road bike; it also allows easy access to the damper adjustments located at the bottom of the fork tubes.

inches of travel and has built-in anti-dive geometry. The Telelever is a thoughtful and practical design that works quite nicely and is very easy to maintain.

In mid-year 1988 Harley-Davidson fitted an updated version of its old spring fork from the 1940s to one of their Softail chassis and created a showroom success, the FXSTS Springer Softail. The fact that the fork continues to work well in the year 2002 is a tribute to the original design,

and to all the work Harley-Davidson put into updating it.

To save money, makers of small, light, and relatively unsophisticated motorcycles, mopeds, and scooters often fit them with el cheapo suspension. Mopeds generally make do with undamped forks. These usually work well enough on these slow-speed machines.

Scooters are usually quite a bit faster, so they are often fitted with either a leading- or trailing-

DIV   *Replacing Fork Seals*

Telescopic forks incorporate a seal between the fork tube and the leg. Its purpose is to keep the oil in and the dirt out. When the seal fails the oil leaks out and the dirt leaks in. As you'd expect, the bike doesn't handle very well and rapid wear can take place between the components. The first indication of a leaking fork seal is oil covering the fork tube, usually accompanied by a smear of dirt. The oil is attracting the dirt of course, so just wiping the area with a rag won't accomplish much.

First, drain the forks and remove the top caps and springs using the instructions in the earlier section on changing fork oil. Then, you need to separate the fork tube and slider before the seal can be replaced. Some motorcycles do have a separate seal holder that can be removed without disturbing the rest of the fork, but they are few and far between these days. There is also a variation in which the seal will come out with the fork tube after a retaining ring is removed.

Follow the instructions in your shop manual regarding fork dismantling. While all bikes are slightly different the basic concept is the same. Often, the lower leg will have a bolt in it that holds the damper rod in place. This bolt will have to be removed before the fork tube can be withdrawn. If you have access to air tools, it's a simple matter to zip the bolt out. If you don't, loosen the bolt before you remove the fork springs; that way the

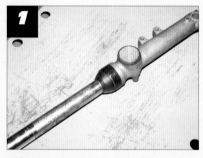

Although the fork doesn't always need to be removed from the motorcycle it generally makes life much easier.

Before removing the leg from the triple clamp, break the fork cap loose; that way you won't have to wrestle with the fork leg while trying to loosen the cap later on. Once the damper bolt is out, remove the fork cap and spring. Remove the fork tube.

Leaving the fork spring installed and under tension will make removing the damper bolt that much easier.

Remove any snap rings and washers.

DIY *Replacing Fork Seals*

5

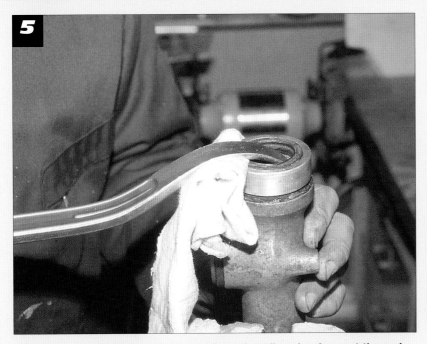

Protect the fork leg with a shop rag or piece of cardboard and pry out the seal. Take care not to scratch the seal seat in the fork leg. A long tire iron works well, and there is no sharp edge to scratch the fork leg. Apply a light coat of grease to the outer edge of the new seal.

6

Use a soft mallet to tap the seal into place. A socket can be used to seat the seal. Replace any washers and snap rings, grease the inner lip of the seal and reassemble the fork leg. Don't forget a new sealing washer on the damper bolt.

spring tension will prevent the damper rod from turning with the bolt.

The alternative may be that the upper tube is fastened via the damper rod to the lower leg; the damper rod threading into the fork cap. This is the general way that cartridge forks are held together. If that's your case, the damper-rod lock nut should be held with the appropriate wrench and unscrewed from the fork cap.

Once the fork tube is removed from the lower leg you'll be able to remove the seal. Most seals are retained in place by a snap ring and washer. Use a pair of snap-ring pliers to remove the snap ring. It'll probably be easier if you use a small screwdriver to pry the snap ring up as you compress it.

Once all the hardware is out of the way, place the end of a pry bar, large screwdriver, or dedicated seal-removing tool under one edge of the seal. Place a folded rag or hunk of cardboard between the fork and the tool to protect the lower leg, and pry the seal free.

The new seal can be tapped into place using a plastic mallet and a socket. Find a socket that just makes contact with the seal's outer lip. Lubricate both the inner and outer surfaces of the new seal with ATF, WD-40 or fork oil. Gently tap the seal in until it bottoms.

Some forks are constructed in such a manner that the inner leg must be installed into the outer before the seal can be installed. These

forks will require the use of a seal driver to install the new seal. These are available to fit specific applications. Normally they cost about $40, but they are well worth owning. Without the correct driver, you could cock a new seal and ruin it during installation. On these forks the seal will slide down over the inner tube, the driver is placed on top of it, and then used to drive the seal into place.

Reinstall the tube and torque the securing bolt(s) to specifications. If your manual calls for it, use the correct sealant on the bolt before installing it. Finally, refill the forks according to the instructions given in the earlier procedure on changing fork oil. ■

(TOP LEFT)
DeCarbon-type dampers keep the nitrogen gas separated from the oil by means of a free-floating piston, which acts as a diaphragm. This way the oil can pass through the damping orifices without interference from the gas bubbles.

(TOP RIGHT)
Reservoir-equipped dampers are a variation of the simplest DeCarbon design. A more consistent oil temperature, and therefore more consistent damping, is provided due to an increased oil capacity; the shock body can be entirely filled with oil since the gas chamber is elsewhere. A rubber bladder is used within the reservoir to separate the nitrogen gas from the damper oil.

(BOTTOM LEFT)
Built in many configurations, the double-damping type provides a damping force on both the compression and rebound strokes. It is the most effective type of shock absorber.

(BOTTOM RIGHT)
Emulsion-type dampers may allow the nitrogen to mix with the oil, or they may incorporate a separator of some sort to keep the oil and nitrogen apart.
(Courtesy American Honda)

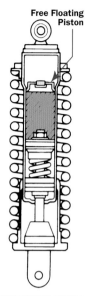

DECARBON TYPE

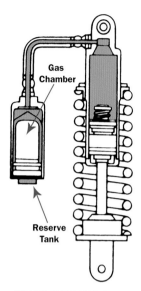

RESERVE TANK TYPE

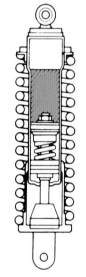

**DOUBLE DAMPING
(DOUBLE EFFECT) TYPE**

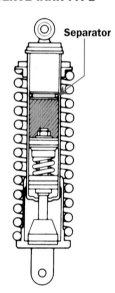

EMULSION TYPE

link fork. These are made of rigid legs that pivot around the steering head, with a small swingarm pivoting on the bottom of each leg and a shock to damp the motion. Leading-link forks were used on BMWs until the late 1960s and are still a popular upgrade for sidecar-equipped bikes.

Maintaining Front Suspension

All front forks need some regular attention. This includes checking and adjusting the steering head bearings and changing the fork oil, see sidebars in this chapter.

In years past it was common to adjust the damping rates of the front fork by changing the fork oil viscosity. In some cases this is still true, however it is not nearly as true as it once was. Modern forks, particularly the cartridge type, tend not to require a viscosity change unless there are some specialized circumstances. More often changes in damping are made through the external adjusters or by replacing internal valving. So my first inclination is tell you to stick with the manufacturer's recommendations as to fork oil weight and height, or capacity. But if you feel that the fork is under-damped, because it pogos or wallows around, its certainly permissible to go to a heavier grade oil. Start by increasing the weight one step at a time. For example, you can go from a 5-weight to a 7.5 or maybe 10-weight without any problem. I'd avoid going from a 5 to a 30-weight though.

Things like this can be a learning experience so be prepared to change lots of oil until the bike feels the way you want it to. Changing the fork oil viscosity is an easy way to modify the front fork. By increasing the viscosity you increase the damping, because it takes more energy to force the thicker oil through the damping orifices.

If you increase the level of the fork oil, the fork will also become slightly stiffer because you have reduced the amount of free air space in the fork. The air in a fork tube acts like a spring. When you decrease its volume by adding more oil you are effectively stiffening the spring. As the fork compresses it compresses the air. Reduce the amount of space the air can fit into and the air will oppose.

This can work both ways; add a little extra oil and the fork gets nice and firm. Add too much and it becomes harsh, mainly toward the end of its travel. This is where your notebook comes in handy. If you feel like experimenting, refill your forks with the prescribed amount of oil. Ride the bike,recording your impressions, add a little to each leg, and repeat. At some point you'll say 'this is great' or 'this sucks'. When you get to the part where it sucks use your turkey baster to lower the oil level back to its great setting. But first I suppose we should learn how to change the fork oil shouldn't we?

REAR SUSPENSION

If your motorcycle was built since the late 1950s, it almost certainly has some form of rear suspension consisting of a swingarm and one or more shock absorbers. Early machines (and many built today) use twin shocks, one on each side of the swingarm. Others use one shock behind the engine, attached directly to the swingarm, or indirectly, by means of a linkage that provide the effect of a progressive rate for both the spring and damping. Still others use one or more shock

SUSPENSION TUNING

Assuming that all is well mechanically, the only thing you really need to do at this point is to formulate a clear idea of exactly what you want to accomplish and how you plan to accomplish it. If you know what you want to improve, it'll be that much easier to fix. But how do you tell what's going on? Initially, that will be the hard part.

Here are three sets of symptoms that will probably be similar to yours:

1. The bike wallows in the turns and is hard to control. The bike may also have ground-clearance problems and straight-line stability may be compromised. The root cause of these symptoms is weak springs and insufficient damping (either rebound or compression). Worn or improper tires can also cause these symptoms.

2. The bike rides rough. It handles okay on smooth roads, but mid-corner bumps, or any bump for that matter, upsets the handling. The root cause is overly stiff springs, and/or too much compression (or to little rebound) damping.

3. When riding through a turn, the suspension compresses further and further, and as it "ratchets," or "pumps" down, the bike tends to run wide on the exits of the turns, and ground clearance becomes an issue. The root cause is too much rebound damping or too soft springs.

Those are the big three; everything else is just a variation on a theme. However, there are other reasons to tweak your suspension. Manufacturers assume that you are an average rider of average size and average ability. In reality, you may be larger or smaller than average, or planning to carry a passenger. You may ride harder than average, or you may not. You may like to tour on rough back roads. You may be short of stature.

All that being said, dialing in your bike's suspension to suit your particular needs is easy, although you should bear in mind that it is a learning experience and may take some time. ■

absorbers mounted underneath the engine or transmission.

The shock absorbers consist of a sealed damper unit with a coil spring over the damper body. Oil and damper units inside the shock provide the damping. Some are adjustable for damping. Your manual will tell you whether or not yours are. Most shocks are adjustable for spring preload by means of a rotating collar with ramps of different heights around the collar. In

Dampers may be installed right side up or upside down. When mounted in the inverted position, unsprung weight is slightly reduced. Not all shocks can be mounted in the inverted position; always check with the manufacturer.

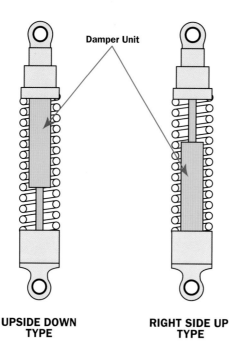

Damper Unit

UPSIDE DOWN TYPE

RIGHT SIDE UP TYPE

the section on improving your suspension, we'll show you how (and why) to use this adjuster to optimize your suspension.

Some shocks use pressurized gas (or even air) to augment the spring. Usually, the gas is nitrogen and pressures are in the 300 psi range. Some even have a piston in the shock or in an external reservoir to keep the gas and oil separate. The latter are known as DeCarbon-type shocks.

The swingarm is part of both the frame and the suspension. We'll cover it in the chapter on frames.

IMPROVING SUSPENSION

One thing you need to realize is that a motorcycle's suspension is more than the forks and rear shock(s). In short, a motorcycle suspension is symbiotic. In addition to the springs and dampers, the suspension encompasses the tires, steering-head bearings, and the swingarm bearings, as well as a few complex factors like frame and fork rigidity, and the frame's basic geometry. We'll discuss those items in the coming chapters, but the reality is that if the tires are worn so thin they won't cast a shadow, you can adjust the suspension all you want, but the bike still won't handle worth a damn.

There are also a few design considerations at work here. Not all bikes have easily-adjusted

suspensions. Quite a few front forks have no provision for external adjustment at all. If you want to change any characteristic you'll need to make a mechanical change inside the fork. This may range from changing the fork oil level or viscosity, to changing the fork spring or internal damper unit. Other forks may have a limited adjustment capability. Perhaps there is a preload adjuster or a damping adjustment. And, of course, some forks have all the bells and whistles.

Rear suspensions are in the same boat. While most have a preload adjustment, fewer have any kind of damping control. If the rear dampers aren't working the way you want them to, the only solution may be replacement.

Preliminaries

So your bike's not handling the way you want it to. Is that what's making you blue? The first question is, did the problem come up suddenly and is it very obvious that something is wrong? Or was it a slow-developing, subtle kind of thing?

If the problem cropped up quickly, it's likely that something mechanical is at fault. In this case, suspect the obvious: low tire pressures, loose steering-head bearings, and wheels that are out of alignment will all cause handling problems. A host of other mechanical faults, like blown fork seals or worn-out rear shocks, are also possible causes.

If the problem came up slowly and is more subtle, finding the problem will take a little detective work. Suspension components do wear out. It may be that the fork springs or rear springs are just sacked. Fork oil deteriorates as well and requires the occasional change. Tires that look fine may have worn to the point where handling starts to fall off. It may also be that the swingarm pivot or steering-head bearings have worn somewhat and need a slight adjustment.

Often overlooked when chasing down a suspension problem are the engine and suspension mounting bolts. Loose or under-torqued hardware can make a bike feel real weird and not handle well. Many frames use the engine as stressed member, so if a mounting bolt works loose it's like having a broken frame member.

DIY Setting Ride Height

To set the ride height you'll first need to measure sag. Your shop or owner's manual should list the specified suspension travel. If it doesn't you'll have to remove the springs and actually measure total travel. Once you have determined the travel, subtract 25–30 percent. For example, rear wheel travel for the Kawasaki Voyager XII is 100mm. Since I like 'em a little tight, I'd use 30mm as a sag figure, leaving 70mm for suspension travel. Now all I have to do is figure out how much sag I actually have.

Measuring front fork sag is pretty easy. With the bike on the center stand support the bike so the front wheel is clear of the ground. Place a tie wrap around the fork tube, forcing it down against the seal. Have a friend support the bike while you sit on it in the normal riding position, off the stand, of course.

If you normally ride with full bags and a passenger, fill the bags and have the passenger or a likely facsimile in place. This may require the use of two friends to support the bike but that shouldn't be a problem for most of you. When the bike is weighted, the fork slider will push the tie wrap up the fork leg. Place the bike back on the center stand and support the bike again so the wheel clears the ground. Measure from the fork seal to the tie wrap. This dimension is your front sag.

Now do the same in the rear. Again support the bike so the rear wheel is clear of the ground. Measure from the center of the rear axle to some point directly above it. Record the measurement and place the bike back on it's wheels, fully laden, as you'd normally ride it. Repeat the measurement. Subtract the second measurement from the first. That number is your rear sag.

Adjusting the sag is straightforward. Simply preload the springs until the desired sag is dialed in. Rear shocks generally have some type of adjuster built into them. Front forks may or may not. The solution is to make a set of spacers to preload the springs. Obtain a piece of PVC pipe that fits inside the fork tube. Find a piece that has an OD (outside diameter) slightly smaller than the fork tube's inside diameter, which should make it approximately the same size as the spring's outside diameter. Place a washer between the pipe and the spring. Cut the PVC to length; I'd start with an inch-long piece. Install it above the spring, and assemble the whole shebang. Then measure your sag again.

You may find that it takes a little trial and error to obtain exactly what you want—which is why my race bike has a handful of quarters stuck between the fork cap and the spring. "How much preload you running in that thing Z-man? About 5 bucks worth." As a side note, this is the one big advantage of touring bikes equipped with air-enhanced suspensions. Sag and ride height settings are just an air chuck away.

If the ride height is now good, but the suspension compresses too much under a load, adding some preload may help. Unfortunately, adding preload is a stop-gap measure at best. Besides, it will alter the bike's ride height, negating all your hard work.

If you find that your bike's suspension is too soft with the correct sag setting, then the right solution is to install stiffer springs. ∎

> **You'll need:**
> - Tape measure
> - Wrench to remove the fork cap
> - Shock adjusting tool
> - PVC pipe, sized to fit
> - Hacksaw
> - A good buddy to give you a hand.

Rear sag: measure from the ground to an easy-to-use point on the motorcycle, like the rear fender.

A tie wrap placed on the front fork can be used to measure both sag and overall suspension travel.

Maybe the bike just isn't working the way it should. One young lady of my acquaintance purchased a new, large, and by all accounts fast, good-handling motorcycle. Fast was no problem. But the handling failed to live up to her expectations. After wrestling the thing around for a few weeks she decided to start turning the adjusters until the bike did what it was told. An hour or two later, she was riding a different bike. This one stuck to the road like the painted line.

Before you attempt to adjust the suspension make sure that everything else is up to snuff. The tires should be properly inflated and have adequate tread. Make sure that the wheels are in line.

NORMAL OPERATION

FULL COMPRESSION

Though the amount of stroke Ⓐ is the same, the amount of stroke Ⓑ becomes greater.

Ⓑ x (2-3)

PRO-LINK

The Honda Pro-Link is typical of rising-rate suspension designs. This type of suspension is characteristically soft during the initial stages of travel while providing increasingly stiffer action as larger hits are absorbed. (Courtesy American Honda)

Unless you're reasonably certain that the rear-wheel adjustment marks are accurate, use a straight-edge to check the wheel alignment. The steering-head bearings should be checked and adjusted as required.

Likewise, check and adjust the swingarm pivot. Not all bikes have adjustable swingarm pivots; if yours doesn't, you'll have to replace the bushings if there is any significant play. (Don't worry, these items are covered in the next few chapters.)

It also helps to write down anything you change. The first thing I do is record the suspension settings before I started fiddling around. That way if I screw things up too badly I can go right back to where I started. I also use a notebook to record each and every change and how the bike felt after I made it. Then I can follow the general drift of where the bike is going. Plus, I don't have to stand around trying to figure out if the last change really did make the bike handle better.

Tuning Stock Components

The first step should be to try and tailor the suspension to your needs without making any serious (read that as expensive) changes. In other words by just twisting the knobs adjusting the preload and if necessary changing the fork oil.

Setting Ride Height and Sag

Setting the correct ride height and sag are the first steps toward making your bike turn and handle the way it should. Among other things, the ride height of your motorcycle determines how much suspension travel is available when impacts force the wheels up and how much is kept in reserve so the wheels can follow dips in the road.

The distance from the ride height to full suspension compression is your available suspension travel. The distance between the ride height and full extension of the suspension is called sag. Normally the sag dimension should be one third to one quarter of your total suspension travel.

Adjusting Rebound Damping

Once the ride height and sag are adjusted you can move onto the damper settings. Not all bikes will have adjustable damping. We'll come back to those that don't in a few paragraphs. The basic theory is that damping must always be proportional to spring rate. Fit stiffer springs and you'll need to increase the damping rate proportionally. The next question is, how do you adjust those suspensions fitted with adjustable compression damping? (see sidebar.)

Adjusting Compression Damping

So much for ride height and rebound damping. The final phase is the compression-damping adjustment. You may have noticed that with only rebound damping the bike tended to ride lower and lower as it worked over a series of bumps. This is the "pumping down" or "ratcheting down," that we discussed earlier. Adding some compression damping helps prevent ratcheting. It also helps stabilize the bike over dips and low spots in the road, especially at low and moderate speeds.

I'd recommend starting your compression damping experiments by returning the setting to the stock position. Repeat the ride. The suspension should feel a little firmer at some stages, but it should also make the bike a bit more stable. Chances are that the stock setting will feel most comfortable, but try turning the compression-damper screw in both directions. If nothing else, it'll show you what the bike feels like with too-soft and too-stiff compression damping.

As you can see there is going to be a fair amount of trial and error involved in this procedure. Which is why keeping accurate notes should prove helpful. It's also a learning process and the more you learn the easier it get.

Adjusting Dampers When There are No Adjusters

What can you do when there are no adjusters to turn and fiddle? Lamentably there isn't much you can do with the rear suspension. If no adjusters are installed on the shock and the damping rates are off, it is time for new rear shocks. This shouldn't be construed as a disaster.

There are plenty of great handling bikes out there with non-adjustable shock absorbers on them. However, if your rear suspenders aren't what you want them to be and have no provision for adjustment, the answer is simple. Bin them and install ones more to your liking.

DIY — Adjusting Rebound Damping

Begin by backing both the rebound and compression all the way off. Do this at the fork and shocks. Record the number of turns or clicks that it took to get the adjusters back to zero. Next take the bike for a slow ride down a familiar road. Notice the way the bike bobs and weaves like Muhammad Ali? That's under-damped suspension at its best. Next add some rebound damping and repeat the ride. I generally go two clicks at a time, because one click is so small that its effect is hardly noticeable. I start halfway between zero and the standard settings. Feels a lot better doesn't it? It's probably still wallowing around a lot but it should feel a more stable. Keep going along this path until you reach full maximum damping, recording the number of clicks and your impression of the ride. At some stage you should see that the bike went from a wallowing pig to good and comfortable, and then proceeded to stiff and overly harsh. Pick the setting you liked best. ∎

You'll need:
- *A small notebook to record your settings*
- *Screwdriver that fits your adjusters*

Now, this is the way to do it. The left side of this Moto Guzzi Le Mans fork contains the compression adjuster. The right side has the rebound adjuster.

Just as sophisticated, the Le Mans features a White Power rear damper. The blue knob adjusts the rear shock's compression damping. There are separate adjusters (not visible) for adjusting rebound damping and spring preload.

I should also point out that the adjusters on a shock or front fork really are trimming devices. They fine tune the suspension and they move the damping curve up or down but they don't change the shape of the curve. Only an internal design change can do that.

The front fork is a fertile playground for suspension minded experimenters. You can start by

DIY *Minimizing Stiction*

Front fork stiction is caused when the fork tubes are out of alignment. Rather than sliding smoothly they fight each other and bind or stick, hence the term stiction. Stiction can also be caused by tight fork seals or physical damage to the legs but in this case we're talking of an alignment problem only.

Modern bikes, those built in the last 15 to 20 years, don't have nearly as many problems with stiction as older bikes did. At least not unless they've been crashed. If the bike has been crashed and the front end twisted you'll need to remove and inspect each component for damage.

However if you suspect that plain old stiction, caused by a slightly misaligned front end is at the root of your handling problems, here's the quick way to check it, and fix it.

Jack the bike up so that the front wheel can be removed and remove it. With the wheel out of the fork, try to insert the axle through the fork legs. If it slides in and out of the legs smoothly the legs are as aligned as you're going to get them with special jigs. If the axle won't slide smoothly something is holding the legs out of plane.

Start by loosening up the fender retaining bolts; don't forget the fender braces as well. Then try the axle again. If it slides freely with the fender loose you've found the problem. Few fenders fit perfectly; many create stiction because the bolts are used to pull the fender into contact with the fork, which preloads it slightly, creating stiction. If that's the case, shim the offending mounting holes with a washer or two, until you achieve a stress-free fit. Fork braces can also create a similar problem.

If the problem doesn't lie in a bolt-on piece, you'll have to loosen up the triple trees and align the forks manually. With the fork loose in the clamps and the top clamp nut loose insert the axle. If it slides in freely, and many times it will, you're in. If it won't, rotate the fork to one fork stop, either left or right. Give the handlebars a very gentle twist against the stop; if the axle won't line up or the misalignment gets worse go the other way. Work slowly and patiently until you get the axle to slide in perfectly.

Once the fit is right, reinsert the axle and wheel. Snug the axle nut down by hand and give the front wheel a good spin, then clamp on the brake and hold it on, while you or a helper torque the front wheel to the recommended specs. Tighten the axle pinch bolts if any. Torque the lower triple clamp pinch bolts.

Place the bike back on its wheels and pump the forks a few times, which will allow them to center themselves in the clamps. Then tighten the upper pinch bolts and fork stem nut. Lastly tighten up the fender and fork brace, making certain they don't preload the fork legs.

Some bikes make it impossible to install or even tighten the front fender after the wheel is installed. If that's the case, install it as you need to, making sure that any gaps are shimmed with washers to prevent the fender from twisting the forks as it's bolted down. ■

changing the weight of your fork oil. The heavier the viscosity the firmer the fork.

You can also change the height of the oil, relative to the top of the tube. If you increase the level of the fork oil, the fork will also become slightly stiffer because you have reduced the amount of free air space in the fork. The air in a fork tube acts like a spring. When you decrease its volume by adding more oil you are effectively stiffening the spring.

If the fork feels under-damped, start by draining and refilling your forks per the manufacturer's specifications. If they don't feel any better try oil that's one viscosity number higher. If it still feels a little soft raise the oil height by 10mm and go for another ride. At some point you'll strike on the right combination. Either that or you'll be on the phone to one of the aftermarket suppliers looking for new damper rods.

Here's the bottom line on suspension adjustment: take notes; if you don't, you can get lost in your work. Besides, if you screw things up at least you have a starting point to return to. Next, make only one change at a time. Evaluate that change and then decide on your next course of action. Don't be afraid to experiment; only you

The Race Tech GOLD VALVE makes an immense improvement in damping. Installation is straightforward and can be performed by anyone. (**Courtesy Race Tech**)

can decide what's right for your riding style and ability.

AFTERMARKET SPRING KITS AND DAMPERS

In years gone by there were all types of aftermarket damping and spring kits available. Today's suspensions are vastly improved and much more sophisticated then they were. Most have enough adjustment to cover the average rider's requirements. If they don't, there are scads of suspension specialists out there that will fine tune your suspension to your particular needs.

For those that would rather do it yourself, the first step is probably going to be an aftermarket spring. In every case, this is a simple out-with-the-old, in-with-the-new procedure. In most cases far less challenging than changing the fork oil.

Damping modifications are a little trickier. The forks will need to be dismantled, and the damping rods replaced or altered in some way. A neat upgrade for those who feel the need is a set of Race Tech's Gold Valve Emulators. Gold Valves are designed to sit on top of the damping unit, under the spring. Spring-loaded orifices control and improve both compression and rebound damping. The emulator is fully adjustable as well. While the Emulator takes some time to install—the original damping unit has to be drilled out—the results are well worth the effort.

Making Telescopic Forks Rigid

Smaller-diameter telescopic forks lack sufficient rigidity. If you doubt that this was a problem find an older bike, something built from the early '90s on down. Straddle the front wheel and grip it with your knees. Then try to turn the handlebars. Many bikes will let the forks twist while the wheel stays stationary; not good.

There are not a whole lot of solutions to this problem. You can upgrade to a better (read that as more rigid) fork assembly. This entails finding a fork that will work, machining up the right spacers and adapters and putting the whole thing together.

I've done this many times and when it all comes together the end result can be extremely rewarding. But it can also be expensive and time consuming. In some cases, aftermarket fork braces are available. These work quite well and are relatively inexpensive and easy to install.

The wheels go 'round and 'round. I can't remember where or when I first heard that ditty, but it must have made a big impression on me. That one line kind of sums it up: if your motorcycle's wheels don't go round or if the wheels aren't round, it's a bumpy ride indeed. In this chapter, we'll tell you how to maintain and improve your wheels and tires, so they keep going 'round and 'round.

WHEELS

Most motorcycles roll on either spoked or cast-alloy wheels, but some are fitted with composite wheels, or even split rims. Each type has advantages and disadvantages.

Spoked Wheels

Spoked wheels are traditional in look, can be very strong, and are rebuildable. They also need regular maintenance to keep them round and true.

Spokers are built up of a rim laced to a hub by spokes. The hub is a casting with two or more bearings in it that rides on the axle. The brakes are also attached to, or cast integrally, with the hub. Arranged around the periphery of the hub are flanges that have countersunk holes in them to locate the spokes. The rim is the hoop-shaped band of metal that carries and supports the tire.

Traditionally, rims were drilled through their centers to accommodate the spokes, which connect the hub to the rim. Because of all those holes, spoked wheels usually require use of an inner tube. A large rubber band or thick tape, the rim band, is placed over the nipples to prevent them from grinding through the inner tube. The

tube rests in the well, over the nipples. Some current rims are built to be run tubeless, however, and these have holes along the outside edges of the rim for the spokes.

Cast Wheels

Cast wheels for everyday street motorcycles gained popularity in the late 1970s, and they are currently popular on all but cruiser-style bikes. They are cast in one piece, usually of aluminum, although magnesium wheels are used on some high-performance machines. Cast wheels can be both light and strong, and they require no maintenance (other than servicing of the wheel bearings).

Magnesium Wheels

Cast wheels were originally developed for racing use. The wheels were cast from magnesium

Once found only on road racers and high-end sportbikes, cast-alloy wheels are now found on nearly every type of motorcycle.

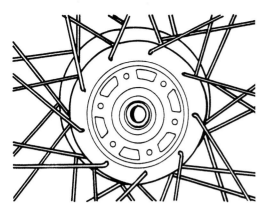

Note how the spokes pull at a tangent; This provides a spoked wheel with its strength.

and then machined to be absolutely true. The wheels were extremely light, extremely strong, and extremely expensive. A further advantage of the cast wheel was that it lent itself to tubeless tire use, which the tire manufacturers applauded.

They also looked really cool and lots of riders began to demand them for their street bikes. However, magnesium is a poor material to use on a wheel that sees lots of daily riding. It's expensive and very prone to corrosion. That's no real problem for a race bike, but a street bike is likely to see a fair amount of damp and wet weather. True, magnesium wheels also have a nasty habit of cracking over prolonged periods of time. For those reasons, street motorcycle wheels are usually made of aluminum alloy, or even malleable cast iron. As a result they are generally heavier then the equivalent-size spoked wheels.

Composite Wheels

Some bikes, most notably Hondas, were fitted with composite wheels built of a cast hub linked to the rim by stamped, star-shaped spoke pieces. Composite wheels can be light and strong, and they require no maintenance, also the rim and/or spokes on some can be replaced if they are damaged.

CHECKING AND ADJUSTING WHEEL ALIGNMENT

Most riders never even consider checking wheel alignment unless there is something radically wrong with the way the bike steers or handles. A motorcycle's rear wheel is usually the focus of our alignment attention. The simple reason

DIY Changing Tubes & Tires

There's no way to sugar coat it, changing a tire or replacing an inner tube is a nasty, dirty job, but it is one of those fundamental jobs that every motorcycle rider needs to become familiar with. Of course, once you become intimately familiar with tire changing you'll figure either it's cake, or you'll have the next one done at your favorite shop.

Your shop manual will give precise instructions on removing and replacing either wheel. Follow them, for safety's sake.

You'll need:
- Tools required to remove the wheel(s)
- A fresh tube
- Tire irons
- Valve-stem removal tool (available from any auto-parts store)
- Rim guards (optional)
- Tire lube or soapy water (tire lube is available commercially or you can use a 50:50 mix of l iquid soap and water as a tire-mounting aid)
- Pail or trash can as a work stand (optional)

Once the wheel is off the bike, the real fun begins. You can either work on the ground, which is even less fun than you may imagine, or try to work standing up, which is only marginally more comfortable. If you elect to work upright, you'll need something to support the wheel. I've found that a 25-gallon steel drum works fine. My second choice is a steel or plastic 5-gallon pail mounted on a sturdy stool or table. You can protect the rim with an old towel or a rag. If you must work on the floor, place a flattened cardboard box or old rug down first to give you and the rim some protection.

Remove the air valve out of the tube's stem. You can use a purpose-built tool, or if you're cheap like me you can find an old tire valve cap that's got the tool built right into it. I'm still using one I found when I was about 15 years old.

Once the air is out of the tube, force the tire bead down into the rim well to break the bond between the tire's bead and the rim. This is called 'breaking the bead' and it can be difficult. You may have to stand on the rim, use a large pair of pliers, or even clamp the tire in a vise to break the bead. Once the first side is

(continued next page)

Besides the common tools needed to remove the wheels, you'll also need (LEFT) tire irons (or spoons if you're a traditionalist), rim protectors, and a valve stem removal tool. (RIGHT) Standard spoked wheel, tire, rim band and inner tube.

DIY **Changing Tubes & Tires**

broken, flip the tire over and repeat for the second side. After the beads are broken, place the tire, sprocket side down, into your barrel. Changing tires is tough enough without chewing your knuckles to shreds on a greasy old sprocket. If you're forced to work on the floor, position the wheel to protect the brake disc.

Now, slip your rim protectors over the rim. If you're the frugal sort, these can be made by slitting a heavy piece of hose down one side and slipping it over the rim.

Next, starting opposite the tire-valve stem, insert your tire irons one at a time and pry the edge of the tire up and over the rim. A little tire lube

or soapy water applied to the bead will make this job a little easier. Work the irons around the tube an inch or two at a time until the bead is removed from the rim. Once the bead is free of the rim, remove the stem lock nut and remove the tube.

Under the tube you're probably going to find a rim band. A rim band is a

Place the wheel on a suitable support.

Remove the valve stem and release all of the air.

Remove the valve stem lock nut.

Break the bead. Since I weigh in at around 230 pounds, I can just bear down on most tires to pop them loose, flip the tire over and break the opposite side as well.

Insert the rim protectors.

Insert the tire irons and pry the bead up and over the rim. Most tire manuals recommend starting at, or close to the valve stem and working your way around the bead.

Changing Tubes & Tires

7

Once the bead is over the rim the tube can be pulled free.

8

The other bead can now be forced over the rim. It may be helpful to use a tire iron to work the edge over the rim, especially if the tire sidewall is a little stiff. Inspect the rim and use a wire brush to remove any corrosion.

10

Make sure the new tube is the correct one for the tire—the information will be stamped directly onto the tube. Inflate the tube just enough (one or two pounds) for it to assume its normal shape. This will prevent the tube from becoming pinched between the rim and tire. Position the tube inside the tire, push the valve stem through the rim, and fasten the nut down finger tight.

9

Replace the rim band, or tape up the rim to prevent the spokes from chafing through the inner tube. This step may be omitted on tubeless tires. Lube the tire. Paying careful attention to any directional arrow, force the first bead down over the rim.

11

Force the bead into place.

12

At some point during installation of the tire, you'll probably need to use tire irons. As with tire removal, start at the valve stem and work your way around the rim.

(continued next page)

Changing Tubes & Tires

Make sure the tire balance mark aligns with the valve stem, then inflate the tire to the correct pressure.

Check the bead indicator; it should be equidistant from the rim all the way around the wheel.

Let the tire sit for a few minutes and recheck the pressure.

If the tire is directional, there will be an arrow molded into the sidewall indicating the direction of rotation.

thin strip of rubber used to protect the inner tube from chafing against the spokes. Not all manufacturers use a rubber band; some bikes may have a plastic compound applied to the rim itself. Pitch the rim band, and substitute a few layers of electrical tape instead. Make sure you punch the hole for the valve stem before replacing the tire.

If you're only replacing the tube, my guess is that's because you've had a flat. If possible, remove the object that caused the flat from the outside of the tire. Then carefully inspect the inside of the tire for any damage or foreign objects. Be prudent when checking the inside of the tire, particularly if you couldn't find anything that may have punctured your tire from the outside. I've seen more than one guy

cut his hand badly on a piece of shrapnel that migrated though the tire and was stuck on the inside.

Unless there is no alternative, I don't recommend patching the inner tube. If you're touring, I'd hope you have the good sense to carry at least a rear tube. If you are going to patch the tube, follow the instructions on the patch kit to the letter and inflate the tube to test it before reinserting it in the tire. Replace the patched tube at the first opportunity with a new one.

Replace the air valve and inflate the tube slightly. You'll need just enough pressure to give the tube some shape. Work the tube back into the tire, inserting the valve stem through the opening and loosely running down the retaining nut. Spray the

bead with tire lube or soapy water, and using hand pressure, start opposite the valve stem and force as much of the bead back over the rim as you can. Use the tire irons only when you can no longer use muscle to force the bead onto the rim. You may find that as you position the bead on the rim the leading edge will try to climb back off. There are tools sold to prevent this from happening, but the resourceful mechanic will use his knee or another tire iron to hold the fugitive portion of the bead in place.

Once the tire is back on the rim, lubricate both beads with your soap solution or tire lube and begin to inflate the tire. At somewhere around 30 to 45 psi, the bead should seat itself on the rim. If it doesn't seat by 60 psi, deflate the tire, and try again. When the tire is seated, the thin rib molded into the tire sidewall will be equidistant from the rim all around the tire on both sides. Check that your valve stem is straight, and if it is, secure the retaining nut. If it isn't, you'll have to break down the tire and start all over again. Bummer. It's also a good idea to partially deflate the tire and bounce it a few times to help work out "wrinkles" in the tube. Then fully reinflate.

If you are changing the tire itself, once the tube has been removed, force the other bead over the rim just like the first. Once the tire has been removed from the rim, inspect the rim for any damage or rust. Remove rust with a wire brush or heavy Scotch-Brite pad.

The new tire has two important markings. First is a directional arrow, perhaps along with the word DRIVE, install the tire so the arrow points in the forward direction. Second is a balance mark, a dab of paint indicating the tire's lightest spot. The balance mark should be placed next to the valve stem. ∎

being that, in almost all cases, the chain is adjusted by moving the rear wheel. Once upon a time, the datum marks stamped on the swingarm were universally distrusted, so most experienced riders would check the wheel alignment any time the chain was adjusted.

Thankfully, most bikes built in the last 20 or so years have pretty accurate markings. A lot of new bikes also use snail-type adjusters to position the rear wheel, which help prevent misalignment. Shaft-driven bikes have no rear-wheel adjustment and bikes with single-sided swingarms use an eccentric pivot that prevents the wheel from becoming misaligned.

An infallible way to check wheel alignment is to lay 8-foot fluorescent bulbs along either side of the rear wheel at floor level. Have a helper hold them in place while you measure the distance between the tubes and the front wheel sidewalls. The distance should be even on both sides and front to back.

If the alignment is off, correct it by using the chain adjusters. If it's way off after you've removed and replaced either wheel, check the wheel spacers. Note that some offset may be permissible, particularly if the bike has shaft drive. Once the wheels are correctly aligned, check your swingarm datum marks for accuracy.

TIRES

Tires are easily the most expensive consumable item fitted to a motorcycle. They also contribute as much, or more, to the enjoyment of riding and to rider safety than almost any other component on a motorcycle. If you doubt me, take a (slow) ride on a bike with incorrect or worn-out tires someday.

Basically, motorcycle tires are of two types: cross-ply and radial. We'll explain those terms in the following paragraphs. Meanwhile, we need to define three other tire terms that are essential to those explanations: beads, sidewalls, and plies, or belts.

Beads are the stiff hoop that touches the rim when the tires are mounted. Sidewalls are the strips around the side of the tire between the bead and the tread area. Plies or belts are stiffeners that are layered under the tread and sidewall during construction.

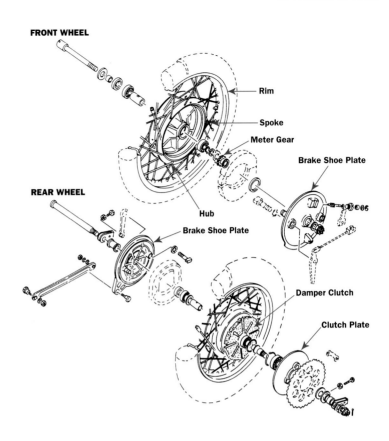

FRONT WHEEL

Rim
Spoke
Meter Gear
Brake Shoe Plate
Hub
Brake Shoe Plate

REAR WHEEL

Damper Clutch
Clutch Plate

Front and rear wheels—don't get confused by the labels "damper clutch" and "clutch plate" applied to the rear wheel parts (LOWER RIGHT). While they may be clutches in a narrow technical sense, they are not true clutches. This is a perfect example of confusing parts manual nomenclature. **(Courtesy Yamaha Motor Corporation)**

Cross-Ply Construction

Cross-ply, or bias-belted, tires are built of plies arranged diagonally, usually at a 45-degree angle, layered one on top of another, running in alternating directions. The plies are not interwoven. If they were, the tire would be extremely stiff and the heat created by the tires flexing would destroy it in short order. For the same reason, the tire manufacturers try to use as few plies as possible. The more plies the tire has the stiffer it is and the more heat it generates while in use.

Tire traction depends to a large extent on the tire's footprint, or contact patch—the area of the tire that is in contact with the road. Because the sidewall flexes, it allows the tire to flatten out slightly where it meets the highway. The softer the sidewall, the more flattening occurs. In gen-

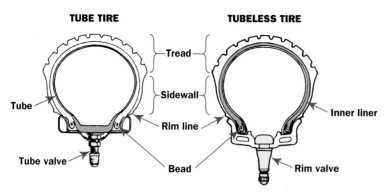

TUBE TIRE   **TUBELESS TIRE**

(LEFT) Tubed tires use an air-filled tube within the tire's casing. Air pressure drops instantly when a nail or other sharp object penetrates the tire and tube.

(RIGHT) Tubeless tires have an inner liner bonded to the inside of the tire instead of a tube. The liner has a special bead area that provides an effective seal against pressure loss. Since the thick liner is not separate from the tire, it does not stretch when inflated and will not burst if punctured. Instead, the liner closes around the puncturing object to prevent substantial pressure loss. (Courtesy American Honda Motor Corporation)

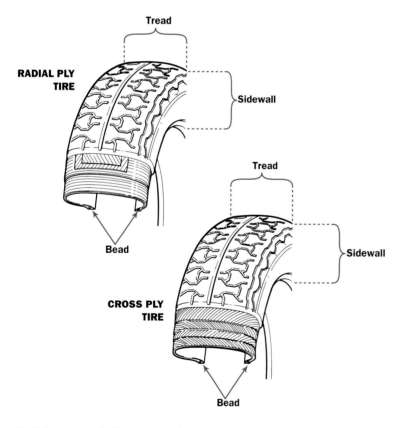

Radial vs cross-ply tire construction; note the lay of the tire plies. Note also that this radial motorcycle has two cross-ply belts that stiffen the tire. (Courtesy Avon Tire)

eral, the larger the contact patch the more traction the rider will have, all other things being equal. Thus, a six-ply tire will likely have a smaller contact patch and thus less traction than a two-ply tire when loaded with the same weight, but the six-ply tire will be able to bear more weight than the two-ply.

Radial Tires

Radial tires are built with their first two plies set at 90 degrees to the beads. Two reinforcing belts are then installed under the tread area only. These reinforcing plies are set at a very shallow angle, somewhere near 20 degrees. This makes for a very flexible sidewall, which allows for a much larger contact patch than that of an equivalent bias-ply tire.

For years motorcycle tire manufacturers tried to make a radial work only to be met with one setback after another. The big problem was that the radial's lack of sidewall rigidity made a bike difficult to steer when radials were fitted. The big breakthrough came about when Avon developed its Mudplugger radial tire for trials bikes. The grip was so much better than the bias-belt tires then in use, that Avon and others were encouraged to develop a street tire. Work on the reinforcing belt under the tread area solved the problems. Currently, radial tires are the hot tip for modern motorcycles, and I expect that to continue for a long time to come.

Some of you, caught up in the moment so to speak, may be tempted to fit radials to motorcycles that originally came with bias-belt tires. In a word, don't. Radial tires require a wider rim to accommodate their wider footprint. If you plan on fitting radials, you'll have to spring for the appropriate rims as well.

Tire Tread

The tread is the outer skin of the tire. It's composed of synthetic rubber which has been compounded to give a calculated compromise between long life and good traction. That compromise is necessary because soft compounds provide better grip at the expense of quick tire wear; harder compounds give longer wear at the expense of grip. A sportbike will generally come with tires that provide lots of traction but wear out in as few as 3,000 miles. A touring bike generally comes with tires that provide less traction but last 10,000 miles or more.

In a perfect world with perfect roads, the ideal tread pattern would be completely smooth, applying the maximum amount of rubber to the road surface at all times. Road-race and drag-race bikes do use smooth tires called slicks. They don't ride in the rain, though, at least not on slicks. On the street, a slick tire would put you in harm's way faster than you can say ouch. In the wet, rain gets trapped between a slick's surface and the road.

On a street tire the tread surface is covered with a network of grooves. These grooves are molded into the tire to create a channel for water to escape. The flexing action of the tire also helps pump water through the tread blocks and out from under the tire. In addition, the grooves help keep the tire a little cooler by increasing airflow across the tire surface.

Each manufacturer creates a tread pattern that they think will work best for a particular rubber compound, application, and condition. There is no best all-around tread pattern. Some designs, like the ribbed pattern once used on front tires, are no longer widely used because they tend to wander when rain-grooves are encountered. Other patterns have been dropped because they were found to cause handling problems when fitted to modern bikes. But by the same token, a pattern that works well on one bike may cause another brand to shimmy at low speeds.

Occasionally, I've installed a tire that just didn't work on a particular bike. Many motorcycles now have a sticker somewhere listing the approved tires for that bike. Any time your bike begins to handle contrarily, suspect the tires, especially if you've just installed a new and different style tire, or if they're getting near the end of their tread. All tire manufacturers have a fitting chart recommending size and tread design for a given motorcycle. Always consult it before fitting a tire other than the original equipment.

Tires and Heat

All tires have an optimum operating temperature. When they reach it, the rubber compound is at its stickiest, and the carcass at it's most flexible. Below that temperature, grip is reduced, and the tire may have a tendency to slide. On the street this isn't much of a problem, unless the bike is very fast, the day exceptionally cold, or the rider foolishly brave. Usually, by the time the engine is up to operating temperature, so is the tire.

If the tire exceeds its optimum temperature, things go wrong very quickly. Excess heat causes the tire tread to degrade. As the adhesives used to bind the tread compound percolate to the surface, the tire becomes very slippery. In severe cases the tire will actually shed chunks of tread. To reduce heat buildup, modern tires are constructed of thin, very strong plies, which cut down on heat buildup generated by flex. Since the carcass runs cooler, a softer tread compound

CHANGING TUBELESS TIRES

Because tubeless tires require much more effort to break down and reseat, I'm a little hesitant to recommend changing them at home. But if you must the procedure is identical to the method outlined for changing tube-type tires. It's just a bit more work.

PATCHING TUBELESS TIRES

In a word, don't do it. Although there are emergency patch kits available to plug a tubeless tire, they are only intended to get you out of the boonies and into the nearest shop, where you can replace the tire. All of the tire manufacturers recommend replacing a damaged tubeless tire because cord damage may have occurred as the tire went flat or when the object penetrated the tread. If you must plug a leaking tubeless tire to get it off the road, fine. Just don't ride the bike any further or faster than you must, and replace the tire as soon as you can. My feeling is that if the object did not cause the tire to go flat, than remove it and keep riding. It's extremely unlikely that the nail or whatever went in any further than the tread. However if the object did any substantial damage to the tread itself the tire should be replaced as a precaution. ■

Tire tread designs are almost infinite in their variety, each manufacturer choosing what he thinks will work best for a given application. From left: Dunlop dirt track, sport, and touring.

Checking & Truing Spoked Wheels

You'll need:
- *A spoke wrench*
- *A good ear*

Over time, all spokes will tend to loosen somewhat. The time-honored method of checking a spoke is to give it a tap with a screwdriver or wrench. If the spoke gives off a nice clear ping, it's still under tension; if the note is flat or dull, it's loose. Loose spokes tend to break, and broken spokes are a bad thing, as they tend to flop around and puncture the inner tube. Besides, one broken spoke can lead to five or six or ten broken spokes, and as you might imagine, a wheel with ten broken spokes is a wheel that's no longer safe. So if your bike has spoked wheels, you should learn how to check and true these wheels.

The first step is to get the wheel you're checking off the ground. Then,

give each spoke a tap and a listen. Don't be alarmed if each spoke isn't tuned to an E sharp because we're not tuning a piano for the philharmonic. If the bike has any real miles on it, chances are you'll find one or more that "thunk" rather than "ping." Use your spoke wrench to tighten the loose spoke a quarter of a turn and then recheck it. Tighten each loose spoke in turn and then recheck them all. If they are still loose, give them another quarter turn and recheck until all are snug. Since tightening one spoke can cause another to loosen, it's easy to start "chasing" loose spokes around the rim if you start trying to tighten them more than a quarter turn at a time.

An alternative method, and one that I prefer to use, is to start at the tire valve stem. Locate the first spoke

after the valve stem and apply your wrench. If the spoke turns with light to moderate effort, move it a quarter turn. Count to the fourth spoke and repeat. Work your way back to the original spoke plus one and repeat the operation, tightening every fourth spoke a quarter turn. Work your way back to the third spoke and begin again. Keep the cycle going until all the spokes are snug. It sounds like a lot of work but it should take less than 10 minutes a wheel, and you only need do it once or twice a year.

During the normal course of use spoked rims tend to twist slightly. This is called run-out. Run-out from side to side is called "wobble," up and down, "hop." In extreme cases run-out can be very difficult to fix; many wheel builders tell me that rather than true a wheel that's really

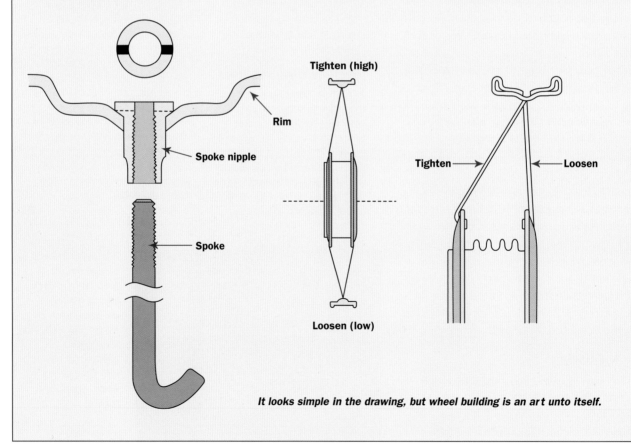

It looks simple in the drawing, but wheel building is an art unto itself.

bad, they'd just as soon loosen everything up and start fresh. For the average rider that's not really a great option.

Obviously, if you can see the rim wobble or hop you know you've got a problem. How much of a problem is debatable. All manufacturers list acceptable wheel runout specs in their shop manuals. As a rough rule, about 0.025 of an inch or one millimeter is acceptable, but check your manual for the specifics, some may allow as much as 3mm of run-out.

To measure the run out, mount a stationary pointer on the fork leg or swingarm. Position it so that it just kisses the rim at the closest point. As you're checking the run out, give the wheel a good shake to check the wheel bearings; if play is obvious, renew the wheel bearings before proceeding.

Measure the rim at its closest point and farthest point. If it's not within spec, you'll need to adjust the spoke tension. To cure up-and-down out of round, you'll need to loosen the spokes on the low side of the wheel and tighten the spokes on the high side to pull the rim into shape. Loosen the spokes only by two or three turns and tighten the opposite side by the same amount. Make certain that you always loosen and tighten an equal amount of spokes on both sides of the rim.

To correct side-to-side run out loosen the spokes on the side of the hub you want to pull away from, and tighten the spokes on the side you want to pull toward. If you end up turning the nipples more than three to five turns to true the wheel, I'd suggest you break down the tire and file down any of the spoke heads protruding from the nipple so they don't puncture the tire.

As you'd expect, this is tedious work and it's easy to make one false move and send the whole wheel out of whack. Experienced wheel builders work as much by feel as anything, which is one reason I recommend you avail yourself of their services if you have any real problems. ■

can be used, enhancing traction. Today's single- or double-ply tire is far stronger than the old four- and six-ply tires of the past. They last a lot longer and provide much better traction because they run cooler.

Air Pressure

Not so very long ago Goodyear Tire Company testers went to a parking lot and randomly checked the tire pressure on a hundred cars. They found that less than 10 percent of the tires were properly inflated. I might add that the test was done in their own corporate parking lot.

I'd hope most motorcycle riders were a little more conscientious about maintaining correct tire pressure, because the tire's profile and your safety depend on the tire being inflated to the correct pressure. When tire pressure is low, the tire flexes more, creating a larger than normal footprint. This creates a lot of heat, which you now know is a bad thing. Over-inflated tires wear out quickly, ride harshly, and reduce traction because the footprint is reduced, although they do run cool.

Check your tire pressure at least once a week and adjust it to the manufacturer's recommendations. Since the air expands when the tire is hot the pressure should always be checked and adjusted when the tire is cool. Do yourself a favor and buy a good tire gauge. Those $1.98 specials at K-Mart may look good in your pocket but they probably won't give you a very accurate measurement.

If you do a lot of riding in the rain—maybe you live in Seattle—you'll find that by increasing your tire pressure by 2–3 psi it may make the bike more resistant to losing traction. Water overwhelms the tread's ability to pump it away; a condition known as aquaplaning. A large tire footprint increases the chances of aquaplaning. By increasing the tire pressure slightly, the footprint is reduced, and the water can escape from beneath the tire before things get too crazy.

What Do All Those Numbers on the Sidewall Mean?

Molded into the sidewall of every tire is a series of letters and numbers that tell you everything you need to know about that particular tire, if you know how to decipher the code.

Learn to decipher the secret codes of the tire wizard, confound your enemies and amaze your friends; or at very least learn what size tires your bike uses.

TIRE CODE

(Inch Indication)

4.00H-18 4PR

Tread width: 4 inch

Speed limit code

Ply No. : 4-ply rating

Rim diameter: 18 inch

Speed Limit Code:

[J]	100 km/h max.
[N]	140 km/h max.
[P]	150 km/h max.
[S]	180 km/h max.
[H]	210 km/h max.
[V]	210 km/h min.
[ZR]	240 km/h min.

(Metric Indication)

170/60 R 18 73 H

Tread width: 170mm

Height/Tread Ratio = 60%

Radial indication mark

Speed limit code

Max. load code

Rim diameter: 18 inch

Height/Width Ratio = %

Height

Width

Initially, tire makers stamped their tires with inch markings (many still do), but metrification has taken over now, so the majority of markings are given in metric sizes. Typical markings may look like this: 4.00H-18 4PR (inch) or 100/90H-18 (metric) or 100/90R18 73 H (metric radial). The preceding nomenclature describes the tire's basic dimensions, speed rating, and whether it is bias-ply or radial. You may also find some tires marked with an alphabetical-numerical code (MM 90-18 Load range B, for example). Tires marked with alphanumeric designations are the least popular, and tires so marked aren't as common, but you do see them. By the way, in case you hadn't suspected, all four tires listed in this paragraph are roughly the same size.

Here's how to decode inch tire sizes, using 4.00 H-18 4PR as our example:

- 4.00 is the tire width in inches.
- H is the speed rating, indicating that this tire is rated for sustained speeds of 130 mph.
- 18 is the rim diameter in inches.
- 4PR indicates the number of plies, four in this case.

Here's how to decode metric tire sizes, using 100/90H-18 as our example:

- 100 is the tire width in millimeters.
- 90 is the aspect ratio, 90 percent, indicating a height of 90mm.
- H is the speed rating, 130 mph in this case.
- 18 is the rim diameter in inches.

The code stamped into a radial tire's sidewall is slightly more complex, but just as easy to decipher. Let's break down a 170/60 R 18 73 H.

- 170 means the tire has a width of 170mm.
- 60 is the aspect ratio; in this case it's 60 percent of 170, or 102mm, meaning this tire is 102mm high.
- R means this tire is a radial.
- 18 is the rim diameter in inches.
- 73 is a code that designates the maximum load that the tire can bear. It doesn't mean much unless you have a load chart to tell you that a tire rated at 73 can support a load of 805 pounds.
- H is the speed rating, 130mph in this case.

Although you may not encounter many, let's take a look at the last category of alphanumeric tires using the example of MM90 18 Load range B.

- M stands for motorcycle.
- M means the width is 4 inches.
- 90 is the aspect ratio, in this case it's 90 percent of 4 inches, meaning this tire is 3.60 inches high.
- 18 is the rim diameter in inches.
- Load range B; this is a curveball. Load ranges are listed alphabetically as well as numerically, A being the lightest.

Tire manufacturers are free to use any marking style and to add any other information they want. Other sidewall stampings will indicate whether the tire is intended to be used with a tube or without and the maximum tire pressure. If the tire is directional (meaning that it is intended to be mounted so it rotates in a given direction) there will be arrows on the sidewall telling you exactly what direction the tire is supposed to rotate. The arrows are generally marked front and rear. The tires should always be mounted so that when the arrow is at the top of the wheel it points forward when the tire rolls forward.

Speed Ratings

Tire-speed ratings indicate the maximum speed at which the tires should be run in continuous operation. Ratings you're likely to see the next time you go to buy tires: S (112mph), T (118mph), U (124mph), H (130mph), V (149mph), and Z (or ZR) (above 149mph). Ratings H, V, and Z (or ZR) are most common for street tires, and often the same size and model of tire is available in two, or all three, of these ratings. Always select tires having the same or higher speed rating as those recommended by the bike's manufacturer. Keep in mind, though, that the faster-rated tire won't make your bike faster. Paying extra for a Z-rated tire on a bike that tops out at 110mph is a waste.

MAINTAINING YOUR WHEELS AND TIRES

Your wheels and tires are the only thing between you and the ground. Take good care of them and they won't let you down. The tires and rims should be inspected as often as possible. Of course, this doesn't mean that you have to get down on your hands and knees before every ride and spend half an hour scouring your tires. But you should get into the habit of checking the tire pressure at least once a week. Look for anything that might indicate a tire problem about to occur; for instance, the head of a screw jammed into the tread is a dead giveaway that trouble is on the horizon. Check the tire tread for scalloping, which may indicate an out-of-balance or low-pressure situation. Keep an eye on the tire tread itself, particularly the wear indicators. Be on the alert for broken spokes or dents in the rims. The best time to check these items is when you're checking the tire pressure or when you're washing the bike.

When to Replace Tires

The smart-ass answer is when they're worn out. That won't do you any good though, will it? Molded into the tread of most tires are a series of bars that run parallel to the sidewall. These are called wear bars; when they become visible the tire is shot, plain and simple. Failing that, any time the tread becomes shallower than one-eighth of an inch, start thinking about replacing the tires.

Picking a New Tire

Of course, you can always replace your worn-out tires with the exact same make and style, if you are 100 percent happy with them. We all know that's not always the case.

There are only a couple of hard-and-fast rules when it comes to replacing the tires. The first is to never replace a tire with one that has a lower speed rating than the original equipment. The second is that rims are designed to support tires of a certain width. Putting on a big fat tire won't

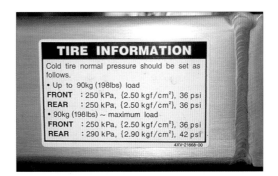

All new motorcycles have a tire pressure and load sticker on them. The sticker will list recommended tire pressures and the maximum load that they can safely carry.

Many tires include a directional arrow and a warning molded into the sidewall.

Checking & Replacing Wheel Bearings & Seals

You'll need:

- *Shop manual*
- *Large brass drift*
- *3 lb hammer*
- *Wheel bearing grease*
- *Small pry bar*
- *Circlip pliers*
- *Bearing drift (optional)*

Chances are that very few of you will be replacing wheel bearings or even wheel seals on a regular basis, but that doesn't mean you shouldn't know how to do it.

Most hubs have sealed ball bearings pressed lightly into the hub. A shoulder machined into the hub or an internal spacer sets the depth of the bearing in the hub.

This wheel has no wheel bearing seals; instead the bearings themselves are sealed. It also has no retainers; the bearing is held in place via the axle spacers. The thin punch is being used to shove the inner spacer to one side.

These bearings are not serviceable. When they show any signs of side play, you need to replace them. While the sealed ball bearing is the most popular, some bikes do use a tapered roller bearing. The tapered roller bearing has the advantage of being adjustable for preload and repackable with grease.

Wheel bearings are usually trouble-free, although street riders that carry heavy loads or rack up very high mileage may wear them out, as will the average dirt rider. One thing that's murder on a wheel bearing is washing your bike down with a high-pressure spray washer or steam cleaner. If you do wash your bike at a coin-operated car wash, avoid directing that high-pressure stream directly at the wheel bearings.

Prop the bike up so that the wheel you want to check is clear of the ground. With your hands on the wheel 180 degrees apart try to move the wheel at a right angle to the axle. If play is felt, you need to find the cause. If no play is felt, great, you're all done.

If play is felt, make sure that it's actually in the wheel bearings by double-checking all of the axle- and wheel-mounting hardware. Assuming the play is in the bearings, replace

them (if they are sealed) or adjust them (if they are tapered rollers). See your shop manual for the specifics on adjusting your tapered bearings.

Start by removing the wheel. The rear wheel may include a separate sprocket carrier with its own seal and bearing. If so, that bearing and seal should also be replaced or adjusted along with the wheel bearings.

Support the wheel so that the hub is clear of the ground by a few inches. A small wooden box will come in handy here. Make sure the hub itself is supported, not just the spokes.

The most common type of bearing and hub arrangement will be two ball bearings separated by a spacer and pressed into the hub. Normally, there will be a seal on each side of the hub that will have to be removed.

Gently pry the seal up and out of the hub. Once the seal is out, you're likely to find that the bearing is retained by a large circlip, or in some cases a threaded ring. Remove the retainer. If it's a threaded ring, a special tool may be required, although a punch can usually be used or a tool cobbled up.

Insert your long punch through one bearing and pry the spacer to one side. A portion of the inner race of the other bearing should now be

Use the brass drift to punch out the bearing.

One bearing and the spacer are out.

The opposite side can then be driven clear.

Clean the hub thoroughly.

DIV Checking & Replacing Wheel Bearings & Seals

visible. Use your punch to drive against the inner race. Work your way around the race to avoid cocking the bearing in the hub.

After the first bearing and spacer are removed, flip the wheel over and remove the bearing on the opposite side. Never reinstall sealed bearings after having driven them out. Since most bearings are generic, you can save a few bucks by picking them up at your local industrial-supply, auto-parts store, or bearing specialist. (Each bearing will have a code number stamped onto it; the number can be cross-referenced by anyone with a bearing catalog.)

Inspect the hub for any galling before installing the new bearings. If the bearing seats are damaged, they should be repaired; minor scrapes and scratches should be polished out with sandpaper. Severe damage may require hub replacement, although a bearing-locking compound like Loctite Stud and Bearing Mount can often be used if the damage isn't too severe.

Unless the bearing is sealed on both sides it should be packed with

I used an old socket that fits the outer race perfectly. Heating the hub will ease the installation of the new bearing. Drive the bearing in until it seats.

high-temperature grease before installation. Install the first bearing using a drift that locates on the outer race. Install any circlip or retainer. Flip the wheel and install the spacer, followed by the second bearing and any appropriate retainers. Press the seals into place with the open side

Install the spacer, then install the opposite side.

facing the bearing. Again use a drift that only contacts the outer edge of the seal. Lightly grease the axle and reinstall the wheel. ∎

---

help much if the rims on your bike are intended to take little skinny ones. Finally, all the information you need to safely choose a new tire is stamped right on the sidewall of your old one.

Balancing Tires

Like any rotating assembly, the tire and wheel assemblies need to be balanced. An unbalanced tire will wear faster, cause handling problems, and in severe cases could cause the rider to lose control of the bike. There are two types of balancing: static and dynamic.

Because spin balancers are "high tech" you might be tempted to think that they are the only proper way to balance tires. They aren't. I've seen road racers with tires that were static balanced run at Daytona with nary a quiver, and these bikes hit over 185mph. Dynamic balancing

is very good, and given the choice I'll use it every time, but if you take your time a static balance job works just fine.

Wheel Building and Truing

Wheel building is an art in itself, as is wheel truing. A good wheelwright can build and true a wheel in less time than it takes me to describe the process in print. If you have a burning desire to build your own wheels, there are books and videos that can walk you through the wheel-building process from start to finish. Frankly, this isn't something the novice mechanic should undertake lightly. Here's a quick look at the process.

Building a wheel is more than just lacing the rim to the hub. First the spoke pattern, or cross, is determined. Does each spoke cross its neighbor twice, three times, or even four? Rim offset is

DIY *Balancing Tires*

You'll need:

- Wheel weights (available at any decent motorcycle shop)
- Tools to remove the wheels, if you plan on taking them somewhere where they can be dynamically balanced.

Spin the tire and wait for it to stop. The heavy spot will settle at the bottom. Mark it. Spin it again. If the tire comes to rest with the same spot at the bottom, it's out of balance. You'll need to add a bit of weight to the point directly opposite.

Wheel weights are available at any motorcycle shop. They come in various shapes and sizes. Mag wheels use either a stick-on weight or one with a little clip that fastens it to the rim. Spoked wheels usually use a weight that's slotted to slide over the spoke. Or you can wrap a few turns of solder around the spokes. It may take a bit of experimenting to get the weight just right, but after awhile you'll get the hang of it. When the wheel is in balance, it will stop randomly each time it's spun. If the tire just won't balance without adding a ton of weight to it, try breaking down the tire and rotating it 90 degrees on the rim.

Most front wheels can be balanced on the bike, so long as there is no drag from the brakes or speedometer cable. In some cases this may involve removing the brake caliper(s). Due to driveline drag, trying to balance the rear wheel on the bike is usually an exercise in futility. The rear wheel will have to be removed and placed in a suitable fixture before it can be balanced. If you have any pretensions toward carpentry, you may want to build yourself a small upright fixture that will support the wheel and axle.

Due to the specialized equipment required, dynamic or spin balancing a tire is best left to a professional. The dynamic wheel balancer is a machine that resembles a cross between a slot machine and a lathe. The wheel assembly mounts to an axle that protrudes from the side of the machine. An electric motor spins the wheel, and while it's spinning a computer determines how much weight the wheel needs and where, in order to perfectly balance the wheel. As you might guess, this type of equipment is fairly expensive, but the shop fees are usually pretty reasonable for this service. Many shops will throw in a free balance if you purchase the tires from them. You can also save a few bucks by bringing in just the wheels. ∎

The ultimate in wheel balancing—the computer-assisted spin balancer.

then measured or looked up in the shop manual (if it lists it). The offset determines where the edge of the rim is located in relation to the hub. Not all rims are offset, of course, but it's a good idea to find out before you dismantle a wheel or start to build one from scratch.

Next, the new inside spokes are all inserted in the hub. The pattern is established and the nipple ends placed in the appropriate holes of the rim. The nipples are greased and installed. Next, the outer spokes are installed and their nipples run down. The wheel is then trued radially (up and down) and finally axially (side to side). See the Do-It-Yourself section for specifics.

IMPROVING WHEELS AND TIRES

Wheel and tire upgrades are becoming extremely popular, particularly among cruiser owners who do it for appearance, and sportbike owners who want to improve performance. Here's a primer on upgrading your tires and rims.

Rim Width and Wider Tires

Cruiser and custom builders love to slap big, fat rubber on their rear wheels. How wide you can go with the tire before you need to change rims is a frequently asked question.

Tire manufacturers recommend that the rim width should be at least half as wide as the tire. Ideally, rim width should approach 60 to 70 percent of the tire's width. When the rim is narrower than the tire, the tire loses support. The bike will develop a mushy or heavy feel. Conversely, while it's rare to fit a tire that's too narrow for a particular rim, it does happen. If the rim is too wide for the tire, the footprint will be too wide and conceivably the rider could run the tire off the edge of its tread during cornering. My advice is to always stick with the manufacturer's recommended tire sizes, unless you want to lace up wider rims.

Installing Wide Rims

Okay, so you want to install a really wide rear tire and rim on your custom. While installing a really wide rear tire on your cruiser may make it look cool, it will create certain problems. First and foremost, the bike will handle differently, and likely not as well as it used to. Second, a wide rim and tire may mean that you have to reposition your drive chain or belt as well as the rear disc assembly to clear the new tire. In some cases, a new swingarm may even be required. If you're intent on installing a fat rear wheel, my recommendation is to read through one of the custom bike builders guides, particularly anything written by Tim Remus (Wolfgang Publishing), before lifting a wrench. He'll give the straight scoop and the step-by-step procedures. He may even try to talk you out of doing it.

Sticky Tires

Everyone wants better traction. One way to get it is by installing sticky tires. Most motorcycles come with a tire compound that's formulated to balance traction against wear. Accordingly, most tire manufacturers may also offer a softer, stick-

A selection of weights make the balancing procedure a whole lot easier. Common weights include the over-the-spoke style and the stick-on type. Solder used to be popular; a length would be cut from a spool and wrapped around a spoke.

ier compound for "sport use." You can read that as being suitable for track days, or a Sunday shoot-out. Many tire builders also offer DOT legal race tires. For example, Michelin offers their splendid Pilot in both race and sport compounds. The race versions offer the ultimate in traction. Although it's primarily a race tire used in supersport racing, it is street legal. However, if used primarily as a street tire, its life expectancy may be less than 2,000 miles. On the other hand, the sport version sacrifices some tractive qualities for a bit better mileage. It is primarily a high performance street tire that's capable of taking in a track day.

Lighter Wheels

Sportbike owners often fit lighter wheels to their bikes. Although this is an expensive modification, it is a worthwhile one. Lighter wheels offer some significant advantages. For example, the reduction in unsprung weight improves the suspension action. Because lighter wheels contribute to an overall reduction in the weight of the motorcycle, acceleration, braking, and handling are all improved. Finally, because the lighter rear wheel has less mass, it allows the engine to accelerate harder, which helps the motorcycle accelerate the wheel quicker, which improves overall acceleration.

Your motorcycle's braking system will be of the disc type, the drum type, or a combination of the two. Drums were the standard until manufacturers gradually began fitting discs, at first just on the front and later on both front and rear.

Today, drums are only used on the front of a few inexpensive entry-level bikes, although they are still used on the rear of more bikes than they should be. Linked hydraulically-actuated disc brakes, some with anti-lock systems, are quite common also. Massive 4- and 6-piston calipers squeeze monstrous floating discs capable of stopping your bike on a dime and returning 8 cents change. And as this book was being written, BMW released a power-assisted brake system, the first motorcycle application of an assisted brake. I can't wait to see what comes next. No matter what type they are, your motorcycle's brakes are a critical safety feature, deserving the best of care. First, we'll look at the parts that make up your system and then show how to maintain and improve the whole.

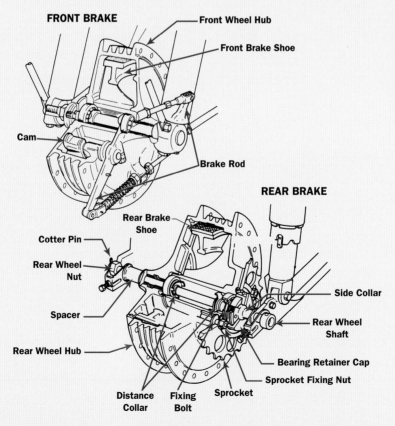

FRONT BRAKE

- Front Wheel Hub
- Front Brake Shoe
- Cam
- Brake Rod

REAR BRAKE

- Rear Brake Shoe
- Cotter Pin
- Rear Wheel Nut
- Spacer
- Rear Wheel Hub
- Side Collar
- Rear Wheel Shaft
- Bearing Retainer Cap
- Sprocket Fixing Nut
- Distance Collar
- Fixing Bolt
- Sprocket

Front drum brakes are no longer as popular as they used to be, especially the twin-leading-shoe variety. However the rear drum brake remains popular. (Courtesy Yamaha Motor Corporation)

DRUM BRAKES

Drum brakes use a drum that spins with the wheel around a backing plate fixed to the forks, frame, or swingarm. Mounted to the backing plate are a pair, or pairs, of brake shoes that, when activated, expand outward to bear on the drum. Friction between the shoes and drum provides the braking force. Springs inside the mechanism retract the shoes away from the drum, when you let go of the brake lever.

Drum brakes typically have two shoes per backing plate (some wheels have a backing plate on each side), but some systems have had as many as four shoes. If each pair is activated by a single cam, they are called single-leading-shoe brakes, for reasons we won't go into here. Some systems have included a second cam, expanding the shoe pairs outward from both ends. These were called double-leading-shoe designs. They offered nearly twice the braking power, but they only worked well in one direction, meaning they were good at stopping the bike, but bad for holding the bike from rolling backward when stopped on a hill.

In general, drum brakes are operated by cables, although some Harleys from the 1950s through early 1970s had hydraulic-drum rear brakes. By the standards of modern disc brakes, even the best drum systems seem weak. Nevertheless, the difference in smoothness and power between properly adjusted drums with high-friction linings and improperly adjusted ones with old, glazed linings is startling. We'll tell you how to optimize yours in the maintenance section.

Disc Brakes

Disc brakes use a metal disc, called the rotor, that spins with the wheel and is gripped by the brake caliper, which is fixed to the forks or swingarm. A piston or pistons inside the caliper extend toward each other when the brakes are activated. These pistons push a pair of brake pads into contact with the rotor. Friction between the pads and rotor provides the braking force. Pads and pistons retract when you release the brake lever.

While there are cable-operated disc brakes, the norm is to use hydraulic actuation. These systems use a master cylinder and hydraulic lines to deliver the brake fluid that activates the

TWO-LEADING-SHOE BRAKE

The two-leading-shoe brake has two cams in the same drum, by which the two brake shoes act as leading shoes. For this reason, the two-leading-shoe brake has greater braking power than the leading-trailing-shoe brake. The rate of wear on the lining is the same for both type brakes. But the two-leading-shoe brake has disadvantages. When the motorcycle stops on a steep slope, both leading shoes are converted to the trailing shoes by the reversing brake drum, and stopping power is halved.

OPERATION THEORY OF THE TWIN-LEADING-SHOE BRAKE

As each cam is turned, the shoes are pushed against the brake drum, and at the same time, friction makes the shoes follow the rotating brake drum, wedging between the drum and the point at which they are anchored. This type of action builds up a tremendous amount of friction, and for this reason gives greater braking power. This is called the servo-effect, or self-energizing effect. ■

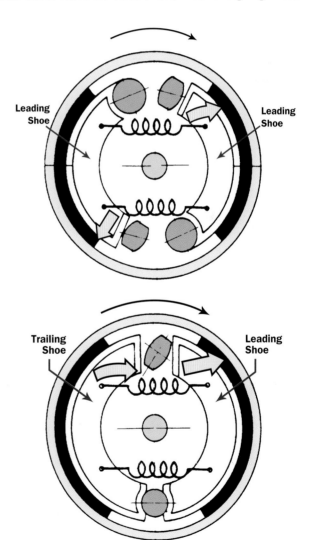

DIY — *Replacing Brake Shoes*

All current and most non-current brake shoes will have some indicator to tell you when they are used up. This may be a line or mark on the lever arm, or a window in the backing plate through which you can examine the shoes. Or it may just mean using a little common sense; if the adjustment is nearly used up, it's time for new shoes.

Replacing brake shoes is somewhat more complicated than replacing a set of pads. For starters, the wheel has to come off. My recommendation is to thoroughly inspect and service the brake anytime the wheel comes off for any reason, such as tire replacement.

Some drum brakes use two different return springs; make sure you identify the springs and mark their correct location. In almost every case, I'd recommend replacing the brake springs along with the shoes, particularly if the brakes have lots of miles on them or the bike is more than two or three years old. If the brake arm is removed from the brake cam, make certain to mark its position on the splines. Normally, the manufacturer will mark the splines with a dot or slash but this isn't always the case.

While there aren't many twin-leading shoe brakes in use these days, there is an off-chance that some of

1 Give everything a good cleaning, preferably over a trash can or something else that'll catch the mung. Resist the temptation to blow the shoes off, as the dust may be contaminated with asbestos, and you really don't need to breathe the stuff.

4 Measure the drum. If it's oversize, it will need replacing (unlikely unless the drum was previously machined or the bike has very high mileage).

2 Clean the drum and give it a light scuffing with a ScotchBrite pad or fine sandpaper if you'd like.

3 Stamped inside the drum will be the maximum drum diameter.

5 Remove any retaining washers.

Replacing Brake Shoes

Remove the shoes, either by lifting them or prying them over the pivot posts.

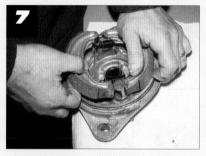

Apply anti-seize to the brake cam and pivot, then install the new shoes.

Install the brake plate into the drum and install the wheel. (A little heavy on the grease there aren't we?)

Adjust the drive chain, tighten the axle, and install a new cotter pin.

Don't forget to tighten the nut on the torque arm and install a cotter pin.

you may own or be restoring a bike that does. When replacing these shoes, or servicing the even rarer four-leading-shoe-type brake (last used around 1972–74), it will be necessary to check the shoe synchronization to ensure that all the shoes contact the drum at the same time. Since each manufacturer uses a different method, you'll need to check the appropriate procedure in your shop manual.

Since many drum brakes are cable operated, some cable inspection and maintenance is required. Inspect the outer cable sheath for tears that could let water in. Small abrasions in the cover can be repaired with electrical or duct tape. Check the cable ends for frays; if the cable has frayed, replace it. Lubricate the cable with a pressure luber before reinstalling it, and don't forget to dab a bit of white grease or anti-seize at the nipple end.

If you really want to do a thorough job, the brake-lever pivot bolts should be removed and given a light coat of grease as well. As an alternative, you can fire a bit of WD-40 or light oil down the pivot to keep things moving smoothly. ∎

DISC BRAKE BASICS

The amount of braking force available depends on the magnitude of force pressing the pads against the discs, the size of the contact area between the brake pads and discs, the distance between the center of the wheel and the center of the brake pads, and on the outside diameter of the tire.

Rectangular brake pads were introduced to increase the area of the pad against the disc. But it was found that these pads do not press against the disc uniformly, so the braking force is not as effective as it could be. Hence, the dual piston caliper was introduced so that a large braking force and uniform pressure against the brake pads is ensured.

Some dual piston calipers have different piston sizes to further balance the braking force across the pad—the trailing piston being larger than the leading piston. Increasing the area of contact between the brake pads and disc increases the braking force. This increased contact means increased heat energy. The increased heat energy requires greater capability for heat dissipation. ∎

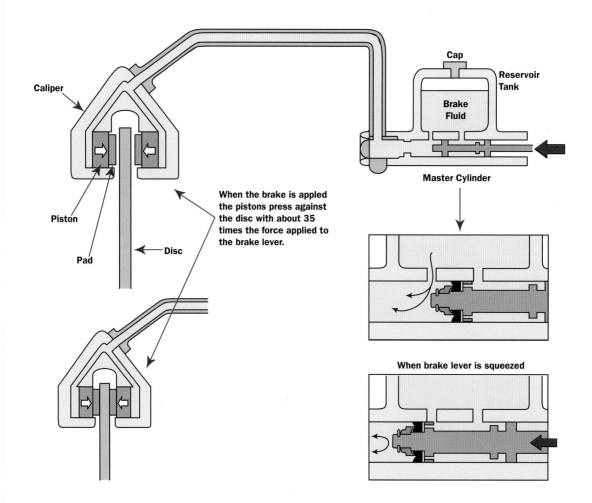

Caliper

Piston

Pad

Disc

When the brake is appled the pistons press against the disc with about 35 times the force applied to the brake lever.

Cap

Reservoir Tank

Brake Fluid

Master Cylinder

When brake lever is squeezed

calipers. If your bike has discs front and rear, it will have a separate master cylinder for each system.

One of two types of brake fluid are used in your brake system: glycol-based (DOT 3 or 4), or silicone-based (DOT 5). Your manual will specify what type of fluid the system is designed to use. Use only that type of fluid.

On older systems, the lines were rubber covered. On many newer systems, they are Teflon covered with a sheath made of braided stainless steel wire. These lines are better at resisting flexing from internal pressure when the brakes are applied, giving more positive braking action.

Calipers come in two basic styles: single-acting and double-acting. Single-acting calipers have a single piston that pushes on the brake disk from one side, whereas double-acting calipers have opposing pistons, which greatly increase the braking power. If your bike was made in the last 20 years, most likely it has double-acting calipers. If not, you might think about upgrading. The best modern calipers have two or three pairs of pistons for really eye-popping stops.

Rotors on early bikes were just solid discs bolted solidly to the wheel. More modern discs are called floating designs. The discs themselves are mounted to the hubs in such a way that the outer part can move a limited amount from side to side to prevent warping. Modern discs are also drilled and/or slotted. This helps keep weight down and allows cooling air to flow through and around the disc. Common rotors are made of cast iron, stamped steel, or stainless steel.

The stopping force of your disc-brake system is governed by several factors: size of and ratio between the master cylinder's piston area and the caliper's (this is known as the hydraulic ratio), by the size of the rotor (the larger the rotor the more leverage the caliper has on the wheel), by the total braking surface contacted by the pad (called the swept area of the brake), and by the coefficient of friction between the pads and rotors.

Anti-Lock Brakes

No discussion of modern brakes would be complete without a discussion of anti-lock brakes. While this is not the prevalent braking system

DIY *Changing Brake Fluid*

Because brake fluid likes to absorb water, it should be changed every two years or so. You could than drain the system and refill it, which as you might guess, would be time consuming and messy. Here's a much simpler method and one that's just as effective. Fasten a hose to the bleed screw, just as you would if you were preparing to bleed the brakes. Go through the pump-and-bleed procedure as if you were bleeding the brake; keep a close eye on the master cylinder, whenever the fluid drops to the add mark, top off the cylinder with fresh fluid. After several cycles of pump and bleed, you should see clean, fresh fluid coming out. Repeat the procedure until only fresh fluid flows. Bingo, you're all done, and your brake fluid is replaced. ■

You'll need:

- *Common tools*
- *A length of hose, preferably clear, that fits your bleed screw,*
- *Container to hold used fluid (the catch can)*
- *Brake fluid*
- *Plenty of clean rags*

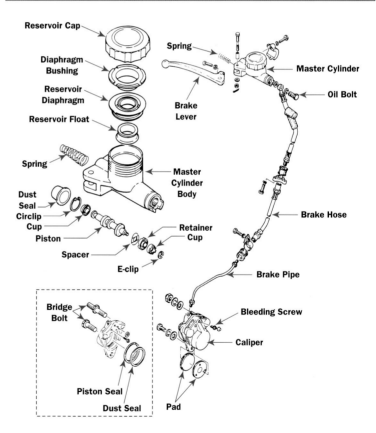

The brake lever and master cylinder are installed on the right side of the handlebar. The caliper assembly, having a pair of pistons and pads, is secured to the front forks. The disc is directly connected to the front hub. The master cylinder is linked to the caliper by means of the brake hose and pipe, through which the brake fluid is forced.
(Courtesy Yamaha Motor Corporation)

DIY *Bleeding Brakes*

You'll need:

- *Common tools*
- *A length of hose, preferably clear, that fits your bleed screw,*
- *Container to hold used fluid (the catch can)*
- *Brake fluid*
- *Plenty of clean rags*
- *Vacuum-pump type brake bleeder (optional)*
- *A helping hand*

Bleeding brakes (or a hydraulic clutch) is nothing more than removing any air bubbles from the hydraulic system. Because air is infinitely compressible, anything stuck inside your brake's hydraulic lines will compromise the ability of the hydraulic fluid to transmit pressure. The worse case being that the air will prevent the brake fluid from doing anything at all.

Depending on the brake system fitted to your bike, the exact procedure may vary. It's best to give your manual a quick read.

The basic principle is that air will become trapped at the highest point of the system. It may also become

trapped in the various nooks and crannies, typically where hoses are routed around the fork tubes, near brake switches and so on.

There are several methods used to bleed brakes. There are also some sophisticated tools that can be purchased, vacuum pumps and pressure bleeders, for example, to make the job easier. In some cases, linked brake systems or those employing ABS, a vacuum pump may be required to bleed the system. If your bike is so equipped, I'd recommend having the system serviced by the dealer, unless of course you're willing to invest in the special tools required.

Normally, brakes will only require bleeding when air has become trapped in the system. Air can enter the system in two ways; Firstly, anytime a major component has been serviced or replaced. Also, if you're an aggressive rider you may be able to get the brake real warm, especially if the fluid is old and has absorbed a

fair amount of water. When the brakes get overly hot the fluid expands, creating gas bubbles, which percolate through the system. After the brakes cool off, the air bubbles remain trapped in the lines; get enough of them in there and the lever goes all mushy. The more water your brake fluid has absorbed, the lower the boiling point; hence, the easier it is to overheat and the more likely it is to need bleeding.

The tried and true method of bleeding goes like this:

Remove the rubber cap from the bleed screw. Attach a piece of hose to the screw. Place the open end of the hose into your catch can. Pour just enough fluid into the catch can to cover the open end of the hose. Assuming the system has fluid in it, top off the master cylinder to the maximum level. Make sure to replace the cap. (If the system is empty, for example if you've changed a hose or replaced a caliper, open the bleed

Select the appropriate brake fluid. When draining the system, I use an old ketchup bottle to hold the used fluid. It's plastic to, avoid breakage, and has a sealable top.

Sometimes a vacuum bleeder is the only way to go.

screw and pump the lever until fluid runs out, then retighten the screw.)

With the bleed screw closed, pump the lever until you feel some resistance. When resistance is felt at the lever, hold it down, as if you were applying the brakes. While holding the lever down, open up the bleed screw. If you're lucky a mix of brake fluid and air bubbles should flow through the hose and into the catch tank. You may find that initially the lever pumps away with no effect whatsoever. That's normal if the system has been completely drained. If that's the case, pump the lever 10–20 times and then open the screw; after a time or two it should start to build pressure.

Close the screw and repeat the process, making sure to check and top off the master cylinder after each pump and bleed session. This can be a long and drawn out procedure; air bubbles have a nasty habit of lodging themselves in every nook and crannie of the brake system. Some mechanics like to "flutter" the lever, that is, pump it rapidly in an attempt to dislodge any air bubbles. Sometimes it works, sometimes it doesn't.

If the system just won't bleed you may need to back flush it. This involves forcing brake fluid into the brake line from the bleed screw end. This requires a special syringe usually sold in auto-parts stores. The syringe works by forcing the fluid into the system under pressure and the air bubbles are pushed upwards toward the master cylinder where they escape into the atmosphere.

Another method requires a vacuum pump to evacuate the brake system. The pump is connected to the open bleed screw, the master cylinder is filled, and the pump activated. As the pump pulls the fluid through the lines, any air is drawn along with it. Most ABS systems require the use of a vacuum pump to bleed them.

Once the lever pressure is nice and firm, tighten up the bleed screw, top off the master cylinder and ride off into the sunset. ∎

DUAL-PISTON CALIPER

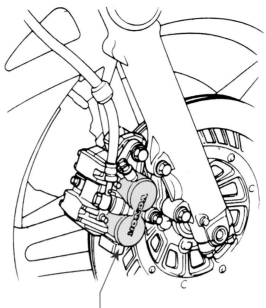

Both pistons located outboard

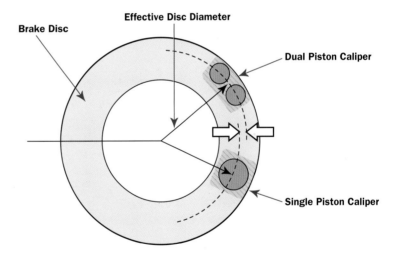

The amount of braking force available depends on the magnitude of force pressing the pads against the discs, the size of the contact area between the brake pads and discs, the distance between the center of the wheel and the center of the brake pads, and the outside diameter of the tire. Rectangular brake pads were introduced to increase the area of the pad against the disc. But it was found that these pads do not press against the disc uniformly, so the braking force is not as effective as it could be. Instead, dual-piston calipers apply uniform pressure against the brake pads and consequently offer superior braking force. Some dual-piston calipers have different piston sizes to further balance the braking force across the pad—the trailing piston being larger than the leading piston. Increased braking force results in increased heat energy, which in turn requires greater capability for heat dissipation.
(Courtesy American Honda Motor Corporation)

DIY   *Installing Braided-Steel Lines*

You'll need:

- *Wrenches*
- *Braided steel lines tp fit the bike*
- *Replacement washers*
- *Teflon paste or tape*

This is a very popular brake system upgrade. Steel-braided lines, which are actually plastic lines covered with a steel or Kevlar cover, are available to fit just about every popular motorcycle made, and some not so popular ones. Additionally, custom lines can be sourced and fitted, if you just can't find what you want.

Installation is quite easy. First drain all the brake fluid from your system. The easiest way is to just bleed the system down until it's empty. Cover and portion off with rags or plas- tic any part of the bike that could be damaged. Remove the old line(s). If banjo fittings are used, re- place the copper or aluminum sealing washers. If the line(s) utilize a screw-in pipe fitting, apply a dab of Teflon paste or a wrap of Teflon tape to the fitting before assembling it. Once the new hose is in- stalled, check for chafe points, pinch points, or any- thing else that might compromise your safety. Once the hose is in place, the system will have to be filled and bled using the standard procedure. ∎

Make sure you have the correct length line and new washers. Start by draining the old fluid.

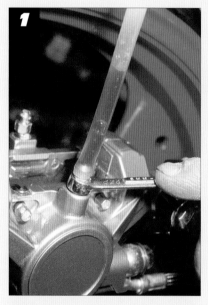

Since this system turned out to be completely contaminated we removed the master cylinder.

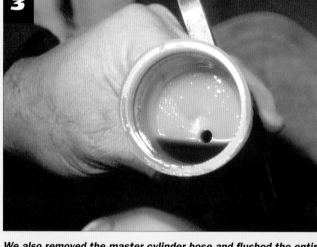

We also removed the master cylinder hose and flushed the entire system.

Install the new hose and don't forget the new sealing washers. Bleed the system as shown previously.

fitted to motorcycles, more and more bikes are now supplied with Anti-lock Brake Systems, or ABS for short. By the way, calling them ABS systems is redundant.

In theory ABS is pretty simple. A small toothed wheel, looking something like a gear, is mounted on one, or often both wheels. A magnetic pickup is positioned so that it counts the teeth on the gear as it goes past. The signal is passed through a small computer, which compares individual wheel speed to the bike's speed. The brake hydraulic system is also connected to the computer through a series of valves that can relieve brake pressure if the computer signals them to. If the wheel speeds vary drastically from either road speed or each other, when the brakes are applied the computer will reduce brake pressure to that wheel or both wheels, if need be, preventing them from locking up.

Due to the requisite electronics, as well as the modification required of the hydraulic system, ABS does add a fair amount of cost to the basic motorcycle. However, the benefits of ABS are indisputable, and in my opinion well worth the additional expenditure.

Integrated Brakes

An integrated brake system is one in which one pedal is used to activate the brakes on both wheels, much like an automotive brake. There are several different systems in use, each differing in detail but substantially the same in theory.

Usually, the rear pedal is used to activate the rear brake and a portion of the front brake. This is accomplished through the use of dedicated hydraulic circuits. For example, one version connects the left front caliper and the rear caliper to the foot brake. Stepping on the brake pedal routes hydraulic pressure to both the rear brake and left front. If you need more front brake pulling, the handlebar lever turns on the right front caliper.

Another system uses calipers with two separate hydraulic circuits. During normal stops engaging the front brake only pumps up the primary circuit of the front caliper. When extra braking force is required, stepping on the foot brake pressures up the rear caliper and the secondary circuit of the front calipers.

The solid disc bolts—or in this case is riveted—directly to the disc carrier. Older discs and carriers are one piece.

Floating discs use buttons between the actual disc and the carrier. The carrier bolts up to the hub, the disc is free to float.

Changing Brake Pads

You'll need:

- *New pads*
- *Brake grease or anti-seize*
- *Thread locking solution*
- *Aerosol brake cleaner*
- *Common hand tools*

Replacing worn-out disc brake pads is one of the easiest maintenance tasks you can perform. Potentially, it's also one of the most dangerous. I can't stress enough how important it is to check and double-check yourself at each step of the operation. While the whole procedure is as straightforward as it seems, I can think of more than one incident when factory racers had the pads drop out on the racetrack. I'll never forget the sight of Kenny Roberts (SR), three-time world 500cc road race champion, wheeling his bike onto the starting grid for the Daytona 200 only to discover that his front brake pads had been installed backward. To say he became a little irate would be a gross understatement.

Most brake pads have some sort of warning line indicating minimum pad thickness marked on their surface. If they don't, your shop manual will provide you with a minimum-thickness dimension.

Take it seriously; if the pads wear to the point that you encounter metal

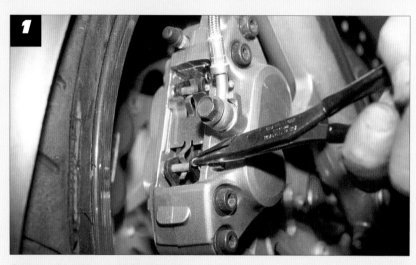

1

Remove the brake retaining pin clips.

2

Remove the pins and anti-rattle springs. Note, the arrow on the stamped steel spring faces up (not all anti-rattle clips will be so marked). Clean the pins until they are bright and shiny.

3

The old pads should slide right out. The pistons will have to be retracted to make room for the new, thicker pads. DO NOT wedge anything between the disc and the piston in an attempt to force the piston back, doing so will likely warp the disc.

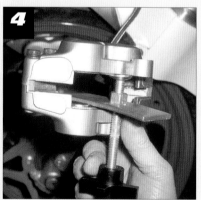

4

Instead, remove the caliper and press the piston back first by inserting the old pads, and then by using a lever between them. The tool shown here is actually a modified automotive tool.

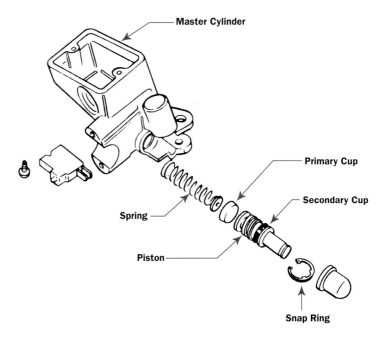

to metal contact, the rotors and possibly the caliper piston will be ruined. As a side note, one indication that your pads have worn to the point of replacement is a drop in the brake fluid level. This happens because as the pads move farther out to compensate for wear, the fluid follows to take up the space. Accordingly, the level drops in the master cylinder. ■

Brake master cylinders are simple, yet highly effective. **(Courtesy American Honda Motor Corporation)**

Insert the new pads.

Reinstall the pins and clips. Don't forget to pump the lever a few times to position the new pads.

The big problem in days past was the need to limit front brake application to prevent wheel lock. Various methods, primarily spring mechanisms on older mechanical systems, and hydraulic valves in the later hydraulic systems, were tried and often found wanting. Modern technology, with computer-controlled ABS shows great promise, and I suspect that fairly soon many more bikes will come equipped with integrated brakes and ABS.

MAINTAINING BRAKES

Without dwelling on the obvious, there are times when your brakes are all that stand between you and utter disaster. Brakes that don't work, fail at inopportune moments (is there ever an opportune moment for brake failure?) or don't work at their full potential can ruin your day, in a very big way. The good news is, that for the most part, brakes are easy to maintain and just as easy to repair, so long as you catch the problem before it catches you.

Maintaining Hydraulics

While hydraulic brakes are by and large trouble free, some periodic maintenance is required. Obviously, anytime you notice a change in braking performance you should inspect and repair as needed. However, a little bit of preventive maintenance should keep those "oh my gawd, she ain't stoppin'" experiences to the minimum.

A quick check for leaks and loose or missing parts should suffice on a weekly basis, perhaps with a more thorough check on a monthly schedule. I'm pretty certain most of you don't bother to inspect your brakes every time you fire up your bike. In fact, you really shouldn't have to. However, a quick tug on the lever to make sure it actually does something never hurts. Likewise,

be on the lookout for chafed hoses and leaks. Generally speaking, when you're washing your bike is as good a time as any to inspect the brakes, after all, you're already down there wiping and polishing. One other thing; never, ever wash down your brakes with a high-pressure stream of water, let alone one of those high-pressure coin-operated washers.

Obligatory Warning

DOT 3 and 4 brake fluid is highly corrosive; it will ruin your paint and can cause grievous

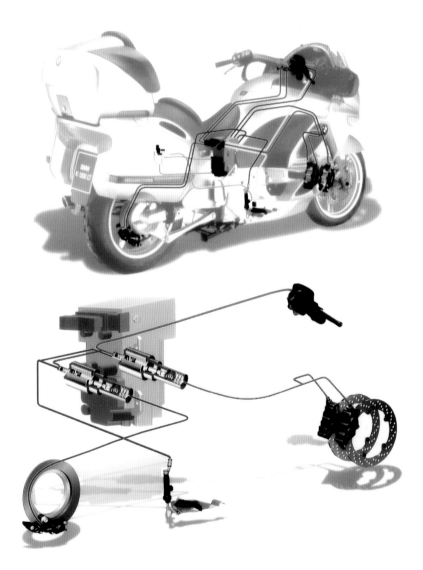

(TOP) BMW incorporates both anti-lock and linked brakes on some of their bikes. The schematic shows the basic layout and sensor positions. (BOTTOM) This illustrates how fluid flows through the BMW integrated brake system. Using the front lever engages both front and rear brakes. Using the pedal activates only the rear. (Courtesy BMW North America)

bodily harm. If any gets on you or your bike wash it off immediately with fresh water. Brake fluid can cause blindness; so anytime you're working with the stuff, please protect your eyes with safety glasses or a clear shield.

Only use the brake fluid recommended for your particular bike. You can upgrade from DOT 3 to DOT 4, but that is it. If the manufacturer specifies a silicone DOT 5, under no circumstances should you use anything else. And never substitute or mix a polyglycol-based fluid with a silicone-based fluid.

REBUILDING CALIPERS

Appropriate Tools

The hardest part of rebuilding the caliper is getting the darned thing apart. Obviously, if it's sticky the piston is most likely frozen into its bore. This may require some special tools or techniques. Once the caliper is apart the cylinder bore may need refinishing. While brake-cylinder hones are inexpensive and easy to use, I'd suggest you have any necessary machine work performed by a brake or automotive machine shop or your local motorcycle shop, at least until you feel comfortable dismantling brake calipers. Other than that, there is nothing special about rebuilding a brake caliper, just the usual warnings to work carefully and safely.

Checking and Changing Brake Lines

The basic problem with rubber hose is that it deteriorates over time, in part due to the constant expansion and contraction of the hose every time the brake is applied. Over time this can give the brake, particularly the front brake, a mushy feel.

Brake lines can't be fixed, so if yours show any cracking or signs of deterioration, you need to replace them. You can replace them with stock lines or upgrade to better lines. We'll cover upgrading in the section on improving brakes.

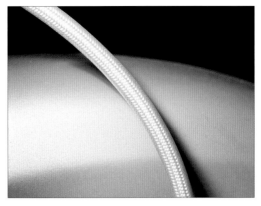

Stainless hoses: a big improvement over the flex-prone, standard-issue rubber hoses.

Brake lines are fastened to their respective components with either a tapered connection, or via a hollow bolt known as a banjo-fitting. Banjo-fittings use soft copper or aluminum washers as seals. Replace these washers every time you remove the fitting.

Most manufacturers recommend periodic replacement of all rubber lines. This has as much to do with liability laws as it does with anything else. That being my opinion, I'd recommend that you inspect the brake lines at least once a month and replace them whenever brake-lever feel becomes objectionably soft.

IMPROVING BRAKES

A popular upgrade is to replace the original and often internally-flexible rubber hose with "stainless steel" lines. This is something of a misnomer as the new lines really aren't made of steel; they couldn't be, as the hose has to flex as the wheel moves with the suspension. In reality, these high-tech brake hoses are plastic inner lines covered with either a stainless-steel braid or Kevlar. Because the rigid, plastic inner liner won't expand like rubber when pressure is applied, the brake has a firmer feel.

Once upon a time I had a very nice BMW R80/7. I bought it new and maintained it like Tammy Faye Bakker maintained her makeup. One fine afternoon I noticed that the steering-head bearings felt a little loose. I kept riding it anyway, planning to adjust them at the next opportunity. I had my steering damper (a BMW option) turned off.

As I descended a steep hill at about 45 to 50 mph, I hit a series of closely-spaced ripples in the road. As soon as the ripples, which were at a slight angle to the road, deflected my front wheel, the handlebars started to oscillate so violently they were literally torn out of my hands. The forks swung from lock to lock with so much force that they broke the steering stop. I was pitched off the bike and landed sitting bolt up-

right in the middle of the road. At that point the bike stopped wobbling and proceeded on its merry way down the road until it ran out of steam and fell over.

While I was recuperating from a broken pelvis I decided to learn as much as possible about frame geometry. And I vowed to never fall behind on my chassis maintenance again.

Speed wobbles and other severe handling ills are rare, especially given a modern bike's high-quality frame and suspension, but they do happen, usually as the result of mechanical neglect. For this reason, you should take your chassis maintenance as seriously as I now do. In this chapter, I'll show you how to keep your chassis in top shape. First, though, let's go through some technical details.

The Harley-Davidson V-Rod has a semi-perimeter steel tube frame. Very trick and well done.

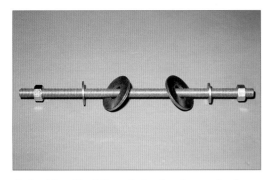

A stout length of threaded rod and some large washers can be used to build a steering head race installation tool.

HOW THE FRAME INFLUENCES HANDLING

Part of the frame's job is to keep the wheels in line, and that includes being able to turn the front one. Another portion of the frame's job is to provide a mounting point for all those little things that make a motorcycle so much fun, like a seat, gas tank, foot rests, and so on. Lastly, the frame provides and accounts for what we call, for lack of a better term, handling.

Handling is a vague concept and can be largely subjective, i.e., if you think your bike handles well, then it does. On the racetrack, handling is quantifiable. Is the rider exhausted from wrestling the bike? Are the tires shredded after three laps? Does the bike look like the world's fastest shopping cart as it wobbles and wallows from pillar to post? If the answer to all of the above is yes, you might have a handling problem. On the street, you're either happy with the way the bike handles or you aren't. Of course, if it goes into a violent wobble every time you change gears, you're probably not too thrilled, but that's an extreme case.

So how does a frame affect the way a bike handles? A frame that flexes excessively is hard to steer, tiring to ride, and can be downright dangerous to ride at higher speeds. By the same token, an overly stiff chassis is hard to ride and hurts traction. As Kevin Cameron points out in his *SuperBike Performance Handbook,* "fork-tube bending, steering-head twist, and swingarm deflection absorb a multitude of small bumps." I would also like to mention that eliminating frame flex can be an expensive and long drawn-

DIY   *Checking Steering-Head Bearings*

Begin your front-end inspection by placing the bike on its stand, or a work stand, so that the front fork is free to pivot.

Hold the bars in the straight-ahead position, and then turn them slowly from side to side. The front end should turn smoothly with equal effort. There shouldn't be any drag, roughness, or notches. If a slight drag is felt, check your cable routing and wiring harness before making any adjustments. A binding cable, or stiff wiring harness that prevents the fork from rotating freely can sometimes mimic a tight steering-head bearing.

If you felt a notch or general roughness during your initial inspection, the bearings should be replaced. As mentioned, steering-head bearings that are worn out often develop a detent or notch in the straight-ahead position that you can easily feel when you start to rotate the bars to either side. At that point, the bearings are done, shot, kaput. Riding the bike in that condition can be lethal. The only cure is to replace the steering-head bearings, and yes, that means both the top and bottom bearings as a set. If nothing untoward is felt, we can move to phase two. But be forewarned, if the bearings have been allowed to become loose, the pounding that occurs during normal riding may have dented them. If that's the case, you'll have to adjust the bearings before you can determine if they are good or bad.

Grasp the front fork by the axle, pull the fork toward you. Be careful! The objective here is to determine if the fork bearings have become so loose they've developed play, not to knock the bike over. Now try pushing away from you, no play should be felt. If movement is felt, the steering stem bearings are overly loose and need immediate adjustment. ∎

Checking steering-head bearings takes less than a minute. Block the motorcycle's front end up off the ground. Grasp the forks as low as possible and try to move them forward and backward. If any perceptible play is felt, or if the turning torque is not within specifications (your manual will provide them), the steering head bearings will need adjustment.

LOAD-BEARING CHARACTERISTICS OF TUBING

Modern frames are normally composed of several different types of tubing, each with unique load bearing characteristics. Note how this Honda sportbike frame makes use of the different types of tubing to create a very light, flex free chassis. ■

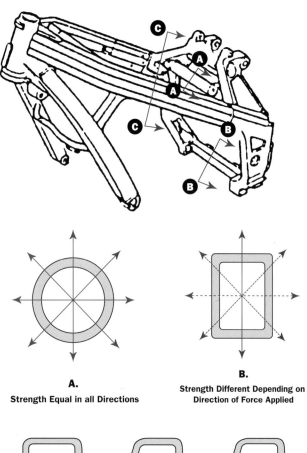

A.
Strength Equal in all Directions

B.
Strength Different Depending on Direction of Force Applied

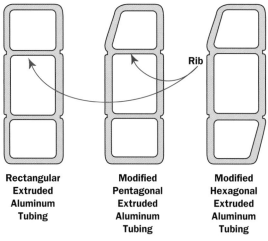

Rib

Rectangular Extruded Aluminum Tubing

Modified Pentagonal Extruded Aluminum Tubing

Modified Hexagonal Extruded Aluminum Tubing

C.

out proposition, and may or may not result in any concrete improvements.

Assuming the frame is built from quality materials, properly designed, and hasn't been twisted out of shape due to an accident, the handling qualities are influenced to a large degree by its basic geometry: the steering head position, wheel base, and swingarm length. Other influences include the suspension settings, overall quality of the suspension, tire condition and pressure, overall mechanical condition, and suitability of the various components that hold the frame and suspension together.

THE MOTORCYCLE FRAME

One of a motorcycle frame's primary functions is to keep the wheels in line. If the frame flexes excessively, it changes the motorcycle from a single-track vehicle to a double-track vehicle, and a double-track vehicle needs at least four wheels to work with any degree of stability. Get the picture? You want it to be rigid.

Frame design and the material used to construct the frame have great influences on frame rigidity. The aluminum spar chassis, common to many high-end sportbikes, is extremely rigid, as is the multi-tube, "bird-cage" space frame favored by Ducati.

Tubing diameter and shape also affect a frame's rigidity. For instance, a large, thin-wall oval tube is stronger and less likely to flex than a round, thick tube of the same diameter. This type of oval-tube frame is currently flaunted on Harley-Davidson's new V-Rod.

Braces and gussets are used to enhance a frame's strength as well; these are often placed at crucial joints to prevent any undue flexing. Frame flex can occur at any point, although the two most common spots are the swingarm pivot and the steering head.

The swingarm flexes because drive-chain pull is always to one side. As torque is applied through the chain, the rear wheel and swingarm are pulled toward the drive side. This is one reason race bikes carry lots of bracing around the swingarm pivot. Conversely, when that torque is removed the swingarm unwinds and returns to the relaxed position. The rear wheel itself also tries to twist the swingarm through side loads

Adjusting Steering-Head Bearings

Most steering-stem adjusters use a castellated nut to adjust bearing preload. These nuts have no flats on them, only slots, hence the need for a special tool. These can be purchased through most motorcycle shops, or a long, thin punch and hammer can be substituted. Follow your shop manual's exact procedure for steering-head adjustment.

Basically it'll go like this; with the front end off the ground, loosen up the fork-tube pinch bolts, loosen the steering-stem locknut. Use the pin spanner to turn the castellated adjuster nut to remove the play. In some cases, apply a slight preload to the steering-stem bearings. Retighten the lock nut and pinch bolts. It sounds easy, and it is for the most part. What gets the novice in trouble is knowing how much preload to apply. The short answer is very little; too much preload is as bad, in fact worse, than not enough. It's easy to put several tons of pressure on the bearing with just a slight twist of the adjuster. Excess steering-head bearing preload will make the bike feel heavy at low speeds and hard to ride in a straight line. It will also ruin the bearings in short order. When in doubt, it's better to leave the bearing preload a little on the loose side.

Occasionally, the manual may specify a fork-rotational preload torque. This means that they want it to take a certain amount of torque to turn the fork. It will also mean a few special tools are needed. A socket or more likely some sort of special adapter is placed on the steering stem nut. A torque wrench is then used to turn the front end. You can read the amount of force needed to rotate the front end directly from the torque wrench, and then adjust the bearings accordingly. This torque setting is crucial; if it's off, the bike's handling will never be up to par. If you don't want to acquire the special tools, have your dealer perform this adjustment.

When the steering-head bearings are correctly adjusted, the fork should swing from side to side without much effort. Here's an easy way to check preload. With the front wheel clear of the ground, hold the handlebars in the straight ahead position. They should remain there, or at most fall gently to one side. If it only takes a slight nudge to get them moving, chances are the adjustment is pretty close. If you've got to give them a shove, they are probably too tight. If so, readjust them, and test again. As I said, when in doubt, it's better to leave the bearing preload a little on the loose side. ■

The forks should turn smoothly from side to side, if any rough spots or dents are felt, the bearings will need replacement.

> **You'll need:**
> - *Shop manual*
> - *Wrenches or sockets to fit your fork-pinch bolts and steering-stem nut*
> - *Torque wrench*
> - *Pin Spanner wrench, often called a hook wrench.*

imposed by cornering stresses and the action of the suspension. As rims and tires have increased in size the swingarm has required more and more bracing.

At the front, the fork imposes torque loading in both directions. Normal fork movement causes the fork to push the upper steering-head bearing backward and pull the lower one forward. When the bike turns, the fork tries to rotate the steering head at right angles to the frame.

TRIANGULATION

The most popular motorcycle frame is composed of tubing, and there are two basic ways to build tubular motorcycle frames. The first is through triangulation: if you want to build something

WHY MOTORCYCLES GO AROUND TURNS

How does a motorcycle go around corners? It's an oft-asked question, and probably one of the least understood physical concepts in motorcycling.

At very low speeds, it is the rider's skill, or lack thereof, that determines whether or not the bike stays on its wheels. However, the faster we go the easier it gets, at least to a point.

Why? In a word, gyroscopes. Remember those little gyroscopes you played with as a kid? As long as they spun merrily along, they'd balance on their own; as they slowed down, they'd get a little wobbly until eventually they'd just tip over. Motorcycles behave in exactly the same way—as a matter of fact, so do most of their riders.

The motorcycle's wheels are, in effect, large gyroscopes. The engine crankshaft, transmission shafts, and clutch also act as gyros to a lesser degree, and like the wheels also contribute to the motorcycle's overall stability. In fact, anything that spins acts to a greater or lesser degree as a gyroscope. Now, having all of these gyroscopes spinning merrily along is what gives a motorcycle its ability to sustain itself in an upright position. Conversely, it's also what gives the motorcycle the ability to navigate turns. That may seem a bit contradictory, and understandably somewhat confusing.

GYROSCOPIC PRECESSION

If the spinning wheel (gyro) contributes so much to straight-line stability, how on earth can it make the motorcycle turn?

A spinning gyroscope when tilted to the left will turn instantly to the left. However, if that same spinning gyroscope were to be rotated around its axis to the left it would actually tilt toward the right. This phenomenon is known as gyroscopic precession.

The best way to demonstrate gyroscopic precession is with an ordinary bicycle wheel. Hold the wheel in front of you and have someone give it a good spin. Spin the wheel away from you. First try tilting the wheel to the left, as if you were leaning your bike into a left-hand turn. The wheel will turn sharply to the left. Now repeat the experiment, friend willing, but this time turn the wheel to the left (without tilting it). The wheel will now lean to the right.

Initiating the Turn

The turning maneuver—that is to say, the initiation of the turn—is controlled by gyroscopic precession. Motorcycles are turned by a combination of banking and countersteering.

Here we are riding off into the sunset. Uh-oh, left turn and a rather sharp one at that. If we turned the wheel in the direction of the turn, gyroscopic precession would cause the bike and its soon-to-be very unhappy rider to be flung (violently) toward the outside of the turn. Conversely, if we steer the bike away from the turn, gyroscopic force will bank the bike into the turn. That's countersteering in a nutshell.

Please don't conclude that this must be a violent maneuver; on the racetrack, yes, it can and sometimes is. On the street, though, countersteering can and should be so subtle as to be almost unnoticeable.

A gentle push on the left handle bar will be all it takes to turn the front wheel to the right. As the front wheel turns slightly toward the right, gyroscopic and centrifugal forces will make the bike turn in the opposite direction. Remember, pushing the left handlebar has the same effect as pulling on the right; the wheel will deflect right and the end result will be a left-hand turn.

Bank and Turn

There are two methods of steering a motorcycle through a turn: banking, or leaning the bike, and countersteering. In reality, an experienced rider combines both methods (subconsciously) into one smooth and fluid action. Unfortunately, there is no cut-and-dry formula for turning a motorcycle. Your own riding style and the circumstances under which you ride will determine how you combine banking and countersteering to get through a given turn. ∎

A spinning bicycle wheel can be used to demonstrate gyroscopic precession.

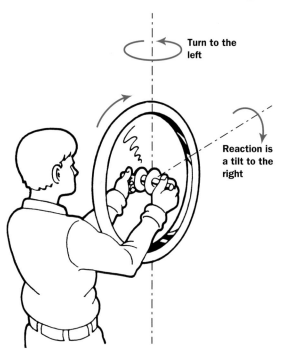

Turn to the left

Reaction is a tilt to the right

that's light, strong, and structurally sound, then a triangle is hard to beat.

The other method of stitching a tube frame together involves using a large diameter tube or tubes to carry the burden. The tube(s) are normally linked to the engine and rear suspension through a series of smaller diameter tubing.

FRAME TYPES

Single Cradle (Single Downtube)

Single-cradle frames have one main backbone above the engine and one down tube in front of the engine. The frame surrounds the engine, a subframe extends rearward to hold the seat and rear suspension. Single-cradle frames are used for off-road bikes and middleweight street bikes. They are easy to build, quite durable, and are usually constructed of mild steel, although aluminum is often used to build off-road frames.

Double Cradle (Double Downtube)

The double-cradle frame is similar to the single-cradle design, except that it uses twin downtubes and twin toptubes; although there are some variations that use a double downtube and single top tube. Doubling up the tubes increases chassis rigidity and also allows the use of a wider engine. Occasionally, a double downtube is incorporated into a frame to facilitate mounting an exhaust system that wouldn't clear a single, centrally placed downtube. Double-downtube frames are used primarily on large-displacement street bikes. Often, one of the downtubes unbolts to ease engine removal.

Stressed Engine

Using the engine as part of the frame is a wonderful, simple idea that works exceptionally well; aluminum engine and gearbox castings are remarkably rigid. By using the engine as part of the frame, you can save lots of weight and build a very strong chassis. To some degree, the engine plays a stiffening role in every chassis. However, when taken to the logical extreme, such as the late model BMW R series, the engine actually becomes the chassis. Sub-assemblies bolted to the engine/gearbox hold the fork and rear suspension, as well as the seat and tank, but there is no true chassis as such.

The Ducati triangulation concept may seem a bit dated compared to some of the other sportbike frames, but rest assured, it works just fine. (Courtesy Ducati North America)

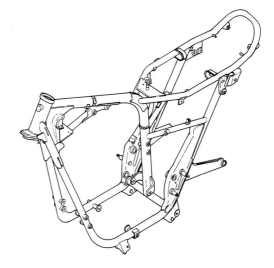

This older, welded steel double-cradle frame was labor intensive to build and heavy by modern standards. However, it was strong, rigid, and able to withstand the heavy vibrations of its parallel twin engine.

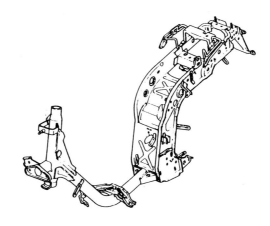

The backbone frame is made with a combination of pressed steel and steel tubing, and can be found mainly on scooters and some of Honda's early motorcycle designs. Backbone construction allows added freedom in the overall design of the vehicle and relatively economical production. (Courtesy American Honda Motor Corporation)

DIY *Replacing Steering-Head Bearings*

You'll need:

- Common hand tools
- Splitter
- Bearing extractor
- Wrenches and sockets for fork-pinch bolts, axle nut, and steering-stem nut
- Torque wrench
- Pin-spanner wrench
- Hi-temp wheel-bearing grease
- Clean rags
- Shop manual
- Dedicated bearing-removal tool
- Long brass drift, or bearing drift
- Bearing-installation tool
- Brass hammer

Despite your best maintenance efforts, steering-head bearings may occasionally need replacing.

Clearly, bikes that see lots of hard use are going to pound the daylights out of the bearings. Off-road and dual-sportbikes are particularly bad in this respect. The combination of hard off-road use, wheelies, and high-pressure car-wash spray washing takes its toll. Guys that like to do lots of wheelies on their muscle bikes will also get to replace their share of steering-head bearings.

Most post-1980 motorcycles have tapered-style steering-head bearings. Many pre-1980 motorcycles have loose-ball-style bearings. Just because your bike came with uncaged steering-head bearings, doesn't necessarily mean you have to replace the worn out ones with the same dated type of bearing. There are conversion kits available for many older bikes that allow the fitting of tapered-roller bearings. Tapered-roller bearings in the steering head will improve handling and withstand a lot more abuse. They may even be cheaper, or at least no more expensive than the races and uncaged balls they replace. If you're replacing the steering-head bearings on your older bike, it's worth checking into.

The procedure for repacking and replacing the bearings is essentially one and the same, so we'll treat it as such.

Note: Bearing removal tools can be quite expensive, and in most cases a brass drift works just as well. However, there is a tool commonly called a race or bearing drift. These are specially shaped punches used to remove bearing races. You'll be able to find them, or at least order them, through tool distributors or auto-parts stores.

Follow your manual's instruction for steering-stem removal. Once the stem is removed, use the bearing-removal tool or work your bearing drift around the perimeter of the lower frame race. (If you're only going to repack the bearings, there is no need to remove either frame race.) Then, remove the upper race in the same manner. The lower bearing should next be removed from the steering stem itself using the splitter or bearing-removal tool. Lacking those, you can often use two tire irons or a pry bar to remove the bearing from the

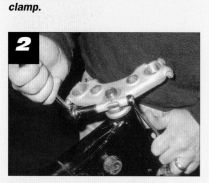

Remove the nut that secures the top clamp.

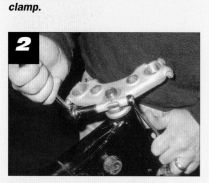

Remove the pinch bolt. Most, but not all bikes, will have some sort of top clamp pinch bolt.

Remove the bearing preload adjusting nut.

If you don't have the correct tool, you can use a punch.

Support the steering stem so that it doesn't drop out.

DIY   *Replacing Steering-Head Bearings*

6

The top balls can be retrieved with a magnet if you don't want to pick them out of the grease by hand.

8

You should end up with the upper and lower outer bearing races, the upper and lower inner races, and in this case 36 loose balls (not shown). If this fork used tapered roller bearings you'd have the outer races and the two tapered bearings.

10

Warm up the bottom inner race as shown.

7

Use a long punch to drive out the lower bearing race.

9

The bottom race is driven using a well-fitting socket or bearing driver.

11

Slide on any dust seals, and then drive the race onto the steering stem. The pipe should locate on the inner lip of the race.

stem. If it just won't budge, resist the effort to drive it off with a chisel or other blunt object. It can be done, but it takes an experienced hand. Better to take it to an automotive machine shop, or other specialist.

Take a moment to examine the old parts. Those dark spots in the races are the dents; if they are deep

enough, you'll be able to feel them with your finger.

If your steering head has tapered-roller bearings, reassemble as follows. If it has loose ball bearings, skip down two paragraphs. Install a new dust seal on the lower stem; this seal protects the bearings from dirt and water. They're cheap, so it's

false economy to try and reuse them. Pack both bearings full of high-quality, waterproof grease (see the appendix for the right way to pack a bearing). The new bearing should then be pressed into place on the stem. To avoid damaging the new bearing, press only on the bearing's inner

(continued next page)

DIY *Replacing Steering-Head Bearings*

Pack the upper race with a stiff wheel bearing grease.

Then insert the correct number of ball bearings. If you're installing tapered bearings, pack the race with grease and pack the bearing itself as described in Chapter 14.

Insert the upper, inner bearing race then pack the lower inner race with grease.

Place the balls on the inner race and pack the bottom race with grease.

Carefully insert the steering stem.

Install the adjuster and snug it down to seat the bearings, then back it off completely and retighten it only enough to remove any play plus 1/8th of a turn.

Install the top clamp and run the nut down until it bottoms.

race. A piece of pipe of the correct diameter, cut to length, works just fine.

To install the outer races into the frame you can use one of several methods. The easiest is to use a dedicated bearing installer, but there are alternatives. Usually, you can tap them into place using a pipe or large socket that rests squarely on their outer edge. Be extremely careful to drive the race in squarely and to avoid nicking the working surface. It will help if the races are placed in the freezer overnight to cool and shrink them. If you feel ambitious, a draw-bolt tool can be constructed from a length of heavy-threaded rod and two large washers or plates. By tightening the bolt, the tool will pull the races squarely into place.

Install the lower stem into the frame, followed by the upper bearing and its hardware. The bearing should be preloaded slightly to seat it, then back it off and re-adjust to specifications. It's normal for new bearings to loosen up and require readjustment after a few hundred miles.

If your steering head has loose ball bearings, proceed as follows. Your shop manual will tell you how many balls go in each race. Normally, both races take an equal number, but there are some exceptions. The races are installed and replaced in the same manner as for the tapered-style bearing.

Once the races are in place, the outer races should be packed full of grease. The balls are then placed into the races, the grease holding them firmly in place. Place only the specified number of balls into each race. It may look like there is room for one more, but trust me there isn't. Adding an extra bearing will prevent the balls from rolling, or skidding in the races, which will ruin them in short order.

Once the bearings are in place gently slide the steering stem into place and reassemble. ∎

DIY *Replacing Steering-Head Bearings*

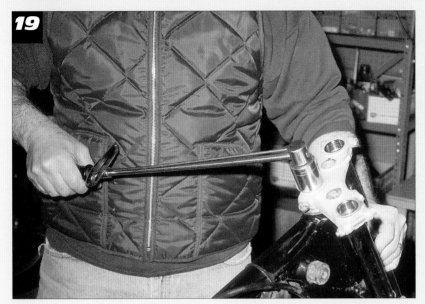
Torque the top nut down to specification and then torque the pinch bolts.

Once the rest of the front end is installed, check the bearing preload and readjust as required.

Spine or Beam Frames (Backbone)

These frames are used primarily on mopeds and other small displacement bikes. Spine or backbone frames, as they are sometimes called, are ordinarily built of steel pressings or steel tubing welded together. They are inexpensive to produce and work well enough when power outputs are moderate.

Ironically, while most backbone frames are used on small utility bikes, there have been some outstanding Grand Prix race bikes that used the design. A German concern, NSU, used a very advanced backbone frame to win a 250cc World Championship or two in the 1950s.

Diamond Frames

This hoary design is still used to build small-displacement motorcycles, and they are still built the same way they were way back when. A single downtube hangs from the steering head, but isn't connected to the rest of the frame. The engine fills the gap and provides the requisite frame strength.

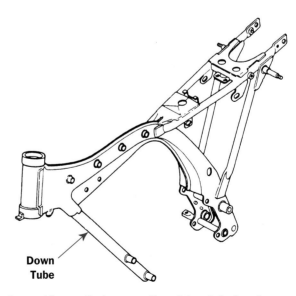

Down Tube

In a diamond frame, the lower section of downtube is not connected with other frame tubes. Instead, the engine forms the final portion of the frame structure and generates the frame strength. The diamond frame is used mainly on small and middle-size vehicles due to the simplicity of its structure and its light weight and excellent serviceability. (Courtesy American Honda Motor Coroporation

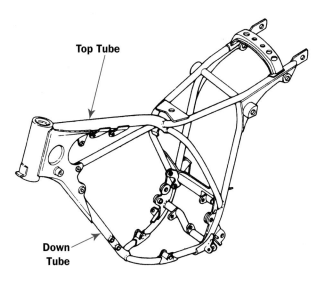

The single-cradle frame has one downtube and one top tube at the front of the engine. The frame's structural material surrounds the engine. This frame is mainly fitted to off-road vehicles and middle-sized, street-going sport models due to its light weight, durability, and ease of serviceability.
(Courtesy American Honda Motor Corporation)

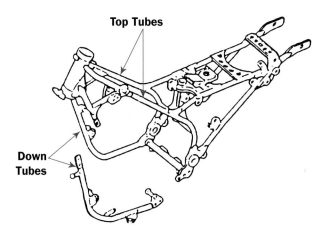

The double-cradle design is similar to the single-cradle frame, but has two downtubes and top tubes, resulting in increased rigidity. A part of the downtube can be removed to facilitate engine removal on some models. This frame is mainly used on large displacement street motorcycles.
(Courtesy American Honda Motor Corporation)

These frames are used on small and mid-weight motorcycles. They are light, provide excellent serviceability, and are simple to design and to build.

Twin-Spar Aluminum Frames (Twin-Spar Beam)

A direct outgrowth of Grand Prix motorcycle racing, the twin-beam chassis uses massive extruded aluminum beams, or spars, to construct a solid and awesomely rigid chassis. Two beams are joined at the steering head and then extended rearward to form a mount for the swingarm (a variation of this frame uses the engine to mount the swingarm). The engine is firmly bolted into the frame and used as a stressed member.

RAKE AND TRAIL

Rake and trail go together like bacon and eggs; while it's possible to have one without the other, it's not nearly so much fun as combining them. For the most part, rake (sometimes referred to as steering-head inclination) and trail (which might be called castor) are to a large degree responsible for how our motorcycles steer, turn, handle, and maintain stability in a straight line. While most riders are familiar with the terms rake and trail, few of us can give a complete and coherent definition of either term.

Rake

Rake may be called steering-head inclination, steering-head angle or steering-axis inclination. It's all the same. Rake is the rearward inclination of the steering head (the part of the frame where the front forks mount) as measured from the vertical. The rake angle and the angle of the front fork tubes are usually identical. I say usually because there are a few instances where the steering-head angle and the fork-tube angle are different. However, these are special circumstances and, for the most part, outside the parameters of normal use. Most street bikes have a rake angle of somewhere between 24 and 36 degrees depending on their intended purpose.

Trail

If you follow the rake angle to its ultimate conclusion, you'll see that a line drawn through the center of the steering stem (the steering axis) will contact the ground somewhere in front of the tire's contact patch. Imagine a second line drawn vertically through the center of the front wheel's axis (at 90 degrees from the road surface). The distance between the point where the rake line

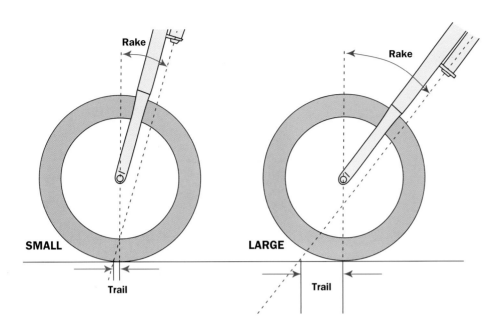

Rake is the rearward inclination of the steering head. Trail is the distance between where the steering axis hits the ground and the center of the tire's contact patch. The smaller the trail dimension, the quicker and easier the bike will steer. Larger trail dimensions slow steering, but improve high-speed stability.

hits the pavement, and the line drawn through the center of the contact patch, is known as trail. In other words, trail is the distance by which the center of the tire's contact patch trails behind the point where the steering axis (which is the equivalent center of the rake angle) contacts the road.

While initial trail dimensions are a result of the rake angle, the final trail settings can be modified quite easily to fine-tune a motorcycle's handling characteristics. Trail is affected by offsetting the fork tubes from the steering stem, or by the position of the front axle. Fork tubes set in the same plane as the steering stem are known as zero offset forks or clamps. Usually the fork tubes are set somewhere forward of the stem and are described as 10mm offset, 25mm offset, and so on. By moving the tire's contact patch forward or backward, relative to the steering stem, we can change the amount of trail.

Occasionally, you'll see a "leading" or "trailing" axle. These designs position the axle in front of or behind the fork tube, respectively. Seventies BMWs are good examples of a leading axle design. While some manufacturers opt to use a leading- or trailing-axle fork to modify trail dimensions, there are a quite a few that mount the axle to one side of the fork for more mundane

The offset front axle is typical of modern off road bikes. Imagine how much taller this bike would be if the axle were positioned beneath the fork.

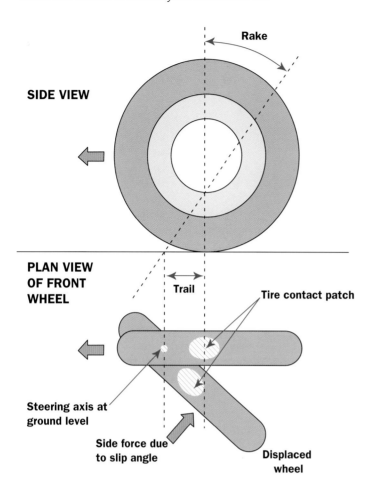

SIDE VIEW

Rake

PLAN VIEW OF FRONT WHEEL

Trail

Tire contact patch

Steering axis at ground level

Side force due to slip angle

Displaced wheel

This illustrates how trail acts as a lever to return the wheel to the straight-ahead position after it has been displaced.

DIY Checking Linkages

Due to the profusion of links and bushings, linkage-type systems can be a little tricky to check, but you should check them anyway at the interval specified in your manual, or whenever servicing the drive chain or rear suspension. First, jack up and support the bike so that all weight is off the rear wheel and suspension. Next, gently lift up on the wheel and feel for any play in the bushings and bearings. You'll feel it as any slight movement of the swingarm or linkages before you feel resistance from the suspension. If there is any play, replace all of the linkage bearings, grease seals, and bushings. You can safely assume that if one has worn out, the rest are soon to follow. My recommendation is to replace all of the bushings and/or bearings at the same time. ∎

reasons. By positioning the axle on the face of the fork tube, rather than below it, the designer can use a long travel fork, without compromising the ride height. In some cases there are three inches or more of fork tube below the front axle, making room for long springs, damper rods, and adjusters. Imagine how tall those bikes would need to be if we always placed the axle beneath the fork.

HOW RAKE AND TRAIL WORK

Trail

The primary purpose of trail is to keep your motorcycle pointed in the right direction and to return it to the straight and narrow when some outside force decides to try and rearrange your travel plans. In essence, the purpose of trail is to provide a degree of straight-line stability and to restore that stability if it's interrupted.

How Trail Affects Steering

Underway, the proportion of the motorcycle's weight carried by the steering head is conducted to the ground through the front tire's contact patch. The weight tends to increase during cornering due to centrifugal force. The weight and resultant centrifugal force also have a tendency to try to turn the steering head to its lowest position. Rake and wheel diameter, as well as trail, affects this angle.

Since we have positive trail, the overall effect is to turn the motorcycle into the corner. In sum, trail (or more correctly the amount of trail designed into a motorcycle) will affect how much torque the rider must apply to turn the motorcycle, as well as how much effort it will take to hold the motorcycle on its chosen path.

The shorter the trail, the quicker the motorcycle will steer. Normally, sportbikes carry very little trail. They steer quickly but are said to be "darty." They may also sacrifice some straight-line, high-speed stability. Touring bikes generally have plenty of trail, they are stable, and relaxing to ride, but most steer slowly and take a fair amount of effort to turn.

Straight-line feel is also dependent on trail. Even in a straight line we are constantly making small steering corrections. As we saw back-and-forth on the handlebars, the front wheel is dis-

DIV Checking & Adjusting Swingarm Bearings

Grease, grease, and more grease. That's the secret to keeping your swingarm bushings and bearings alive and well. Modern linkage suspensions use lots of little needle bearings and bushings, all of which live in close proximity to the rear wheel, right where they can get a nice blast of water, grit, and dirt. If you lube those bearings and bushings every time you change the oil, they should last a reasonable amount of time. If you don't, well I suppose you'll learn how to replace them.

Here's how you check the swingarm bearings. First, block the bike up so that the rear wheel and swingarm hang unsupported. If the bike is equipped with a centerstand, this won't present any problems. If the bike doesn't have one, you'll need to jack the bike clear off the ground. All weight must be removed from the rear wheel and suspension.

Grasp the rear wheel and try to wiggle it from side to side, parallel to the ground. If movement is detected, the swingarm bearings are shot or need adjustment. Swingarm bearings on most motorcycles are non-adjustable, though, and will have to be replaced. If yours are adjustable, consult your manual for the exact method.

To replace the bearings, you'll need to first remove the rear wheel and suspension from the bike, as well as anything else in the way. Then press or drive out the old bearings or bushings. Install the new ones as shown below.

Note: disconnecting the shocks and chain will make any play much more obvious, although if the bushings are truly worn out you should be able to feel it with everything still connected. ∎

You'll need:

- *Common hand tools*
- *Large hammer*
- *Bushing drive kit*
- *Torque wrench*
- *Grease gun*
- *Clean rags*
- *Shop manual*

A bushing driver set will make removal and replacement that much easier. Remove the swing arm according to the shop manual instructions and thoroughly clean it.

Using a wooden box to support the swing arm, a length of steel rod can be used to drive out the old bearings. After the bearings are removed, clean and de-burr the area and then coat with anti-seize or white grease.

The bushing driver locates only against the bearing's outer race, preventing damage to the bearing surface.

Carefully drive the new bearing in until it's flush with the surface or seated against an inner shoulder, according to the service manual.

Give the inner axle or pivot a good coating of high-pressure grease before assembly.

placed, creating a corresponding restoring force or torque. This restoring torque is dependent on surface adhesion (grip), tire design, and trail.

Obviously, any steering input we receive is relayed from the road surface, up through the tire, and to the handlebar. What we do with it is up to us. As a rule of thumb, lots of trail will reduce the feedback, while in many cases short trail tends to provide more information than we can process.

Usually, some other force comes into play; an out-of-balance front tire, loose steering-head bearings, or too much luggage carried too high and too far toward the rear of the bike are all likely culprits. How do you avoid it? First, keep your bike in good mechanical repair, pack sensibly, and install a steering damper. Those are the practical solutions. In theory, you could also reduce trail, stiffen the frame, or reduce the mass of the front-fork assembly.

Rake

Way back, when the velocipede was the hot set-up for adventurous young men, some budding

Some very bright people have spent years trying to find a replacement for the telescopic front fork. By and large their efforts have not been well received. **(Courtesy Tony Foale)**

rocket scientist realized that by inclining, or raking, the fork backward the effect of trail could be enhanced to the point where the velocipede would become fairly stable at moderate speeds. In fact, it could be ridden with no hands, which must have impressed the lovelies of the day to no end.

As rake is increased, the effect of trail decreases (even as the trail dimension increases). That's why a designer will add trail as he adds rake. Cruiser bikes with their front ends raked way out in front of the frame typically have correspondingly-increased trail. Decrease the rake for a given amount of trail, and trail-induced instability can become a problem. So, if we increase the rake, do we increase high-speed stability? Absolutely.

At the opposite end of the spectrum, experiments by noted frame builder Tony Foale have proven many times that zero degree rake works as well, if not better, than the traditional values, provided that trail is adjusted. In fact, Foale noted that fork stiction decreased, brake dive was eliminated, and low-speed maneuverability was enhanced.

Other benefits included a constant steering-head height and zero-degree camber change as the bike was banked. In the real world, rake angles run from an extreme of around 21 degrees, found on roadracers and pure sportbikes, to about 36 degrees, found on cruiser-style or custom bikes.

By now you should have a basic understanding of what rake and trail are all about and how they interact. You should also understand why a sportbike has a steering-head angle of maybe 22 or 23 degrees and a trail measurement of perhaps 4.75 inches, while a cruiser carries maybe a 33-degree steering-head angle and around 6 inches of trail.

Let's sum it all up; rake and trail are inherently connected. A change in one demands and creates a need for a change in the other. Rake can only be changed by moving the steering head or by changing the position of the forks relative to the steering head. Trail can be changed by offsetting the front axle or by using a set of triple clamps to relocate the fork tubes either closer or farther from the steering stem. Changing rear

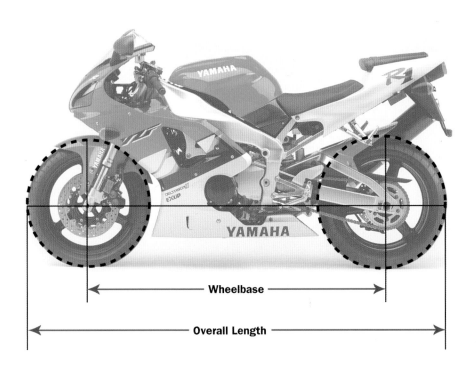

Wheelbase is the distance between the center of the wheels' contact patches. (Courtesy Yamaha Motor Corporation)

Wheelbase

Overall Length

suspension or front suspension lengths will also affect both rake and trail. To make a bike steer quicker, simply install longer rear shocks or slide the fork tubes up in the clamps; this reduces rake. To slow down the steering, shorten the shocks or drop the fork tubes; this increases rake.

The Bottom Line

Bikes that prize quick steering and maneuverability over ocean liner-like stability will have steep rake angles and short trail, and vice versa.

As long as motorcycles have forks and wheels, rake and trail will be discussed, modified, and argued over. Obviously, rake and trail, while at the top of the frame geometry list, are by no means the entire list.

WHEELBASE

Wheelbase is defined as the distance between the wheel centers. As a rule of thumb, the longer the wheelbase, the more stable the motorcycle as a whole and the more resistant to changes in direction. The longer the wheelbase, the farther the front wheel needs to be turned to traverse a given bend and the more effort you will need to turn the bike as well. As a bonus, things that go bump in the road will have less effect on stability. A long wheelbase also diminishes the effects of

weight transfer under braking and acceleration. Short-wheelbase motorcycles tend to be very nimble, but can exhibit a degree of instability at high speed. Again, there is always a trade-off.

MAINTAINING THE CHASSIS

Frame maintenance is one of those things that few of us ever think about. After all, what kind of maintenance do a few hunks of welded pipe need? Truthfully, not much, but it's absolutely critical that you maintain those parts that need it.

Periodic Checks

Your shop manual will provide a list of all the fasteners and their torque settings. At least once a year, go over the entire bike and check the torque on every major and minor bolt. This includes the engine mounting bolts, the swingarm and suspension-linkage bolts, and the mundane stuff like the handlebar clamps. You'll be appalled at how much stuff has worked its way loose. The whole job, start to finish, should take less than 15 minutes. I generally perform this job whenever I do a major service on my bike.

All front forks, except BMW's Telelever design, pivot on either tapered roller bearings, caged ball-bearings, or loose, uncaged ball-bearings. Both bearing designs use a hardened-steel

DIY **Bolt Checking**

You'll need:

- Torque wrench
- Torque settings (service manual)
- Sockets
- Socket extension

Vibration from normal operation can loosen fasteners over time. You'll want to regularly check to make sure all the fasteners on your bike are appropriately tight.

I recommend going over the entire motorcycle and checking the torque on each bolt—from all-important engine mounting bolts and handlebar clamps, to minor bolts that hold bodywork in place—at least once a year.

Do this as part of a major service and, depending on the type of bike, it shouldn't take more than 15 minutes to complete. ∎

When checking to make sure bolts are tight, start with the fasteners at one end of the bike. I like to start at the fork and work my way rearward.

Don't forget to check the small out-of-the-way fasteners such as this sub-frame bolt.

Large bolts, like the swing arm pivot, should be checked with a torque wrench.

outer race pressed into the frame. The lower outer race is pressed onto the steering stem, the upper outer race is located under the top clamp. The bearings themselves fit between their respective races.

Regardless of the type of bearing used, some maintenance is required. The bearings themselves require periodic adjustment and intermittent replacement. Since the grease used to lubricate the bearings deteriorates with age, they will also need to be removed, cleaned and repacked with fresh grease on occasion; your shop manual will specify the intervals.

As the bearings loosen up, the bike may develop a vague feeling in the front end. The fork may also tend to shimmy, particularly under hard acceleration, or during deceleration, particularly around 40 to 45mph, when the bars are loose in your hands. Really loose bearings will make themselves known with a clunk whenever the front brake is applied.

Symptoms of worn steering-head bearings include vague handling and wander in a straight line. When the bearings are severely worn they become dented; a noticeable indentation may be felt when the forks are held in the straight-ahead position. The hard part is that the bearing decay may take place so slowly that it's not obvious to the rider.

CRASH DAMAGE

Anytime the motorcycle is involved in a serious accident, the frame will need to be checked for

What can I say? This one's done for.

alignment. This is a job that should only be performed by an experienced technician. The frame will have to be stripped, checked, and possibly straightened; or in the worst case, replaced. This is not a job that should be undertaken lightly. Due to liability issues, many shops won't even get involved in frame repair. From both a legal and a practical standpoint, it's easier and cheaper for them to replace a frame that's been damaged than to attempt a repair.

I can hear the groans now. Nothing on a motorcycle seems to confuse more people or create less interest than the electrical system. From a theoretical standpoint, nothing seems harder for the mechanic, let alone the layman, to grasp. I suspect this is because unlike a purely mechanical device, the workings of electrical systems are all performed at a subatomic level. And if you can't see it work, why fuss with it? In reality, electrical systems are fairly simple to understand and to troubleshoot. Even better, they rarely need much in the way of either service or repair.

So why bother to learn about them? Look at it this way: in the off-chance that your electrics do act up, some simple troubleshooting procedures and a basic understanding of how the components function may make the difference between a brief roadside inconvenience and a long walk home.

Furthermore, if you plan to add any electrical accessories, you're much better off knowing how to safely install them and how many you can add before your charging system packs it in.

Besides, the pursuit of knowledge for its own sake is an admirable undertaking. So quit whining.To make this subject a little more palatable for you we'll divide it into two separate chapters; the first will cover some basic principles and charging systems; the second, lights, horns, switches and the various components.

ELECTRICAL BASICS

All matter—you, me, your motorcycle—is made up of molecules. All molecules are made of atoms. Atoms consist of subatomic bits and pieces called "protons" and "neutrons" (which make up the center, or nucleus, of the atom) and other bits called "electrons" (which whirl around the nucleus). Some electrons orbit the nucleus rather closely, while others orbit at some distance. Protons have a positive electrical charge, neutrons have no charge, and electrons have a negative charge.

Electricity can only flow when the electrons in the outermost orbit are free to move. When a material has a lot of these so called "free electrons," it is said to be a good conductor of electricity, or simply a good conductor. Most metals are good conductors. When a material has few or no free electrons, it is called an insulator. Rubber and plastic are both good insulators.

This battery has been sorely neglected; in a word it's shot!

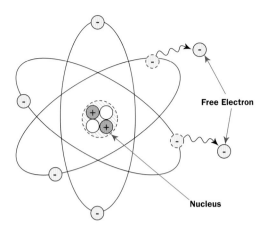

For all of you who were snoozing in physics class, electricity flows when the electrons are free to move outward from their orbits.

Electron Flow

Common thinking used to be that electrons flow from positive to negative. In recent years, it's been proven that electrons actually flow from negative to positive. Since no one felt like rewriting all of the technical manuals, it was decided that for convenience's sake things would remain as they were. To placate the scientific community, it was decided that electrical current would be considered to flow from positive to negative, while electron flow would be from negative to positive.

If that seems confusing look at it this way: electricity can only flow when there is an excess of negatively charged electrons. Materials with an excess of electrons are said to have a negative charge; materials that have deficiency of electrons, a positive charge. When a negatively charged material is connected via a conductor to a material with a positive charge, the excess electrons will flow from negative (too many electrons) toward positive (too few electrons).

To further add to the confusion, the electrons don't actually flow. What they really do is bump into each other and transmit their energy along, much the way a long string of dominoes does when you push the first one over. For practical purposes, however, electrical energy is considered to flow, analogous to the way water does. The flow of electrons is called current. The rate of flow is called amperage.

Battery Maintenance

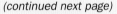

As a general rule of thumb, charging systems don't need a whole lot of preventive maintenance. Maintenance chores revolve around the battery and, less often, attention to some of the ancillary connections. Normally, a motorcycle battery should last about three years. Most don't, mainly because they receive little or no maintenance. At every major service, or at least twice a year, the battery should be serviced, more often if the bike is used infrequently.

Bear in mind that a battery is more or less a plastic box full of acid, which gives off explosive and easily ignited gases. Here are a few things to keep in mind when working with batteries:

No smoking. Don't smoke near a battery, while servicing one, installing one, or removing one. Battery acid is highly corrosive. It can eat through a steel motorcycle frame in very short order, and it will eat through your skin even quicker. Protect yourself with rubber

(continued next page)

You'll need:
- *Tools to remove the battery*
- *Voltmeter*
- *Hydrometer*
- *Distilled water (available at most grocery stores)*

Disconnect the ground, or negative, side first.

The specific gravity of the battery fluid should be checked with a hydrometer. The reading for a fully charged battery should be between 1.265 and 1.280.

If you are using a voltmeter to test the battery condition, the reading should be between 12.5 and 13.2 volts for a fully charged wet-cell 12-volt battery.

Battery Maintenance

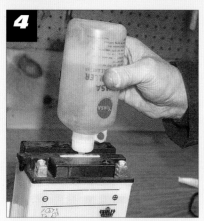

If the battery requires topping off, use only distilled water. Avoid using tap water and never use battery acid.

Charge the battery as required, preferably with a "smart charger". The plastic container isn't affected by acid spills. Since this battery is being charged at very low amperage the caps can be left in place. Were it being charged at 1 amp or more the caps should be removed to prevent gas build up.

After charging the battery, wash it down with cool water and dry it thoroughly.

Reinstall the battery in the bike, making sure all hold-downs and terminal covers are in good condition and that the vent hose is connected and properly routed.

gloves, long sleeves, and long pants, and preferably by wearing a shop apron. Above all, protect your eyes. If battery acid splashes into your unprotected eyes, there is a very good chance it will blind you. If you are foolish enough to service your battery without wearing some sort of eye protection, you're a dim bulb indeed.

Inexpensive eye protection is available. Buy some, and wear it!

Also, keep plenty of fresh water and baking soda on hand. If the acid does spill, use a solution of 1 pound baking soda to 1 gallon of water to neutralize the acid.

If possible, the battery should be removed from the motorcycle before servicing it. I understand that some

motorcycles have batteries that are a real headache to remove. All I can say is in that case, be extremely careful. Always make sure the ignition switch is off before disconnecting the battery. This prevents errant sparks from igniting any residual gases. Disconnect the ground side of the battery first. This will normally be the negative terminal.

After the battery is removed, spray the terminals down with electrical contact cleaner and then buff them until they are shiny and bright using a small, stiff-wire brush, old toothbrush, or a piece of emery cloth. Wash the battery down with cool water and dry it with a paper towel. Most batteries have a clear plastic case or strip that allows you to check the electrolyte level. If the level is low, top it off using only distilled water. Never add more acid after the initial filling.

If the bike doesn't see much use, check the charge using either a hydrometer or a voltmeter. If you use a hydrometer, buy yourself a good one that actually measures the specific gravity. The ones that just have the floating balls in them are next to useless. Specific gravity for a fully-charged battery should be 1.265 to 1.280, per cell. If it's less than 1.200, the battery requires recharging. If you elect to go with a voltmeter, measure the voltage across the terminals. Voltage for a fully charged 6-volt battery should be between 6.2 and 6.6 volts. A fully charged 12-volt lead-acid battery should read between 12.5 and 13.2 volts.

If the battery requires recharging, use only a motorcycle or small-battery-specific charger, or one that can be regulated down to 2 amps or less. These are available at most motorcycle shops. A motorcycle battery should never be charged at more than one-tenth its rated amp-hour capacity. If your battery is rated at 20 amp-hours, then it can only be safely charged at 2 amps per hour.

After the battery is fully charged, it should be allowed to cool down for one half hour, rinsed off, and then reinstalled in the bike. Take care not to pinch the breather tube. Install the hold-down, and then connect the terminals, starting with the positive. Some technicians like to cover the battery terminals with dielectric-silicone grease, petroleum jelly, or a dedicated battery-terminal protector. Some even use a copper-based anti-seize compound. This will prevent corrosion from attacking the battery terminals. However, I prefer to inspect my battery on a regular basis and, if need be, clean the terminals, rather than cover them up with a greasy substance. When the bike is in use, it's a good idea to periodically give the battery a few swipes with a damp rag. Dirt and grease can accumulate on the battery top, creating a path between the positive and negative terminals. The battery can "short" across the dirt pathway, and eventually you'll end up with a dead battery.

Unfortunately, some of us just can't ride as often as we'd like. For a battery to work properly and stay alive for any length of time, it needs to be kept fully charged. Most battery manufacturers recommend keeping the battery on a charger if it sits idle for more than two weeks at a time. If that's your situation, I'd recommend you purchase what's called a "smart charger," or more accurately a pulse charger. Pulse chargers are state-of-the-art in battery charging. They work by constantly monitoring the state of the battery and adjusting the charging rate accordingly. They can be left on indefinitely without harming the charger or the battery. Most come with an adapter cord that can be permanently attached to the battery, making the hookup a breeze. In any event, you'll need one when we come to the section on winter storage, so you might as well buy one now. ∎

ALTERNATING CURRENT

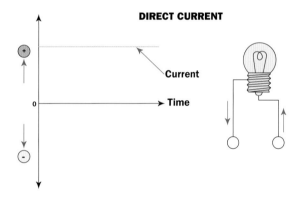

Alternating current changes its voltage and polarity over time. AC flows in one direction until peak voltage is reached. It then drops back to zero, changes polarity and reverses direction again until peak voltage is reached. From zero to peak positive voltage, to peak negative and back to zero is one full cycle. Alternating current cannot be stored in a battery, it must be changed or "rectified" into DC for storage.

DIRECT CURRENT

Direct current remains constant in both strength and direction. Direct current can be stored in a battery.

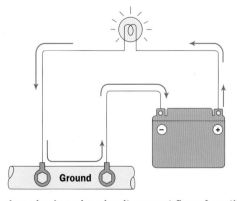

In a simple series circuit, current flows from the positive terminal of the battery, through the bulb, back to ground. In this example we could eliminate the ground (which is actually intended to illustrate the frame) and connect the other side of the light bulb directly to the battery's negative terminal. The frame (or ground) merely serves as a conductor for part of the circuit.

TROUBLESHOOTING THE CHARGING SYSTEM

Many, certainly the majority of us, are more than likely going to ride our motorcycles for a very long time without ever experiencing a catastrophic charging-system failure. Of course, that doesn't mean we won't run into the occasional dead battery or other charging system glitch. In most cases, some simple troubleshooting procedures and a little common sense will have you back in the saddle ASAP.

Lots of charging system faults can be traced to either poor maintenance or bad electrical connections, including broken wires and bad grounds.

Frequently, the first sign of charging-circuit problems is hard starting. The bike may turn over slowly or not at all. Your first inclination may be to simply replace the battery at this point and hope for the best—don't.

First, check the charging voltage using a voltmeter. If the voltage is within specifications, remove the battery, service it, and charge it. If you find something obviously wrong, for instance, a dry cell or two, or a bad battery connection, it's more than likely you've found your problem. If the charge rate is low, look for corrosion at the system-component connections. All of the connections need to be in good, clean condition. If they aren't, make them so before reconnecting the component. Coat the terminals with a dielectric silicone grease to prevent any further problems. Use your wiring diagram to locate all of the connections and their grounds. Separate each connection and thoroughly clean the terminals. Likewise, remove each ground, clean

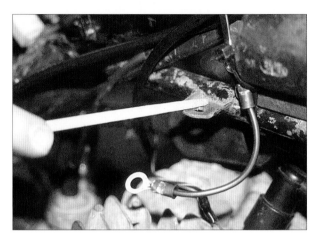

All grounding points on the chassis must be shiny clean. If they aren't, use a file or piece of sandpaper to clean the surfaces.

the terminal, and clean its grounding point, usually the frame. Don't be afraid to get a little aggressive here. A small file or piece of sandpaper should be used to reach bright, shiny metal.

Use your brain. If the problem cropped up just after you installed some kind of high-zoot electrical accessory, disconnect the item to see if the problem goes away. Likewise, if the problem cropped up after you removed some component or bodywork for service, you may have inadvertently left a ground wire or connection loose.

Investigate. Some alternator connections are routed perilously close to drive chains, hot exhausts, or pinch points. If the charging indicator suddenly comes on, it may be due to a broken or melted wire. A quick charging-system check for bikes not normally equipped with a charging indicator is to simply watch the headlights at night. At idle many lights will

dim slightly, especially if the turn signals or brake lights are applied. As you rev the engine up, the light should become slightly brighter. This is by no means an accurate test, but it does give you some indication that the charging system is functioning.

If all else fails, and your charging system does go belly up, don't be afraid to improvise. An ignition system can run for three or four hours on battery power alone. I've seen all types of bodges used to get the bike home: spare batteries strapped to the luggage rack or stuck in the saddlebags are popular. Once, two friends of mine were on tour when the rectifier in one bike packed it in. The nearest replacement was about a three-hour ride away. Since both bikes used a similar-sized battery, they rode halfway, swapped batteries from the bike that wouldn't charge to the one that did, and rode the rest of the way to the dealership, where the new rectifier was installed. ∎

Alternating Current and Direct Current

There are only two types of electrical current: alternating current and direct current. Fundamentally, these are as different as night and day. Nevertheless, since many motorcycles use electrical systems that encompass both alternating and direct current components, a full understanding of each will prove helpful.

Alternating current is a current where the magnitude and polarity vary like a wave. In other words, the voltage rises from zero to a positive peak, back to zero, down to a negative peak, and back to zero. This roundtrip is called a cycle. Since the current alternates between positive and negative peaks, we call it alternating current, or AC for short.

AC power has several advantageous characteristics. It can be stepped up to a higher voltage or down to a lower one by using a transformer. Secondly, a small, compact, AC generator can easily produce quite a bit of current. A serious disadvantage is that alternating current cannot be stored in a battery.

Direct current is current whose magnitude and direction remain constant, and I'll bet you've already guessed that the abbreviation is DC. Unlike AC, DC current cannot be stepped up or down. But the big advantage of DC is that it can be stored in an accumulator, or as most of us call it, a battery.

At one time, all motorcycle charging systems used a DC generator. The current (pun intended) situation is just the opposite: I can't think of a single new motorcycle that uses DC generation. The norm now, and it's been this way for 30 years or more, is to generate AC current and then convert it into DC so that it can be stored in a battery. The components requiring DC voltage can then draw the required power from the battery.

Occasionally, you'll run into bikes that use AC power exclusively. The most common are off-road bikes, such as motocross or enduro bikes. But some small road bikes and mopeds also use AC power exclusively. As we learned in chapter 2, AC ignition systems work just fine. But what happens when we want to power up the headlight or taillight on our off-road bike or moped? When a headlight, or any other component for that matter, is operated on AC, the device will turn off as the current falls and reverses polarity, and then come back on as the current rises. Fortunately, this on-off cycle is repeated so many times a second that it's not really noticeable. At very low speeds, however, you might notice that the lights dim or flicker and the horn will have a tendency to warble.

A Few More Terms

When discussing electrical devices we need to define and understand a few simple terms.

Voltage is electrical pressure. The oft-used analogy is water. Imagine we have two water tanks. One is full of water and set some distance above the other, which is empty. When the two are connected, water will flow from the upper

tank to the lower. The flow is the direct result of the pressure difference between the two tanks. So it is with electricity; the pressure difference between the power source and the component we want to turn on is called the electrical-potential difference. This is just a complicated way of saying voltage. The amount of electrical force we have available, the pressure so to speak, is measured in volts.

Amperage is the rate at which the current flows past a given point. Using the water analogy, amperage tells us how much water is flowing between the tanks. Amperage is measured in amperes, "amps" for short.

Resistance is the reluctance of an object to allow the flow of current. Using our water analogy

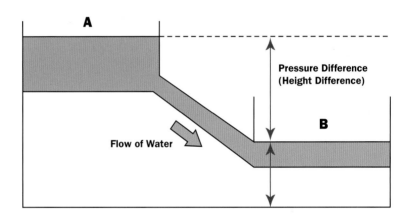

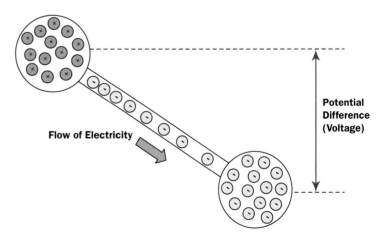

The flow of electricity can be compared to the flow of water. Water will flow from the upper to the lower tank because a pressure difference exists between the two tanks. The same concept may be applied to electricity. In this case, the pressure difference is called the electrical-potential difference and it is measured in volts. Simply put, when the voltage is high at one end of a complete circuit it will flow toward the low end.

These symbols represent the most common electrical components used on motorcycles. (Courtesy American Honda Motor Corporation)

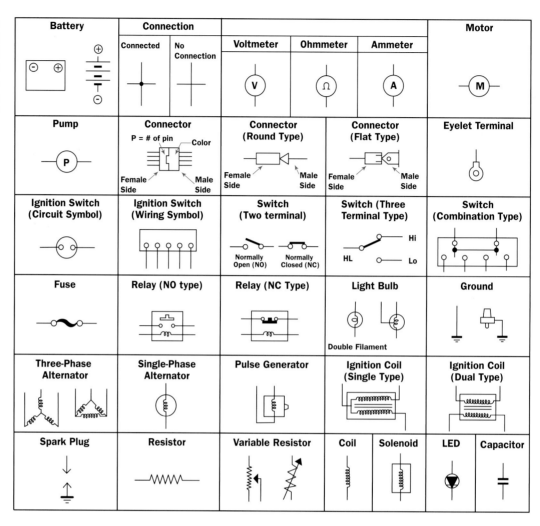

again, if the pipe between the tanks is large, resistance will be low, and lots of water will flow with little pressure. Conversely, if our pipe is reduced in diameter, it will take a lot of pressure to force a small amount of water to flow between the tanks. Resistance is measured in ohms, which is most often represented by the Greek letter omega(Ω).

Conductors are devices used to carry current, such as a piece of wire or anything else that allows current to pass through it. An electrical circuit can be thought of as a complete pathway; from the source of the voltage, through all the components connected to the voltage, and then back to the source. Normally, there are two different types of circuits used on motorcycles: series and parallel. A third type, the series-parallel, is used less often.

A series circuit connects components from positive to negative, like a string of old-fashioned Christmas-tree lights. Current flows through each component before reaching the next. If one component fails, breaking the connection, none of them will work. In a parallel circuit, all of the positive terminals are connected together, as are all of the negative. If one component fails, no current will flow through it, but the others will keep functioning.

Electrical Components

There are also a few components that we need to define and at least have a passing familiarity with before we continue. We're not going into a lot of depth here.

For our purposes, knowing what they do is more important than knowing every nuance of how they do it. We also need to know what they look like on a wiring diagram so we can identify them. A battery is a device that stores electrical energy. As I said, it does not create electricity, it merely stores it for later use.

An AC generator is a device that generates AC power, which is converted into DC and used to charge the battery. It is sometimes called an AC dynamo, although most Americans call it an alternator. AC generators are cheap, require virtually no maintenance, and deliver a lot more power than DC generators.

An AC magneto is a device that generates ignition-source current plus an AC lighting and charging current. They are used in electrical systems that normally don't use a battery.

A DC generator is a device that generates DC power. Until about 1960, most motorcycles, especially the larger ones, used a DC generator to recharge their batteries. The sole advantage in using the DC generator lay in the fact that the current output could be used without conversion. DC generators were expensive, needed somewhat more maintenance than an alternator, and had less output for a given size than the equivalent-sized alternator, particularly at low speed.

A Regulator/Rectifier is a device that changes the current from AC to DC and regulates the amount of current being fed to the battery. It used to be common to separate these two functions using a rectifier to change AC to DC, and a regulator to control current flow. With the advent of semiconductors, manufacturers began to combine the functions into one unit. Because they use semiconductors, these units generate a fair amount of heat. For that reason, the units themselves are normally sealed into a finned, aluminum case. A rectifier uses one or more diodes to regulate the direction of the current flow. A diode acts as an electrical valve; it permits current to flow in one direction but not the other. There are several types of rectifiers in use, which we'll discuss in turn.

Zener diodes are as old as dirt, but they are still used and worth discussing. A Zener diode is nothing more than a one-way, electrical "pressure-relief valve." A Zener diode works by diverting anything over a pre-specified voltage straight to ground. Normally, a Zener turns on at

INSTALLING A NEW BATTERY

Despite our best efforts at maintaining our batteries, we sometimes need to replace them. How a new battery is initially prepared, determines in large part on how long it will last in service.

Most motorcycle batteries are shipped dry, without any electrolyte solution. The acid is added at the point of purchase. The acid should be added up to the full mark, and the battery left to sit for a few minutes. The plates will absorb some of the acid, so you'll have to recheck the battery and top it off as required. The battery should then be left to settle down for at least half an hour.

The next step is to charge the battery. As with any motorcycle battery, the normal charge rate is one-tenth of its rated amp-hour capacity. But for how long? Good question. Most manufacturers recommend charging a new, conventional lead/acid battery for at least three to five hours.

Before you install the charged battery in your bike, wipe the exterior with water and dry it. Again, when you install it, make sure the vent hose is properly routed. ∎

about 14 volts. If you increase the electrical load by, say, turning on the lights, and voltage drops below 14 volts, the Zener turns off. It's a simple and effective device.

HOW WET-CELL BATTERIES WORK

Motorcycles use lead-acid wet-cell batteries. Wet-cell batteries are compact and have low internal resistance, which allows a heavy current to be drawn without losing a lot of battery voltage. They are also more or less infinitely rechargeable, which makes them ideal for motor-vehicle use.

All lead-acid batteries are constructed to work on the same basic principles. A typical lead-acid battery is constructed of individual cells. These cells contain alternating plates. One plate gives off a positive charge, the other a negative. The positive and negative plates are separated by an insulator and are connected together by group. All the positive plates are joined to each other, as are all the negative plates.

The cells are housed in a plastic case. Since each cell is connected in series to its neighbor, the total voltage it generates is the aggregate of the voltage of the individual cells in the battery. Each cell has a nominal voltage of about 2.2 volts. Thus, a battery with three cells produces about 6.6 volts; one with six cells will produce about 13.2 volts.

This is a dated drawing of an AC flywheel magneto, (note the use of the points and a condenser) yet the basic AC magneto is still used, albeit in updated form, on many motorcycles.

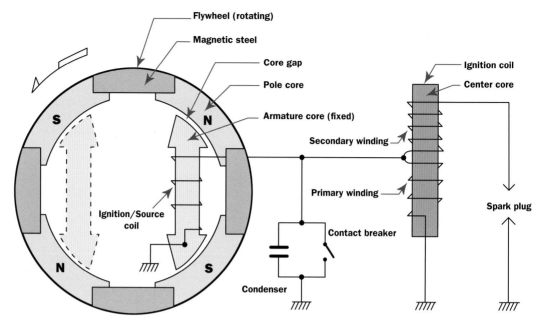

The negative plates are made of spongy lead (Pb), and the positive plates of lead peroxide (PbO_2). The electrolyte, or battery acid, is just that: a dilute mixture of water and sulfuric acid. When the electrolyte is poured over the lead plates, a chemical reaction takes place. It's this reaction that allows the battery to store electrical energy.

When the battery terminals are connected to a closed circuit, the battery discharges electrical current. As the battery discharges, the negative and positive plates absorb the acid in the electrolyte, and the chemical reaction that takes place turns the lead of the original compounds to lead sulfate ($PbSO_4$). During discharge, the electrolyte becomes increasingly weaker (although it'll still burn holes through anything it touches). And if the process goes on long enough, the battery may not be rechargeable.

You may have heard the term sulfated used to describe a battery that won't take a charge. This means that the plates have degenerated to the point where they are covered with a telltale white deposit of lead sulfate crystals. I know I just told you that the plates turn into lead sulfate during discharge, but, in reality, the lead sulfate is a crystal. If the discharge isn't interrupted periodically by recharging the battery, the sulfate crystals grow and blossom into a condition beloved by battery salesmen the world over. Once sulfation takes place, it's unlikely that the battery will ever accept a full charge, and it's time for a new one.

During the discharge process, the water in the battery decomposes, generating hydrogen (from the negative plates) and oxygen gases (from the positive plates). Contaminated with sulfuric acid, these gases are corrosive, highly explosive, and need to be vented. Always make sure that a vent hose is fitted (if required). Also check that it's routed so that it won't be pinched and is well away from anything it might damage (the chain, for instance).

Battery capacity is the quantity of electricity the battery can pump through a load when the battery is fully charged. Capacity is measured in amp-hours, that is, the number of amps the battery can deliver, multiplied by the number of hours it can deliver them. The common figure used for hours is 10. Since capacity actually varies according to rate of discharge, this measure can be misleading.

A battery discharged slowly or intermittently will produce current for quite a while, even if it's not recharged. On the other hand, a battery discharged quickly won't last very long. Let's say we have a 20-amp-hour battery. If we discharge it at 2 amps, it should last 10 hours. If we discharge it at 10 amps, I'd be surprised if it lasted an hour and a half, let alone the full two hours. Still, the amp-hour rating provides a good basis of comparison between batteries and is a convenient way to determine which battery your motorcycle needs.

How Flywheel Magnetos Work

Back in Chapter 2 we briefly discussed flywheel magnetos. Let's take an in-depth look at how they function. Flywheel mags, to use the shorthand, are simple to build, easy to maintain, and light in weight. Unfortunately, their output is on the low side; for that reason, they are generally used on bikes that don't require much in the way of electrical power, such as smaller bikes and off-road machines.

Flywheel magnetos have two sections: the flywheel, which is located on the end of the crankshaft; and the stator, which fits underneath it. Variations on the theme include the inverted flywheel (the stator, in that case being mounted to the crankcase cover and fitting inside the flywheel) and the internal flywheel (in which case the stator surrounds a small flywheel). Since the other types can be considered AC generators, we'll confine this section to the simple, external flywheel magneto.

The flywheel is located on the crankshaft and revolves with it. The stator has one or more coils of very fine wire, each wrapped around a laminated iron core. The coils provide energy for lighting, ignition and in some cases charging. The functional theory is the same no matter what the coil's purpose.

Embedded in the flywheel is a series of magnets. As the magnets rotate, they induce a current in the coils. In the bad old days, contact points were connected in parallel between the primary-ignition coil, which generated the voltage, and the secondary-ignition coil, which generated the spark. When the points were closed, current flowed through the primary coil; when the points were opened, current flow was transferred to the primary side of the ignition coil, inducing a current flow in the secondary side and creating a spark. Nowadays, all the manufacturers I can name have replaced the points with some form of electronic ignition, generally a CDI (capacitor-

Quick Charge Test

On occasion, you may want to check the charging rate, if for no other reason than to satisfy your mind that all is well. The simplest way to perform a quick check is to use a voltmeter.

You'll need:
• A voltmeter

Set the voltmeter to the 20-volt scale and connect it across the battery terminals. Your shop manual will give you a voltage-output figure for a given rpm, which should be something like 14.5 volts at 3,000rpm. Start the engine and bring it up to the recommended rpm while watching the voltmeter. If the voltage reading is correct, all is well. ∎

The voltmeter will let you know in an instant if all is well in the charging department.

discharge ignition), but the theory remains the same. A point to note is that AC secondary-ignition coils are wired in parallel with whatever controls them, DC coils, in series.

Some bikes also stick a charging and lighting coil under the flywheel. If a charging coil is provided, the AC current needs to be changed or rectified into a DC current.

One neat feature of an AC flywheel magneto is that as engine speed increases, the frequency of the AC current becomes high as well. The greater the AC frequency becomes, the higher the coil's internal resistance. This self-limiting feature keeps voltage in check, and helps prevent component damage.

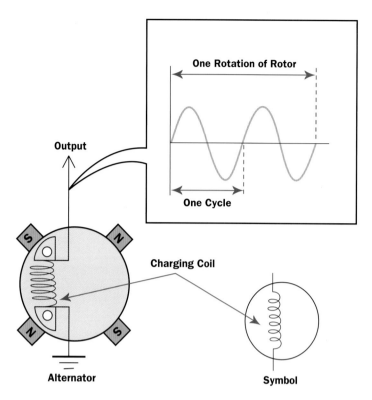

Since a single-phase output alternator uses only one charging coil, the output voltage is a single-phase AC wave. The output frequency varies depending on the number of magnets on the rotor, and the speed of the rotor. The generator in the diagram on the right has two pairs of magnets, and its output has two cycles for every rotation of the rotor. Single-phase output is low, and its small size is best suited for engines of small displacement and a small electrical load.

(Courtesy American Honda Motor Corporation)

GENERATING CURRENT

A long time ago, a fellow (with some knowledge of electricity) called me up to ask for some help. It seems his motorcycle battery kept dying on him, leaving him stranded. Since he had an understanding of the basics, I asked him if he'd taken a voltage reading at the battery terminals with the bike running. He had and he stated it was 12 volts. There's your problem, I said, the alternator isn't putting out. Yes, it is, he insisted, it's a 12-volt system.

As tactfully as I could, I pointed out that for a battery to charge you have to put in more voltage than is taken out. Therefore, charging voltage must be something more than 12 volts. He got mad at me and hung up in huff. But here is the point, when troubleshooting a charging system, remember that to recharge the battery you'll need a higher voltage than the battery itself provides. For 12-volt systems, this is normally 14.5 to 15 volts. ∎

As I stated before, the drawback to a flywheel magneto is its limited output. In the main, this is caused by the need to limit the size and amount of the coils in order to fit them under, or in some cases around, an appropriately-sized flywheel.

How Alternators Work

The basic theory of the alternator is identical to that of an AC flywheel: voltage is induced by cutting magnetic lines of force. Alternators come in several different forms. Some are mounted to the end of the crankshaft, a few are externally mounted and driven by a belt or chain, some are gear driven, and at least one comes mounted behind the clutch.

Construction details vary from unit to unit, but, in general, an alternator is built like an inside-out version of a flywheel magneto. Since there are variations in design, we'll discuss each one as we come to it, starting with the simplest.

Single-Phase Alternator

This is the simplest and least efficient form of alternator. Nevertheless, it has worked quite well for many years. Bolted to the end of the crankshaft is a small, steel cylinder, called a rotor. The rotor is keyed to the crankshaft. Embedded in the rotor are (generally) six permanent magnets. Surrounding the rotor is a laminated iron ring, bolted firmly to the crankcase. The ring holds six coils of fine copper wire. The generating coils are usually encapsulated in epoxy, or some other resin, to protect them.

This is where the rectifier comes in. A single-diode rectifier does work, but it blocks half of the alternator output. Remember, a diode acts as a one-way electrical valve, permitting current flow in one direction only. Because they block half of the output, they are known as half-wave rectifiers.

Since the object of using the alternator in the first place is to create power, wasting half of it seems somewhat extravagant. But half-wave rectifiers do work well, especially where current demands are limited, such as on mopeds and small utility bikes.

A better solution is to build a rectifier that uses as much of the alternator's output as possible. These are known as bridge or full-wave rectifiers. A full-wave rectifier captures 63 percent of the alternator output, as opposed to 37 percent for a half-wave rectifier. Even with full-wave rectification, the single-phase alternator's output is limited. For that reason, they are found mostly on small bikes with limited electrical requirements.

Three-Phase-Output Alternators

Modern motorcycles place extremely heavy demands on their electrical systems. To cope with the demands of electric starters, electronic ignitions, numerous lights, and more recently ABS and fuel-injection systems, the three-phase alternator was developed. The three-phase alternator wires three coils together. The energy output of the three-phase alternator is higher and the pulses are much closer together. This provides a high, smooth, and consistent flow of power.

From a theoretical standpoint, the three-phase alternator functions much like the single-phase variation. Magnets rotate around coils of wire, inducing current flow. The AC output is rectified into DC and stored by the battery.

Your bike's three-phase alternator will probably have a lot more coils than the three normally shown on the wiring diagram. This is because there isn't enough physical room in most alternators for three large stator coils, so to save space a bundle of three or four smaller coils are connected in a series to form one large one. The three coil groups are then connected to each other.

Three-phase alternators sometimes use electromagnets, instead of the permanent magnets we've been discussing so far. These types of alternators are called excited-field alternators, or sometimes claw-pole alternators. The rotor uses a central core of copper wire surrounded by what look like two claws. Battery current is fed into the central core, via a slip ring and carbon brushes.

The battery current excites the coil and creates a strong electromagnet. By regulating the strength of the magnet, alternator output can be controlled. A slight modification on this idea is the brushless alternator. The brushless version uses a separate coil to magnetize the rotor. As you'd expect, rectifying a three phase current is a little more complicated than a single phase. In

practice, six diodes are used, as opposed to four, with each phase being rectified separately.

How Voltage Regulators Work

If we didn't regulate the alternator's output, at some point it would rise high enough to damage the wiring and fry most of the motorcycle's electrical components. We could just switch different coils in and out of the circuit, and at one time that's how a lot of single-phase systems worked. One set of coils recharged the battery during daylight operation. When the lights were switched on, another set of coils was connected through the light switch, which increased output.

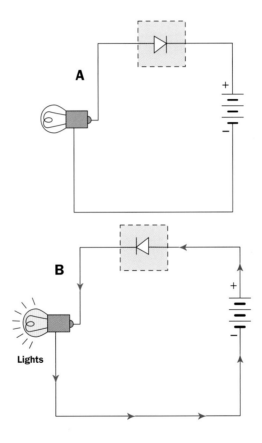

By placing a silicon rectifier (also called a diode) as shown in A, the current flow from the positive terminal will be blocked by the diode. Since the current cannot flow from the positive to negative terminal the light will not come on. If we reverse the diode the current flows, lighting the lamp. If we substitute an alternator for the battery in the drawing, current will flow first in one direction, then reverse and try to flow in the other. The rectifier will block current flow in one direction. Half of the output produced will be lost; however the other half will become rectified DC current. These so-called half-wave rectifiers are inefficient but cheap and reliable.

A further refinement was the addition of a Zener diode to help prevent overcharging.

One problem with the Zener is that it creates a lot of heat, and so needs to be mounted where it gets plenty of cool air. The other problem is that the Zener, as originally used, did nothing to actually regulate the alternator; it merely dumped excess voltage to ground.

The next development integrated the Zener with a thyristor or two (a thyristor meaning an electrical semiconductor switch) and an integrated circuit containing a resistance. By switching current paths through the regulator unit, AC voltage could be controlled, saving a lot of wear and tear on the alternator.

When the three-phase alternator came into popular use, regulators became more sophisticated. Initially, mechanical units were used. These are only found on very old bikes. All modern regulators are non-serviceable, diode-controlled sealed units that work by monitoring the battery voltage and adjusting the alternator output accordingly. Using a claw-pole or field-excited alternator makes voltage regulation much simpler. The regulator varies current to the electromagnet according to the battery's requirements. This instantly increases or decreases the alternator's output on an as-needed basis.

BATTERY BREATHER

Conventional lead-acid batteries have one big disadvantage for motorcycle use: they emit acid vapors that can discolor chrome, peel paint, and even cause chain breakage. Because of this, you should only buy batteries designed for motorcycles. These batteries will have a vent hose to carry those vapors to a place where they'll cause little or no harm.

Resist the temptation to save money by buying a cheap garden-tractor battery at Sears or Wal-Mart. These batteries vent through their caps, so all those corrosive gases will waft out over everything near the battery, causing quick and lasting damage. And if your bike tips over, acid will dribble out, ruining paint, chrome, rubber, and metal.

Even with a real motorcycle battery, vent routing is critical. Many motorcycles will have a diagram, pasted somewhere near the battery, detailing the correct battery vent-hose routing. Failing that, common sense should tell you that the vent hose should be routed so that it can't be pinched, and so that any vapors emitted won't damage anything. You don't want to route the hose anywhere near the drive chain or anything made of metal. Occasionally, a replacement battery may come with a short vent hose. If that's the case, simply slip a piece of fuel line over the vent to lengthen it. Then route the hose anywhere you want.

Sealed Batteries

The first and only practical alternative to a standard lead-acid motorcycle battery, in my book, is

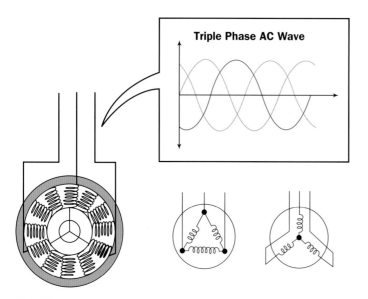

Triple Phase AC Wave

Triple-Phase Alternator

Symbol

The triple-phase alternator uses three groups of coils connected in series to produce three single-phase AC wave forms, each 120 degrees apart. These alternators are used on bikes with heavy electrical loads. The symbol is represented by just three coils to save room. The bottom symbol illustrates a three-phase, excited-field coil alternator, a variation that uses a field coil to magnetize the rotor.

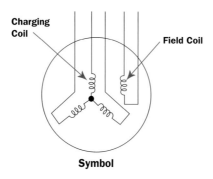

Charging Coil

Field Coil

Symbol

the sealed battery. Sealed, non-spillable batteries are relatively new to the motorcycle world. Sometimes called "maintenance-free" or "AGM" (Absorbed Glass Mat) batteries, sealed batteries differ from conventional batteries in several respects and offer a number of advantages.

Since they are sealed, they can't leak and don't need topping off. The negative plates never become fully charged, so no hydrogen gas is produced, and oxygen produced by the positive plates is reabsorbed by the electrolyte. While there's no vent to spew corrosive fumes all over the place, in the event that the battery is overcharged, a safety valve prevents any gases that are created from rupturing the case.

Sealed batteries are particularly useful on dual-sportbikes and bikes on which battery access is compromised by location. Unfortunately, you can't just run out and buy a sealed battery for every motorcycle. At least for the time being, they're only built in a few specific sizes. Furthermore, to use a sealed battery, your bike must have a charging system with a regulated output of 14.0 to 14.8 volts. This may preclude their use in vintage motorcycles.

A sealed battery tends to hold its charge longer when it's not being used, compared to a conventional battery, but that doesn't mean you can ignore it completely. When the bike is going to sit for any length of time, the battery should still be connected to a trickle charger.

Cold Weather and Your Battery

Because chemical activity is a function of temperature, extreme cold will sap your battery's strength. If you plan on doing some winter riding, using a pulse charger or trickle charger makes a lot of sense. If you use a trickle charger, plug the charger in once a week or so to keep the battery at full charge.

To prevent overcharging and possible battery damage, never leave a trickle charger unattended for more than eight hours at a time. It isn't a good idea to just start-up the bike or drive it once around the block, as that won't be enough to charge the battery. As a side note, remember that a discharged battery is susceptible to freezing. If it cracks the case, the acid spill when it thaws in the spring can be a real bummer.

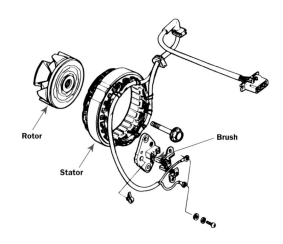

Excited-field-coil alternators with brushes have a field coil placed inside the rotor. Current flows through the brushes to the field coil and electromagnetically induces the rotor. This generator has a strong magnetic force, large output, and is small and lightweight. (Courtesy American Honda Motor Corporation)

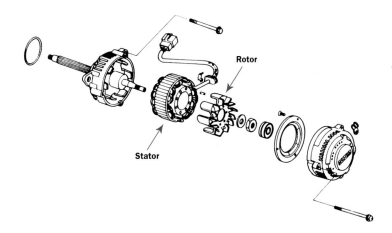

Unlike the other alternators, this brushless excited-field-coil alternator is exposed outside the engine because it is air-cooled. In general, the rotor speed is multiplied by gears or chains connected to the crankshaft. This type is the most powerful among the triple-phase alternators and is primarily used for power on large displacement motorcycles. Excited-field-coil type alternators do not utilize a permanent magnet. Instead, the field coil magnetizes the rotor and generates power as the rotor passes the coil. (Courtesy American Honda Motor Corporation)

In previous chapters, we discussed some electrical theory while explaining how the ignition and charging systems functioned. When it comes to electrical systems, those two are pretty much the stars of the show. Without them, our motorcycles go nowhere. But our motorcycles go nowhere on the street unless they're equipped with a few other important electrics: headlights, taillights, turn signals, and a horn. Many motorcycles also have other circuits that make riding more enjoyable: electric start, radio, heated grips, power-adjustable windshield, or onboard air compressor.

In this chapter, we'll look at some of these circuits and how the devices that are used in them work. We'll also take a look at the instruments, mainly the speedometer and tachometer, and how they work.

LIGHT BULBS

In principle, the electric light bulb hasn't changed much since Thomas Alva Edison uttered those immortal words, "I've got 'er now. I bet I can sell a skillion of these things and make a mint." Well, old Tom was right; he did sell a skillion of them, and he did make a mint. While modern bulbs throw a lot more light, and live much longer, they haven't really changed.

An electrical current is passed through a finely drawn piece of wire, called a filament. The most common filament material is tungsten, which is durable, cheap, and able to withstand the high temperatures involved in incandescent lighting. The filament is placed inside a glass bulb. The only other thing in the bulb, besides the filament, is nothing—a vacuum. The ends of

the filament are connected to terminals in the base of the bulb. When an electrical current is passed through the filament, the wire naturally offers some resistance to flow. The resistance causes the filament to heat up, and it reaches white heat instantly. Because there's no oxygen in the bulb to oxidize the filament, the bulb

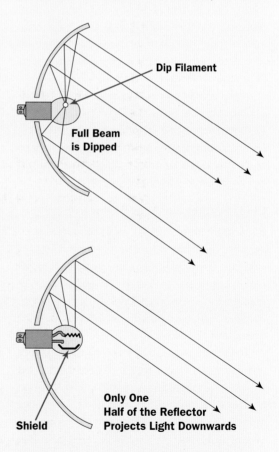

Two ways of focusing the low beam: An offset filament (TOP); or a small shield used to redirect the beam (BOTTOM).

provides us with light instead of a fireworks display.

Wattage and Brightness

Wattage is the rate at which an electrical device uses power. The higher the wattage, the more power a device consumes. Bulbs are measured in watts and the higher the wattage the brighter the bulb. The wattage of the bulb is determined by the resistance of the filament.

If the bulb were just hanging in the headlamp, the light would shoot off in every direction, making it impossible to see beyond a foot or two. To focus the bulb's output, it is positioned in the center (or close to it) of a silvered reflector. The reflector gathers up the beams of light and aims them forward. The glass lens of the light then focuses those beams so they can illuminate our way. In the past, motorcycle headlights used a replaceable bulb, the reflector and lens being separate pieces. But building the headlight as one unit, called a sealed-beam headlight, offers several advantages; the main one being that there is no possibility of the reflector becoming tarnished and reducing light output.

Many bulbs use two filaments, allowing high- and low-beam patterns. Headlights normally carry a high-beam filament, positioned to throw the broadest possible beam of light, and a low-beam filament positioned slightly above the high beam so that its light is reflected downward toward the road and off to one side. A variation on that idea fits a small shield in front of the low beam filament; the shield aims the light toward the upper half of the reflector, which results in the beam being focused downwards.

Tungsten bulbs work well enough when speeds are low, and they also work well where being seen is more important than seeing. For example, a turn signal or taillight is visible for quite a distance, despite its relatively weak strength. A headlamp is a different kettle of fish.

I'm as blind as a bat at night. The brighter the headlight, the better I like it. If I could figure out a way to mount and power it, I'd fit one of those World War II anti-aircraft searchlights to the front of my bike. Since they weigh as much as a small car, the idea seems a little impractical. A better solution would be a brighter type of light,

DIY Checking Resistance

Resistance checks tell us if a component is working properly, or if a wire is broken. Resistance checks can also turn up bad grounds and faulty connections. Diodes are also tested with ohm meters. Since a working diode should only pass current in one direction an ohm meter can be used to indicate in which direction(s) the current is flowing.

The ohmmeter is only used to check resistance; ohmmeters will be destroyed if current passes through them. If you're checking a circuit make absolutely certain it's not "live." When checking a component always disconnect it from the circuit before testing.

Analog meters will have to be zeroed to obtain the correct measurement. With the meter on, touch the ends of the probe together and turn the adjusting knob to zero. Digital meters normally don't have a zero adjustment.

Set the scale to the appropriate calibration for the device you're testing. The correct settings are ordinarily listed in your shop manual. Unless you're checking a diode, ohmmeters are not polarity sensitive, either probe can be attached to either side of the component. The ohmmeter will give you a direct reading, which can be compared with specifications.

Meters can be funny things, over the years I've seen quite a few guys look at their meter, see the problem and ignore it. They then go on to search fruitlessly for some other problem. For some reason, they just don't trust the instruments. Take it from me, meters don't lie. Learn to use your meter, learn to trust it. Once you do, electricity will lose a lot of its mystery. ∎

You'll need:
- *Volt-Ohm Meter*

With the voltmeter set on the AC scale we can read un-rectified AC voltage; set on the OHM scale the same meter is used to measure a coils resistance.

Amp meters are always connected in series with the circuit whose current you are measuring. Many meters use a separate connection for the amp terminal to protect the rest of the meter.

built to a manageable size. Fortunately, for me and everyone else, the quartz-halogen headlight has become universal for all but the cheapest motorcycles.

Brighter Lights

If we fill a tungsten filament bulb with an inert gas, such as nitrogen or argon, we can raise the internal temperature of the bulb, providing more illumination. If we do that, we'll also need more wire in the filament. To keep the size of the bulb reasonably compact the filament is wound into a coil, allowing us to pack more wire into the same space. The drawback to this plan is that the higher temperature will cause the outer layer of the filament to vaporize more quickly, only to re-

appear as a black shadow on the inside of the bulb after the vapor has cooled and condensed. This black residue will in turn create even more heat. Pretty soon, poof! No more light.

In some cases, the filament may evaporate so rapidly that the bulb takes on a silver appearance. This is usually caused by a sudden electrical overload. If it happens, don't just admire your shiny, dead bulb prior to replacing it with a new one. Look for the reason it overloaded, often you'll come across a bad ground or a regulator on the way out.

So, how do we make a bulb burn brighter without burning out? Start by building the bulb out of quartz instead of glass. Next, replace the inert gas with something that's got a little pizzazz to it. Quartz bulbs use an atmosphere based on a krypton gas. This isn't the stuff from Superman's home planet. Rather, it's a gaseous halogen, usually, but not always, iodine.

Here's how it works: a temperature difference exists within the bulb between the filament and the glass. Initially, at around 2,700 degrees, the tungsten that evaporates from the filament will combine with the halogen gas to form a halide. A halide is a volatile-metallic compound, which isn't capable of attaching itself to the walls of the bulb. Instead, it drifts around in the bulb until it comes back in contact with the filament, which is a blistering 3,500 degrees. The high heat causes the tungsten and halogen to separate, and the tungsten recombines with the filament. In this way, the filament is self-regenerating.

Since the tungsten-halogen is only gaseous above 475 degrees, the bulb must be kept small so it stays hot. Quartz is used as the bulb material because it withstands high temperatures. A side benefit is its greater strength as compared to a glass bulb, which allows it to contain a greater gas pressure. The greater pressure slows the filament-evaporation rate.

The result is a bulb that has a longer life and provides about 50 percent more light for a given wattage. The quality of the light also is much improved, being more blue-white than yellow. While there are a few small problems associated with the quartz light, in the main, it's a vast improvement over the tungsten-filament, glass-bulb lamp.

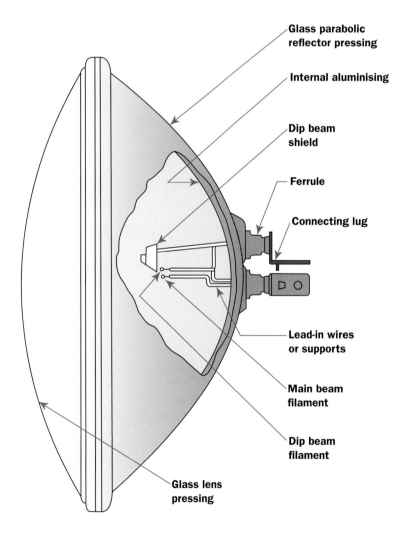

Glass parabolic reflector pressing

Internal aluminising

Dip beam shield

Ferrule

Connecting lug

Lead-in wires or supports

Main beam filament

Dip beam filament

Glass lens pressing

Detail drawing of the sealed-beam headlight.

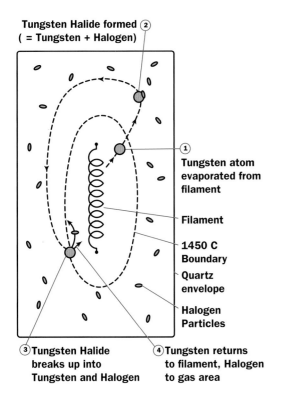

Tungsten Halide formed ② (= Tungsten + Halogen)

① **Tungsten atom evaporated from filament**

Filament

1450 C Boundary

Quartz envelope

Halogen Particles

③ **Tungsten Halide breaks up into Tungsten and Halogen**

④ **Tungsten returns to filament, Halogen to gas area**

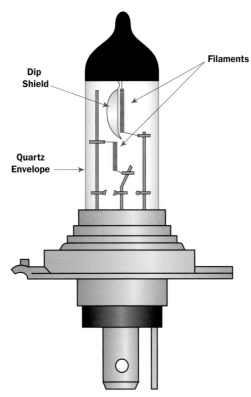

Dip Shield

Filaments

Quartz Envelope

A quartz bulb with Tungsten Halide construction is not much different internally than a plain old incandescent version. The chemistry is what makes it better.

Quartz Bulb Construction

Quartz bulbs require some special handling. Perspiration or grease from your fingers can create a hot spot on the quartz bulb that allows the glass to expand at different rates, and quite probably will shorten the life of the bulb. Quartz, in particular, is easily etched by acids and the normal body salt found in perspiration. Never handle a quartz bulb by anything but its metal base. If you do touch it, clean it before use with a rag and alcohol or contact cleaner.

Future Bulbs

Few of us buy a bike because of its bright lights. Consequently, light technology changes slowly. Still, new technologies—such as using different gases in halogen lights and computer-designed, multifaceted headlight reflectors—are producing ever better illumination.

Light-Emitting Diodes are currently (get it?) very popular. LEDs use little power, weigh close to nothing, and have an extremely long life, all of which makes them attractive for motorcycle use. Besides, the less power required to run the lights, the more you'll have to run the fuel-injection

system. And, as motorcycle electronics become more sophisticated, more electrical power will be required to run the computer systems. The fly in the ointment is that LED luminescence is low. They make great indicators, and tail lights, but their use as headlights is impractical at this time.

Brake-Light Circuit

The taillight often uses a two-filament bulb. One filament is switched on with the ignition, providing the bike with a taillight; the other uses a second filament that only comes on when the brake is applied. The switches are either mechanically-operated or hydraulically-activated pressure switches. Mechanical switches are found on both cable and hydraulic-brake systems; pressure-activated switches only on hydraulic-brake systems.

When the lever or pedal is moved, the switch contacts close. Current flows through the appropriate wire into a pin at the base of the bulb, and the ground connection is made through the bulb's base. When the lever is released, contact is broken and current stops flowing. It doesn't get any simpler. If the brake light doubles as a tail-

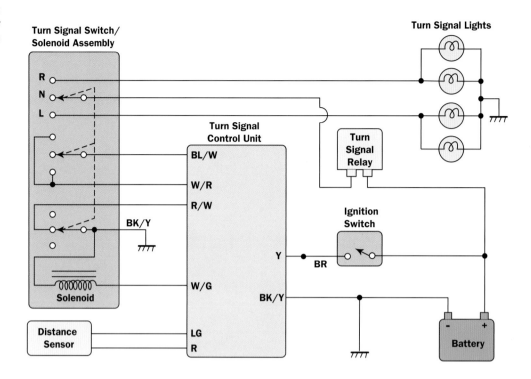

Self-canceling turn signals normally measure both time and distance.

light, a second filament, of lower wattage is positioned in the bulb, and a second pin installed in the light's base. Current flows from the light switch into the pin, through the filament and back to ground, the taillight circuit being entirely separate from the brake-light circuit.

Turn-Signal Circuit

I can remember when turn signals on a bike were something of an anomaly. I also remember debates as to whether they were even safe. Thankfully, those days are long gone.

The turn-signal circuit includes stalk- or fairing-mounted lights that can be activated by a switch to indicate changes in the rider's direction of travel. Some systems also incorporate a separate switch to activate all the lights simultaneously to indicate a hazard. The lenses are amber colored to avoid confusing the signal with a stop or taillight, and they generally flash at between 60 and 120 cycles per minute. Most systems also feature some sort of self-canceling device. This keeps you from driving your riding buddies batty by leaving the signals on for an hour at a time. Many signal switches also feature

a push-to-cancel function. When you push the signal button inwards the signals shut off.

The heart of the turn-signal circuit is the turn-signal relay or flasher unit. Although there are differing methods in use, the underlying principle is the same: the current flowing through the relay to the signal lights is used to turn the relay off and on, which in turn causes the lights to flash. There are two main types of flashers in general use: bimetal and capacitor. Capacitor flashers are preferable because their flash rates aren't affected by voltage fluctuations or by vibration.

Self-Canceling Turn Signals

Self-canceling turn signals are a relatively new feature on motorcycles, and not all bikes come equipped with them. Some of these systems use a simple timing device, after so many seconds the timer just cancels the signal. Of course, if you get stuck at a long red light you may end up going through a cycle of on-off-on for a minute or two.

To overcome this glitch a second feature was added to some systems, one that measures distance. A counter is built into the speedometer that measures pulses, much the way an ignition pickup does. The timer tracks the pulses. The signals won't self-cancel until both the distance and the time criteria have been met. This way, when you're passing that long line of campers going up a hill, the flashers stay on until the timer shuts them off. Conversely, when you're parked at a stoplight for what seems like hours, the timer won't turn off the signals until the bike starts to roll and the counter has clicked X amount of feet. Of course, you can always cancel the signals manually.

Horn Circuit

Until very recently, motorcycle horns tended to be somewhat ineffectual. In fact, many still are. Electric horns are simple, and while they may differ slightly in construction, they all work on the same essential principles.

The horn circuit consists of a button on the handlebars, the horn, and often a relay to take the electrical load off of the horn switch.

Modified versions of the common electric horn use a trumpet to increase or change the tone of the horn. Most electric horns are fitted with a small screw for adjusting the internal contact points as they wear. Sometimes, a dead horn can be restored to life by giving the screw a quarter turn or so to increase the current flow.

Switches

Switches are devices that control current flow and direct it to the various components. Switches work by using a movable contact that can be positioned to engage a fixed contact. Some switches, such as ignition switches and light switches, use clusters of contacts to perform more than one function. Some switches are what's called momentary contact, meaning that you have to hold them on. Starter buttons, horn buttons, and the headlamp flasher are momentary-contact switches. The other type is the latching switch, which is more or less self-explanatory. Latching switches include the ignition switch, on-off type kill switches, and high-low beam switches.

Switches generally use what's called a self-wiping design. This means that they clean themselves every time they're used. Barring mechani-

cal failure, they're normally long-lived and trouble-free. However, large quantities of water, especially when forced into them with a pressure washer, can shorten their life span considerably.

When I was about 16, I attempted to dismantle a light switch and rebuild it. It turned out to be a bad move, as lots of the tiny components were spring-loaded. The predictable thing occurred, and I had to enlist the aid of an older and much wiser mechanic to help me put it back together. He simply handed me a used one and said, "Kid, rule of thumb. Never dismantle a switch; they are inscrutable."

If a switch stops switching, I suggest spraying the guts of it with either WD-40 (in fact, a shot or two every time you wash the bike won't hurt either) or a proprietary electrical-contact cleaner. If that doesn't work, replace the switch. If you're an inveterate tinkerer, go ahead and take the thing apart. You'll probably end up replacing it anyway, but at least you'll see what it looks like on the inside.

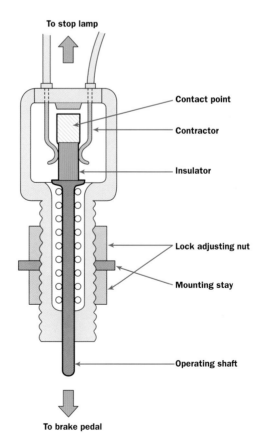

To stop lamp

Contact point

Contractor

Insulator

Lock adjusting nut

Mounting stay

Operating shaft

To brake pedal

The basic brake light switch. When the pedal is depressed the shaft moves downward, the contact connects the two wires, and the brake light comes on. This type of switch is widely used on rear brakes.

Basic Wiring Technique

You'll need:

- *Electrical breadboard*
- *Crimping pliers*
- *Electrical connectors and terminals (various sizes)*
- *Shrink tubing*

With so many electrical accessories available in the aftermarket, from electric vests, gloves, and chaps to heated grips, sound systems, driving lights, or even something as simple as a cigarette-lighter style outlet to recharge a cell phone, it's not uncommon for motorcycle owners to want to modify their bikes' electrical systems.

Using appropriate basic wiring techniques will help avoid potential problems such as short circuits or drained batteries. An electrical breadboard is one way to plan the circuit you want to add, with assurance that all components are in good working order before they're installed on the bike. ■

1

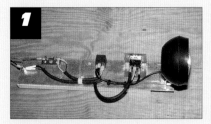

An electrical breadboard is used to illustrate the circuits and connections as they would appear on a bike without the complication of all the motorcycle's other circuits and switches. In this case it's used to illustrate a typical installation of a spotlight. From the front to the rear, spotlight, switch, relay, and fuse. Using the electrical breadboard as an example, power is first routed to the fuse. All wiring should be protected by a loom and securely fastened by either cable clamps or tie-wraps.

3

Use good crimping pliers to secure the terminals.

2

All wiring should be protected by a loom and securely fastened by either cable clamps or tie-wraps. Use only quality crimp-on or solder-on terminals, and protect the joints with heat shrink tubing.

4

A heat gun or (in this case) a bottle torch can be used to shrink the tubing. DO NOT use the torch any where near the motorcycle. If you must shrink some tubing on the bike itself use only a heat gun or hair drier.

5

The finished connections should be clean, strong, and waterproof.

Wiring Harnesses and Connectors

The miscellaneous wires in your wiring harness are joined to each other with a medley of crimped or soldered connectors. At one time, individual connectors were used but the multitude of circuits used on modern bikes makes this impractical. Today multi-pronged cannon connectors are used. These utilize dedicated clips to ensure they can only be joined in one way.

Repair kits containing an assortment of connectors and a wire stripper/crimping tool can be purchased at any hardware or auto parts supplier for under $20. Keeping a basic electrical-repair kit on hand will make it a lot easier to perform electrical repair, add any accessories, or repair Mom's toaster.

Fuses

I'm hard-pressed to think of a single road-going motorcycle that doesn't have at least one fuse in its electrical system. Fuses act as an electrical safety valve, sacrificing themselves to protect the wiring and other electrical equipment. The fuse is located between the battery and the component it's meant to protect. When current flow exceeds the fuse's amperage rating, usually due to a short circuit, the fuse will melt or "blow," preventing current from flowing.

Most motorcycles have a fuse to protect each circuit, although smaller machines may have only one central fuse. Normally, the fuses are found in a holder located under the seat or a body panel, generally close to the battery.

There are three types of fuses in general use: the glass-body fuse (which is found primarily on older bikes), the ceramic fuse (which is common to older European machines), and the flat-bladed fuse (which is found on most new motorcycles). The glass-body fuse and the flat-bladed fuse are rated at their fusible value: 10 amps, 20 amps, and so on. The ceramic fuse is rated according to how much continuous current they can carry, which is half of the fusible value.

There are two basic fuse rules: first, never replace a blown fuse with one carrying a higher rating; second, try to locate whatever it was that caused the fuse to blow in the first place before replacing the bad fuse. Otherwise, you'll spend the rest of the day replacing blown fuses. A little

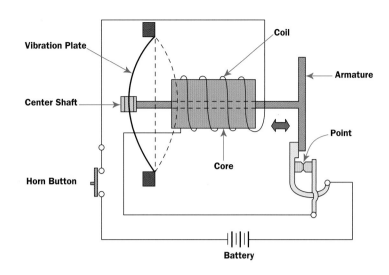

This simplified drawing omits a few minor parts but certainly covers the high points. When the button is depressed, current flows through wire coil. This creates a magnetic field in the core, which attracts the armature. The armature is attached to the vibration plate (diaphragm) as the armature moves it causes the vibration plate to flex. At the same time the points are pulled apart by the armature breaking the circuit; the armature then returns to its resting position, the plate flexes again, the points close, current flows and the cycle is repeated; the horn sounds.

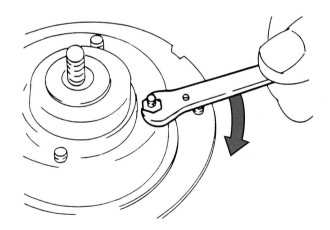

Over time the points wear on horns, reducing current flow and causing the tone to change. Most horns have some sort of adjusting screw that can be used to restore the tone.

common sense goes a long way here. If everything was fine until you switched on the turn signals, the problem is probably in the turn-signal circuit. Investigate the signal circuit before continuing.

BASIC CIRCUIT FACTS

As the current flows from source to ground and back again, we expect it to earn its keep and perform a little work. That work is generally in the form of cranking a starter motor, lighting a lamp, or igniting the fuel-air mixture that propels our motorcycles down the road. The electrical current flows through any number of wires, from source to load, to ground and back to the source. This pathway is known as a circuit, or more accurately, a complete circuit.

The motorcycle's electrical system encompasses many separate circuits. While there is some circuit overlap, by and large, each circuit should be considered a separate entity. The wiring diagram will help you to identify each circuit and the pathways particular to it. By using a wiring diagram and a simple $4.95 test light, you can trace the current flow from the battery, through the circuit, to the component and back to the battery. Before we get too involved, a brief discussion on circuit overlap may be in order.

Occasionally, a fault in one circuit can and will affect another. Suppose your right-side turn signal stops working because the ground wire broke off. Everything else should work fine. The only thing that won't work is the right-side turn signal. This is a perfect illustration of an isolated failure in an independent circuit.

Now let's assume the power lead to the same light chafed against the frame until the insulation wore through. Every time you try to signal, it blows the main fuse and the bike stops. That's circuit overlap. A problem in the turn-signal circuit has affected the entire motorcycle. In reality, modern bikes usually fuse each circuit independently to prevent just such an occurrence. Way back when, though, there was often only one fuse: the main. If it blew, you fixed it or pushed.

Another example of circuit overlap, probably the best one, would be the charging system. A charging system problem can affect all the other circuits. Low battery voltage means the lights go dim, the ignition can't fire the engine, and the starter stops turning. Pretty soon you're on foot. It's that simple.

Finally, there's one circuit that works in concert with all the others: the ground circuit. But since most bikes use the frame as a ground, a total system failure isn't often a problem. Occasionally though, I have seen bikes that ran all of their ground wires to a common terminal. Once that terminal became corroded, bye-bye ground, which meant that nothing worked.

Instruments

Instruments are kind of like magical black boxes. If they break, there really isn't a whole lot you can do about it. In days past, instruments, particularly the speedometer and tachometer, were purely mechanical. If they failed to work, 9 times out of 10 you could trace it to a broken cable or drive unit. The 10th time you could actually pull the unit apart and possibly fix it or send it to a specialist that could.

As with other aspects of the motorcycle in recent years, the instruments have become more complex. As such, they are for the most part sealed units that cannot be repaired. Substitution is the only avenue open to the mechanic, even at the dealership level.

If the instrument stops working, check the electrical leads to it and the connections. If they appear to be in good condition, consult your shop manual for the appropriate checks.

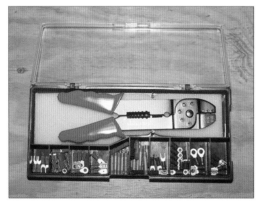

An inexpensive electrical repair kit can be purchased for around $10. It should contain almost everything you need to make a quick and safe repair or add an electrical accessory.

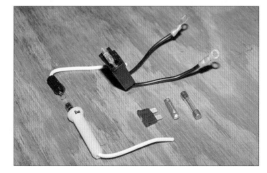

Make sure you pack the correct fuse in your tool kit. This is a selection of the most common fuses and fuse holders.

Fuel gauges, temperature gauges, and oil-level gauges rely on sending units to provide them with the correct information. When one of these gauges goes haywire, suspect the sending unit first.

Many speedometers are still driven from either one of the wheels, most often the front or the transmission via a cable. If the speedometer becomes erratic or stops working altogether, take a look at the cable, and/or its drive unit, especially if the drive unit has been disturbed during wheel removal.

Electronic instruments can pass on to the rider far more information than a mechanical instrument can. It's not uncommon these days to find a speedometer that includes elapsed time, mileage, and even fuel consumption. Electronic speedometers use an electronic "counter" to measure wheel revolution, each time a toothed wheel on the hub passes the pickup a signal is sent through a wire connected to the speedometer. Because they aren't dependent on spinning cables, electronic instruments respond faster than mechanical ones. This is most noticeable on revy bikes.

MAINTAINING ELECTRICS

This is one of those out-of-sight, out-of-mind things. I consider myself to be at the top of the heap maintenance-wise, and yet, in all honesty, I can't tell you the last time I checked my bike's taillight. Most of us will only find out a bulb is blown when the sun goes down, or that the horn doesn't work when we actually need it. So, the first order of business is to get into the habit of checking your electrics on a regular basis. Do it while the bike is warming up.

Assuming you have no major electrical catastrophes on the horizon, electrical maintenance should be routine and easily accomplished. Since the battery is the main power source, keep a close eye on the electrolyte level, especially if you've added electrical accessories over the years. Current has to flow from the battery to the electrics via an assortment of wires and connections. High resistance will create plenty of problems. Starting at the battery, ensure that all of the connections are clean and tight, particularly the battery terminals and chassis ground.

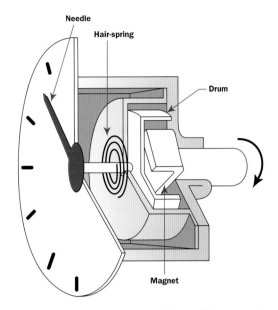

Mechanical speedometers are fairly straightforward: as the magnet rotates, it "drags" the drum magnetically in the same direction, rotating the indicator needle with it. The faster the magnet rotates, the farther the needle will advance against the hair-spring that holds it back. For the most part, these have been replaced with electronic versions on modern bikes.

COOLANT-TEMPERATURE SENSOR/ WATER-TEMPERATURE GAUGE NOT WORKING

Coolant-temperature sensors make use of thermocouples to change the amount of amperage flowing to the water-temperature gauge. Put as simply as possible, these are devices that change resistance based on temperature. As the resistance changes, so does the amperage passing through to the gauge. The gauge's needle position is dependent on the amount of amperage passing through it. Vary the amperage, and the needle changes position.

Trouble-shooting one is relatively easy. As always, check your shop manual for the specifics. In many cases, it will go something like this: with the ignition turned on and the motor off, disconnect the wire from the temperature sensor. Using a jumper wire, ground it. If the gauge needle swings to the hot end of the scale, disconnect the jumper instantly. The sensor is bad and should be replaced. If the gauge didn't move, check for voltage at the sensor connection. If voltage is present, you've got a bad coolant gauge. If no voltage is present, trace the feed using your manual's wiring diagram.

Testing a temperature sensor itself is somewhat more complicated. Most procedures call for heating the sensor in a pan of coolant, normally a 50:50 mix of water and antifreeze, while you measure the resistance at a specific temperature. It's somewhat time consuming and, in my opinion, of importance only when you're trying to isolate a calibration problem or intermittent-gauge problem. ■

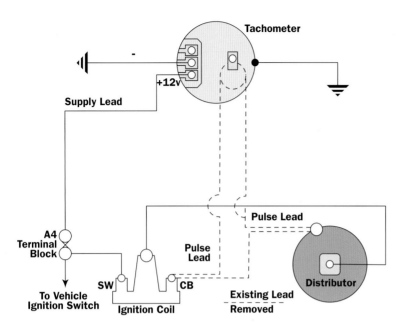

Tachometer

Supply Lead

+12v

-

A4 Terminal Block

To Vehicle Ignition Switch

SW

Ignition Coil

Pulse Lead

CB

Pulse Lead

Distributor

Existing Lead Removed

Electronic tachometers are much easier to install, and tend to be somewhat more accurate than the average mechanical instrument.

Repeated bulb failures, or intermittent working of any electrical component, can often be traced to a bad ground. If it seems you're replacing an awful lot of left rear-turn signals or that the new ones aren't as bright as they should be, the first thing to check is the ground connection. Quartz lights are also particularly sensitive to temperature. If its working temperature is reduced, the life expectancy drops off dramatically. High resistance causes low voltage, which causes the temperature to decrease. If bulb life is short, suspect corroded wiring or connectors.

Chafing is always a problem, mainly where the wires turn or exit components and body panels. Wires that run underneath the fenders are always subject to damage and should be given the occasional glance. While you're checking the wiring, also take a look at the connectors. It's not uncommon to find the "green death" (corrosion) lurking between snap connectors. A little WD-40 and a Scotch-Brite pad should clean things up.

When assembling your newly-cleaned connection, take a moment to pack it with a dielectric silicone grease (available at any auto-parts or electronics store) to prevent any future problems.

I almost feel silly telling you how to replace a light bulb, but, what the heck. Most headlight bulbs these days are halogen. Replacing one is simply a matter of removing the headlight unit, releasing the spring clip, and removing the bulb.

Again, make sure you grab the new bulb by the terminal end. Do not touch the glass part with bare fingers. If you do, wash the fingerprints off with alcohol.

To access the signal or taillight bulbs, remove the plastic lens, which is usually retained by two screws. To remove the bulb, push down, and give it a slight twist to the left.

The socket should be inspected and any corrosion removed before a new bulb is inserted. If the bike sees a lot of wet weather or lives in a corrosive environment, it's not a bad idea to apply a little Copper Coat or other conductive lubricant around the stem of the bulb. Just try to keep it off the contacts at the base.

Adding Electrics

Riders add all sorts of extras to their bikes, including a whole host of electrical devices. Common additions include fog lights, GPS receivers, radios, marker lights, grip heaters, and many others.

Every one of these devices draws a current. When the total amount of drawn current (amps) is less than the total supplied by the charging system, everything works fine. Exceed the system's capability, and you've got problems. That's the law of the jungle when it comes to installing electrical components. The corollary to that is the load can slightly exceed system output, if (and this is a big if) you don't use all of the components at the same time. Adding additional lights, as long as you stay within the limits of your electrical system, shouldn't present any problem. But how do you figure out what those limits are?

All of the electrical components on your motorcycle have a wattage rating. If you want to know how much power it takes to run all of your components, simply add up the wattage of each component. (Bulb wattage is listed in the manual and should actually be stamped or printed on the bulb itself.) Compare the total wattage to your charging system's output. If your owner's man-

ELECTRICAL DO'S AND DON'TS

Whenever you work on the electrical system, disconnect the negative side of the battery. By the same token, when you remove the battery disconnect the negative side first as well.

- Always connect the positive terminal first when installing the battery.
- Whenever you insert a probe, try to do it without puncturing the wire;

go to the nearest connector and test there first.

- Always make certain electrical connectors are clean and well-seated.
- Wiring harnesses should be routed away from sharp edges and the protruding edges of screws and bolts. The harness should be secured to the frame with clips or tie wraps.

- Never route wiring harnesses too tight or too slack.
- Avoid pinching the harness when installing a component or body panel.
- Never replace a fuse with one carrying a higher rating.
- When using a meter, read the instructions.
- Above all think. ■

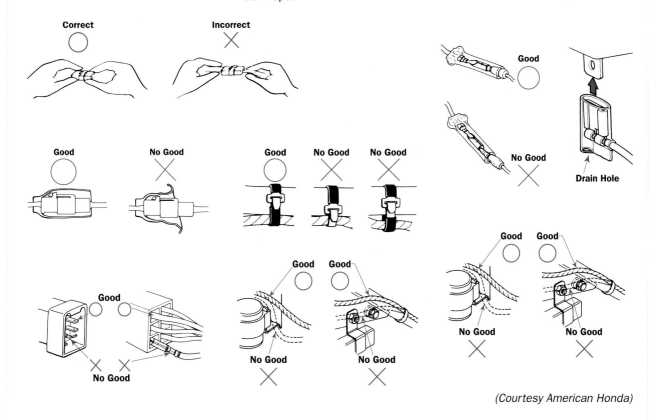

(Courtesy American Honda)

ual doesn't list the alternator output in watts, the formula is simple: watts equal voltage multiplied by amperage.

For example, the Kawasaki Voyager has a rated alternator output of 35 amps and 13.5 volts at 7,500 rpm. Meaning that, under optimum conditions, we have 472.5 available watts of power (35 x 13.5 = 472.5). Let's say that the headlight low beam requires 55 watts, the four taillights (8 watts each) consume 32 watts, and the ignition system uses something around 20 watts. Other stuff like the instrument bulbs, radio, running

lights, and fuel pump use up maybe another 50 watts. We won't count the intermittent stuff like the blower fan or cruise control. So, 55 + 32 + 20 + 50 = 157. That's how many watts are needed just to go down the road, leaving 315.5 watts available for other things.

Since I like to leave a good-size fudge factor to account for things like low-speed driving (when the charge rate drops slightly) and also because we do have intermittent draws like the cooling fan (around 80 watts) and high beam (60 watts), let's call it an even 250 watts of reserve. If we add two fog lights at 35 watts each and a few 5-watt marker lights, that's another 90 watts, leaving us with 140 watts in reserve for mundane chores like battery charging, operating the brake lights, and using the cigar lighter.

If you add any electrical devices, the cardinal rules are to make sure the installation is done properly and to make sure your wattage requirements don't exceed your charging system's capability. If you have to have heated grips, fine, just remember that using them, your running lights, and your CB radio while sitting in traffic may exceed your alternator's ability to keep up.

Common sense should tell you that accessories should be wired through a dedicated circuit and that each circuit should have its own fuse. In the case of factory options, there may be a circuit already built into the harness. If there isn't, it's a simple matter to install one. I recommend tapping into battery power either at the battery's positive terminal, or the battery connection at the starter solenoid.

All additional circuits need to be safely wired and individually fused. The fuse should be placed between the battery and the device, or its relay. If you plan to run multiple accessories, it's not a bad idea to install a small fuse-block. These are available at auto-parts stores and Radio Shacks. They allow you to run several devices, each with its own circuit and fuse, from one source connection.

All connections and terminals should be crimped or soldered. If a splice is required, it should be soldered and sealed with heat-shrink tubing. All added wiring should be protected with an outer sheath, and, if possible, secured to the main harness or tie wrapped to the frame.

If everyone rode stock motorcycles, lighting considerations would be simple and straightforward. But adding lights to our bikes is a time-honored tradition. Whether it's for practical or aesthetic reasons, lots of us like to hang a few extra lights.

When I was a kid I got a big kick out of lead-sled competitions, where guys would vie to see who could mount the most colorful lighting on his bike. It was nothing to see 80 to 100 taillights mounted to an old 74-inch Harley. Back then, I never gave much thought to the technical aspects of those displays, but I do now.

Bolting on additional lights, or any electrical accessory for that matter, places increased demands on your motorcycle's electrical system. If the additions are well thought out and the installation performed in a workmanlike manner, the impact to your charging system should be negligible. If you fail to think everything through, you're liable to end up with problems ranging from hard starting, to smoldering wires, or a melted electrical system.

FUEL-LEVEL-SENDING UNITS; FUEL GAUGE INOPERATIVE OR WILDLY INACCURATE

While there are several types of gauges and sending units in use, they are all based on the same principle. A float is connected, via a movable arm, to a contact point. The float moves up and down according to the level of gas in the tank. As it does, the contact moves along a coil of wire. Collectively, this is a variable resistance called a "rheostat." As the contact point moves across the wire, it varies the resistance. As the resistance varies, so does the amperage flowing through the fuel gauge. As the amperage varies, so does the position of the needle.

In the old days, troubleshooting a non-working fuel gauge was pretty simple; you grounded the hot lead of the sending unit, and if the gauge swung to full, you knew you had a bad sending unit. These days, I'd be a bit more circumspect and only ground the unit if the service manual specifically called for it. If the gauge checks out, your next check should be for continuity between the sending unit and the gauge. If that's present, you should proceed to check the power lead for voltage. Assuming everything checks out there, then the problem must be in the sending unit itself. Lastly, you should remove the sending unit from the tank, connect an ohm meter across the terminals, and move the float by hand while watching the gauge. If the resistance readings are screwy, replace the sending unit. If they are within spec, retrace your steps starting at the gauge. ∎

TROUBLESHOOTING ELECTRICAL SYSTEM

Without the ability to read and interpret a wiring diagram, you're not going to be able to troubleshoot the most basic electrical problems, nor will you be able to safely install electrical accessories. We also need to recognize some basic electrical symbols (refer to the chart in Chapter 11). As will be explained, not everyone uses the same symbols, but most are readily understandable and also listed in your motorcycle's shop manual.

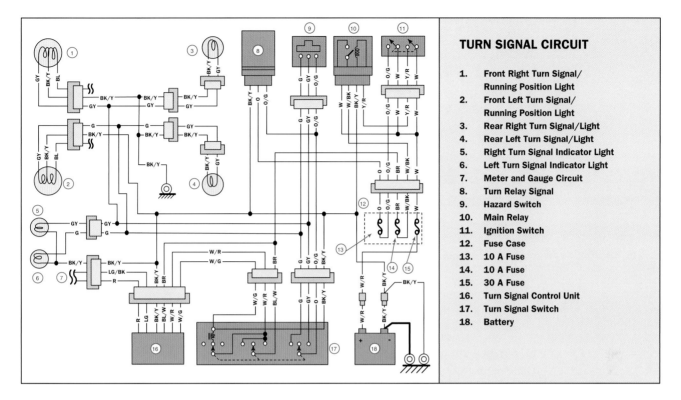

TURN SIGNAL CIRCUIT

1. **Front Right Turn Signal/ Running Position Light**
2. **Front Left Turn Signal/ Running Position Light**
3. **Rear Right Turn Signal/Light**
4. **Rear Left Turn Signal/Light**
5. **Right Turn Signal Indicator Light**
6. **Left Turn Signal Indicator Light**
7. **Meter and Gauge Circuit**
8. **Turn Relay Signal**
9. **Hazard Switch**
10. **Main Relay**
11. **Ignition Switch**
12. **Fuse Case**
13. **10 A Fuse**
14. **10 A Fuse**
15. **30 A Fuse**
16. **Turn Signal Control Unit**
17. **Turn Signal Switch**
18. **Battery**

A typical wiring diagram is like a road map of the electrical system. The various circuits are clearly indicated as are the components that make up those circuits.

The wiring diagram that's found in every service manual represents a road map of the circuits. The odd little symbols scattered throughout the diagram are pictorial representations of the devices that transfer, control, or use electricity. Japanese diagrams generally use pictures that look like the object they represent, as do most American and British manuals. European motorcycles usually use the German DIN (Deutsche Industrial Norms) symbols. DIN symbols can be a little confusing. However, the ever-efficient Germans specify a terminal designation and a wire-color code for each and every component. For instance, anything made in Germany—lawnmower, motorcycle, car, truck, or airplane—uses the same terminal designation and color code for its electrical components. For example, terminal 15 is always an ignition switch. A green wire always runs from the 15 terminal on the switch to the 15 terminal on the secondary-ignition coil, end of discussion.

Unfortunately, there is no real standardization in the United States. Each manufacturer is free to do as it pleases. Thankfully, certain conventions

have been adopted. It's safe to say that manufacturers generally find a system of colors and symbols they like and stick with them. For instance, most manufacturers in this country use red to indicate a "hot" wire and black to indicate ground.

Take a few minutes to familiarize yourself with the particulars of your bike's wiring diagram. You don't have to memorize it, but at least take a look at it: which leads go where, what colors the individual circuits use, and what the pictures represent. Preferably, do this before you have to look for an electrical fault at 2am, in the rain.

Basically, electricity is a lazy fellow that doesn't want to work if it doesn't have to. What it wants to do is return as quickly as possible to its source, which in this case is the battery. If the circuit is open, like when a wire is broken but isn't shorted, the electrons can't flow. They get to stay home. If the wire breaks and shorts out against the frame, bingo, they return home via a short cut, probably blowing the fuse in the process. Finally, if the ground is bad, they don't bother even

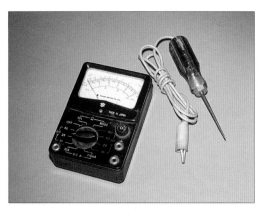

While the test light works fine for simple tasks, the Volt-Ohm Meter will be needed for more sophisticated tests.

trying to work. As you may surmise, electricity always takes the short cut. In essence, our job is to make sure the laggard does his job.

Test Lights Vs. Multimeters

This is a controversial subject among engineers and electrical technicians. Every once in awhile I run into some self-appointed expert that climbs up on a soapbox and proclaims, "The only proper way to troubleshoot an electrical circuit is with a VOM." That's a volt-ohm meter, or multimeter to us mortals. Let me go on record stating that, yes, that view is 100 percent correct. Let me also state that in the real world of day-to-day repairs, which is where I've spent the better part of the last 30 years, more often than not, the test lamp is still the first troubleshooting device the technician picks up when there is an electrical problem.

When I refer to a test lamp, what I'm talking about is a device that lights up whenever one end is grounded and voltage is applied to the other end. Usually, these look like an awl with a light bulb attached, and that's where the problem lies. A lot of "mechanics" like to check for current by poking a hole in the wire, perhaps in the hope that the electricity will leak out and they'll see it. Poking holes in wires is generally a bad move. Once you've got a hole in the insulation, electricity can leak out, which is called a short. The other problem, which is a lot more common, is that water can leak in. A much better idea is to disconnect the wire at some junction and check it there. If you must poke a hole in the wire, and

sometimes it is necessary, seal it afterward with a little dab of silicone and a wrap of tape.

The other problem with a test light is that you can only use it to check current flow and the condition of the ground. With a little experience you can also ascertain a circuit's resistance, but only within broad criteria. For example, if the bulb barely lights, the circuit's resistance may be too high. That's all you'll know, though, whereas a multimeter can precisely measure voltage, resistance, voltage drop, current flow, and so on. By all means, if you have the knowledge and the meter, use it instead of a test light. But if you're simply checking voltage, do it the easiest possible way and use a test light.

Most of the electrical faults you'll diagnose on the road fall into one of three broad categories: shorts, bad grounds, and failed components. Outside of replacement, there's not much you can do with a blown ignition module. However, shorts and bad grounds can be repaired or bypassed easily. All you have to do is find them and that's where the test light comes in.

If you're troubleshooting a component, the horn, for instance, place the probe at the positive terminal of the horn. If the light comes on when you press the horn button on the handlebars, you know that (a) you have current to the horn and (b) the horn circuit from the battery to the horn itself is in good shape. By extension, there are only two things left that could be at fault: either the horn is bad or the horn's ground is bad. How do you tell which one? Disconnect the ground side of the horn, place the alligator clip on the ground lead, the probe tip on the horn's ground tab, press the button. If the light comes on it means the ground and its lead are good. Bingo! That means you need to replace or adjust the horn as required.

There is one serious problem that crops up when using a test light. Computers often use less than 12 volts as a reference voltage. If you probe the wrong circuit with a test light you can cause some very expensive problems. My suggestion is to only use a test light to troubleshoot things like horns, turn signals, and other non-computer driven components.

Don't confuse the test light with its near cousin, the continuity tester. The continuity

DIY   *Checking Sending Units*

In essence, a sending unit is little more than a switch. Some, like an oil-pressure sensor, are simple on-off devices. Others, such as coolant-temperature sensors or fuel-level indicators, need to be somewhat more sophisticated.

Certain sending units work by completing a circuit or by grounding it; others work by varying the resistance in a circuit. Essentially, when a sensor-controlled gauge or warning light stops working, you'll be faced with three possibilities: a bad gauge, a bad wire or a bad sending unit.

Since all manufacturers have their own designs and methods of troubleshooting, you'll have to refer to your shop manual for the specific test procedure appropriate to your motorcycle and situation. What follows is a brief description of three representative predicaments.

Faulty oil-pressure sensor: the oil-pressure light doesn't come on when the ignition switch is turned on.

Most oil-pressure-indicator sensors are simple on-off switches. The sensor is screwed directly into an oil passage. A small hole allows oil to enter the sensor. Inside the sensor is a contact. A light spring holds the contact against a seat; the seat is usually grounded through the sensor body, although a separate ground wire may also be used. The spring determines how much oil pressure is required to separate the contacts.

In a typical oil-pressure sensor/ warning-light circuit when the ignition is on, but the engine isn't running, current flows from the battery through the ignition switch to the warning light. It then enters the sensor, and passes through the contact to ground, which completes the circuit turning on the indicator light at the instrument panel.

When the engine is started, oil enters the sensor, lifting the contact of its seat, which breaks the circuit

causing the light to go out. If oil pressure drops while the engine is running, the spring forces the contact to close which turns on the light.

As an alternative, some sending units use the contact to open the

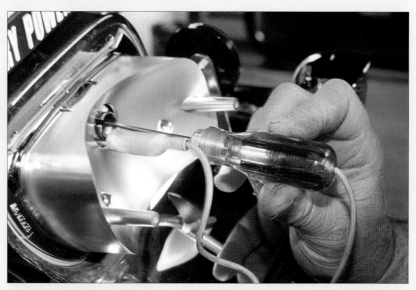

A test light is only used to check a live circuit. With the switch turned on, the probe of the test light is inserted into the socket, and the alligator clip is connected to a good ground. If current is present the indicator lamp should glow.

power side of the circuit, rather than make or break a ground. Obviously, if the light comes on when you're riding, you've got a potentially serious problem. The bike should be stopped as soon as possible, and not ridden or started until the problem is repaired.

But what if the light fails to come on when the ignition is turned on? Normally I'd tell you to check the bulb first, but in this day and age that may involve removing quite a few parts just to get to it. Better to be certain it's the bulb than to guess. Besides, since current normally flows from the bulb to the sending unit, there's a much simpler way to determine if the bulb is good or bad. First and foremost, consult your shop manual for the appropriate test procedure be-

The continuity tester is only used to check a circuit when the power is turned off. In the photo the tester is connected between the ground terminal of the taillight and the taillight socket. Since the tester bulb is on we know there is a good path to ground.

(continued next page)

DIY Checking Sending Units

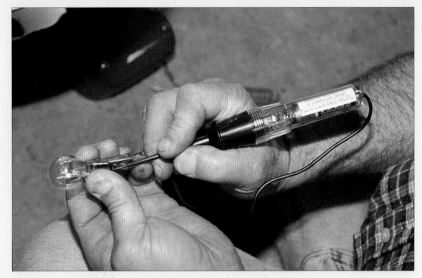

cause it may differ from the one described here. But assuming you have a typical, on-off type sensor here's the skinny.

Start by turning the ignition on, (engine off). Use a test light or voltmeter to check for voltage between the hot lead of the sensor and ground.

If voltage is present, then you know that the bulb is good, as is all of the wiring up to the sensor. If that's the case replace the sensor. As a double check, you can ground the hot lead, which should cause the light to come on.

If voltage isn't present, you'll need to work backward, using your manual to show you the current-feed path. Although, in the above case, the most likely culprit is probably a burned-out bulb. ■

This is an awkward way to test the bulb, but it does work. Because the filaments are intact the self-powered continuity tester comes on. Me? I'd just substitute a new bulb. However, this is one way to tell if that $40 projection-beam bulb is actually burned out, before you spring for a new one.

---

tester is a self-powered device used to check for continuity only. If it's inadvertently hooked up to a power source, the result is usually tester meltdown.

While test lights have their good points—chiefly, low cost and ease of use—nothing beats a good multimeter. Another problem with a test light, outside of its tendency to be misused, is the fact that it can't measure voltage or current, let alone resistance.

Meters will tell you if you have 10 volts or 12.5. The lamp may glow dimly, but is it dim because there's a bad ground or low voltage? Test lights are fine for a quick and dirty check; however, if you plan on serious troubleshooting, particularly at the component level, a meter is the only way to go.

Open Circuits and Bad Grounds

Let's start with an easy one. The right rear-directional signal is out. The right front isn't. Nothing could be easier. You replace the bulb with a new one, right? Uh-oh, it's still out. Now what, another new bulb? Don't laugh. I once watched a supposed mechanic, and I use the term loosely, pop in four bulbs before realizing the problem went a little deeper. Obviously, we have either no power to the light socket or no ground to complete the circuit. How do we find out where the problem lies?

You'd start by clipping the alligator clamp of your test lamp to a good ground; the ideal spot would be to the battery ground terminal itself. If this isn't possible, any good ground, the engine block, for example, will do. Next, touch the tip of the test light to the center terminal of the signal lamp (don't forget to turn on the signal). If the light doesn't come on, we have no power to the socket; if it does come on we have a bad ground.

Lets assume for the moment that the light doesn't come on, indicating a lack of power. First, just for your own peace of mind if nothing else, verify that you do have a good ground by touching the tip of the test lamp to a known power source; the positive battery terminal is best. If the light doesn't come on, recheck your ground and perform your test over.

By looking at the wiring diagram of the turn signal circuit a few pages back, you can see that current flows from the battery (18) via the wire marked W/R to the fuse (15). On the other side of the fuse the wire changes color and is now marked W, it proceeds to the ignition switch (11). When the ignition switch is in the ON position it energizes the main relay (10). Current flows from the relay, via a wire marked W/BK back to fuse (14). At the fuse, the wire again changes color and is now marked BR. Wire BR carries current to the signal switch (17) and also to turn-signal control unit (16). The ignition switch also routes current via wire O/G to fuse (13). At the fuse, the wire changes color again and is marked O; it connects to the turn-signal relay (8). The relay is connected to the hazard switch (9) via the lead marked O/G. Exiting the hazard switch, you'll see a lead marked GY. The GY lead connects both the turn-signal switch and the hazard switch to the right-side signal light and the indicator. Lead G from the hazard switch connects the left-side signals. The ground circuit is BK/Y.

Anytime the ignition switch is on, current flows through it to the main relay, the signal relay, the turn-signal control unit, and both the signal switch and hazard switch. The switches control current flow to the signals themselves.

You could start at the battery and trace the circuit out—a long and laborious process. Eventually, you'd find a point where you lost current, most likely a break in the wire or a corroded connection. Or, we can start at the light and work our way forward until we find power. A quick glance at the wiring diagram tells us that there is a cannon connector located close to the signal. Since either wire in the connector is a prime candidate for trouble, we may as well start there. Besides, logic tells us that since the front signal and both left ones work, power must be reaching the switch and flowing through the rest of the circuit. If power is reaching the switch and the left-side light works, we know that the problem is somewhere between the signal and its power source.

If we disconnect the cannon connector, we can check for current in the GY (green and yellow) wire. If there were no power, we'd keep checking it until we found the break. As you can see from the diagram, the GY wire comes from the switch, to the indicator bulb (5), to a joint between the two cannon connectors that feed the signal. Since we know the front signal works, logic and the wiring diagram tell us that the break has to be between the joint and the rear connector. Granted, the illustration I've used is about as basic as it gets, but I think you see where we're going.

The key to electrical troubleshooting is patience, and a fair amount of practice. Hopefully, you have more of the former than the latter. With a test light, a little bit of knowledge, and a wiring diagram, you can generally find the cause of most of the problems that crop up on the road and in the garage. With the aid of a diagram and some basic understanding of the various systems, you can usually bypass many of the electrical problems that put a lot of bikes on the trailer. You may not be able to fix a shorted or broken wire on the side of the highway, but if you know where it terminates, you can easily disconnect and bypass it with that spare wire you keep rolled up in the tool kit.

Big Disclaimer

Gauges and sending units are tricky things, it's easy to burn one up using the wrong troubleshooting methods. For that reason I can not stress enought how important it is to troubleshoot gauges and sending units using only the manufacturers' approved tools and methods.

It's time to have a little fun. In the first 12 chapters we learned a lot of boring technical stuff. By now, you should have a pretty good idea of what makes a motorcycle tick internally. In this chapter, we'll discuss how to make your bike fit you, how to keep it looking spiffy, and how to lay your bike up for storage.

WASHING, WAXING, AND POLISHING

Keeping your motorcycle clean and shiny accomplishes several objectives. First, it shows pride of ownership. Second, periodic washing will often help you find any little problems before they become big ones.

I can't tell you how many times I've spotted loose motor-mount bolts or a small oil leak while washing my bikes. Clean bikes also hold their value longer and are more pleasant to work on. And a good coat of wax will prevent bugs and road dirt from getting a good grip on your paint job.

Everyone has their own theory and method when it comes to cleaning their motorcycle. Some guys (ones I ride with actually) never wash their bikes. They prefer to use dedicated spray cleaners that are available through most motorcycle shops, or to just take the occasional ride in the rain. Me, I'm kind of traditional and enjoy spending the odd Saturday morning washing and waxing my bike.

Washing your bike can be a very satisfying, almost Zen-like, affair when you do it right. Washing a bike the right way is pretty easy. In reality, there is no wrong way, although I don't recommend steam cleaning your motorcycle, or running it through the car wash on a regular basis. Even those coin-operated car washes should generally be avoided. The high-pressure sprays

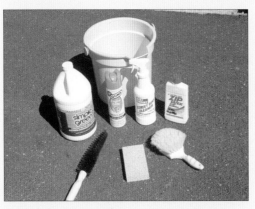

Let's see, I got my degreaser, my bucket, my soap, sponges, and spoke brushes. What did I forget? Oh yeah, water.

Small pressure washers work great, particularly if you do a lot of off-road riding and have to hose off lots of mud. Careful around those bearings and seals though. Pressure washers can force water into a lot of places it shouldn't go.

tend to force a lot of water into places you don't want it to go, like the electrical system, the wheel bearings, and the carburetor.

That said, I often use one of those little pressure washers available at any home-improvement center to hose down my off-road bikes, just because it's so easy. However, I am very careful about hosing down any sensitive areas.

Lots of riders like to use commercial prewashes; S-100 or Simple Green, for example, are popular cleaners. All of the products I've ever tried have worked well, and made washing the bike that much easier. The big advantage in using a dedicated cleaning product is that you can essentially spray the stuff on, following the appropriate instructions, of course, and then just hose it off.

This works really well if the bike is semi-clean to start with. But if the bike is really grungy, particularly around the engine and rear wheel, I like to use plain old spray Gunk. If you've never actually had a whiff of Gunk, it can be a little pungent. Personally I like the smell, but then again my olfactory senses are pretty tired.

The bike should always be pre-sprayed, either with a prewash or plain water. This should remove the majority of the loose road dirt and surface grime. If a prewash is used, it should be left to sit for a while (the instructions will specify how long), and then rinsed with clear water. At this point, you can wash the bike with soap and water, or simply dry it off.

If the bike is going to be hand-washed, start with a good rinse first, then hand-wash the bike using a soap formulated for automotive or motorcycle finishes. In general, I find that dishwashing soaps don't do a good job and will dull the paint, in some cases permanently.

You can use a sponge or old rag to wash the bike, or a soft-bristle brush. Years ago, I picked up a tapered brush that's perfect for working in and around the spokes. These are still available through motorcycle shops and are worth acquiring, if only to keep you from busting a knuckle trying to wash around the rear sprocket. Old toothbrushes can be put to good use scrubbing out all those hard-to-reach nooks and crannies as well.

DIY *Saturday Morning Bath*

Since I try to ride to work every day my bikes can get pretty grungy by the end of the week. All things being equal, I like to give them a little spit-and-polish on Saturday morning, particularly if I plan on taking a Sunday ride. Normally my Saturday morning wash ritual takes no more than an hour, leaving me plenty of time to mow the lawn, and think about where I'll be headed on Sunday!

(continued next page)

You'll need:

- *Wash bucket*
- *Car wash soap*
- *Sponge*
- *Soft bristle brush*
- *Gunk or other grease remover*
- *Pre wash- something like S-100*
- *Clean terrycloth toweling*
- *Clean rags*
- *Wax*
- *Armor All*
- *Metal polish*
- *Running water*

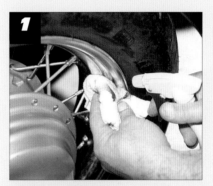

First, I like to clean off all the heavy stuff, such as chain goo, bird droppings, and splattered bugs. I use WD-40 to wipe the rear wheel clean before I wet down the bike.

Then I spray degreaser around the engine, or anywhere else that's oily, greasy, or hard to scrub.

Pre-wash is used if the bike has a lot of road film on it.

DIY *Saturday Morning Bath*

After the degreaser has had a few minutes to do its job, the bike gets rinsed with cool water. Once the bike is good and wet, it's time to get out the soapy water and elbow grease.

I use a soft bristle brush on unpainted parts, a new sponge or clean rag on everything else. By the way, if you have kids, this is the perfect time to introduce them to the joys of motorcycling.

At this point, a good paste wax can be applied. After it's hazed over, buff to your heart's content. If it shines, polish it.

Rinse thoroughly with cool water, and then towel dry the bike. Or cheat and blow it dry with your compressor (but once again be wary of blowing water into bearings and seals).

Lastly, it never hurts to apply a little Armor All or similar product to the soft parts. If you decide to buff up your tires, apply the conditioner only to the sidewalls and take great care not to lather up the tread with anything that will compromise traction.

The bike should then be dried with a clean towel. If possible, wash the towel before its next use. Dirty towels don't absorb as much water as clean ones and they tend to put fine scratches into the finish. As an alternative, the bike can be blown dry with compressed air, a leaf blower, or even a blow drier. After the bike is dried off, I like to take a quick spin around the block; this removes any residual water from all the nooks and crannies and helps dry out the brakes, exhaust, and engine.

After the bike is clean and dry, you can, if you're feeling ambitious, apply a wax or spray polish. In the past few year, I've become a big fan of spray cleaners and waxes, like Pro Honda Spray Cleaner & Polish. They go on easy and buff out quickly. Spray cleaners are also terrific if you just want to buff up your bike a little and don't have the time or inclination to do a full bucket wash. If you're on tour, a spray cleaner, like S100's Detail & Wax, can be stowed in your saddlebag with a piece of clean toweling and used to remove light road grime and the inevitable bug splatter at the end of each day's ride.

If you prefer a good old paste wax, go for it. Paste waxes come in two formulations: carnauba-based, which is a natural wax, and silicone-based. Carnauba-based waxes take a little extra effort to apply, but the final result is well worth it. If the finish is damaged, the wax can be easily stripped to allow touch-ups or repainting. Silicone waxes give you an outstanding finish, but they can be difficult to remove and tend to trap dirt particles beneath the coats. They make touch-ups difficult because they are hard to get out completely enough so that paint will adhere. Given a choice, I'll use a carnauba wax every time.

Follow the instructions on the side of the tin regarding application, and then buff off using a clean piece of toweling. Toothpicks, small paint brushes, or an old toothbrush can be used to remove the wax from around tank badges and other tight spots. Paste waxes regularly applied will go a long way toward protecting your bike's finish. Rubber parts can be dressed with Armor-All or a tire dressing; just don't get any on the brake discs or tires. The seat can also be buffed up with Armor-All, but please forgo drenching the grips and tires in the stuff.

Aluminum parts are often coated with clear lacquer, making them difficult to polish unless the lacquer is first removed. Removing the clear coat can be tedious. If you must, use lacquer thinner, or stripper, to remove the lacquer, but remember you'll be polishing the aluminum for a long time to come.

In my experience, the best polishes for aluminum are Simichrome, which is almost universally available, and Autosol, which may prove harder to come by. I've also used Cape Cod Metal Polishing Cloth to brighten dull aluminum. Cape Cod comes with its own impregnated cloth. You tear off a small piece, using it until it turns black, at which point it's basically used up.

You then polish off the residue using a clean rag. Cape Cod is less labor-intensive to use than the paste-type polishes and produces a nice shine, but it works less well at removing heavy stains and tarnish.

Nevr-Dull is another aluminum cleaner that works well. This stuff is chemical-soaked cotton batting. You wipe down the dull parts with it, scrubbing aggressively if need be, and then polish the part with a rag. Nevr-Dull works well, but care must be taken to avoid getting it on any painted or vinyl surfaces.

Dull chrome should be cleaned and shined with chrome polish, such as Dupont No. 7 and then protected with any proprietary wax. To remove surface rust from chrome, spray down the tarnished area with WD-40 or some other penetrating type of oil. Next, polish the area with steel wool, a Scotch-Brite pad, or very fine emery paper. Once the rust has been removed, use a clean, dry piece of toweling and Simichrome to remove any residual scratches.

It's easy to accumulate all kinds of products you never knew existed. Waxes, metal polish, leather conditioner; pretty soon you won't have any room for the bike in the garage.

Aerosol Spray Painting

You'll need:

- Primer
- Paint
- Wire brush
- Sandpaper
- Masking tape
- Newspaper

A very credible finish can be had using aerosol spray paint. I've seen entire bikes painted with a "spray bomb" that came out very nicely. My advice is to start out with small parts first, before you tackle the big jobs.

As with any paint job, 90 percent of the work is in the preparation. That means removing any trace of rust, grease, or dirt before painting. If the finish is really pitted, you may need to use a primer or surfacer to build up the surface.

Spray-paint colors vary slightly from manufacturer to manufacturer, and even from can to can. However, all cans are marked on the bottom with a batch number. If you anticipate a lot of painting pick up several cans from the same manufacturer, and try to get cans with the same batch number. Doing so will prevent color variations from appearing between coats or between parts.

By the same token, I don't recommend mixing paints and/or primers from different manufacturers because they may be incompatible. I once ruined a paint job because halfway through I ran out of a particular paint. I let the first coat dry, but applied the next coat without using a sealer. The paint formulations didn't agree, and ten minutes later I had a gooey mess on my hands that had to be completely stripped and repainted. ∎

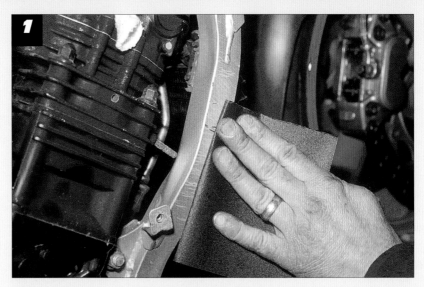

Strip the old paint completely and wash the part down with a good solvent. Brake cleaner will do, but lacquer thinner is better.

If you prefer to paint the part on the bike, or if the part is a portion of the bike that can't easily be removed, mask the surrounding areas with newspaper and masking tape. You can buy masking paper at a body shop supply store, but for most home projects newspaper will work fine.

Prime the part to be painted and let it dry. Than apply the top coat. Let stand (if required) and then apply the clear coat.

Blue Pipes

Discolored exhaust pipes are always a headache. My advice: learn to live with them if you can. All single-wall chrome head pipes will eventually discolor. But if you absolutely, positively have to remove the blueing from your head pipes, use a product called Blue-Away. Put some on a clean rag, rub like the dickens, and repeat. The luster won't be perfect, but it'll be pretty good.

Spiffing up your bike can be a chore, or you can make it fun. I prefer to play whenever possible, so here are my rules for primping bikes: first, never wash or wax a bike in direct, hot sunlight. Two, keep a few cold drinks handy. And three, always have a radio handy so you can listen to your favorite tunes.

PAINT BASICS

Here's a quick primer on paint (sorry, I couldn't resist). As a motorcycle owner/amateur mechanic, paint and its care will, or might, assume some importance. How much importance depends on the individual and the type of bike he's riding. I'd say that dirt-bike riders are on the low end of the scale, while owners of customs are at the top. The rest of us fall somewhere in between. The primary function of paint is to protect the base metal. I suppose the secondary function is to attract the buyer on the showroom floor. Oddly enough, when I was a motorcycle dealer I found that very few new buyers made a decision based on color.

Unless you plan to get involved with custom painting you really don't need to know a lot about the chemical makeup of paint so we'll just hit the basics.

Primer is a general term for any base or preparatory coat of paint. The primer is used to create a bond between the base metal and the finish coat. It is also used to fill in and level off small surface imperfections. Most primers are porous, so a primed piece will rust if left to sit for any length of time. If you like the primed look (a la Ducati's Monster Dark) you'll need to use a primer/sealer to keep moisture at bay.

For our purposes, there are basically two families of paint: enamel and lacquer. Within those families there are dozens of variations but for the most part enamel and lacquer are all we need to concern ourselves with. Enamels are tougher, but lacquers are easier to repair if you scratch the paint or make a mistake.

SETTING UP THE BIKE TO FIT YOU

Very few riders take the time to actually make their bike fit them. I don't know how many times I've seen riders struggle with awkwardly positioned handlebars, levers that were set at an angle guaranteed to cramp their wrists, and foot controls that were just plain clumsy to use. I do a lot of road-testing for a particular motorcycle magazine and I'd say at least half the bikes I receive are improperly set up, ergonomically. The

DIY   *Touching Up Paint*

Fortunately, most nicks and scratches can be repaired fairly easily. Since rust starts to bloom within a day or two, I'd recommend repairing any chips as they occur.

Most motorcycle manufacturers sell touch-up paint sticks. These usually include a small brush in the cap. The brush can be used to dab a bit of paint into the chip or a matchstick or toothpick can be used. The dinged spot should first be cleaned with solvent to remove any traces of wax. Let the repaired spot dry for a day or two before applying any wax or compound. Two-part finishes will also need a dab of clear after the color has thoroughly dried. ∎

You'll need:

• *Touch up paint (available through the OEM or aftermarket)*

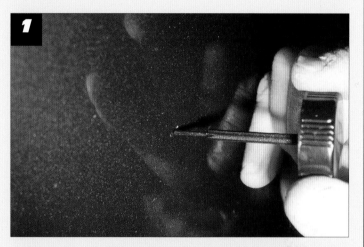

Let the paint roll off the end of the brush until it fills the chip.

In some cases a toothpick or paper match stick will be a bit easier to use for touch-up work.

Making the Bike Fit You

You'll need:

- *Common hand tools, sized to fit your controls*

Setting up the bike is relatively simple. Start by sitting on the bike. Your hands should drop to the bars in a natural position. If they don't, it's time to adjust the bars or replace them.

If your bike has non-adjustable bars, consider a replacement kit from one of the aftermarket companies. Often these bars use the original cables to simplify installation. Bear in mind that the wider the bar, the more leverage you'll have. If your bike is heavy and wears you out on the back roads, you may want to replace the factory bar with something offering a bit more leverage.

If the bars feel good, check the levers. If you have to bend your wrists like a contortionist just to reach them, something is wrong. Loosen them up and set them where you want them. If the levers require too much reach, put them where you want them. Again, you may have to go to the aftermarket to find what you want, but chances are it's out there.

Does your throttle have to be wound up like an old-fashioned alarm clock before it'll start to move the slides? If it does, adjust it to take that excess play right out of the cable. Most manufacturers recommend somewhere between 2 and 4 millimeters of free-play at the throttle cable. When is the last time you checked yours? Remember, you need some free-play or the throttles will lift every time you move the handlebars. This may cause the engine to rev up at inopportune moments, possibly causing an accident.

Foot controls should be adjusted to their most comfortable position. The rear brake on most bikes has an independent height adjustment that shouldn't affect free play. Set the brake pedal to its most comfortable position. For most of us, that should be slightly below the footpeg. The shift lever should also be positioned where it's most convenient. Many shifters have some sort of adjusting mechanism, or they can be rotated on their splines. If it still doesn't feel right, trot on down to your local dealer and find a longer or shorter lever, or modify yours the way you want it.

If the footpegs aren't where you'd like them, find more comfortable ones, or reposition the ones you have. You can make up a sanitary mount for your pegs by bolting a plate of aluminum to the stock location and then mounting your pegs to the plate

Don't put up with a bike that doesn't fit you. Adjust the handlebars.

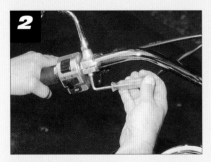

Then adjust the levers and turn the shift and brake lever adjusters until you're comfortable.

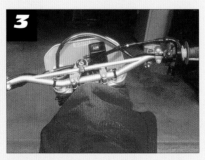

Use a shop rag or old towel to protect the fuel tank. Remove the clutch and brake levers by loosening the brackets (lever mounts).

(continued)

DIY   *Making the Bike Fit You*

4

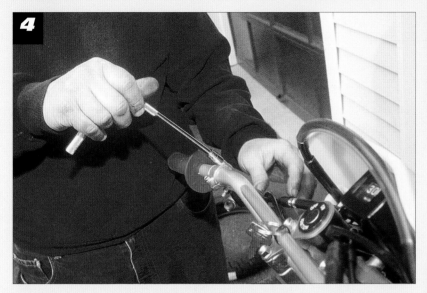

This bike has split brackets making them easy to unbolt. If your bike has one-piece mounts the throttle grip and left hand grip will have to be removed. You can then slide the lever assembly off the end of the handlebar. Hydraulic master cylinders should be tie wrapped to some convenient spot on the forks in an upright position to prevent air from entering the system. This may be easier after the bar clamps have been removed. It's rare that hydraulic lines will need to be removed unless the handlebar height is being radically changed.

5

Remove all the electrical switches if they haven't come off along with the lever mounts.

6

Many handlebar clamps are asymmetrical. Asymmetrical clamps have a punch mark indicating which way they should face.

7

Remove the handlebar clamps, followed by the bars. Install the new handlebars, then slide on the levers as required before reinstalling the handlebar clamps. Run the handlebar clamp bolts down only enough to prevent the bars from flopping around.

8

Before installing the throttle use a little light grease to lubricate the handlebar end.

Making the Bike Fit You

If possible, position the levers so they don't protrude beyond the ends of the handlebars. Tighten the lever mounts only enough to keep them from moving, but not so tight that they can't rotate if you apply some pressure. That way, if the bike tips over the handlebars will protect the lever ends and if the levers do hit something they will rotate out of the way, rather than break off.

in a location that suits you better. The seat is where you'll spend most, if not all, of your riding time. If the stock seat feels more like a device used to extract confessions during the Inquisition, chuck it. There are lots of aftermarket seats out there.

Grips can be a real source of annoyance, but that's why they make razor blades. Slice the old ones off, and install a pair you like.

Lower or taller windshields are always an option worth considering, if buffeting is a problem. If you can't find one you like, grab a jigsaw and make one you like better.

Here's the bottom line on ergonomics: make the bike fit you; don't adapt your body to fit the bike. ∎

Center the bars in the clamps. Check all lever adjustments, and make sure the throttle and switches work properly before riding the bike.

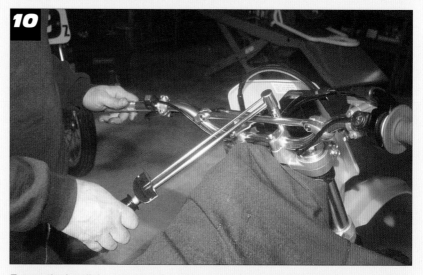

Torque the handlebar clamp bolts down according to the specifications in your service manual.

worst part of it is that correctly setting up the bike only takes maybe half an hour.

Some riders may accept a bike that's somewhat uncomfortable as the cost of doing business. Sportbike riders often seem to think that if their bikes aren't excruciating to ride, then something isn't right. Trust me, kids, real racers go to great lengths to make their bikes as comfortable to ride as possible.

Another factor that comes into play, particularly when someone has owned and ridden a bike for some time, is the general wear that takes place. A cable in daily use eventually starts to stretch, clutches and brakes wear and need adjustment, throttles develop too much free-play, and so on. This wear takes place so gradually that many riders aren't even aware it's occurring.

It's hard to ride a bike smoothly if every time you release the clutch, it engages in series of slips and sticks because the cable is dry as a bone. Likewise, if the throttle has half an inch of free-play, it's going to make on-off throttle transitions a little weird.

So, the first rung on the ergonomic ladder is to make sure you keep up your maintenance program. Routine checks of free-play and cable adjustment will help keep your bike operating smoothly and make it easier to ride. If it takes the strength of Godzilla to pull in the clutch, lube the cable, or replace it with a new one before your next ride.

In his excellent book, *The Sportbike Performance Handbook,* Kevin Cameron placed the chapter on fitting the bike at the very front, for the simple reason that you can ride farther, faster, longer, and with more confidence on a comfortable bike than you can on one that isn't.

WINTER STORAGE

No one likes to put his or her bike away for the winter, or for any extended period for that matter. What's even less fun is trying to resurrect the poor thing when the riding season finally arrives. Many a rider has parked his sweet-running, good-looking machine in the garage at the first sign of cool weather, expecting the same bike to be there the following spring. When the last snows have melted and the crocuses popped through, he heads out to the garage. What he often encounters is a dirty, rusty, hard-starting motorcycle that won't idle.

I'm of two minds when it comes to winter storage. I like to ride a lot. I'll generally ride my street bike and trail bike right up until snow makes the road a slippery mess and the trails impassable. Then, I'll go ice racing. I will continue to ride my street bike at least once a week, even if it's only for an hour or so. Basically, I try to bypass the whole storage issue, but I also have a heated shop to work in and warm water to wash the road salt and grime off my bike. So one side

of my brain thinks, "Sod winter, I'm going riding." But the other portion, the logical side, small as it may be, realizes that isn't practical for most motorcyclists. There is nothing wrong, for a wide variety of reasons, with parking your bike for a few months every year.

If the bike is ridden hard and put up wet, you're likely to have a few headaches when it comes springtime. On the other hand, if the bike is stowed away with a modicum of care, resurrecting it come springtime should be a breeze.

Winter storage is also the perfect time to perform any long-term projects or major overhauls you've had in mind. When I store a bike for the winter, I often stretch out any scheduled maintenance jobs. One weekend I may go out and adjust the valves. The next I may replace the tires, or whatever. By the time spring rolls around, about the only maintenance left should be to reinstall the battery, air up the tires, and wash any preservatives from the bike. It's nice to have the luxury of time to perform all of those little, fiddly things that are such a pain in nice weather. In my book, there are few better ways to spend a snowy winter Saturday than working on a motorcycle. And there is nothing finer than rolling a freshly-tuned motorcycle out of the garage on

A prospective buyer gets the lowdown. My advice for novice used bike buyers is to always start at your local motorcycle shop.

DIY Storage Procedure

You'll need:

- *Common hand tools*
- *Drain pan*
- *Engine oil*
- *Fuel stabilizer*
- *WD-40 or some other moisture displacing lubricant*
- *Battery charger*
- *Motorcycle cover (optional)*

Start by giving the bike a thorough wash and wax. I mean, really go over that baby from top to bottom. When you're done, take a ride. You want to get the motorcycle completely dry. Ride the bike for as long as you want, but before you return home, fill the tank to the brim. This will prevent condensation from forming in the tank. When you park the bike, add a bit of fuel stabilizer to the fuel tank (if the ride home from the gas station was of any length, top up the tank again when you return home).

Your next project is going to be to drain the carburetor float bowls. If you can, drain the bowls manually by opening a drain screw, or whatever. On some bikes that may be more trouble than it's worth. If so, you can just run them dry. If your bike has a manual petcock, turn it to off and let the bike idle until the engine stops. If the petcock is vacuum-operated, disconnect and plug the vacuum line to keep the petcock from opening. If the bike has fuel injection, don't worry about anything.

Next, it's time to change the fluids: engine oil, tranny oil, and primary oil (if applicable). If you've got shaft drive, the rear-end oil as well. Let the old stuff drain out and replace it with new. Change any oil filters at the same time. Do not restart the bike. Disconnect the battery and remove it.

Spray a little WD-40 or other moisture-displacing lubricant into the exhaust pipe and then seal the opening with duct tape. Likewise, seal the air-filter opening to prevent it from becoming a mouse condo.

Once the bike is placed in its storage facility, you can set it on its centerstand or a work stand. Block the tires clear off the ground and drop the tire pressures by around 20 percent.

The final step is to cover the bright work with a very light coat of WD-40 or some other light oil. Some guys I know go so far as to spray the whole bike down with oil or Cosmoline. This complicates cleanup in the spring slightly but positively guarantees that you won't find any rust. I used this method to protect my restored classics over several long New England winters, and the results were outstanding. I'd park the bikes on large sheets of cardboard, spray an entire can of WD-40 or CRC 556 over them and then let them sit. In the spring I'd Gunk them down, wash them off, and they looked terrific. The only drawback is that working on a slippery, oil-covered motorcycle can be a real drag. If you have a motorcycle cover, pop it over your baby, and then kiss it goodnight.

Lately, I've seen storage bags for motorcycles for sale. These are giant-sized baggies that you can roll your bike into. Desiccant is placed into the bag, and then a vacuum cleaner used to evacuate any moisture-filled air. One version even has a built in fan and filter to keep vapor-free fresh air circulating inside the bag. These are expensive and I think a little over-the-top, but they do work.

I almost forgot about the battery. The battery should be washed down and dried off. The water should be topped off and the battery stored in a cool, dry place, where it won't freeze. If the battery is stored in an unheated location, keep it charged, preferably with a smart charger. If a trickle charger is used, check the water level at least bi-weekly.

Winter storage advice always used to include a line or two about removing the spark plugs and pouring a teaspoon of oil into the cylinders to prevent rust from forming on the cylinder walls. Many owner's manuals still recommend doing just that. Personally, I don't believe in doing it. My feeling is that all it really does is gum up the rings. The best thing you can do, if you're the least bit ambitious, is to pop the bike into high gear and then turn the engine over using the rear wheel. Do that once or twice a month and you won't have any problems with either ring sticking or cylinder rusting. If you disagree with me, by all means oil up your cylinders, but I'd recommend using a very light fogging oil. Fogging oil is a preservative oil created to prevent rust from forming in the cylinders of engines that sit for long periods of time, primarily snowmobile engines and outboard motors. Many bike shops carry it, as do marinas and sled shops. If you opt to use it, follow the instructions printed on the container. ■

the first warm day of spring and going for a ride to reward yourself for planning ahead.

Finding a location to store the bike is sometimes tricky. The worst place is in the basement. Forget about the dangers of keeping a fully-fueled motorcycle in the house. Imagine the disaster that would result should a spark from the oil burner or water heater ignite some stray gasoline vapors. Another issue is that temperatures in basements fluctuate widely, due to the aforementioned heaters. It's not unusual to see a 20-degree temperature difference when the burner kicks on. Those ups and downs in the temperature cause condensation to form on your motorcycle's metal surfaces creating rust. A better solution is to store your bike in a garage, protected from the elements. Unheated garages are perfectly fine, provided the bike is stored out of direct sunlight.

Spring Unveiling

If your bike is properly maintained and properly put away for the winter, the spring restart should be cake. Simply reinstall the battery, air up the tires, and wash the goo off the bike. Then go for a ride. If you just parked Old Paint figuring you'd gas'er and go, good luck. If the bike only sat for a month or two, you'll probably get away with doing just that. But if you've run out of luck or winter lasted a whole lot longer than you thought it would, sorry pard; you'll need to read the next chapter on troubleshooting.

Everything we've discussed so far has been, for the most part, about the nuts and bolts of motorcycling. In this final chapter, we're going to get right down and really get our hands dirty. In the first section we're going to learn what to do when our bikes are broken and, in the second section how to do all sorts of neat things to repair them.

I'm going to divide troubleshooting into two categories. The first, for lack of a better title, is called what to do when the bike won't start. The second is titled, just as creatively, what to do when the bike won't run. To the novice mechanic that may seem a bit redundant. But by not running, I mean either that bike lacks performance, or that it was running and shut off. After all, a bike that won't start in the first place and one that was running fine and then shut off suddenly are two completely different things. I've also provided a chart that should help shortcut the troubleshooting procedure considerably.

WHAT TO DO WHEN BIKE WON'T START

There is nothing worse than strolling out to the garage, all bright-eyed and bushy-tailed, primed for a terrific ride and not being able to start your bike. When I was much younger and rode a lot of really tired iron, I made it a point never to put my helmet and jacket on until I actually saw a few signs of life in whatever old crock I planned to ride. Only after the bike was good and warmed up, would I don my riding gear.

Assuming the bike was running fine when it was last put away and also assuming that it

He looks a little shaky doesn't he? He'll get over it; it's natural to be a little nervous anytime you attempt something new, but work slowly and patiently, you'll do just fine.

wasn't put away six months prior to the current attempt to start it, troubleshooting a no-start situation is relatively simple.

Will the Bike Turn Over?

First, does the bike turn over with the electric starter? If the bike spins normally but just won't start, we can discount a dead battery. Obviously, if all you get are a few clicks and a groaning sound when you hit the starter button, the battery is probably dead. If the battery appears to be dead, check it with your voltmeter. If it reads anything below 12.5 volts, it's time for a battery charge. Of course, you'll have to find out why the battery went dead in the first place after the bike is started, but that's a separate issue. Kickstart-only bikes aren't as susceptible to dead battery problems; most have a magneto ignition of some sort and should start, dead battery or not.

What if the battery checks out normal, but nothing happens when you thumb the starter? First, make absolutely certain you are following the correct starting procedure. Some bikes will only start with the clutch in and the kickstand up. Others may start with the kickstand down, but only if the bike is in neutral. It's easy to forget the drill, particularly if you're unfamiliar with the bike. Another often-overlooked item is the kill switch. Always check that first, especially if the bike is parked where idle and curious children can get hold of it.

If everything checks out but the engine still won't spin, it's time to get out the service manual and start tracing circuits. You may be dealing with anything from a faulty clutch, kickstand-safety switch, starter relay, or just a bad connection. The only way to find out is to troubleshoot the electrical system, step by step, with the aid of your test light or voltmeter and the shop manual. Start at the battery and work your way forward; blown fuses, dirty or bad switches and broken wires are all likely suspects, as is the occasional bad starter motor.

If the bike spins over normally, it's time to move forward. In the first chapter we learned that engines need three things to run: fuel, compression, and spark. If any one of those three items is deficient, the engine simply won't start.

DIY Go with the Flow

Without fuel our motorcycle goes nowhere. If your motorcycle suddenly refuses to start or sputters to a stop lack of fuel is always a suspect. Before you start pulling things apart though, make certain that there is fuel in the tank and that the petcock is open. ■

You'll need:

- *The appropriate wrenches or screwdriver to remove the carburetor drain plug, and fuel lines.*
- *Small drain pan to catch spilled fuel.*

Usually the easiest place to check fuel flow is at the carburetor float bowl. This race bike has a drain plug. More common, particularly on street bikes, are small drain screws, located on the side of the float bowl.

If fuel is flowing, you know the problem lies elsewhere.

If no fuel flows, remove the fuel line at the petcock and check flow. If your bike uses a vacuum petcock, turn the lever to prime.

If fuel flows from the petcock, but it's not reaching the carburetor float bowl, the likely culprit is a plugged fuel filter.

DIV Checking for Spark

You'll need

- *Spark plug wrench*
- *New plug or known good one*
- *Spark testing device (optional)*

We need fuel, spark and compression to make an engine run. If the fuel is there than the next logical step is to check for spark. A word of warning, before checking for spark make sure that any and all fuel that may have spilled is cleaned up. Even a very weak spark can ignite raw gas and turn your motorcycle into molten mass of plastic and alloy. ∎

Remove the plug wire from the spark plug and plug it onto the tool. Clip the ground end of the tool to the engine or other good ground. Spin the engine over; if the tool flashes you know you have enough current to fire the spark plug. However, it's always possible that the plug itself may be bad, so if the bike still won't start it's worth checking the plug.

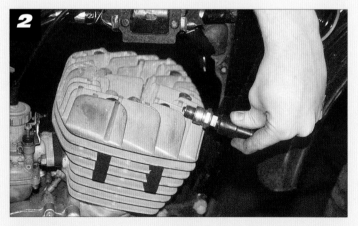

Since time immemorial—or at least for the last 100 years or so—we've been checking for spark by unscrewing the plug, plugging the lead back onto it and holding the base against the head while someone spins the motor over. The technique still works. Ideally the spark should be fat and blue. Careful, this is also a good way to get a real jolt, especially if the ground is less than good.

Check for Fuel

Fuel is the easiest item to check and the one that probably causes the most problems. If the tank is low and you have a manual petcock, move it to PRIME or RESERVE and try to start the beast again. Crank it for short periods of time, no more than about 10 seconds each try. If the tank has no petcock, just a warning light, or as I call them a "walk light" and it's on, you may have found your problem. If it's not on, check the tank anyway. If you can't see or hear any fuel sloshing around, add a little into the tank, and try again.

Even if there appears to be plenty of fuel in the tank it may not be getting into the carburetor. The easiest way to check is to place a small container beneath one of the float bowls and loosen the drain screw. Fuel should run out. If no fuel appears, or if a mixture of fuel, slime, and water come out, you've probably found the problem. If fuel just dribbles out a bit and then stops, go back and check the level in the tank. If it's full, then chances are that there is either a blockage in the fuel line or the fuel-tank vent is blocked. Try opening the cap. If fuel starts to flow, somehow the fuel-tank vent has become blocked. Check for a pinched vent hose, or on older bikes with vents in the cap, an obstruction in the vent itself. Overzealous waxing can sometimes plug up the small vent in the top of the cap, something to check if you're a shine-a-holic.

Check for Spark

If you've gotten this far and the bugger still won't light, it's time to check the spark. This can be tricky, especially since you've just been checking the fuel, and if you're like me probably gave yourself a good dousing with the stuff.

The easiest way to check for spark is to remove a spark plug from the cylinder head, plug it back into the wire, and lay it on the cylinder head. Crank the engine over and observe the spark. If there isn't any, substitute a new or known-good plug and try it again. If you now have a fat blue spark jumping to ground, replace the plugs with new ones, and see what happens. While fouling a plug is a relatively rare occurrence these days, it still happens.

If you don't feel up to pulling the plugs, just pull the wire and substitute a new plug or use a spark-checking device (see illustration). While you won't be able to ascertain the condition of the plugs in the engine, you will at least be able to determine if the ignition system is functioning.

If you've no spark, you'll have to troubleshoot the ignition system. Since all new bikes rely on electronic-ignition systems, you may not be able to get very far, but remember the problem may not be in the ignition system as such. A bad kickstand-safety switch, a bad ignition or kill switch, or a bad clutch-interlock switch can all cause the sparks to go out. On some Harley-Davidson models there is even a roll-over-shut-off sensor. When the bike tips too far to one side it kills the engine. These switches hardly ever go bad, but the cheesy bracket that holds them breaks off every once in awhile. This lets the switch flop around like a hooked bass until it eventually shuts the engine off. These switches can also cause obscure running problems, but I'm getting ahead of myself.

Check for Compression

The last piece of the non-starting puzzle is compression. Without good compression, the engine just won't run. Sudden and dramatic losses of compression usually make themselves known in other ways, but hard starting or no starting may be traced to a gradual tightening of the valves or a worn-out top end. Taking a compression test varies from the fairly simple to the very involved, depending on the type of bike you're riding.

A compression test involves removing the spark plug(s) and screwing in an adapter hooked to a gauge. When the engine spins over, the gauge takes a direct pressure reading inside the cylinder. The reading is then compared to the factory specifications. The service manual will also tell you how much the actual reading can deviate from the factory recommendation.

If the battery has been run down, make sure it's fully recharged before attempting to check the compression, otherwise the slowly-spinning starter will give you a false low reading. On single-cylinder engines the reading will be whatever it is, good or bad. On multiple-cylinder engines, the cylinders should be no more than 10 psi apart, from the highest reading to the lowest.

DIY Checking Compression

Uh-oh, you've got fuel and spark and she still won't light? Now it's time to get serious. The last piece of the puzzle is compression, without it the engine just isn't going to run. ■

You'll need
- *Spark plug wrench*
- *Compression gauge*

Remove the plug and thread in the gauge.

Compression must be within the specifications provided by your service manual.

It's also more important that the readings remain fairly level.

For instance, if the factory-recommended compression for a four-cylinder engine is 150psi and your check reveals pressures of 145, 140, 150 and 145, I wouldn't be too concerned; the bike should run just fine. However, if you get something like 150, 145, 150, 60, you've got a problem.

Troubleshooting Engine Problems

Problem: Engine won't start, but turns over with electric starter or kickstarter.

Cause Lack of fuel, lack of spark, low compression.

Solution Check the petcock. Is it on? Is there clean, fresh fuel in the tank? Is it getting to the carburetor? The first two problems have obvious solutions.

If fuel is not reaching the carburetor, work from the petcock down. If it's a vacuum petcock, turn the lever to PRIME or RESERVE. If fuel doesn't flow, suspect a plugged petcock. Make certain the fuel line is clear. If fuel is reaching the carb inlet, but not flowing into the float bowl, tap the bowl with the handle of a screwdriver. If the float is sticking, the rap should free it up. If no fuel flows, the float needle may be frozen.

In any event, you'll need to remove the float bowl to determine the problem. If fuel doesn't appear to be the problem, your next check should be for spark. To check for spark, remove one of the spark plugs, laying it on the head and turning the engine over. Be extremely careful to wipe up any spilled fuel before performing a spark check. If there is no spark or a very weak one, replace the spark plug with a known, good plug.

If the spark seems adequate with the new plugs, replace any gas-fouled plugs, and try to start the engine. Fouled plugs are rare on modern street bikes, but there is always a chance that the engine was over-choked during a cold start, or that the choke was left on too long after the bike started, fouling the plugs. If the new plugs have no spark, troubleshoot the ignition system as required.

Problem: Engine will not turn over with electric starter

Cause Dead battery, safety switch engaged, blown main fuse, or bad starter solenoid.

Solution Check battery by turning on the ignition switch. If the lights work and the horn blows, chances are that the battery and main fuse are good and the problem lies elsewhere. Make sure that you are following the correct starting procedure: transmission in neutral, kickstand up, clutch pulled in, kill switch is on. If nothing comes on, check the main fuse first.

If the fuse is good, check the battery with a voltmeter and charge or replace as required. If the battery tests good but engine still won't turn over, likely suspects include a bad starter-safety interlock (not all bikes have these), bad starter relay, or even a bad starter motor.

Make sure the interlock, if there is one, is working. Troubleshoot the starter circuit as required. Refer to your service manual here, as it's likely to have a "no-start" troubleshooting tree listing the most common scenarios and their solutions.

Problem: Engine turns over, has good spark and good fuel, but still won't start

Cause Low compression or slipped timing.

Solution If a compression-check reading indicates low cylinder pressure, adjust the valves and recheck. If it's still low, you'll have to examine the top end. If compression checks out good, retrace troubleshooting procedure.

Let me point out here that sudden loss of compression in one or more cylinders indicates a serious problem. On the other hand, a low average compression reading just means the engine is getting tired.

Slipped ignition timing is a somewhat obscure problem, but it does occur, especially on kickstart-only bikes. If the woodruff key that locates the ignition rotor has sheared, the rotor can slip on its taper. The ignition will still have spark, it'll just occur at the wrong time. This can be a tough problem to find. The easy way is to set the engine at TDC and see if the timing marks still line up. Fortunately, the repair is normally straightforward: replace the key, retorque the nut, and go on your way.

Problem: Engine starts hard, idles poorly, and runs erratically

Cause This may occur after washing the bike, or after it's sat for a long period of time. It's often caused by water in fuel or dirty carburetors.

Solution Drain the carbs, and see how it runs. If big globs of water pour out you've found the problem. In severe cases you may need to remove the float bowls and blow out the jets.

Cause Restricted fuel flow.

Solution Check the fuel-tank vent, and replace fuel filters, check the lines for obstructions, and check the float needle and seat for dirt or sticking.

Cause Bad plugs.

Solution Replace, with known-good plug(s). If the situation occurred gradually a tune up is indicated. Adjust valves, replace plugs, replace fuel and air filters, and clean and adjust carburetors.

Troubleshooting Engine Problems

Problem: High-speed misfire

Cause Misfires generally come on over time and often just mean that it's tune-up time. Common causes include worn or dirty spark plugs, dirty air filters, and contaminated fuel filters.

Solution If the problem occurred after an aftermarket exhaust system or air filter was installed, the bike's jetting should be checked.

Problem: Engine hesitates or dies when the throttle is opened fully

Cause Plugged main jet.

Solution Remove and clean.

Cause Pilot mixture too weak.

Solution Adjust the pilot mixture to factory specifications and recheck.

Cause Water in float bowl.

Solution Drain float bowl.

Problem: Engine surges at moderate speeds, especially when you try to maintain a steady throttle

Cause Lean carburetion.

Solution Raise the needle one clip. If the needle has no adjustment, or if the problem is really bad, you may have to install an aftermarket jet kit.

Problem: Overall power loss, sluggish response

Cause Worn-out top end. Lots of times, other symptoms will appear: high oil consumption and/or smoking, for example. If your bike generally feels lazy and you start to blow lots of oil out of the breather, or smoke billows out the exhaust every time you roll on the throttle, chances are the top end is on the way out.

Solution Check compression and repair top end as indicated. This usually means semi-major surgery at the very least.

Problem: Overheating of water-cooled engines

Cause Low coolant, bad thermostat, bad fan or fan switch.

Solution Check and refill. It's also a good idea to find out where the coolant went. Check the hose clamps, radiator cap, and water pump for leaks. Repair any that are found. If the coolant level drops dramatically and quickly, and the bike starts to run rough or lose power, suspect a bad head gasket or other major internal leak.

Cause Bad thermostat.

Solution Replace the thermostat.

Cause Bad fan motor or bad fan sensor, if so equipped.

Solution Lots of times the bike won't overheat when the fan goes bad until you're stuck in a traffic jam or some other situation that prevents air from flowing across the radiator. If the temperature gauge climbs into the red zone without the fan coming on, you've got a problem. Troubleshoot the electric fan according to your manual and repair as required.

Problem: Overheating of air-cooled engines

Cause Clogged fins. This is more of an off-road problem. Mud and debris can build up to clog the fins. The junk acts to prevent cool air from carrying the heat off.

Solution Stop, clean the junk out, and let the engine cool off a little.

Problem: low oil level

Cause This is a no-brainer isn't it?

Solution Look for and correct any leaks; check more frequently.

Problem: Detonation (pinging or pinking)

Cause Low-octane fuel.

Solution Use the manufacturer's recommended grade of fuel.

Cause Too hot a spark plug. The wrong heat-range plug can cause pre-ignition, leading to detonation.

Solution Use the correct grade of plug. If a lot of hard riding is anticipated, you might want to go a range colder. This is more of a concern to riders of older or air-cooled motorcycles than it is to riders of newer, or liquid-cooled machines.

Cause Lugging the bike. Running the bike in too high a gear for the load causes the bike to overheat, as the engine struggles to develop enough torque to pull the load.

Solution Downshift into a lower gear, particularly when traveling uphill or carrying a heavy load.

Cause Over-advanced ignition timing. This is not the problem it once was, but it does occur.

Solution Reset the timing to factory specifications.

Cause Lean mixture. Lean mixtures create heat, and heat leads to detonation.

Solution Richen mixture slightly; an aftermarket jet kit may help.

Problem: Engine backfires during deceleration

Cause Air leaks or anything else that creates a lean condition.

Solution Check for air leaks at the exhaust-head pipe(s) or intake manifold. Adjusting the pilot screw a half turn or more richer will normally prevent backfires.

Troubleshooting Engine Problems

Problem: Backfire with aftermarket exhaust or air filter

Cause Again, this is caused by a lean mixture.

Solution Often when an aftermarket exhaust or air filter is installed, the bike tends to run a little lean. My feeling is that anytime anything affecting the intake or exhaust system is changed, the carburetors should be re-jetted to match the new parts.

Problem: Excess engine vibration

Cause Loose engine mount bolts, mounting plates, or head stays.

Solution Torque all bolts to spec. Actually, you should be checking and tightening all the bolts at every major service, or at least once a year.

Cause Carburetors out of sync

Solution Synchronize carburetors. Again, this is something that should be taken care of during a normal tune-up procedure.

Cause General engine tune, or lack thereof. An out-of-tune engine, be it single or multiple cylinder, will run rough and vibrate.

Solution Follow your owner's manual recommended service intervals.

Cause Cracked frame.

Solution This is more common on off-road bikes, but if your bike has sustained accident damage it's worth checking. Anytime you feel a weird or undue vibration that occurs after the bike has been in an accident, it may be due to damaged, bent, or cracked structural members. This isn't something you want to take lightly if the bike has been in an accident, especially one that bent the forks or damaged a rim. Have someone you trust inspect the frame and suspension components, preferably a shop that has experience dealing with accident-damaged bikes.

Problem: Excess oil consumption, evidenced by a drop in the oil level or smoking.

Cause Bad rings, worn cylinders, and worn out pistons.

Solution Replace the rings and hone the cylinders. If wear is severe or the cylinders are out of round, a rebore and oversize pistons will be required.

Cause Worn valve guides or valve-guide seals.

Solution Replacement of the valves and guides is the only real solution if they are worn.

Cause Overfilled sump.

Solution Overfilling the sump can cause the engine to burn the excess oil. Only fill the crankcase to its recommended level. You'd be amazed how many people like to add "a little bit extra" oil.

Overfilling the oil sump makes the oil and engine run hotter than normal because the crankshaft now has to churn its way through the extra oil. It also reduces crankcase volume, leading to engine breathing problems. The excess oil may be drawn through the breather into the air cleaner and from there to the combustion chamber. Once it starts to burn it gums up the valves and rings leading to other, more serious problems.

Troubleshooting Clutch & Transmission Problems

Problem: When you try to accelerate, the engine revs, but the bike doesn't move any faster

Cause Clutch slip.

Solution Start by checking and adjusting the clutch free-play. If the free-play is within specs, and the problem persists, the clutch plates, and possibly the clutch springs are worn out and in need of replacement.

Problem: The clutch won't fully disengage; when you put the bike in gear it clunks and stalls or creeps forward

Cause The clutch is dragging.

Solution Clutch drag can be caused by an assortment of problems, but the most likely and the easiest one to rectify is excess free-play. Excess free-play creeps into the clutch gradually; it happens so slowly that you may not even notice it, at least until you start grinding gears. As in the case of reduced free-play, the cure is simple: adjust the cable-free play.

Cause Oil level too high, the oil is of the wrong viscosity (too heavy), or an additive was used.

Solution An overfilled primary case can cause drag, as can oil of a heavier viscosity than recommended. The excess oil or the thicker oil can prevent the plates from separating cleanly. You can imagine what happens to those same plates when something like STP is added to the oil.

Cause Air in hydraulic system or low fluid level.

Solution When air is trapped in a hydraulic clutch, the release will behave exactly like a mechanical system with excess free-play in the cable. The solution is to refill the clutch master cylinder to the correct level and bleed the system.

Problem: The transmission is hard to shift

Hard-shifting gearboxes may or may not be the result of internal mechanical damage. Before ripping into the tranny or carting the bike to the nearest dealer take the time to investigate the little things.

Cause Oil of the wrong viscosity. Filling the transmission with an overly heavy oil will make changing gears difficult, and it won't necessarily offer any better protection.

Solution Use only the manufacturer's recommended weight and grade of oil.

Cause Shift linkage out of adjustment or not properly adjusted for the rider.

Solution This would seem to be more of a problem on a new bike, but occasionally internal wear or even a new pair of boots will require an adjustment to the shift linkage. Obviously, not all bikes have adjustable shift linkages, but if yours does, make sure that it's adjusted to make shifting as effortless as possible.

Cause Bent shift shaft. This is a sometimes obscure cause of hard shifting. It usually occurs after the bike has fallen and landed on the shift lever.

Solution If the bike starts to shift hard after a major accident or even a minor topple, it's worth removing the shaft for a look-see before pulling the transmission apart.

Cause Internal mechanical damage. Too many wheelies, holeshots, or slammed shifts can bend shift forks, chip gears, and tear up bearings. The only real way to determine what's damaged is to tear down and examine the shift drum, the gears, and the shift forks.

Problem: The transmission jumps out of gear or refuses to go into a particular gear

Cause Worn shift dogs, bent shift fork(s), bent shift-fork shaft.

Solution Sorry, but the only solution here is a tear-down and investigation.

Cause Broken linkage spring. I saved this one for last because it's an unusual problem. If the bike suddenly stops changing gears, either up or down but exhibits no other problem, it's possible that the shift spring that locates the shift mechanism on the shift shaft has broken. Normally, when this occurs, you can only change gears in either one direction, or possibly not change them at all.

Solution You'll have to do a fair amount of work to replace the spring, but at least you won't have to split the cases.

Troubleshooting Drum-Brake Problems

Problem: Poor performance; a high effort is required to stop, or the bike just won't stop when the brake is applied

Cause Adjustment out of spec.

Solution Check and adjust the brake cables, or rod, according to the service manual.

Cause Worn-out brake linings.

Solution Replace the brake linings.

Cause Cables or linkage are binding and not applying the brake when the levers are activated.

Solution This is usually caused by dirt or rust gumming up the works. The cure is to replace the cable and lubricate any pivot points. You might also want to consider devising a little more rigorous preventive-maintenance program.

Cause Glazed or contaminated linings.

Solution Rough-up glazed linings with sandpaper or a file (always wear a respirator to protect your lungs). Clean contaminated linings and drums with brake cleaner.

Problem: Brakes stick

Cause Cables or linkage are binding and preventing release of the brake.

Solution This is usually caused by dirt or rust gumming up the works. The cure is to replace the cable and lubricate any pivot points. You might also want to consider devising a little more rigorous preventive-maintenance program.

Cause Brake cams are dry and/or sticking.

Solution Dismantle the brake assembly, remove the cams, and lubricate them using anti-seize compound, per your shop manual.

Problem: Brakes squeal, annoying you, the neighbor's cat, and your riding buddies

Cause Dirt in the drum or overly-hard linings.

Solution You'll need to wash everything down with brake cleaner. Sometimes you may be able to find a slightly softer lining that resists squeal.

Troubleshooting Electrical Problems

Problem: Battery won't hold a charge

Cause Electrolyte level

Solution Top off the battery with distilled water and recharge it.

Cause Poor grounds either at the battery or at ground points on the frame. Inspect and correct.

Cause Battery is sulfated.

Solution Visually check the battery for sulfation. If you are in doubt as to its condition, charge and load-test the battery.

Cause There is a draw on battery.

Solution Use an ammeter connected in series between the battery and its ground cable to determine the battery draw when the bike is sitting; if it's excessive, disconnect the circuits one at a time until it's eliminated.

Problem: Battery won't charge (assuming you are using a known-good battery)

Cause Bad rectifier/regulator or a bad alternator.

Solution Test the charging system per the service manual. Once you locate the problem or bad component, repair or replace it as required.

Problem: Battery overcharges (overcharge symptoms include a battery that uses lots of water, frequently blown bulbs or a voltmeter that reads above 15 volts for long periods of time)

Cause Bad regulator.

Solution Replace regulator. This is more likely to be a problem on an AC-ignition bike. Normally tested by measuring the resistance between regulator terminals with an ohmmeter.

Troubleshooting Chassis Problems

Problem: Hard steering; it takes a lot of effort to get the bike to turn, especially at low speed

Cause The first thing to check is tire pressure. Low tire pressure can make the bike difficult to turn and impart a heavy feel to it.

Solution Adjust the tire pressures to the recommended specifications.

Cause Over-tightened steering-head bearing. When the bearings have been over-tightened, the bike will tend to fall from side to side at low speed. However, as the speed increases, the handling will improve.

Solution The steering-head bearings should be adjusted so that the front end swings freely from side to side without binding, yet not so freely that it flops around like a hooked bass. This takes a delicate touch. Some manuals will list a turning torque that can be measured.

Problem: You feel a detent, or dent, in the bearings when the fork is positioned straight ahead

Cause Worn or notched steering-head bearings. The bike really shouldn't be ridden in this condition. Handling will feel heavy at low speeds, and the bike may resist turning as the speed picks up.

Solution Replacement is the only real solution; periodic repacking of the bearings and routine checks on the adjustment help prevent wear.

Problem: Front end clunks when brake is applied

Cause Loose steering-head nut or bearings, which allows the fork to pivot at the frame.

Solution Adjust the bearings and torque the securing nut to proper specification.

Problem: Bike won't track straight. It may wander from side to side or turn better to one side than the other. Tire wear may increase on one side.

Cause Misaligned wheels.

Solution Carefully align the wheels. Use a straightedge to ensure that the datum points on the chain adjusters are accurate.

Cause Worn-out swingarm-pivot components.

Solution This problem usually only shows up when the bike has lots of miles on it. Replace the worn components as necessary.

Cause Bent frame.

Solution Bent frames are usually caused by severe accidents. Some frames are repairable, but generally they should be replaced.

Problem: Front end dives excessively under braking or when a small bump is encountered

Cause Soft, worn-out or broken springs, or insufficient preload.

Solution Increase preload or replace springs. If the bike has an air-assisted fork, you can add a bit of pressure.

Cause Insufficient damping, particularly on the compression side.

Solution You can increase fork-oil viscosity or firm up the compression damping using adjusters. You can also add a bit of fork oil; it won't change the damping rate, but it will reduce the air volume in the fork, which will have a similar affect to stiffening the spring.

Problem: Front fork feels stiff and reacts harshly to small bumps

Cause Too much compression damping.

Solution Use the clickers to reduce the compression damping.

Cause Too much rebound damping. This may seem odd, but if there is too much rebound damping the suspension will ratchet down. That is, after you hit a bump, the excess rebound damping prevents the suspension from returning to its correct ride height. You lose travel and, as more of a load is placed on the suspension, it has less ability to respond. Eventually you run out of travel.

Solution Simple, back off the rebound damping a little and see what happens.

Cause Overly-stiff fork springs.

Solution Fit softer fork springs or fit progressive springs.

Cause Too much oil.

Solution Use a fork-level gauge to accurately measure the fork oil level. Reduce the oil height slightly.

Cause Fork oil too thick. This will actually cause both rebound and compression to become overly stiff.

Solution Use lower viscosity.

Problem: Rear suspension is harsh

Cause Springs are too stiff.

Solution Reduce preload or fit softer springs.

Cause Incorrect damper adjustment.

Solution Back off clicker to factory recommendations.

Troubleshooting Hydraulic-Brake Problems

Problem: Spongy brakes

Cause Air trapped in brake lines.

Solution Bleed brakes and change brake fluid periodically.

Cause Lines flexing.

Solution Rubber brake hoses, especially well-aged ones, expand when pressure is applied. Brake feel is lost, and as you'd expect, the force required to expand the hoses subtracts from the force applied to the pads. The answer is simple: replace the cheesy OEM lines, especially if they are old and soft, with some high-zoot stainless-steel aftermarket lines.

Problem: Poor brake action or poor response

Cause Worn-out pads. This might seem like a straightforward issue, but you'd be amazed at how many people are riding around with worn-out brakes.

Solution Check your brakes on a weekly schedule. Replace them before they've worn past the point of no return.

Cause Contaminated pads. If the brakes worked fine before the bike was washed and doused with a spray wax or silicone, they have become contaminated. Leaking wheel seals, leaking calipers, and leaky fork seals can also contaminate brake pads.

Solution Clean the pads with brake cleaner or alcohol. If they can't be cleaned, replace them. Clean the rotors as well, and eliminate the source of the contamination.

Problem: Caliper is stuck or frozen (this usually occurs after the bike has been sitting for long periods of time)

Cause Water has settled in the brake caliper, rusting the bore, and possibly corroding the brake's sliding or pivoting surfaces.

Solution Remove the calipers and clean any rust or corrosion from the pivot point or slide surface. The caliper should be removed, dismantled, and rebuilt. If the inner surface of the caliper is badly pitted it should be replaced.

Problem: Brake lever pulses whenever the brakes are applied, or you feel a shudder through the handlebars

Cause Warped discs (rotors).

Solution Rotors warp for a variety of reasons, but mostly because they've been overheated. While some rotors can be machined back into shape, the best solution is to replace them.

Problem: Brake lever comes back too far

Cause Improper adjustment. Many bikes have a lever adjuster installed on the front brake. This can take the form of a large externally-adjustable eccentric, or a distance screw and lock nut. Some Lockheed master cylinders, used on older British and Italian bikes, use the lever-pivot screw as an adjuster. Adjust the lever until it feels comfortable for you.

Cause Worn-out pads

Solution Replace worn-out pads immediately.

Cause Low brake-fluid level.

Solution Refill the master cylinder and check pads, as a low fluid level indicates either worn pads or a leak.

Problem: Brakes drag

Cause Improper lever adjustment. The brake lever must have some play in it to ensure that the return port of the master cylinder doesn't become blocked.

Solution Adjust to spec. This is a serious problem. A dragging brake creates a lot of heat. This in turn results in brake fade, brake-fluid loss, and warped discs.

If one or more cylinders are low, you can squirt a little oil into the cylinders and re-try the test. The oil will act as a temporary seal to help the rings hold compression. If the compression comes up, you know the rings are worn. If the compression remains low, the problem is most likely in the valve train. Before tearing down the engine though, check your valve clearances and adjust as required. It's always possible that a valve is a little tight, reducing compression.

As an aside, every so often someone tells me that their engine is burning oil, but they know the top end is okay because they took a compression test and it read fine. Wrong line of reasoning. A compression test only tells you that the compression rings and valves are good. Even if the oil-control ring were left out of the engine you wouldn't see it on a compression gauge. However, if the compression is uniformly low, it is a good indication that the top end is worn and should be overhauled in the near future.

Bolt Head Marking Chart

Grade Marking	Specification	Material	Nominal Size, Dia. Inch	Proof Load PSI (MPa)	Tensile Strength Min. PSI (MPa)	Bolt Rockwell Hardness		Nut Rockwell Hardness	
						Min.	Max.	Min.	Max.
	ASTM A307 Grade A SAE J429 Grade 1	Low carbon steel	1/4 thru 1/2	33,000	60,000	B70	B100	—	—
	SAE J429 Grade 2	Low carbon steel	1/4 thru 3/4 3/4 to 1 1/2	55,000 33,000	74,000 60,000	B80	B100	—	C32
5.8	ISO SAE J1199 Property Class 5.8	Low or medium carbon steel	M5 thru M24	55,100 (380)	75400 (520)	B82	B95	—	C32
	ASTM A449 Type 1 SAE J429 Grade 5	Medium carbon steel, quenched & tempered	1/4 thru 1 1 to 1 1/2	85,000 74,000	120,000 105,000	C25 C19	C34 C30	—	C32 C32
8.8	ISO/DIN SAE J1199 Property Class 8.8	Medium carbon steel, quenched & tempered	M3 thru M16 M17 thru M36	84,100 (580) 87,000 (600)	116,000 (800) 120,350 (830)	C20 C23	C30 C34	—	C32
	SAE J429 Grade 5.1 (SEMS)	Low or medium carbon steel, quenched & tempered with assembled washer	No. 6 thru 5/8	85,000	120,000	C25	C40	—	—
9.8	ISO SAE J1199 Property Class 9.8	Medium carbon steel, quenched & tempered	M1.6 thru M16	94,250 (650)	130,500 (500)	C27	C36	—	C32
	SAE J429 Grade 7	Medium carbon alloy steel, quenched & tempered, roll threaded after heat treament	1/4 thru 1 1/2	105,000	133,000	C28	C34	—	—
	SAE J429 Grade 8.2	Low carbon boron martensite steel, fully killed, fine grain, quenched & tempered	1/4 thru 1	120,000	150,000	C35	C42	—	—
10.9	ISO SAE J1199 Property Class 10.9	Medium carbon alloy steel, quenched & tempered	M6 thru M36	120,350 (830)	150,800 (1040)	C33	C39	C26	C36
12.9	ISO Property Class 12.9	Medium carbon alloy steel, quenched & tempered	M1.6 thru M36	140,650 (970)	176,900 (1220)	C38	C44	C26	C36

This chart lists common bolt head markings and specifications.

DIY   *Removing a Seized Bolt*

You'll need

Depending on the severity of the problem
- *Penetrating oil*
- *Heat source*
- *Wrenches*
- *Vice grips*
- *Stud removers*
- *Ez-outs*

Frozen bolts can be a real headache, though not nearly so much of a headache as a broken off bolt. When you encounter a seized bolt resist the temptation to use brute force. Most of the time you'll find that a lot of penetrating oil, some heat and gentle persuasion work better in the long run.

∎

It's a lot easier to gently work the bolt loose than it is to drill it out. Start by applying some penetrating oil and let the bolt sit.

If the bolt still resists, apply some heat.

Apply steady, firm pressure, don't force it. If the bolt resists, apply more oil followed by more heat. Be careful though, as the oil can easily catch fire.

RUNNING PROBLEMS

A motorcycle that starts to run poorly is often harder to troubleshoot than one that won't run at all. Usually, once you find out why the bike won't run and rectify it, your troubles are more or less over. One that develops an intermittent problem or even an ongoing running problem can be a real headache.

Start by logically examining the problem. Let's assume that your bike, which used to run like a well-oiled watch, has acquired a high-speed misfire. At anything above sixty it now spits and sputters like Elmer Fudd.

The first question is, did this occur after some action on your part, or did it just crop up? If the problem started after you fueled up or washed the bike, it is most likely to be related to some type of contamination in the carburetor. Either water or dirt has made its way into the float bowl and the solution is to drain the float bowl and see if anything that doesn't belong there has migrated into it.

If the problem seemed to come on gradually, it's more likely that it's being caused by a general deterioration in the motorcycle's overall tune; especially if the bike is getting hard to start, won't idle smoothly or displays other symptoms consistent with a need for a tune up. If that seems to be the case the solution is pretty straightforward: tune the bike up.

One scenario that every motorcyclist eventually finds him or herself in involves breakdowns on the road. Again, the logical approach will work a lot better than blind panic. First, get yourself off the road and into a spot where you can at least work safely, even if this means pushing the bike down the road a bit to a protected location.

If the engine died suddenly with no warning, the problem is generally electrical in nature. Look for a blown main fuse, disconnected switch, broken wires, bad ground wire, and so on. Unfortunately, sudden electrical failures are often traced to the ignition module or other "black box," and may render the bike temporarily out of action.

If the bike started to buck and hesitate before expiring, the problem is usually fuel related; switch to reserve, and try starting the bike. At high speed, running out of fuel can sometimes mimic the sudden stop of an electrical failure, so the rule of thumb is always check fuel first. In most respects, once the bike shuts off, treat the condition as you would any other no-start situation. Remember it's fuel, spark, compression, and then cell phone.

Obviously, there are a wide variety of problems that can affect our bikes. Not all of them are engine-related. The following list details some of the more common problems most of us will run into, likely causes, and reasonable solutions.

BASIC HOW-TO: THINGS THAT TOOK ME YEARS TO LEARN

In this, the final section I'm going to teach you all of those silly little things that it took me years to learn. Some of the tips may seem odd or silly or even self-evident, but trust me they'll all come in handy.

Wrench Sizes and Bolts

When I was a kid I was fortunate to work for an old timer named Mac McCullough. Mac was a stickler for detail, and he taught me early on that a wrench is sized by the width of its jaws or box end. Or, perhaps more accurately, the width across the flats on the bolt head that the wrench fits. A bolt is sized by the diameter of its thread. For example a 10mm wrench fits a hex that's 10mm across its flats. Normally, a 6mm bolt has a 10mm hex head. Many people ask for a 10mm bolt when they really want a 6mm. If you ask for a 10mm bolt you're going to get a pretty big bolt; in fact the diameter of the threaded portion will measure 10mm—just under 7/16 inch. Try to familiarize yourself with the more common hardware sizes. Be aware that while it is customary for a bolt of a certain size to use a hex head of a given size, it is not a strict requirement and a manufacturer may fit whatever size hex head they feel is appropriate.

What Do Those Marks Mean on Hex-Head Bolts?

Did you ever notice those marks or numbers etched on the heads of hex bolts and wonder what they meant?

All hex bolts manufactured and sold in the United States have a stamping on the head indicating the tensile strength of the bolt. Bolts made

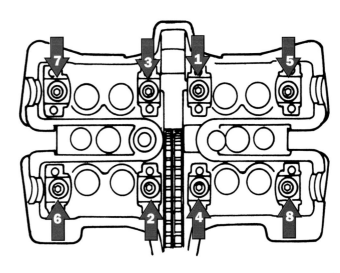

Head bolts are torqued in stages, (normally 25 percent increments of the final torque specification) and in a diagonal pattern, starting from the inside and working your way to the outer edges of the head.

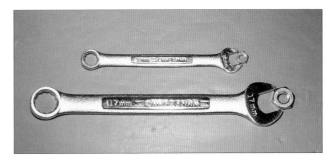

The designation on the wrench describes the distance between the flats. Not the size of the fastener. For example the top wrench is a 10mm, the nut between its jaws is a 6mm nut. The 17mm wrench on the bottom fits a 10mm nut

specifically for a manufacturer or imported may or may not have any identification marks embossed on the head. But all US-made (and foreign made) replacement bolts will have a symbol on them representing the bolt's strength. Your service manual will tell you what class of bolt is required for a particular application. If you know what to look you can easily find the correct replacement bolt by reading the symbol on the head of the bolt. The rule of thumb here is when in doubt go up a class, for instance you can replace a metric class 10.9 bolt with a class 12.9 but never the opposite. The chart in this chapter indicates the most common markings.

How To Torque a Bolt

A properly tightened fastener is one that applies the correct clamping force, or preload, to a bolt or stud. Think of a bolt or stud as a spring. As the bolt is tightened it stretches slightly. As it stretches, it applies a compressive load to the parts being held together. This load may be applied by threading the fastener into a tapped hole or by use of a nut. The load applied by the fastener to the parts being held together must be equal to or greater than the load the parts are expected to bear. The load capacity of the fastener must be equal to or greater than the load it is expected to bear.

Like any spring, the fastener must not be stretched too far. If it is, it will just lose its ability to remain elastic, or in the case of a bolt it will probably snap. Obviously if it's left loose it won't compress enough to accomplish its task. The solution is to accurately measure how much stretch or preload we place on the bolt. Although there are other methods, this can best be accomplished by using a torque wrench to tighten the bolt. While many bolts are secured without using a torque wrench, from a technical point of view, all bolts should be tightened using a torque wrench.

Your shop manual will specify the amount of torque to be used on the fastener, whether the bolt should be installed dry, or lubricated, and how many stages should be used to torque the bolt(s). It will also illustrate the pattern to be used on multiple fasteners that hold down large assemblies. For example, a cylinder head should always be torqued in multiple stages, starting with a relatively low torque figure and working progressively toward the final figure.

At the same time a very specific pattern should be used, starting with the inner bolts and working in a diagonal pattern toward the outside.

In the last few years some manufacturers have recommended torquing certain bolts, usually head bolts, to a given torque. They then recommend giving them a further twist by a specified amount, usually one-quarter to three-eighths of a turn. This procedure is now common in the auto industry; if it applies to your motorcycle, the manual will spell it out.

What To Do When You Strip a Screw

No matter how careful you are (or try to be), inevitably you'll be forced to deal with a stripped screw head or rounded-off nut or bolt. Phillips-head screws are particularly damage prone, most screws being made of fairly soft material. Lots of damage can be avoided simply by using an impact driver and the correct bit, but trust me, at some point you'll end up dealing with a stripped screw head. The following procedure details removing a screw or bolt that has had the head stripped or rounded off.

Once the head of the screw strips, STOP. Assess the situation, collect your wits, and take a deep breath before proceeding. Can the screw can be grabbed with a Vise-Grip? If it can, that should be your next step. Most of the time you won't be so lucky.

Plan B is usually to saw a slot in the screw and remove it with a straight-blade screwdriver. Most of the time, plan B fails because there isn't enough room to cut the slot. My favorite method is to take a small chisel or very sharp punch, set the tool on the edge of the screw, and angle it so that the force of the blow tends to loosen the screw. Give the punch a good whack or two. The screw should loosen.

If it doesn't, the final method is to drill dead center through the screw head using a drill bit that is slightly larger then the diameter of the screw shank. Drill into the head until it pops off the shank. Remove whatever the screw was holding on, usually a cover of some sort. The shank

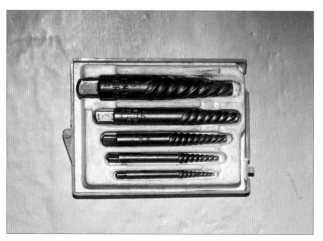

I've had this venerable E-Z Out set since 1970 and it hasn't let me down yet.

Removing a Stuck Screw

1

Most of the small screws found on our motorcycles seem to have all the structural integrity of cheese. Sometimes it seems like the buggers come pre-stripped right from the factory. Be that as it may, while a stripped screw can be a bear to remove, it can always be done. ∎

You'll need:

- *Impact driver*
- *Small very sharp chisel and hammer*
- *3/8 drill and bits*
- *EZ-OUT or other screw remover*

I hate when this happens, and trust me, I didn't stage it on purpose.

2

For argument's sake, I tried to catch one end of the screw head with a small sharp chisel, driven at a shallow angle. The theory is that the shock of the blow will loosen the screw. It works about 75 percent of the time.

4

Normally all the information you'll need will come with the extractor, often embossed on the shank of the tool or in the lid of the box. Note the rags in use here to protect the other parts from flying metal chips. Select the extractor that fits the hole and tap it into place.

3

When the chisel technique fails, it's time to start drilling. Drilling out a Phillips headed screw is fairly easy— the cross-slot provides a dead center for the bit to start in. On large bolts start with a small bit and bore a pilot hole. The final bit size will be determined by the size of the fastener and the size of the extractor that you're going to use.

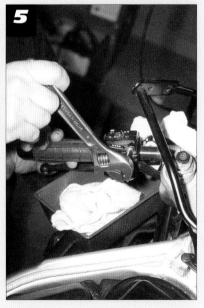

5

Use the adjustable wrench, or better yet a tap-handle, and twist the extractor and what's left of the old screw out.

A stud extractor can sometimes be used to remove a bolt that's sheared off.

of the screw can now be gripped with a Vise-Grip and spun right out.

When I was putting this section together I came across one other method. Honestly, I've never attempted to remove a screw like this but I'll bet it works. Take a punch slightly larger than the screw head and rest it directly on the stripped cross-slots. Using the punch and the appropriate hammer tap the slots back together. Next, find an impact bit that's a close fit in the mangled screw head, and use your hammer to drive it into the slots. Fit the impact driver to the bit and fetch it a stout blow, as they say in the old BSA manuals.

When refitting the cover or whatever it was you were trying to remove in the first place, consider replacing the silly Phillips head screws with Allen bolts.

Rounded-off bolt heads and nuts can largely be prevented by using the correct size box wrench or socket, preferably in six-point configuration. If the nut rounded because it seized to the bolt, a little heat and some penetrating oil will usually free it up enough to permit removal with a Vise-Grip or small pipe-wrench tool. A nut can often be split, either by using a cold chisel, hacksaw, or die grinder equipped with a cutting disc, or by using a nut-splitting tool. Normally, a rounded bolt can be gripped with a Vise-Grip or the head drilled off if it isn't too hard.

A dodge I've employed more than once is to use a slightly smaller socket or a metric socket on a fractional bolt and vice versa. The socket

can be pounded on with a hammer, and then the bolt can be spun off. I've also seen an old screw-driver blade jammed between one side of the damaged nut or bolt and the jaw of an open end wrench.

The big question is why was the bolt head rounded off in the first place? If it was from carelessness, that's one thing, but if it was because the bolt was seized in its thread that's something else that we'll need to deal with.

Removing Seized Bolts and Screws

Fasteners seize for lots of reasons, the most common being either corrosion, which acts to weld the threads together, or the wrong-length fastener being used. If an over-length screw is used it will bottom out in the threaded hole. This causes the threads to distort, jamming everything together.

Debris in the hole will also cause the threads to bind up. This can be a real problem if a part is sandblasted or glass beaded and not thoroughly cleaned prior to reassembly. Seized bolts can be very difficult to remove. If you use force you're just as likely to end up with a broken bolt as you are with a removed one.

If the bolt moves at all, count your blessings and then apply as much penetrating oil as you can. Let the stuff work for a few minutes while you take a break. The longer you can wait the better the results are likely to be. Start your removal by working the bolt back and forth a little bit at a time, first to the left and then to the right, all the while flooding the bolt hole with penetrating oil. Eventually, the bolt will start to move a little further each time you apply pressure and hopefully it will eventually come free. A little heat can be applied to speed things up.

Be very careful because most penetrating oils are flammable, which is a complication that you really don't need. Instead of using a torch try using a hot-air gun, like the ones used for stripping wallpaper or paint. The secret to success in the case of a seized fastener is going to be patience, lots of lubricant, and heat.

What to Do When the Fastener Breaks

I hate when this happens! Broken bolts, screws, or studs are really a worst-case scenario. The problem is that in 90 percent of the cases the fas-

DIY *Heli-Coil Installation*

Stripped holes are fact of life around motorcycles. Especially where you're threading a steel bolt or screw into soft aluminum. Fortunately there are several solutions to the problem that provide a neat and permanent repair. ■

You'll need:

- Helicoil kit
- Tap handle
- Cutting oil (you can substitute any light oil)
- 3/8 Drill
- Small magnet
- Small punch and hammer
- Needle-nose pliers

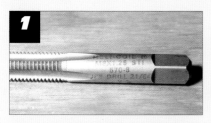

1 The information stamped on the tap tells you what size hole and thread pitch the tap will repair and what size drill to use.

4 The finished threads should look something like this.

7 The Helicoil should be threaded down a half thread or so below the surface.

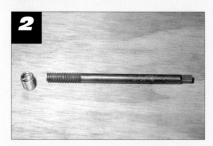

2 The tang on the insert (left) fits into a notch on the mandrel (installation tool).

5 Install the insert onto the mandrel, making sure the tang engages the drive slot on the tool.

8 The drive tang can be snapped off with a pair of pliers or small punch and retrieved with a magnet.

3 Use plenty of lubricant when tapping a hole. In many situations you'll be threading a blind hole, so the flutes of the tap should be packed with grease to retain the chips.

6 Insert the tool into the hole and thread the insert into it.

9 Repair complete.

DIY *Lubing a Control Cable*

You'll need:

- *Cable luber tool*
- *Cable lubricant*

My personal opinion is that most cables aren't lubed often enough. How often is of enough? Good question, many owners manuals call for 5,000 mile intervals, my recommendation is to halve that. ■

1

All you really need are a decent cable lube tool and a can of lubricant. The tool and lubricant can be purchased from any motorcycle shop.

2

Remove the cable from the control lever at the handlebar. It looks like this cable has seen better days.

3

Clamp the tool over the open end of the cable and tighten it down. The aerosol straw is inserted into the port on the tool. Spray until lube runs out the other end of the cable.

tener breaks because it's seized solid in its hole. The rest of the time the bolt breaks because someone gets a little antsy and wrings the end off with an oversized wrench or over-tightens the fastener.

Bolts that have simply been broken by an overzealous hand can often be spun straight out once you get a grip on the left-over piece. Sometimes you luck out, and the bolt snaps clean at the head. You can then remove the cover or mechanism and spin the busted piece out using a stud extractor or Vise-Grip.

The big headaches happen when the bolt gets wrung off because it is seized in the hole. Frankly, there is seldom an easy solution, chiefly because the blasted screw generally breaks off flush or slightly below the surface of the hole.

The first step is going to be drilling a small pilot hole, dead center into the broken bolt. Start by center-punching a dimple into the center of the bolt. This is tricky but it's the most important step. If you can, file the end of the break flat, but unfortunately this isn't always an option.

Next, using lots of oil and a very sharp drill bit, bore a pilot hole through the broken fastener. Be extremely careful to keep the drill centered and to ease up pressure as you approach the bottom of the hole. The last thing you need at this point is a broken drill bit stuck in a broken bolt.

On the bright side, the very act of center-punching the bolt and drilling it may collapse and loosen the bolt enough to allow it to be easily removed. Left-hand twist drills can often help the process along. In fact, the broken part may walk itself out during the process. You can obtain left-hand bits, cut specifically for the removal of broken bolts, at any good tool supplier.

Once the pilot hole is drilled you can open the hole up with progressively larger drill bits. Make the hole as large as you can without cutting into the original threads. Screw removal tools come in several different styles. The most common is the E-Z Out (easy out).

Essentially an E-Z Out is a hardened, tapered and fluted device. It is gently hammered into the broken fastener where it wedges solid. A tap handle or adjustable wrench is then used to spin the broken bolt out. A variation on the same idea uses a straight, fluted piece of tool steel. This style is driven into the fastener and turned using an adapter that fits over it.

There is also a device called a Drill-Out, this combines a small drill and an extractor into one unit. The Drill-Out uses the torque of the drill to remove the seized fastener.

Repairing Ruined Holes

Sometimes the worst possible scenario occurs. That broken bolt, stud, or screw just isn't going to come out. Or if it does it brings most of the original threads with it. If that happens, you're going to need to drill out the broken fastener and re-thread the hole. This is actually easier in many situations than extracting the broken bolt in the first place. But my advice is to always try to remove the broken fastener first. If that doesn't work, you can always proceed to drill the bolt out and start anew. You may also encounter a simple stripped hole.

Most threads are stripped because of continued over-torquing, which tends to pull the threads, bolt, or screw like any other wedge-type puller. Another culprit is under-torquing, which allows the fastener to move about in the hole until the threads are literally eroded away (which is commonly known as fretting).

The introduction of dirt between the fastener and the thread area also creates problems, as the dirt will seize the threads together. Of course, plain old carelessness in the form of cross-threading, jamming a fine-threaded bolt into a coarse-threaded hole (and vice versa), not to mention the almighty half-inch drive air impact gun, all account for their fair share of ruined threads.

One last thing should be mentioned: occasionally a bolt that went in fine comes out with some or most of the threads dangling from it. This is usually the result of dissimilar metals (steel or stainless steel into aluminum or cast iron) being assembled without adequate lubrication. Anytime you install a steel or stainless-steel bolt, which covers almost all bolts today, into aluminum or cast iron, it should be lubricated with a light oil or anti-seize compound, preferably one based on a colloidal copper compound, these are sold under a variety of trade names, I

DIY Hand-Packing a Bearing

This is fun, kind of like being a kid and making mud pies, plus it really packs the grease into those old bearings. Don't forget to remove the gloves or wash your hands before using the guest towels. ∎

You'll need:
- Grease
- *Your hands*
- *Rubber gloves (optional)*

1 Grab a handful of grease in one hand and the bearing in the other. Since I m right handed I hold the bearing in my right and use the left to glom up the grease.

2 Place the large end of the bearing so that it faces the grease, press the bearing down as you drag it across the grease. The grease will work its way into the bearing and should start to roll out of the narrow end.

3 Not too bad. Before installing the bearing wipe the circumference with grease and pack the inner race.

BEARING AND SEAL NUMBERS

All bearings and seals have a generic part number listed on them. Usually this takes the form of a code number such as 6204 or some such. Once you know the code number you can purchase the bearing or seal at any auto parts store or bearing house. If you can't find the code or the great big bearing interchange book doesn't list it, the part number can usually be determined by measuring the bearing outside and inside diameters and width, as shown in the photos. ■

personally like the Permatex line of anti-seize lubricants. Obviously, some torque specs call for a dry, clean fastener. This is often the case with head bolts, but check your shop manual if there is any doubt. Since a stripped hole and one intentionally drilled are repaired in the same manner we'll treat both cases as one.

The first and most obvious solution that may come to mind is simple: re-drill the hole and re-tap it to the next-over size. Fine idea if you have the room to do it. In many instances, it may be possible to enlarge the hole, say from 6mm to 8mm or 1/4 to 5/16 inch, and thread the hole accordingly. The problem is that this doesn't always work.

If the stripped hole is in a tight location, say an alloy primary or timing cover, there may not be enough room to use the next larger bolt size. Besides, there may not be enough meat in the stripped hole to proceed that way. Finally, while the repair itself may prove satisfactory, its appearance may leave something to be desired. A better and more permanent repair is a Heli-Coil-type insert. It's also the only way, short of welding up the hole and starting from scratch, to repair a stripped spark plug hole.

Heli-Coil kits are available at most industrial supply shops and many auto parts stores. The kit consists of a dozen or so spring-steel inserts, a purpose-ground tap, and a mandrel for installing the inserts. You supply a drill bit of the correct size (the appropriate size is listed on the package), a 3/8-inch drill motor, and a steady hand.

Normally, drilling out the stripped hole presents little, if any, problem. Make sure the drill bit is positioned true to the hole, use a moderate speed and pressure, and you'll find the bit will basically guide itself. In some cases, especially with small holes like the ones for tank badges, you can use a tap handle to turn the bit. Remember, you're not removing much material. In fact, I'd recommend using a tap handle to turn the bit whenever possible.

Once the hole is drilled and the chips removed, the hole is tapped like any other using the supplied tap and the proper lubricant, which is kerosene in aluminum, a light mineral oil for steel and cast iron. In a pinch, WD-40 or motor oil can be substituted, though the threads probably won't be as nicely formed. Most industrial suppliers carry a variety of cutting oils under names like Thread-Eze or Kool-Kut that are worth picking up if you plan to do any serious threading.

Now that your hole is drilled, tapped, and cleaned, it's ready to accept the Heli-Coil insert. The insert is first threaded into the mandrel, and when the end is visible it's introduced to the hole. If you've done everything just right to this point, it can be screwed in without further ado. When the uppermost thread is about half a turn below the surface, stop turning and remove the mandrel. Break off the drive tang by giving it a sharp blow with a hammer and a punch. The tang can then be removed with a magnet or a pair of tweezers.

The neat thing about this kind of repair is that you can use the same style, size, and pitch of fastener as the original, and usually the repair can be accomplished in place. The exceptions are spark plugs and drain plugs. These two pieces present a unique problem because the chips created during the cutting operation have nowhere to go other than the bowels of the engine. I have personally installed Heli-Coils in spark plug holes with the head in place when I had absolutely no other choice, but I certainly wouldn't recommend doing so.

For those inclined to risk it, here's the procedure: the spark plug kit utilizes a tapered tap to open up the hole so no drilling is required. By packing the flutes of the tap with grease, it's possible to keep most of the chips out of the engine. The tang is removed by breaking it off with a pair of needlenose pliers. Again, I don't recommend it, but in a pinch it can be done.

Drain bolts, on the other hand, present less of a problem. Some engine oil drain bolts are carried in a separate bolt-on plate that mounts to the crankcase, or in a removable oil pan. If that's the case remove the sump plate from the engine and perform the repair on the workbench.

If the drain bolt is located in a portion of the crankcase that isn't removable, the solution is fairly straightforward. Since drain plugs invariably point down, drain the engine oil. Apply grease to the flutes of the drill bit, then open up the hole using the drill's slowest speed. Then wash the hole with brake cleaner or some other solvent. Pack the threads of the tap with grease, thread the hole, and wash again.

Transmission drain plugs and rear end drives can be repaired in the same manner. And remember the more washing out you do, the less chance there is of a chip remaining inside to do any damage. In theory as well as practice, you'll find that most of the chips stayed in the greasy tap. If you're really worried, you can finish up by cleaning the area with a cotton swab soaked in solvent.

Heli-Coils come in a variety of pitches, diameters, and lengths. In a pinch, one that's slightly long can be cut down to the correct height. Once you've bought the installation kit, the coils themselves are cheap. Prices vary, but expect to pay somewhere between $25 and $50 for a standard kit such as 3/8 inch or 8mm/1.25. The spark plug kit is about double.

One last piece of advice: while lots of parts can be repaired in place, do yourself a favor and evaluate the expediency versus aggravation factors well before picking up the first tool. Putting yourself in a bad position isn't worth the time you might save by not removing what might be in the way. In fact, it may end up taking longer doing it the wrong way especially if (or when) the drill gets away from you and tap-dances across your fresh paint, polished cases, your arm, or all of the above. Take your time, do it right, and consider it a learning experience.

DIY *Applying Gasket Sealer*

No doubt about it silicone type sealers are among the best thing to happen to motorcycling since John Dunlop invented the pneumatic tire. Unfortunately it's always possible to have too much of a good thing. Shown is the right way to apply it. ■

You'll need:
- *Recommended gasket sealer*
- *Acid brush*

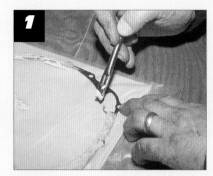

Brush the sealer onto the side of the gasket that faces the removable cover. This will make future disassembly much easier. The sealer should be applied as thinly as possible; an almost translucent coating is all that's required.

Position the gasket and torque down the cover.

Removing & Replacing a Seal

You'll need:

- Pick or center punch
- Sheet metal screw
- Screwdriver
- Vice grip
- Brass hammer
- Socket or piece of pipe sized to fit the seal's OD.
- Seal puller (optional)

Most of us will need to replace a seal at one time or another. My guess is that the countershaft seal is the most commonly replaced seal on the motorcycle. Mainly because it's constantly covered in chain lube and grit, which makes for a fine grinding compound.

Seal replacement techniques vary greatly depending on who is replacing the seal and where it's being installed. Some manufacturers recommend installing the seal wet; that is with some oil on both its ID and OD. Some want it installed dry or with just a dab of oil on the OD. My personal feeling is that unless otherwise specified a driven-in seal should always be installed with a light coating of oil on both the OD and ID. ∎

Often a seal can be removed by prying it out with a screwdriver or by using a tool called a seal puller.

Use a sharp center punch to put a small hole in the outer lip of the seal.

As an alternative you can use an awl or even an old ice pick.

Thread a sheet metal screw into the hole. Screw it in until it bottoms, but don't force it into the seal seat. About half the time just punching the hole will dislodge the seal enough to pop it out.

Once the oil seal is out, thoroughly clean the area and inspect the seal cavity for damage. If any nicks or burrs are found, smooth them over with a fine jewelers file or light sandpaper. Check any shafts or spacers that pass through the seal the same way. High spots can be smoothed over. Low spots may have to be built up or the component replaced to get the component to seal properly.

DIY Removing & Replacing a Seal

Using only hand pressure locate the seal in its cavity, centering it as accurately as you can.

Using a socket that will fit on the edge of the seal or a dedicated driver, tap the seal in until it seats.

Heli-Coil Alternatives

There are several alternatives to the Heli-Coil. However, there are only two that I would recommend. The first is Loctite's Thread Restorer. This is an epoxy-like compound that can be mixed on the spot and used to repair any noncritical fastener up to three-eighths inch in diameter. The operative phrase here is non-critical. If you plan on using it temporarily to repair a stripped 6mm bolt on a valve cover, fine. But if you are going to use it to repair an 8mm bolt from a brake caliper or handlebar clamp, no way.

Loctite's Thread Restorer is definitely a handy item to keep in the tool kit for an impromptu roadside repair. I would not recommend using it on a part whose loss could compromise your safety (nor does Loctite). But used in the proper manner, Thread Restorer is a viable alternative to a mechanical repair.

The second alternative is called a Time-Sert. Rather than using a coiled wire to re-thread the hole, the Time-Sert is a one-piece steel shell. The installation process is similar to that of the Heli-Coil except that the top of the hole is chamfered with a special tool to accept a matching chamfer on the Time-Sert. Another special tool is used to screw the Time-Sert into its hole. As it's drawn tight it expands the bottom of the insert slightly, thus locking it firmly in place.

How to Use Gasket Sealers

I think that gasket sealers are often overused and abused. Here are a couple of suggestions for using the stuff. To start with, if your service manual recommends using a specific sealer, then that's what you should use. It goes without saying that any joint that seals liquid and doesn't use a gasket is going to require some sort of sealer. But what about the joints that use a gasket, should you apply sealer there as well? Well, yes, maybe, and no.

My feeling is that if the factory didn't apply any sealer then you shouldn't either. The problem is that line of thinking presupposes that the

DIY   *Changing Hydraulic Fluid*

As I mentioned in the text brake fluid is hygroscopic; that is, it absorbs water from the atmosphere and requires periodic changing. As a rule of thumb, the brake fluid and clutch fluid should be changed every two years or whenever it turns brown. Remember that most brake fluid is corrosive and will attack paint, as well as your eyes, so take care not to splash the stuff around.

There are two methods you can use to change brake fluid. The first involves pumping up the system, opening the valve, letting the fluid out, closing the valve, and adding fresh fluid to the reservoir. This is identical to bleeding a brake and is somewhat tedious.

The other method involves leaving the bleed screw open while you pump the reservoir down, then adding fresh fluid as the fluid level drops. If air enters the master cylinder you will have to bleed the whole system down. You must also keep an eye on the bleeder to make sure no air is sucked back into the caliper. You can make this part a little easier by keeping the end of the hose submerged in old brake fluid. The second method goes a lot faster, and does a slightly better job. ∎

1 *Hydraulic fluid, which on motorcycles most often means brake fluid, should be changed on a yearly basis, but most of us don't bother to do that.*

4 *There are two methods you can use to change brake fluid. The first involves pumping up the system, opening the valve, letting the fluid out, closing the valve, and adding fresh fluid to the reservoir. The other method involves leaving the bleed screw open while you pump the reservoir down, then adding fresh fluid as the fluid level drops.*

2 *The easy way to change hydraulic fluid (brake fluid or hydraulic-clutch fluid), is to follow a procedure similar to the one we'd use to bleed brakes. First loosen the master cylinder cover.*

3 *Connect a snug fitting hose over the bleeder screw and place the other end of the hose in a container, preferably submerged in the brake fluid to prevent any air from getting back into the system.*

Keep the fluid level above the minimum mark at all times! If we hadn't changed the fluid when we did, it could work it's way through the system, possibly ruining the master and slave cylinder.

gasket surface is in perfect shape, the gasket is perfect, and that the cover is installed perfectly. In the real world this seldom happens.

My suggestion is to sparingly apply a thin coat of gasket sealer to any gasket surface that contains oil or water under pressure, unless your manual specifically tells you not to. If the sealant is properly applied, and we'll come to that in a moment, it won't cause any harm, and if the sealing surface is less than perfect it will prevent any annoying leaks. It's also my practice to use sealant on any gasket that's in an awkward spot or that will be a real nightmare to replace if it springs a leak somewhere down the road.

Applying Gasket Sealant

No question that the current generation of anaerobic sealers, loosely called silicone sealant or room-temperature vulcanizing (RTV) sealant have been a great boon to motorcycling. My only problem with them is most mechanics.

The rule of thumb for their use is simple: use as little of it as possible. Lots of guys squeeze that tube like it's toothpaste. They leave a huge bead of the stuff smeared all over the joint they're trying to seal. When they assemble the parts together a rope of gasket sealer as round as your finger oozes out of the joint.

Joe Wrench wipes the goo up with his bandanna and figures he's done a terrific job of sealing that leaky case. What Joe overlooked is that whatever was forced out of the joint on the outside was forced out of the same joint on the inside. So now he has big snakes of plastic goo swimming through his engine ready to find their way into oil passages and bearings where they can create all sorts of mischief.

Here's the right way to apply silicone-type sealers. Get an acid brush. These are sold in every hardware store in the world for under 50 cents. Cut the bristles down about two-thirds of the way until you have a very short, stiff brush. Dip the brush into a bead of sealer. Paint the joint or gasket with the sealer leaving only a very light, translucent coating of the stuff. When you assemble the case halves very little if any material should be forced out.

This is what we found when we popped the top off the master cylinder. Because the slope of the cylinder was away from the intake port no real harm was done. Still think that hydraulic fluid looks ok?

Hand-Packing a Bearing

After the old grease is washed out the new grease has to be pushed in; sure, there are tools for accomplishing this, but not everyone has them. The photo sequence shows the good old-fashioned method of hand-packing a bearing.

Lubing a Control Cable

Lubricating control cables has become almost a lost art. It shouldn't be, though, because there are lots of bikes out that still use mechanical clutch cables, and every bike I can think of still uses a traditional throttle cable. Cable lubers are cheap and available at most motorcycle shops. In the photo sequence I demonstrate how to use one.

Changing Hydraulic Fluid

The first time I changed hydraulic brake fluid it was a real disaster. First I drained the old fluid out then I replaced it with new fluid and spent two hours bleeding the system. In the ensuing 35 years I haven't learned much but I've certainly figured out a better way of changing brake fluid. The photo sequence shows how.

Appendix: Tools

High quality hand tools can found at just about any auto parts store, home improvement center, or Sears.

PRECISION MFG, & SALES CO., INC
P.O. Box 149
Clearwater, Fl 34617
800-237-5947

Precision supplies tools for the motorcycle trade, they carry everything from boring bars to feeler gauges.

AMERICAN KOWA SEIKI
13939 Equitable Road
Cerritos, CA 90703
800-824-9655

Kowa carries a really neat and reasonably priced line of metric hand tools and brand-specific tools. They supply most of the special tools used by the big-four Japanese manufacturers.

LINCOLN MANUFACTURING
4001 Industrial Ave.
Box 30303
Lincoln, NE 68503

Lincoln makes a full line of jacks and roll stands.

WESTERN MANUFACTURING
705 South Third Avenue
P.O. Box 130
Marshalltown, IA 50158
515-752-5446

Western builds air- and electric-powered lifts, as well as jacks and work tables.

WHITEHORSE PRESS TOOLS
Whitehorse Press
P.O. Box 60
North Conway, NH 03860-0060
800-531-1133
www.whitehorsepress.com

In addition to this book and just about every other you'll ever need to work on your bike Whitehorse Press carries a comprehensive line of tools from degree wheels to drill bits. You can actually pick up almost everything you'll ever need from Whitehorse.

MOTION PRO SPECIALTY TOOLS
867 American Street
San Carlos, CA 94070
650-594-9600
www.motionpro.com

Motion Pro supplies all sorts of special tools and parts to the motorcycle industry. They sell a wide range of custom-designed tools, mostly to shops and serious do-it-yourselfers. Motion Pro products are available only through authorized dealers.

CRUZ TOOLS
P.O. Box 250
Standard, CA 95373
209-536-0491
www.cruztools.com

Cruz Tools supplies the best take-a-long tool kits in the business. These things are the Swiss Army knives of tool kits. The kits are well thought out, compact and of extremely high quality.

Over the years I've spent a small fortune and considerable time and energy amassing a library of motorcycle related literature. Now, not everyone is as interested in motorcycles as I am, and not everyone is willing to pony up thousands of dollars to read about them. But if you're serious about motorcycles, here's a selection of books I suggest you start collecting:

FOUR-STROKE PERFORMANCE TUNING
by A. Graham Bell, Haynes Publishing
ISBN 1 85960 435 8

This might be a little intimidating for the novice, and the focus is really geared toward racecars but it's an easy-to-read and informative guide to the high-performance four-stroke engine.

MOTORCYCLE BASICS MANUAL
by Pete Shoemark, Haynes Publishing
ISBN 1 85010 083 7

Pete's book explains all the basics and a few not so basic concepts in a straightforward and easy-to-read manner. This book is straight theory—there are no repair sections. It's worth having for the technical drawings alone.

TUNING FOR SPEED
by Phil Irving
Turton & Armstrong Publishers
ISBN 0 908031 29 7

This is the definitive book on basic high performance, a little dated by now and hard to find but still worth reading. Besides, it gives you great insight into the mind of the man largely responsible for the design of the legendary Vincent motorcycle.

SPORTBIKE PERFORMANCE HANDBOOK
by Kevin Cameron
MBI Publishing
ISBN 0 7603 0229 4

Mr. Cameron's credentials are impeccable. As Cycle World's technical guru, his columns and articles are probably the most widely read in motorcycling. He's insightful, entertaining, and very, very clever. His book covers all aspects of the performance street bike, but more than that he discusses many very basic issues that apply to all motorcycles.

MOTORCYCLE DESIGN AND TECHNOLOGY
by Gaetano Cocco
Giorgio Nada Editore Publications
ISBN 88 7911 189 2

This is a very heady tome, written by the head of Aprilia's race team. Cocco's book is heavy on theory with lots of math. If you can wade through it, and at times that's saying something, you'll be rewarded with an in-depth understanding of how motorcycles work.

MOTORCYCLE CHASSIS DESIGN: THE THEORY AND PRACTICE
by Tony Foale and Vic Willoughby
Osprey Publishing
ISBN 0 85045 560 X

Foale is a noted chassis designer. His book literally walks you through every aspect of frame design and construction from how they work to how to build them.

MOTORCYCLE WORKSHOP PRACTICE MANUAL
by John Fidell and Pete Shoemark,
Haynes Publishing
ISBN 1 85960 470 6

Written in basic shop-manual style, this book is a terrific guide to everyday workshop techniques. It's not big on specific bikes, but it's invaluable when it comes to the day-to-day methods and tools required to repair motorcycles. In typical English fashion, there are some very useful "bodges" that can be used in place of the requisite factory tools and fittings.

MOTORCYCLE ELECTRICAL MANUAL: A COMPREHENSIVE GUIDE
by Tony Tranter
Haynes Publishing
ISBN 0 5696 446 8

Tony has just published a second edition with lots of updates. The first edition is written in a textbook/workbook style. It's not much fun to read but it is informative, particularly so if you own or want to restore an older British bike. There is a lot of really good basic electrical theory here, written so that the layman can understand it.

MOTORCYCLE CARBURETOR MANUAL
by Pete Shoemark
Haynes Publishing
ISBN 0 85696 603 7

This is another easy to read and useful manual. Pete discusses the design and maintenance of all popular carburetors. A good book on both a theoretical and practical level.

AUTOMOTIVE HANDBOOK
Bosch Technical Publications
ISBN 3 18 418004 2

Bosch publishes a new edition of this little desktop reference book every few years. This manual is intended for use by automotive engineers and technicians who need quick information on everything from how many trucks were registered in Gabon in 1984 (7500) to the operating principles of the internal combustion engine. There is way more stuff here than most of us can ever use but it's a neat book to read through.

MACHINERY'S HANDBOOK
Industrial Press Inc.
ISBN 0 8311 2625 6

My copy is so old that it doesn't even list an ISBN number. However this book is available through any bookstore or industrial supply shop; Whitehorse Press also carries it. This book is the standard metalworking reference used by engineers, machinists, and hobbyists the world over. It may not seem to fit in here, but trust me, if you have any interest in things mechanical or creating your own parts, you need this book.

Index

Index

Index

Mark Zimmerman has been completely enthralled by motorcycles for 40 of the last 49 years. After spending 20 years repairing them he began writing about them. Mark is a freelance author, specializing in the technical and historical aspects of motorcycling and is currently the Technical Editor of *Motorcycle Cruiser Magazine*. In addition to *Essential Guide to Motorcycle Maintenance* he has written several books on motorcycle restoration, history, and repair as well as a buyers guide or two. Mark enjoys all aspects of motorcycling, particularly racing his vintage flat-trackers and riding off-road. On the street he prefers cruising, preferably to somewhere that has great barbecue. Other hobbies include collecting motorcycle memorabilia, particularly printed matter; fishing, and gardening. He lives in Connecticut with his wife Brenda, and their dog Hannah.

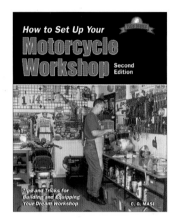

Softbound
8-1/4 x 10-1/2 inches
176 pages
Approx. 200 b/w illus.

ISBN: 1-884313-43-4
Order Code: MASI2
Price: 19.95

How to Set Up Your Motorcycle Workshop (2nd Ed.)

by C. G. Masi

Everything you need to know about designing, building, and equipping a workshop, with practical information that will help you make the most of your space and budget. New edition includes profiles of real-world workshops, from small garage spaces to purpose-built restoration and race-prep shops.

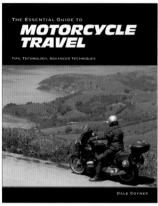

Softbound
8-1/4 x 10-1/2 in.
192 pages
color illus.

ISBN: 1-884313-59-0
Order Code: EGMT
Price: 24.95

Essential Guide to Motorcycle Travel

by Dale Coyner

This book is written to help motorcyclists prepare themselves and their motorcycle for traveling long distances over extended periods. Whether you are getting ready for a weekend trip beyond your home turf, or for a transcontinental odyssey lasting several years, Coyner's book details the fundamentals for riding in comfort, safety, and convenience.

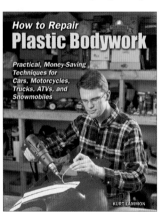

Softbound
8-1/4 x 10-1/2 inches
144 pages
color illus.

ISBN: 1-884313-37-X
Order Code: PLAS
Price: 19.95

How to Repair Plastic Bodywork: Practical, Money-Saving Techniques

by Kurt Lammon

It's a familiar story—a simple accident in the driveway results in cracked and broken bodywork that costs thousands of dollars to replace. Lammon shows the reader how to assess the damage and determine whether it can be repaired, then provides step-by-step procedures for identifying the kind of plastic from which the part is made, and fixing everything from a simple scratch to a major break.

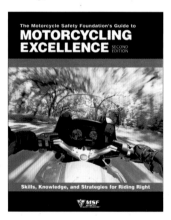

Softbound
8-1/4 x 10-1/2 in.
192 pages
color illus.

ISBN: 1-884313-47-7
Order Code: MCX2
Price: 24.95

Motorcycling Excellence: Skills, Knowledge, and Strategies for Riding Right (2nd Ed.)

by The Motorcycle Safety Foundation

Here is a book for the motorcyclist who wants to do it right—the most complete, authoritative book ever published on safe riding techniques and strategies. This book is the culmination of what MSF has learned about teaching students of all ages and experience. It is the perfect refresher for anyone who has taken an MSF course and will be an eye-opener for those who have not yet discovered them.